7TH - Edition

CELEBRITY DIRECTORY™

7
T
H
-
Edition

CELEBRITY DIRECTORY™

 Axiom Information Resources

ISSN 1083-1614

ISBN 0-943213-23-1

Printed in the United States of America

SPECIAL SALES

The Celebrity Directory™ is available at special quantity discounts.
For information, write:

Axiom Information Resources Inc., P.O. Box 8015-T, Ann Arbor, Michigan 48107 U.S.A.

Introduction

Welcome to the new and expanded Seventh edition of the Celebrity Directory™. This new edition incorporates many changes suggested by our readers' enthusiastic response to previous editions. As always, our aim is to provide the reference librarian, speaking engagement coordinator, general researcher or fan with the easiest-to-use, most accurate and comprehensive collection of celebrity names and addresses available anywhere.

The editors have researched and arranged data on thousands of prominent persons engaged in all fields of human accomplishment throughout the world. If a person is famous and worth locating, it's almost certain that his or her name and address is listed in the convenient, alphabetically-arranged Celebrity Directory™.

Most of the celebrities listed in this directory welcome correspondence concerning their lives and work. Please remember when writing to a celebrity, as well as writing to Axiom Information Resources Inc., it is always best to enclose a stamped, self-addressed envelope. Of course, the editorial staff and publisher cannot guarantee that listed celebrities will respond to correspondence.

We have made every effort to ensure that the information contained in the Celebrity Directory™ is up-to-date and accurate. We cannot accept responsibility for inaccuracies created by a celebrity's moving or changing his or her mail arrangements after the directory went to press.

We welcome any suggestions or inquiries concerning the Celebrity Directory™, and we sincerely hope this new edition will provide our readers with even more entertainment and information. All inquiries concerning this book should be sent to Axiom Information Resources Inc., P.O. Box 8015-T, Ann Arbor, Michigan 48107 U.S.A.

A

Beverly Aadland
P.O. Box 1115
Canyon Country, CA 91350
"Actress"

Henry Aaron
1611 Adams Drive S.W.
Atlanta, GA 30311
"Ex-Baseball Player"

Bruce Abbott
4526 Wilshire Blvd.
Los Angeles, CA 90010
"Actor"

Dihanne Abbott
460 West Avenue #46
Los Angeles, CA 90065
"Actress"

Gregory Abbott
P.O. Box 68
Bergenfield, NY 07621
"Singer"

John Abbott
6424 Ivarene Avenue
Los Angeles, CA 90068
"Actor"

Philip Abbott
5400 Shirley Avenue
Tarzana, CA 91356
"Actor, Director"

Paula Abdul
14755 Ventura Blvd #1-1710
Sherman Oaks, CA 91403
"Singer"

Kareem Abdul-Jabbar
1436 Summitridge Drive
Beverly Hills, CA 90210
"Basketball Player"

Abdullah The Butcher
1000 S. Industrial Blvd.
Dallas, TX 75207
"Wrestler"

Akeem Abdul Olajuwon
10 Greenway Plaza E.
Houston, TX 77046
"Basketball Player"

Ian Abercrombie
1040 North Gardner
Los Angeles, CA 90046
"Actor"

F. Murray Abraham
40 Fifth Avenue #2C
New York, NY 10011
"Actor"

Leslie Abramson
4929 Wilshire Blvd.
Los Angeles, CA 90010
"Attorney"

Ray Abruzzo
20334 Pacific Coast Hwy.
Malibu, CA 90265
"Actor"

Bella Abzug
2 Fifth Avenue
New York, NY 10011
"Politician"

AC/DC
46 Kensington Ct. St.
London W8 5DP ENGLAND
"Rock & Roll Group"

Sharon Acker
6310 San Vicente Blvd. #401
Los Angeles, CA 90048
"Actress"

Bettye Ackerman
302 North Alpine Drive
Beverly Hills, CA 90210
"Actress"

Forrest Ackerman
2495 Glendower
Los Angeles, CA 90027
"Author"

Leslie Ackerman
4439 Worster Avenue
Studio City, CA 91604
"Actress"

Joss Ackland
76 Oxford Street
London W1N OAX ENGLAND
"Actor"

David Ackroyd
12425 Otsego Street North
North Hollywood, CA 91607
"Actor"

Timothy Ackroyd
33 Chepstone Road
London W2 5BP ENGLAND
"Actor"

Jay Acovone
3811 Multiview Drive
Los Angeles, CA 90068
"Actor"

Acquanetta
4415 North Arcadia Lane
Phoenix, AZ 85018
"Actress"

Deborah Adair
9300 Wilshire Blvd, #555
Beverly Hills, CA 90212
"Actress"

Red Adair
8101 Pinemont
Huston, TX 77040
"Fire Extinguishing Expert"

Brooke Adams
248 S. Van Ness Avenue
Los Angeles, CA 90004
"Actress"

Bryan Adams
406-68 Water Street
Vancouver BC V6B 1A4 CANADA
"Singer"

Cindy Adams
1050 Fifth Avenue
New York, NY 10028
"Actress"

Don Adams
2160 Century Park East
Los Angeles, CA 90067
"Actor, Writer, Director"

Edie Adams
12925 Valleyheart Drive
Studio City, CA 91604
"Singer, Actor"

Joey Adams
1050 Fifth Avenue
New York, NY 10028
"Actor, Writer, Director"

Julie Adams
1535 Magnolia Blvd. #429
Sherman Oaks, CA 91403
"Actress"

Maria Adams
247 S. Beverly Drive #102
Beverly Hills, CA 90212
"Actress"

Mason Adams
900 Fifth Avenue
New York, NY 10021
Actor"

Maud Adams
1930 Century Park West #403
Los Angeles, CA 90067
"Actress, Model"

Richard Adams
26 Church Street
Whitechurch, Hants. ENGLAND
"Author"

Tom Adams
29-31 Kings Road
London SW3 ENGLAND
"Actor"

ADC Band
17397 Santa Barbara
Detroit, MI 48221
"Rock & Roll Group"

Herb Adderly
8 Pelham Road
Philadelphia, PA 19119
"Musician"

Wesley Addy
88 Central Park West
New York, NY 10023
"Actor"

Merv Adelson
600 Sarbonne Road
Los Angeles, CA 90077
"TV Producer"

Isabelle Adjani
2 rue Lord Byron
F-75008 Paris, FRANCE
"Actress"

Lou Adler
3969 Villa Costera
Malibu, CA 90265
"Director, Producer"

Margot Adler
c/o National Public Radio
2025 "M" Street N.W.
Washington, DC 20036
"News Correspondent"

King Bhumibol Adulyadey
Villa Chiralada
Bangkok, THAILAND
"King Of Thailand"

Aerosmith
P.O. Box 882494
San Francisco, CA 94188
"Rock & Roll Group"

John Agar
639 North Hollywood Way
Burbank, CA 91505
"Actor"

Andre Agassi
8921 Andre Drive
Las Vegas, NV 89113
"Tennis Player"

Spiro T. Agnew
10000 Coastal Hwy #1108
Ocean City, MD 21842
"Politician"

Martin Agronsky
4001 Brandywine Street
Washington, DC 20016
"TV Producer"

Jenny Agutter
6882 Camrose Drive
Los Angeles, CA 90068
"Actress"

A-Ha
P.O. Box 203
Watford WD1 3YA ENGLAND
"Rock & Roll Group"

Danny Aiello
4 Thornhill Drive
Ramsey, NJ 07446
"Actor"

Troy Aikman
1 Cowboys Parkway
Irving, TX 75063
"Football Player"

Roger Ailes
440 Park Avenue South
New York, NY 10016
"Producer, Director"

Anouk Aimee
201 rue du Faubourg St. Honore
F-75008 Paris, FRANCE
"Actress"

Danny Ainge
2910 North Central
Phoenix, AZ 95012
"Basketball Player"

Air Supply
14755 Ventura Blvd. #1-710
Sherman Oaks, CA 91403
"Rock & Roll Group"

Franklin Ajaye
1312 South Orange Drive
Los Angeles, CA 90019
"Comedian, Actor"

Emperor Akihoto
The Imperial Palace
1-1 Chiyoda - Chiyoda-Ku
Tokyo, JAPAN
"Emperor of Japan"

Alabama
P.O. Box 529
Ft. Payne, AL 35967
"C&W Group"

Buddy Alan
600 East Gilbert
Tempe, AZ 85281
"Singer"

Alarm
47 Bernard Street
St. Albans, Herts ENGLAND
"Rock & Roll Group"

President Hafez Al-Assad
Presidential Office
Damascus, SYRIA
"President of Syria"

Capt. Lou Albano
P.O. Box 3859
Stamford, CT 06905
"Wrestler, Manager"

Edward Albee
14 Harrison Street
New York, NY 10013
"Writer, Producer"

Anna Marie Alberghetti
10333 Chrysanthemum Lane
Los Angeles, CA 90077
"Actress, Singer"

Eddie Albert
719 Amalfi Drive
Pacific Palisades, CA 90272
"Actor"

Edward Albert
1930 Century Park West #403
Los Angeles, CA 90067
"Actor"

Marv Albert
c/o NBC Sports
30 Rockefeller Plaza
New York, NY 10012
"Sportscaster"

Prince Albert
Palais De Monaco
Boite Postal 158
98015 Monte Carlo Monaco
"Prince of Monaco"

Dolores Albin
23388 Mulholland Drive
Woodland Hills, CA 91364
"Actress"

Lola Albright
P.O. Box 250070
Glendale, CA 91225
"Actress"

Medeleine Albright
799 United Nation Plaza
New York, NY 10017
"U.S. Ambassador to the U.N."

Dr. Tenley Albright
2 Commonwealth Avenue
Boston, MA 02117
"Skater"

Alan Alda
641 Lexington Avenue #1400
New York, NY 10022
"Actor"

Antony Alda
15 Seaview Drive North
Rolling Hills, CA 90274
"Actor"

Ginger Alden
4152 Royal Crest Place
Memphis, TN 38138
"Model"

Norman Alden
106 North Croft Avenue
Los Angeles, CA 90048
"Actor"

Dr. Ed "Buzz" Aldrin, Jr.
233 Emerald Bay
Laguna Beach, CA 92651
"Astronaut"

Frank Aletter
5430 Corbin Avenue
Tarzana, CA 91356
"Actor"

Kyle Aletter
5430 Corbin Avenue
Tarzana, CA 91356
"Actress"

Denise Alexander
345 North Maple Drive #361
Beverly Hills, CA 90210
"Actress"

Jane Alexander
1100 Pennsylvania Ave. NW #520
Washington, DC 20506
"Actress"

Lamar Alexander
1109 Owen Place NE
Washington, DC 20008
"Ex-Governor"

Jason Alexander
6230-A Wilshire Blvd. #103
Los Angeles, CA 90048
"Actor"

Shana Alexander
156 Fifth Avenue #617
New York, NY 10010
"News Correspondent"

Kim Alexis
345 North Maple Drive #185
Beverly Hills, CA 90210
"Model"

Kristian Alfonso
P.O. Box 3037
Brockton, MA 02404
"Actress"

Muhammad Ali
P.O. Box 187
Berrien Springs, MI 59103
"Former Boxing Champion"

Tatyana Ali
410 North Rossmore #207
Los Angeles, CA 90004
"Actress"

Alicia-Ana
9744 Wilshire Blvd. #308
Beverly Hills, CA 90212
"Actress"

Alice in Chains
207 1/2 First Avenue South, #300
Seattle, WA 98104
"Grunge Band"

Jed Allan
P.O. Box 5302
Blue Jay, CA 92317
"Actor"

Betty Allen
645 St. Nicholas Avenue
New York, NY 10030
"Mezzo-Soprano"

Chad Allen
6489 Cavalleri Road #204
Mailbu, CA 90265
"Actor"

Corey Allen
8642 Hollywood Blvd.
Los Angeles, CA 90069
Actor, Writer, Director"

Debbie Allen
607 Maguerita Avenue
Santa Monica, CA 90402
"Actress, Dancer, Singer"

Elizabeth Allen
P.O. Box 243
Lake Peekskill, NY 10537
"Actress"

Joan Allen
40 W. 57th Street
New York, NY 10019
"Actress"

Jonelle Allen
8730 Sunset Blvd. #480
Los Angeles, CA 90069
"Actress, Singer"

Karen Allen
P.O. Box 237
Monterey, MA 01245
"Actress"

Marcus Allen
1144 Ravoli Drive
Pacific Palisades, CA 90272
"Football Player"

Marty Allen
1991 Pago Court
Las Vegas, NV 89117
"Actor, Comedian"

Mel Allen
21C Weavers Hill
Greenwich, CT 06830
"Baseball Commentator"

Nancy Allen
9150 Wilshire Blvd., #205
Beverly Hills, CA 90212
"Actress"

Rex Allen
P.O. Box 430
Sonoita, AZ 85637
"Singer"

Rex Allen, Jr.
128 Pine Oak Drive
Hendersonville, TN 37075
"Singer"

Sean Barbara Allen
1622 Sierra Bonita Avenue
Los Angeles, CA 90046
"Actress, Writer"

Steve Allen
16185 Woodvale
Encino, CA 91316
"Actor, Writer, Comedian"

Tim Allen
9601 Wilshire Blvd. #620
Beverly Hills, CA 90210
"Actor"

Woody Allen
930 Fifth Avenue
New York, NY 10018
"Actor, Director, Comedian"

Kirstie Alley
4526 Wilshire Blvd.
Los Angeles, CA 90010
"Actress"

Michael Allinson
112 Knollwood Drive
Larchmont, NY 10538
"Actor"

Mose Allison
34 Dogwood Street
Smithtown, NY 11787
"Pianist, Composer"

Greg Allman
18 Tamworth Road
Waban, MA 02168
"Musician"

Christopher Allport
121 North San Vicente Blvd.
Beverly Hills, CA 90211
"Actor"

Gloria Allred
6380 Wilshire Blvd. #1404
Los Angeles, CA 90048
"Attorney, Feminist"

June Allyson
1651 Foothill Road
Ojai, CA 93023
"Actress"

Maria Conchita Alonso
P.O. Box 537
Beverly Hills, CA 90213
"Actress"

Felipe Alou
4525 De Coubertin Ave.
Montreal, PQ, H1V 3P2 Canada
"Ex-Baseball Player"

Herb Alpert
31930 Pacific Coast Hwy.
Malibu, CA 90265
"Musician"

Hollis Alpert
P.O. Box 142
Shelter Island, NY 11964
"Writer"

Carol Alt
111 East 22nd Street #200
New York, NY 10010
"Actress"

Jeff Altman
5065 Calvin Avenue
Tarzana, CA 91356
"Comedian, Actor"

Robert Altman
502 Park Avenue #15G
New York, NY 10022
"Writer, Producer, Director"

Robert Altman
9200 Harrington Drive
Potomac, MD 20854
"Financier"

Luigi Alva
via Moscova 46/3
20121 Mailand ITALY
"Tenor"

Christiane Amanpour
25 rue de Ponthieu
75008 Paris, France
"Broadcast Journalist"

Rodney Amateau
133 1/2 South Linden Drive
Beverly Hills, CA 90212
"Film Writer, Producer

Nicolas Amer
14 Great Russell Street
London WC1 ENGLAND
"Actor"

America
8730 Sunset Blvd., PH
Los Angeles, CA 90069
"Rock & Roll Group"

Ed Ames
1457 Claridge
Beverly Hills, CA 90210
"Singer"

Rachel Ames
303 South Crescent Heights
Los Angeles, CA 90048
"Author"

Trey Ames
15760 Ventura Blvd. #1730
Encino, CA 91436
"Actor"

Madchen Amick
9200 Sunset Blvd. #625
Los Angeles, CA 90069
"Actress"

Idi Amin
Box 8948
Jidda 21492 SAUDI ARABIA
"Deposed Ruler"

Clevland Amory
200 West 57th Street
New York, NY 10019
"Writer"

Deborah Amos
c/o National Public Radio
2025 "M" Street N.W.
Washington, DC 20036
"News Correspondent"

Famous Amos (Wally)
215 Lanipo Drive
Kailua, HI 96734
"Cookie Entrepreneur"

John Amos
P.O. Box 587
Califon, NJ 07830
"Actor"

Tori Amos
P.O. Box 8456
Clearwater, FL 34618
"Singer"

Morey Amsterdam
1012 North Hillcrest Road
Beverly Hills, CA 90210
"Actor, Comedian"

Barbara Anderson
P.O. Box 10118
Santa Fe, NM 87504
"Actress"

Bill Anderson
P.O. Box 888
Hermitage, TN 37076
"Singer"

Brad Anderson
13022 Wood Harbour Drive
Montgomery, TX 77356
"Cartoonist"

Daryl Anderson
5923 Wilbur Avenue
Tarzana, CA 91356
"Actor"

Ernie Anderson
4141 Knobhill Drive
Sherman Oaks, CA 91403
"Actor"

Gillian Anderson
110-555 Brooks Bank Avenue #10
No. Vancouver BC V7J 3S5
CANADA
"Actress"

Harry Anderson
2305 Ashland Street #C-506
Ashland, OR 97520
"Actor, Comedian"

Jack Anderson
1200 Eton Court N.W.
Washington, DC 20007
"News Correspondent"

John Anderson
Nova University
Center for Law
Ft. Lauderdale, FL 33314
"Politician"

Loni Anderson
3355 Clerendon Road
Beverly Hills, CA 90210
"Actress"

Louie Anderson
8033 Sunset Blvd. #605
Los Angeles, CA90046
"Comedian"

Lynn Anderson
4925 Tyne Valley Blvd.
Nashville, TN 37220
"Singer"

Mary Anderson
1127 Norman Place
Los Angeles, CA 90049
"Actress"

Melissa Sue Anderson
20722 Pacific Coast Hwy.
Malibu, CA 90265
"Actress"

Melody Anderson
301 E. 64th Street #18-B
New York, NY 10021
"Actress"

Michael J. Anderson
6930 Lennox Avenue #25
Van Nuys, CA 91405
"Actor"

Pamela Anderson-Lee
5433 Beethoven Street
Los Angeles CA 90066
"Actress"

Paul Anderson
1603 McIntosh Street
Vidalia, GA 30474
"Weightlifter"

Richard Anderson
10120 Cielo Drive
Beverly Hills, CA 90210
"Actor"

Richard Dean Anderson
2049 Century Park E. #2500
Los Angeles, CA 90067
"Actor"

Sheri Anderson
3633 Willowcrest Avenue
Studio City, CA 91604
"TV Writer"

George "Sparky" Anderson
4077 North Verde Vista
Thousand Oaks, CA 91360
"Baseball Manager"

Terry Anderson
50 Rockefeller Plaza
New York, NY 10020
"News Correspondent"

Ursula Andress
Via F. Siaci 38
I-00197 Rome ITALY
"Actress"

John Andretti
P.O. Box 59244
Indianapolis, IN 46259
"Race Car Driver"

Mario Andretti
53 Victory Lane
Nazareth, PA 18064
"Race Car Driver"

Michael Andretti
471 Rose Inn Avenue
Nazareth, PA 18604
"Race Car Driver"

Prince Andrew
Sunninghill Park
Windsor, ENGLAND
"England Royalty"

Anthony Andrews
503 The Chambers
Chelsea Harbour
London SW10 ENGLAND
"Actor"

Julie Andrews
P.O. Box 666
Beverly Hills, CA 90213
"Singer"

Maxene Andrews
14200 Carriage Oak Lane
Auburn, CA 95603
"Singer"

Patti Andrews
9823 Aldea Avenue
Northridge, CA 91354
"Singer"

Tige Andrews
4914 Encino Terrace
Encino, CA 91316
"Actor, Writer"

Vanessa Angel
9830 Wilshire Blvd.
Beverly Hills, CA 90212
"Actress"

Maya Angelou
2720 Reynolda Road #MB-9
Winston-Salem, NC 27106
"Writer, Poet"

The Angels
P.O. Box 3864
Beverly Hills, CA 90212
"Rock & Roll Group"

Jean-Hughes Anglade
151 El Camino Drive
Beverly Hills, CA 90212
"Actress"

Jim Angle
c/o National Public Radio
2025 "M" Street N.W.
Washington, DC 20036
"News Correspondent"

Philip Anglim
2404 Grand Canal
Venice, CA 90291
"Actor"

Edward Anhalt
500 Amalfi Drive
Pacific Palisades, CA 90272
"Writer, Producer"

Jennifer Aniston
5750 Wilshire Blvd. #580
Los Angeles, CA 90036
"Actress"

John Aniston
4872 Topanga Canyon Blvd. #311
Woodland Hills, CA 91364
"Actor"

Paul Anka
10573 West Pico Blvd. #159
Los Angeles, CA 90064
"Singer"

Ann-Margaret
2707 Benedict Canyon Drive
Beverly Hills, CA 90210
"Actress"

Annabella
1 rue Pierret
92200 Neuilly, FRANCE
"Actress"

Princess Anne
Gatcombe Park
Glouchestershire, ENGLAND
"England Royalty"

Wallis Annenberg
10273 Century Woods Place
Los Angeles, CA 90067
"Magazine Executive"

Francesca Annis
2 Vicarage Court
London W8 ENGLAND
"Actress"

Michael Ansara
4624 Park Mirasol
Calabasas, CA 91302
"Actor"

Susan Anspach
473 16th Street
Santa Monica, CA 90402
"Actress"

Adam Ant
503 The Chambers
Chelsea Harbour, Lots Road
London SW10 0XF ENGLAND
"Singer"

Lysette Anthony
501 West Genoaks Blvd. #521
Glendale, CA 91202
"Actress"

Ray Anthony
9288 Kinglet Drive
Los Angeles, CA 90069
"Orchestra Leader"

Susan Anton
16830 Ventura Blvd. #300
Encino, CA 91436
"Actress"

Lou Antonio
530 Gaylord Drive
Burbank, CA 91505
"Actor, Writer, Director"

Michelangelo Antonioni
Via Vincenzo Tiberio 18
Rome, ITALY
"Film Director"

Gabrielle Anwar
5 Denmark Street
London WC2H 8LP ENGLAND
"Actress"

Rocky Aoki
8685 N.W. 53rd Terrace
Miami, FL 33155
"Food Entrepreneur"

Luis Aparicio
Calle 73 #14-53
Maraciabo, VENEZUELA
"Ex-Baseball Player"

Christina Applegate
20411 Chapter Drive
Woodland Hills, CA 91364
"Actress"

Apollonia (Kotero)
8200 Wilshire Blvd. #218
Beverly Hills, CA 90212
"Actress"

John Aprea
727 North Martel Avenue
Los Angeles, CA 90046
"Actor"

Michael Apted
111 Richmond Street W., #400
Toronto, Ontario
M5H 264 CANADA
"Film Director"

Corazon Aquino
c/o Pius XVI Center, UN
Manila PHILIPPINES
"Politician"

Yassir Arafat
c/o PLO Office
1730 "K" St. NW #703
Washington, DC 20006
"Politician"

Alan Arbus
2208 North Beverly Glen
Los Angeles, CA 90077
"Actor"

Loreen Arbus
8841 Appian Way
Los Angeles, CA 90046
"Writer"

Eddie Arcaro
11111 Biscayne Blvd.
Miami, FL 33161
"Ex-Jockey"

Anne Archer
13201 Old Oak Lane
Los Angeles, CA 90049
"Actress"

Bernard Archer
Holt Barton
Witham Frairy
Somerset ENGLAND
"Actor"

Beverly Archer
606 North Larchmont Blvd. #309
Los Angeles, CA 90004
"Actress"

Dennis Archer
2 Woodward Avenue
Detroit, MI 48226
"Mayor"

Jeffrey Archer
93 Albert Embankment
London SE1 ENGLAND
"Author"

Army Archerd
442 Hilgard Avenue
Los Angeles, CA 90024
"Columnist"

Dotti Archibald
10372 Tennessee Avenue
Los Angeles, CA 90064
"Comedienne"

Toni Arden
34-34 75th Street
Jackson Heights, NY 11372
"Singer"

Moshe Arens
49 Hagderat
Savyon, ISRAEL
"Politician"

Oscar Arias
Casa Presidencia
San Jose, COSTA RICA
"Politician"

Ben Aris
47 West Square
London SE11 4SP ENGLAND
"Actor"

Adam Arkin
2372 Veteran Avenue
Los Angeles, CA 90064
"Actor, Director"

Alan Arkin
8942 Wilshire Blvd.
Beverly Hills, CA 90211
"Actor"

Samuel Z. Arkoff
3205 Oakdell Lane
Studio City, CA 91604
"Film Producer"

Roone Arledge
535 Park Avenue #13A
New York, NY 10021
"TV Producer"

Giorgio Armani
Palazzo Durini 24
1-20122 Milan ITALY
"Fashion Designer"

Joan Armatrading
27 Queensdale Place
London W11 ENGLAND
"Singer, Guitarist"

Rep. Dick Armey (TX)
House Cannon Bldg. #301
Washington, DC 20515
"Politician"

Russell Arms
2918 Davis Way
Palm Springs, CA 92262
"Actor, Singer"

Anne Armstrong
Armstrong Ranch
Armstrong, TX 78338
"Politician"

Bess Armstrong
151 El Camino Drive
Beverly Hills, CA 90212
"Actress"

Curtis Armstrong
3867 Shannon Road
Los Angeles, CA 90027
"Actor"

Garner Ted Armstrong
P.O. Box 2525
Tyler, TX 75710
"Evangelist, Author"

Neil Armstrong
777 Columbus Avenue
Lebanon, OH 45036
"Astronaut"

R.G. Armstrong
3856 Reklaw Drive
North Hollywood, CA 91604
"Actor"

John Arnatt
3 Warren Cottage
Woodland Way
Surrey KT10 6NN ENGLAND
"Actor"

Desi Arnaz, Jr.
P.O. Box 2230
Pine, AZ 85544
"Actor"

Lucie Arnaz
RR #3 Flintlock Ridge Road
Katonah, NY 10536
"Actress"

James Arness
P.O. Box 49599
Los Angeles, CA 90049
"Actor"

Jeanetta Arnette
9024 Dorrington Avenue
Los Angeles, CA 90048
"Actress"

Alison Arngrim
P.O. Box 46891
Los Angeles, CA 90046
"Actress"

Eddy Arnold
P.O. Box 97
Brentwood, TN 37027
"Singer"

Tom Arnold
PO Box 15458
Beverly Hills, CA 90209
"Actor"

David Arnott
P.O. Box 70185
San Diego, CA 92167
"Baritone"

Francois Arnoul
53 rue Censier
F-75005 Paris FRANCE
"Actress"

Stefan Arnsten
1017 Laurel Way
Beverly Hills, CA 90210
"Actor"

Alexis Arquette
1930 Century Park West #303
Los Angeles, CA 90067
"Actor"

David Arquette
8942 Wilshire Blvd.
Beverly Hills, CA 90211
"Actor"

Patricia Arquette
9560 Wilshire Blvd. #500
Beverly Hills, CA 90212
"Actress"

Rosanna Arquette
7704 Woodrow Wilson Drive
Los Angeles, CA 90046
"Actress"

Rod Arrants
260 S. Beverly Drive #308
Beverly Hills, CA 90212
"Actor"

Arrested Development
9380 SW 72nd Street #B-220
Miami, FL 33174
"Music Group"

Gus Arriola
P.O. Box 3275
Carmel, CA 93921
"Cartoonist"

Beatrice Arthur
2000 Old Ranch Road
Los Angeles, CA 90049
"Actress"

Maureen Arthur
9200 Sunset Blvd. #625
Los Angeles, CA 90069
"Actress"

Robert Arthur
1711 Kings Way
Los Angeles, CA 90069
"Producer"

Mary Kay Ash
2708 Fairmont Street
Dallas, TX 75201
"Cosmetic Executive"

Dana Ashbrook
151 El Camino Drive
Beverly Hills, CA 90212
"Actress"

Daphne Ashbrook
10683 Santa Monica Blvd.
Los Angeles, CA 90025
"Actress"

Jane Asher
644 North Doheny Drive
Los Angeles, CA 90069
"Actress"

Peter Asher
644 North Doheny Drive
Los Angeles, CA 90069
"Record Producer"

William Asher
54-337 Oak Hill Blvd.
La Quinta, CA 92253
"Writer, Producer"

Renee Asherson
28 Elsworth Road
London NW3 ENGLAND
"Actress"

David Ashford
53 Moat Drive
Harrow, Middlesex ENGLAND
"Actor"

Evelyn Ashford
818 Plantation Lane
Walnut, CA 91789
"Athlete"

Ashford & Simpson
254 West 72nd Street #1-A
New York, NY 10023
"Vocal Duo"

Vladimir Ashkenazy
Sonnenhof 4
6004 Lucerne, SWITZERLAND
"Pianist"

Edward Ashley
4054 Pylon Way
Oceanside, CA 92056
"Actor"

Elizabeth Ashley
1223 North Ogden Drive
Los Angeles, CA 90046
"Actress"

Jennifer Ashley
11130 Huston St. #6 .
North Hollywood, CA 91601
"Actress"

John Ashley
18067 Lake Encino Drive
Encino, CA 91316
"Actor, Producer"

John Ashton
700 Hinsdale Drive
Ft. Collins, CO 80526
"Actor"

Luke Askew
8383 Wilshire Blvd., #954
Beverly Hills, CA 90211
"Actor"

Leon Askin
624 North Rexford Drive
Beverly Hills, CA 90210
"Actor, Director"

Asleep At The Wheel
P.O. Box 463
Austin, TX 75767
"Rock & Roll Group"

Edward Asner
P.O. Box 7407
Studio City, CA 91604
"Actor"

Armand Assante
RD #1, Box 561
Campbell Hall, NY 10916
"Actor"

Pat Ast
1412 1/4 North Hayworth Avenue
Los Angeles, CA 90046
"Actress"

Robyn Astaire
1155 San Ysidro Drive
Beverly Hills, CA 90210
"Widower of Fred Astaire"

John Astin
P.O. Box 49698
Los Angeles, CA 90049
"Actor, Director, Writer"

Mackenzie Astin
4526 Wilshire Blvd.
Los Angeles, CA 90010
"Actor"

Sean Astin
5438 Norwich Avenue
Van Nuys, CA 91411
"Actor"

Rick Astley
Box 29, Newton-le-Willows
Mercyside WA12 OES ENGLAND
"Singer"

William Atherton
5102 San Feliciano Drive
Woodland Hills, CA 91364
"Actor"

Chet Atkins
1096 Lynwood Blvd.
Nashville, TN 37215
"Guitarist"

Christopher Atkins
7072 Park Manor Avenue
North Hollywood, CA 91605
"Actor"

Tom Atkins
10100 Santa Monica Blvd. #2500
Los Angeles, CA 90067
"Actor"

Rowan Atkinson
47 Dean Street
London W1 ENGLAND
"Actor, Comedian"

David Attenborough
5 Park Road
Richmond Green
Surrey ENGLAND
"TV Producer"

Sir Richard Attenborough
Old Friars
Richard Green, Surrey
ENGLAND
"Writer, Producer"

Rene Auberjonois
8428-C Melrose Place
Los Angeles, CA 90069
"Actor"

Jacques Aubuchon
20978 Rios Street
Woodland Hills, CA 91364
"Actor"

Louis Auchincloss
1111 Park Avenue
New York, NY 10028
"Author, Critic"

Stephanie Audran
95 Bis rue de Chezy
92200 Neuilly-sur-seine
FRANCE
"Actor"

Red Auerbach
151 Merrimac Street
Boston, MA 02114
"Basketball Executive"

Ira Augustain
3900 Ramboz Drive
Los Angeles, CA 90063
"Actor"

Jean Pierre Aumont
4 Allee des Brouillards
F-65018 Paris FRANCE
"Author"

Jean Aurel
40 rue Lauriston
F-7016 Paris, FRANCE
"Writer"

Karen Austin
3356 Rowena Avenue
Los Angeles, CA 90027
"Actress"

Patty Austin
400 Kelby Street #9C
Ft. Lee, NJ 07204
"Singer"

Teri Austin
4245 Laurel Grove
Studio City, CA 91604
"Actress"

Tracy Austin
26406 Dunwood Road
Rolling Hills Estates, CA 90274
"Tennis Player"

Alan Autry
10100 Santa Monica Blvd. #2496
Los Angeles, CA 90067
"Actor"

Gene Autry
P.O. Box 420187
Atlanta, GA 30342
"Actor, Singer, Executive"

Frankie Avalon
1652 Aldercreek Place
Westlake Village, CA 91362
"Singer"

MichaelAngelo Avallone
80 Hilltop Blvd.
East Brunswick, NJ 08816
"Author"

Richard Avedon
407 East 75th Street
New York, NY 10021
"Photographer"

Hy Averback
9830 Wilshire Blvd
Beverly Hills, CA 90212
"Film & TV Director"

James Avery
2311 Waverly Drive
Los Angeles, CA 90068
"Actor"

Margaret Avery
P.O. Box 3493
Hollywood, CA 90078
"Actress"

Val Avery
84 Grove Street #19
New York, NY 10014
"Actor"

Hoyt Axton
644 Fred Burr Road
Victor, MT 59875
"Singer, Songwriter"

Dan Aykroyd
8455 Beverly Blvd.
Los Angeles, CA 90048
"Actor"

Leah Ayres
15718 Milbank
Encino, CA 91436
"Actress"

Lew Ayres
675 Walther Way
Los Angeles, CA 90049
"Actor"

Hank Azaria
6435 Bryn Mawr Drive
Los Angeles, CA 90068
"Actor"

Paul Azinger
4520 Bent Tree Blvd
Sarasota, FL 34241
"Golfer"

Charles Aznavour
76-78 ave. des Champs Elysses
F-75008 Paris FRANCE
"Singer"

Candice Azzara
1155 North La Cienega Blvd. #307
Los Angeles, CA 90069
"Actress"

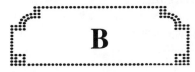

B-52
P.O. Box 60468
Rochester, NY 14606
"Rock & Roll Group"

Shirley Babashoff
17254 Santa Clara Street
Santa Ana, CA 92708
"Swimmer"

Sec. Bruce Babbitt
Department of Interior
"C" St. Between 18th & 19th NW
Washington, DC 20240
"Secretary of Interior"

Harry Babbitt
7 Rue St. Cloud
Newport Beach, CA 91660
"Conductor"

Barbara Babcock
530 West California Blvd.
Pasadena, CA 91105
"Actress"

Tai Babilonia
933-21st Street #6
Santa Monica, CA 90402
"Ice Skater"

Baby's
1545 Archer Road
Bronx, NY 10462
"Music Group"

Babyface
8255 Beverly Blvd.
Los Angeles, CA 90048
"Singer"

Lauren Bacall
1 West 72nd Street #43
New York, NY 10023
"Actress"

Barbara Bach
1541 Ocean Avenue #200
Santa Monica, CA 90401
"Actress"

Cathrine Bach
14000 Davana Terrace
Sherman Oaks, CA 91403
"Actress"

Burt Bacharach
10 Ocean Park Blvd #4
Santa Monica, CA 90405
"Composer, Pianist"

Don Bachardy
145 Adelaide Drive
Santa Monica, CA 90402
"Writer"

Bachman-Turner-Overdrive
1505 West 2nd Avenue, #200
Vancouver BC V6H 3Y4 Canada
"Rock and Roll Group"

Wally Backman
160 S.E. 39th Street
Hillsboro, OR 97123
"Baseball Player"

Henny Backus
10914 Bellagio Road
Los Angeles, CA 90077
"Actress"

James Bacon
10982 Topeka Drive
Northridge, CA 91324
"Actor"

Kevin Bacon
9830 Wilshire Blvd.
Beverly Hills, CA 90212
"Actor"

Sarah Badel
4 Ovington Gardens
London SW3 1LS ENGLAND
"Actress"

John Badham
100 Universal City Plaza
Bldg. #507, 3E
Universal City, CA 91608
"Film Director"

Max Baer, Jr.
10433 Wilshire Blvd. #103
Los Angeles, CA 90024
"Film Director"

Parley Baer
4967 Bilmoor Avenue
Tarzana, CA 91356
"Actor"

Joan Baez
P.O. Box 1026
Menlo Park, CA 94025
"Singer"

Vince Bagetta
3928 Madelia Avenue
Sherman Oak, CA 91403
"Actor"

F. Lee Bailey
1400 Centre Park Blvd. #909
West Palm Beach, FL 33401
"Attorney"

G.W. Bailey
4972 Calvin
Tarzana, CA 91356
"Actor"

Jim Bailey
5909 West Colgate Avenue
Los Angeles, CA 90036
"Actor"

Joel Bailey
6550 Murietta Road
Van Nuys, CA 91401
"Actor"

Razzy Bailey
P.O. Box 62
Geneva, NE 68361
"Singer"

Barbara Bain
1501 Skylark Lane West
West Hollywood, CA 90069
"Actress"

Conrad Bain
1230 Chickory Lane
Los Angeles, CA 90049
"Actress"

Beryl Bainbridge
42 Albert Street
London NW1 7NU ENGLAND
"Author"

Scott Baio
3130 Dona Sarita Place
Studio City, CA 91604
"Actor"

Anita Baker
804 North Crescent Drive
Beverly Hills, CA 90210
"Singer"

Carroll Baker
P.O. Box 480589
Los Angeles, CA 90048
"Actress"

Colin Baker
2-3 Golden Square #42-43
London W1R 3AD ENGLAND
"Actor"

Diane Baker
8877 Tulare Drive #314-D
Huntington Beach, CA 92646
"Actress, Director"

Ginger Baker
4230 Del Rey Avenue, #621
Marina Del Rey, CA 90292
"Musician"

Howard Baker
P.O. Box 8
Huntsville, TN 37756
"Former Senator"

Janet Abbott Baker
450 Edgeware Road
London W2 ENGLAND
"Mezzo-Soprano"

Joe Don Baker
23339 Hatteras
Woodland Hills, CA 91364
"Actor"

Raymond Baker
P.O. Box 5617
Beverly Hills, CA 90210
"Actor"

Brenda Bakke
12754 Sarah Street
Studio City, CA 91604
"Actress"

Roy Ward Baker
125 Gloucester Road
London SW7 4TE ENGLAND
"Film Director"

James (Jim) Bakker
P.O. Box 94
Largo, FL 33649
"TV Evangelist"

Tammy Faye Bakker-Messner
72727 Country Club Drive
Rancho Mirage, CA 92270
"TV Evangelist"

Scott Bakula
9560 Wilshire Blvd. #500
Beverly Hills, CA 90212
"Actor"

Bob Balaban
390 West End Avenue
New York, NY 10024
"Actor"

Belinda Balaski
1434 1/2 N. Curson Ave.
Los Angeles, CA 90046
"Actress"

Rebecca Balding
8831 Sunset Blvd. #304
Los Angeles, CA 90069
"Actress"

Adam Baldwin
P.O. Box 5617
Beverly Hills, CA 90210
"Actor"

Alec Baldwin
1033 Gayley Ave. #208
Los Angeles, CA 90024
"Actor"

Daniel Baldwin
151 El Camino Drive
Beverly Hills, CA 90212
"Actor"

Stephen Baldwin
8730 Sunset Blvd. #490
Los Angeles, CA 90069
"Actor"

William Baldwin
955 S. Carrillo Drive #200
Los Angeles, CA 90048
"Actor"

Christian Bale
151 El Camino Drive
Beverly Hills, CA 90212
"Actor"

Darla Balenda
15848 Woodvale
Encino, CA 91316
"Actress"

Marty Balin
436 Belvedere Street
San Francisco, CA 94117
"Singer, Songwriter"

Fairuza Balk
9830 Wilshire Blvd.
Beverly Hills, CA 90212
"Actress"

Carl Ballantine
6767 Forest Lawn Drive #115
Los Angeles, CA 90068
"Actor, Comedian"

Christine Ballard
11501 Chandler Blvd.
North Hollywood, CA 91601
"TV Writer, Director"

Hank Ballard
11457 Harrisburg Road
Los Alamitos, CA 90720
"Singer"

Kaye Ballard
P.O. Box 922
Rancho Mirage, CA 92270
"Actress, Singer"

Lucinda Ballard
180 East End Avenue
New York, NY 10028
"Costume Designer"

Mark Ballou
9169 Sunset Blvd.
Los Angeles, CA 90069
"Actor"

Talia Balsam
1999 Avenue of the Stars #2850
Los Angeles, CA 90067
"Actress"

Anne Bancroft
2301 La Mesa Drive
Santa Monica, CA 90405
"Actress, Writer, Director"

Prince Bandar al-Saud
601 New Hampshire Avenue N.W.
Washington, DC 20037
"Royalty"

Antonio Banderas
201 South Rockingham Avenue
Los Angeles, CA 90049
"Actor"

Sal Bando
104 West Juniper Lane
Mequon, WI 52092
"Ex-Baseball Player"

Moe Bandy
P.O. Box 748
Adkins, TX 78101
"Singer"

Victor Banerjee
10 East Harrington
Calcutta 700071 INDIA
"Actor"

Abolhassan Bani Sadr
Auvers-Sur-Oise
FRANCE
"Politician"

Ernie Banks
P.O. Box 24302
Los Angeles, CA 90024
"Ex-Baseball Player"

Jonathan Banks
909 Euclid Street #8
Santa Monica, CA 90403
"Actor"

Tyra Banks
170 Fifth Avenue, 10th Floor
New York, NY 10010
"Model"

Ian Bannen
1999 Avenue of the Stars #2850
Los Angeles, CA 90067
"Actor"

Bob Banner
2409 Briarcrest Drive
Beverly Hills, CA 90210
"Director, Producer"

Sir Roger Bannister
1 Church Row
Wandsworth Plain
London SW18 ENGLAND
"Actor"

Jack Bannon
5832 Nagle Avenue
Van Nuys, CA 91401
"Actor"

Christine Baranski
8942 Wilshire Blvd.
Beverly Hills, CA 90211
"Actress"

Adrienne Barbeau
P.O. Box 1334
North Hollywood, CA 91604
"Actress"

Glynis Barber
19 Denmark Street
London, WC2H 8NA ENGLAND
"Actress"

Joseph Barbera
12003 Briarvale Lane
Studio City, CA 91604
"Film Producer"

Paula Barbieri
10660 Wilshire Blvd.
Los Angeles, CA 90024
"Actress, OJ's Girlfriend"

John Barbour
4254 Forman Avenue
Toluca Lake, CA 91602
"Writer, Comedian"

Brigitte Bardot
La Madrigue F-83990
St. Tropez Var, FRANCE
"Actress"

Bobby Bare
1210 West Main Street
Hendersonville, TN 37075
"Singer, Songwriter"

Bob Barker
1851 Outpost Drive
Los Angeles, CA 90068
"TV Show Host"

Ellen Barkin
836 Greenway Drive
Beverly Hills, CA 90210
"Actress"

Charles Barkley
10 Greenway Plaza E.
Houston, TX 77046
"Basketball Player"

Roger Barkley
5435 Burning Tree Drive
La Canada, CA 91011
"Actor"

Carl Barks
P.O. Box 524
Grants Pass, OR 97526
"Cartoonist"

Peter Barkworth
47 Flask Walk
London NW3 ENGLAND
"Actor, Comedian"

Randy Barlow
5514 Kelly Road
Brentwood, TN 37027
"Singer"

Dr. Christian Barnard
Box 6143, Welgemoed 7538
Capetown SOUTH AFRICA
"Heart Surgeon"

Binnie Barnes
838 North Doheny Drive #B
Los Angeles, CA 90069
"Actress"

Joanna Barnes
267 Middle Road
Santa Barbara CA 93108
"TV Writer"

Priscilla Barnes
3500 W. Olive Ave. #1400
Burbank, CA 91505
"Actress"

Barney
300 E. Bethany Road # 8000
Allen, TX 75002
"Cartoon Personality"

Doug Barr
515 South Irving Blvd.
Los Angeles, CA 90020
"Actor"

Julia Barr
420 Madison Avenue #1400
New York, NY 10017
"Actress"

Steve Barr
P.O. Box 395
Mt. Laurel, NJ 08054
"Cartoonist"

Marie-Christine Barrault
2429 Beverly Avenue
Santa Monica, CA 90406
"Actress"

Majel Barrett
P.O. Box 691370
W. Hollywood, CA 90069
"Actress"

Rona Barrett
1122 Tower Road
Beverly Hills, CA 90210
"TV Personality"

Barbara Barrie
15 W. 72nd Street #2A
New York, NY 10023
"Actress"

Maurice Barrier
18 rue de Gravelle
F-75012 Paris, FRANCE
"Actor"

Sydney Biddle Barrows
210 West 70th Street
New York, NY 10023
"Alleged Madam, Socialite"

Dave Barry
1 Herald Plaza
Miami, FL 33101
"Comedian"

Gene Barry
10100 Santa Monica Blvd. #2490
Los Angeles, CA 90067
"Actor"

John Barry
540 Centre Island Road
Oyster Bay, NY 11771
"Composer"

Len Barry
3096 Janice Circle
Chamblee, GA 30341
"Singer"

Marion Barry
3607 Suitland Road
Washington, DC 20004
"Mayor"

Patricia Barry
9229 Sunset Blvd. #710
Los Angeles, CA 90069
"Actress"

Philip Barry, Jr.
12742 Highwood Street
Los Angeles, CA 90049
"Writer, Producer"

Raymond Barry
4526 Wilshire Blvd.
Los Angeles, CA 90010
"Actor"

Sy Barry
34 Saratoga Drive
Jericho, NY 11753
"Cartoonist"

Drew Barrymore
11288 Ventura Blvd. #159
Studio City, CA 91604
"Actress"

John Blyth Barrymore
144 South Peck Drive
Beverly Hills, CA 90212
"Actor"

John Barrymore III
7551 Sunset Blvd. #203
Los Angeles, CA 90046
"Actor"

Lionel Bart
8-10 Bulstrode Street
London W1M 6AM ENGLAND
"Lyricist, Composer"

Jean Bartel
229 Bronwood Avenue
Los Angeles, CA 90049
"Actress"

Paul Bartel
7860 Fareholm Drive
Los Angeles, CA 90046
"Actor, Director"

Bonnie Bartlett
3500 West Olive #1400
Burbank, CA 91505
"Actress"

Peter Barton
2265 Westwood Blvd. #2619
Los Angeles, CA 90064
"Actor"

Billy Barty
4502 Farmdale Avenue
North Hollywood, CA 91602
"Actor"

Mikhail Baryshnikov
157 W. 57th St.#502
New York, NY 10019
"Ballet Dancer"

Basia
2100 Colorado Ave.
Santa Monica, CA 90404
"Rock & Roll Group"

Carmen Basilio
67 Boxwood Drive
Rochester, NY 14617
"Boxer"

Kim Basinger
11288 Ventura Blvd. #414
Studio City, CA 91604
"Actress"

Angela Bassett
9911 West Pico Blvd. PH#1
Los Angeles, CA 90035
"Actress"

Jennifer Bassey
Chelsea Hotel
222 West 23rd Street
New York, NY 10019
"Actress"

Shirley Bassey
24 Avenue Princess Grace #1200
Monte Carlo MONACO
"Singer"

William Bast
6691 Whitley Terrace
Los Angeles, CA 90068
"Screenwriter"

Charles Bateman
303 South Crescent Heights
Los Angeles, CA 90048
"Actor"

Jason Bateman
2628-2nd Street
Santa Monica, CA 90405
"Actor"

Justine Bateman
11288 Ventura Blvd. #190
Studio City, CA 91604
"Actress"

Alan Bates
122 Hamilton Terrace
London NW8 ENGLAND
"Actor"

Kathy Bates
2829 West Shore Drive
Los Angeles, CA 90068
"Actress"

Randall Batinkoff
P.O. Box 555
Ferndale, NY 12734
"Actor"

Kathleen Battle
165 West 57th Street
New York, NY 10019
"Opera Singer"

Belinda Bauder
15301 Ventura Blvd. #345
Sherman Oaks, CA 91403
"Actress"

Bruce Bauer
12456 Ventura Blvd. #1
Studio City, CA 91604
"Actor"

Hank Bauer
12705 West 108th Street
Overland Park, KS 66210
"Ex-Baseball Player"

Jamie Lyn Bauer
3500 West Olive Avenue #1400
Burbank, CA 91505
"Actress"

Steven Bauer
8033 Sunset Blvd. #102
Los Angeles, CA 90046
"Actor"

Sammy Baugh
c/o General Delivery
Rotan, Texas 79546
"Ex-Football Player"

Jon "Bowzer" Bauman
3168 Oakshire Drive
Los Angeles, CA 90068
"Actor, Singer"

Meredith Baxter
151 El Camino Drive
Beverly Hills, CA 90212
"Actress"

Stanley Baxter
2 Ormond Road, Richmond
Surrey TW10 6TH ENGLAND
"Actor, Comedian"

Bay City Rollers
27 Preston Grange Road
Lothian, SCOTLAND
"Rock & Roll Group"

Birch Bayh
1575 "I" Street #1025
Washington, DC 20005
"Ex-Senator"

Don Baylor
56325 Riviera
La Quinta, CA 92253
"Manager & Baseball Player"

Elgin Baylor
3939 South Figueroa Street
Los Angeles, CA 90037
"Ex-Basketball Player"

Beach Boys
4860 San Jacinto Circle #F
Fallbrook, CA 92028
"Rock & Roll Group"

Michael Beach
10100 Santa Monica Blvd., #2500
Los Angeles, CA 90067
"Actor"

Stephanie Beacham
P.O. Box 6448
Malibu, CA 90264
"Actress"

John Beal
205 West 54th Street
New York, NY 10019
"Actor"

Jennifer Beals
151 El Camino Drive
Beverly Hills, CA 90212
"Actress"

Abe Beame
1111-20 Street N.W.
Washington, DC 20575
"Ex-Politician"

Alan Bean
26 Sugarberry Circle
Houston, TX 77024
"Astronaut, Painter"

Orsen Bean
444 Carol Canal
Venice, CA 90291
"Actor, Comedian"

Sean Bean
76 Oxford Street
London W1N OAX ENGLAND
"Actor"

Amanda Bearse
4177 Klump Avenue
North Hollywood, CA 91602
"Actress"

Emmanuelle Beart
9 rue Constant-Coquelin
75007 Paris, FRANCE
"Actress"

Allyce Beasley
2415 Castilian Drive
Los Angeles, CA 90068
"Actress"

Beastie Boys
298 Elizabeth Street
New York, NY 10012
"Rap Group"

Queen Beatrix
Kasteel Drakesteijn
Lage Vuursche 3744 BA
HOLLAND
"Royalty"

Ned Beatty
2706 North Beachwood Drive
Los Angeles, CA 90027
"Actor"

Warren Beatty
13671 Mulholland Drive
Beverly Hills, CA 90210
"Actor, Director, Writer"

Beavis & Butt-Head
1515 Broadway #400
New York, NY 10036
"Music Group"

Gary Beban
6133 N. River Road, #600
Rosemont, IL 60018
"Track Athelete"

Gilbert Becaud
24 rue de Longchamp
Paris 16e FRANCE
"Singer, Songwriter"

Jeff Beck
11 Old South Lincolns Inn
London WC2 ENGLAND
"Singer, Guitarist"

John Beck
12424 Wilshire Blvd. #840
Los Angeles, CA 90025
"Actor"

Kimberly Beck
11330 West Olympic Blvd. #610
Los Angeles, CA 90064
"Actress"

Marilyn Beck
P.O. Box 11079
Beverly Hills, CA 90213
"Columnist, Critic"

Michael Beck
15301 Ventura Blvd. #345
Sherman Oaks, CA 91403
"Actor"

Boris Becker
Nusslocher Str. 51
6906 Leiman, GERMANY
"Tennis Player"

Sidney Beckerman
10490 Wilshire Blvd. #906
Los Angeles, CA 90024
"Film Producer"

Bonnie Bedelia
8942 Wilshire Blvd.
Beverly Hills, CA 90211
"Actress"

Brian Bedford
10100 Santa Monica Blvd. #2500
Los Angeles, CA 90067
"Actor"

Kabir Bedi
8271 Melrose Avenue #202
Los Angeles, CA 90046
"Actor"

19

Molly Bee
6430 Variel Avenue #101
Woodland Hills, CA 90211
"Actress, Singer"

The Bee Gee
P.O. Box 2429
Miami Beach, FL 33140
"Rock & Roll Group"

David Beecroft
4558 Longridge Avenue
Sherman Oaks, CA 91423
"Actor"

Geoffrey Beene
550-7th Avenue
New York, NY 10018
"Fashion Designer"

Leslie Bega
9229 Sunset Blvd. #710
Los Angeles, CA 90069
"Actress"

Ed Begley, Jr.
3850 Moundview Avenue
Studio City, CA 91604
"Actor"

Sam Behrens
9229 Sunset Blvd. #315
Los Angeles, CA 90069
"Actor"

Nina Beilina
400 West 43rd Street #7D
New York, NY 10036
"Violinist"

Harry Belafonte
151 El Camino Drive
Beverly Hills, CA 90212
"Singer, Actor"

Shari Belafonte-Harper
662 North Van Ness Avenue #305
Los Angeles, CA 90004
"Actress, Model"

Christine Belford
12747 Riverside Drive #208
North Hollywood, CA 91607
"Actress"

Barbara Bel Geddes
15 Mill Street
Putnam Valley, NY 10579
"Actress"

Belita
Rose Cottage
44 Crabtress Lane
London SW6 6LW ENGLAND
"Actress, Belleria"

Albert Bell
c/o Cleveland Stadium
Cleveland, OH 44114
"Baseball Player"

Archie Bell
P.O. Box 11669
Knoxville, TN 37939
"Singer"

Bell Biv Devoe
413 South Broad Street
Philadelphia, PA 19147
"R&B Group"

George Bell
324 West 35th Street
Chicago, IL 60616
"Baseball Player"

Griffin Bell
206 Townsend Place NW
Atlanta, GA 30327
"Ex-Government Official"

Laura Lee Bell
7800 Beverly Blvd. #3305
Los Angeles, CA 90036
"Actress"

Tom Bell
108 Torriano Avenue
London NW5 ENGLAND
"Actor"

Bellamy Brothers
Rt. 2, Box 294
Dade City, FL 33525
"Vocal Duo"

Bruce Belland
6226 Elisa Place
Encino, CA 91436
"TV Writer"

Kathleen Beller
11288 Ventura Blvd. #304
Studio City, CA 91604
"Actress"

Melvin Belli
30 Hotaling Place
San Francisco, CA 94133
"Attorney"

Marco Bellocchio
Viale Mazzini 117
00195 Rome, ITALY
"Film Director"

Saul Bellow
1126 E. 59th Street
Chicago, IL 60637
"Writer"

Louie Bellson
12804 Raymer Street
North Hollywood, CA 91605
"Drummer"

Pamela Bellwood
7444 Woodrow Wilson Drive
Los Angeles, CA 90046
"Actress, Photographer"

Jean-Paul Belmondo
9 rue des St. Peres
F-75007 Paris FRANCE
"Actor"

Robert Beltran
924 Westwood Blvd. #900
Los Angeles, CA 90024
"Actor"

James Belushi
8033 Sunset Blvd. #88
Los Angeles, CA 90046
"Actor"

Richard Belzer
9000 Sunset Blvd. #1200
Los Angeles, CA 90069
"Actor"

Pat Benatar
5721 Bonsall Road
Malibu, CA 90265
"Singer"

Brian Benben
3854 Ventura Canyon Ave.
Sherman Oaks, CA 91423
"Actor"

Johnny Bench
617 Vine Street
Cincinnati, OH 45202
"Ex-Baseball Player"

Peter Benchley
35 Boudinot Street
Princeton, NJ 08540
"Author"

Michael Bendetti
3151 Cahuenga Blvd. West #310
Los Angeles, CA 90068
"Actor"

Billy Benedict
1347 North Orange Grove Avenue
Los Angeles, CA 90046
"Actor"

Dirk Benedict
P.O. Box 634
Bigfork, MT 59911
"Actor"

Nick Benedict
3816 Laurel Canyon
Studio City, CA 91604
"Actor"

Paul Benedict
84 Rockland Place
Newton, MA 02164
"Actor"

Tex Beneke
2275 Faust Avenue
Long Beach, CA 90815
"Orchestra Leader"

Annette Bening
13671 Mulholland Drive
Beverly Hills, CA 90210
"Actress"

Richard Benjamin
719 North Foothill Road
Beverly Hills, CA 90210
"Actor, Director"

Bruce Bennett
2702 Forester Road
Los Angeles, CA 90064
"Actor"

Hywell Bennett
15 Golden Square #300
London W1R 3AG ENGLAND
"Actor"

Tony Bennett
101 West 55th Street #9A
New York, NY 10019
"Singer"

Willaim Bennet
1776 "I" Street NW #890
Washington, DC 20006
"Ex-Government Official"

Joan Benny
1131 Coldwater Canyon
Beverly Hills, CA 90210
"Wife of Jack Benny"

Joan Benoit
R.R. #1 - Box 145AA
Freeport, ME 04302
"Track Athlete"

George Benson
519 Next Day Hill Drive
Englewood, NJ 07631
"Singer, Guitarist"

Robby Benson
P.O. Box 1305
Woodland Hills, CA 91364
"Actor, Writer"

Michael Bentine
433 N. Hermosa Drive
Palm Springs, CA 92262
"Actor, Comedian"

John Bentley
Wedgewood House
Peterworth
Sussex ENGLAND
"Actor"

Barbi Benton
40 North 4th Street
Carbondale, CO 81623
"Actress, Model"

John Beradino
1719 Ambassador Drive
Beverly Hills, CA 90210
"Actor"

Tom Berenger
P.O. Box 1842
Beaufort, SC 29901
"Actor"

Berry Berenson
2840 Seattle Drive
Los Angeles, CA 90046
"Mrs. Anthony Perkins"

Marisa Berenson
80 Avenue Charles de Gaulle
F92200 Neuilly, FRANCE
"Actress"

Patty Berg
P.O. Box 9227
Ft. Meyers, FL 33902
"Golfer"

Peter Berg
433 North Camden Drive #500
Beverly Hills, CA 90210
"Actor"

Candice Bergen
955 South Carrillo Drive #200
Los Angeles, CA 90048
"Actress"

Mrs. Edgar Bergen
1485 Carla Ridge Drive
Beverly Hills, CA 90210
"Actress"

Polly Bergen
11342 Dona Lisa Drive
Studio City, CA 91604
"Actress"

Senta Berger
Robert-Koch-Stasse 10
D-82031 Grunwald, GERMANY
"Actress"

Lee Bergere
2385 Century Hill
Los Angeles, CA 90067
"Actor"

Alan Bergman
714 North Maple Drive
Beverly Hills, CA 90210
"Lyricist"

Ingmar Bergman
P.O. Box 27127
S-10252 Stockholm SWEDEN
"Film Director"

Marilyn Bergman
714 North Maple Drive
Beverly Hills, CA 90210
"Lyricist"

Peter Bergman
4799 White Oak Avenue
Encino, CA 91316
"Actor"

Sandahl Bergman
9903 Santa Monica Blvd. #274
Beverly Hills, CA 90212
"Actress, Model"

Luciano Berio
11 Colombaig Radiocobdoli
53100 Siena, ITALY
"Composer, Conductor"

Elizabeth Berkeley
4526 Wilshire Blvd.
Los Angeles, CA 90010
"Actress"

Steven Berkhoff
9255 Sunset Blvd. #515
Los Angeles, CA 90069
"Actor"

David Berkowitz #78A1976
Sullivan Corr. Fac., Box AG
Fallsburg, NY 12733
"Prisoner"

Milton Berle
10750 Wilshire Blvd. #1003
Los Angeles, CA 90024
"Actor, Comedian"

Warren Berlinger
10642 Arnel Place
Chatsworth, CA 91311
"Actor"

Shelley Berman
268 Bell Canyon Road
Bell Canyon, CA 91307
"Comedian"

Crystal Bernard
10866 Wilshire Blvd. #1200
Los Angeles, CA 90024
"Actress"

Ed Bernard
18851 Braemore Road
Northridge, CA 91326
"Actor"

James Bernard
29/33 Berners Street
London W1P 4AA ENGLAND
"Composer"

Edward L. Bernds
6455 Woodman Avenue
Van Nuys, CA 91401
"Writer"

Sandra Bernhard
11233 Blix Street
North Hollywood, CA 91602
"Comedianne, Actress"

Kevin Bernhardt
9300 Wilshire Blvd. #410
Beverly Hills, CA 90212
"Actor"

Collin Bernsen
401 North Poinsettia Place
Los Angeles, CA 90036
"Actor"

Corbin Bernsen
3500 West Olive #920
Burbank, CA 91505
"Actor"

Elmer Bernstein
3301 Barham Blvd. #201
Los Angeles, CA 90068
"Composer, Conductor"

Jay Bernstein
9360 Beverly Crest Drive
Beverly Hills, CA 90210
"Talent Agent"

Kenny Bernstein
1105 Seminole
Richardson, TX 75080
"Race Car Driver"

Yogi Berra
19 Highland Avenue
Montclair, NJ 07042
"Ex-Baseball Player & Manager"

Chuck Berry
Buckner Road
Wentzville, MO 63386
"Singer, Songwriter"

Halle Berry
1368 North Doheny Drive
Los Angeles, CA 90069
"Actress"

John Berry
17060 Central Pike
Lebanon, TN 37087
"Singer"

Ken Berry
4704 Cahuenga Blvd.
North Hollywood, CA 91602
"Actor, Dancer"

Michael Berryman
P.O. Box 902802
Palmdale, CA 93590
"Actor"

HRH Prince Bertil
Hertigens av Halland
Hungl Slottet
11130 Stockholm, SWEDEN
"Royalty"

Valerie Bertinelli
12711 Ventura Blvd. #490
Studio City, CA 91604
"Actress"

Bibi Besch
3500 West Olive Avenue #1400
Burbank, CA 91505
"Actress"

Ted Bessel
1454 Stone Canyon Road
Los Angeles, CA 90077
"Actor, Dancer"

Luc Besson
24 rue Ives Toudic
F-75010 Paris FRANCE
"Director"

James Best
433 Pine Hill Blvd.
Geneva, FL 32732
"Actor"

Kevin Best
P.O. Box 1164
Hesperia, CA 92345
"Actor"

Martine Bestwicke
131 South Sycamore Avenue
Los Angeles, CA 90036
"Actress"

Ivy Bethune
8033 Sunset Blvd. #221
Los Angeles, CA 90046
"Actress"

Zina Bethune
8033 Sunset Blvd. #221
Los Angeles, CA 90046
"Actress"

Gary Bettenhausen
2550 Tree Farm Road
Martinsville, IN 46151
"Race Car Driver"

Tony Bettenhausen
4941 McCrary Street
Speedway, IN 46224
"Race Car Driver"

Lyle Bettger
P.O. Box 1076
Pai, HI 96779
"Actor"

Richard Bey
445 Park Avenue #600
New York, NY 10022
"TV Show Host"

Turhan Bey
1443 North Doheny Drive
Los Angeles, CA 90069
"Actor"

Troy Beyer
9229 Sunset Blvd. #710
Los Angeles, CA 90069
"Actress"

Richard Beymer
1818 N. Fuller Avenue
Los Angeles, CA 90046
"Actor"

Benazir Bhutto
70 Clifton Road
Karachi, PAKISTAN
"Politician"

Mayim Bialik
1525 North Cahuenga Blvd. #304
Los Angeles, CA 90028
"Actress"

Sen. Joseph Biden, Jr.
6 Montcham Drive
Wilmington, DE 19807
"Politician"

Michael Biehn
3737 Deervale Drive
Sherman Oaks, CA 91403
"Actor"

Thom Bierdz
1888 N. Crescent Heights Blvd.
Los Angeles, CA 90069
"Actor"

Ramon Bieri
19963 Arce Street
Northridge, CA 91324
"Actor"

Ronald Biggs
201 rua Monte Alegre
Santa Teresa
Rio de Janiero, BRAZIL
"Train Robber"

Roxanne Biggs-Dawson
1999 Avenue of the Stars #2850
Los Angeles, CA 90067
"Actress"

Theodore Bikel
1131 Alta Loma Road #523
Los Angeles, CA 90069
"Actor, Singer"

Tony Bill
73 Market Street
Venice, CA 90291
"Actor, Director"

Barbara Billingsley
P.O. Box 1320
Santa Monica, CA 90403
"Actress"

Peter Billingsley
1115 North Larrabee #302
Los Angeles, CA 90069
"Child Actor"

Sir Rudolph Bing
160 Central Park South
New York, NY 10019
"Opera Executive"

Juliette Binoche
10 Avenue George V.
F-75008 Paris FRANCE
"Actress"

Matt Biondi
1404 Rimer Drive
Moraga, CA 94556
"Swimmer"

Thora Birch
9560 Wilshire Blvd., #500
Beverly Hills, CA 90212
"Actress"

Billie Bird
9255 Sunset Blvd. #515
Los Angeles, CA 90069
"Actress"

Larry Bird
6278 N. Federal Hwy. #298
Ft. Lauderdale, FL 33308
"Basketball Player"

Jane Birkin
28 rue de la Tour
F-75016 Paris, FRANCE
"Actress"

David Birney
20 Ocean Park Blvd. #11
Sanata Monica, CA 90405
"Actor"

Elvin Bishop
816 West Evergreen
Chicago, IL 60622
"Singer, Guitarist"

Joey Bishop
534 Via Lido Nord
Newport Beach, CA 92660
"Actor, Comedian"

Stephen Bishop
2310 Apollo Drive
Los Angeles, CA 90046
"Singer, Composer"

Jacqueline Bisset
1815 Benedict Canyon Drive
Beverly Hills, CA 90210
"Actress"

Josie Bissett
8033 Sunset Blvd. #4048
Los Angeles, CA 90046
"Actress"

Yannick Bisson
55A Sumuch Street
Toronto, Ontario
M5A 3J6 Canada
"Actor"

Cilla Black
Greener House
66-68 Haymarket
London SW1 7AG ENGLAND
"Singer/Actress"

Clint Black
P.O. Box 299386
Houston, TX 77299
"Singer"

Jay Black
360 Central Avenue
Lawrence, NY 11559
"Musician"

Karen Black
3500 W. Olive Avenue #1400
Burbank, CA 91505
"Actress"

Blackjack
35 Brentwood
Farmingville, NY 11738
"Rock & Roll Group"

Black Oak Arkansas
1487 Red Fox Run
Lilburn, GA 30247
"C&W Group"

Honor Blackman
11 Southwick Mews
London W2 1JG ENGLAND
"Actress"

Harry Blackstone, Jr.
11075 Santa Monica Blvd. #275
Los Angeles, CA 90025
"Magician"

Nina Blackwood
22968 Victory Blvd. #158
Woodland Hills, CA 91367
"Music Correspondent"

Taurean Blacque
4207 Don Ortega Place
Los Angeles, CA 90008
"Actor"

Ruben Blades
521 - 12th Street
Santa Monica, CA 90402
"Singer, Actor, Songwriter"

Nell Walden Blaine
3 Ledge Road
Gloucester, MA 01930
"Painter"

Betsy Blair
11 Chalcot Gardens
England's Lane
London NW3 ENGLAND
"Actress"

Bonnie Blair
N34W23-38 B Grace Avenue
Pewaukee, WI 53072
"Skater"

Janet Blair
21650 Burbank Blvd. #107
Woodland Hills, CA 91367
"Actress"

Linda Blair
8033 Sunset Blvd. #204
Los Angeles, CA 90046
"Actress"

Lionel Blair
68 Old Brompton Road #200
London SW7 3LQ ENGLAND
"TV Personality, Dancer"

Robert Blake
11604 Dilling Street
North Hollywood, CA 91608
"Actor"

Stephanie Blake
14332 Dickens Street #8
Sherman Oaks, CA 91423
"Actress"

Whitney Blake
P.O. Box 6088
Malibu, CA 90265
"Actress"

Susan Blakely
421 North Rodeo Drive #15-111
Berverly Hills, CA 90210
"Actress"

Michael Blakemore
11A St. Martin's Almhousees
Bayham
London NW1 ENGLAND
"Film Director"

Ronee Blakley
8033 Sunset Blvd. #693
Los Angeles, CA 90046
"Singer, Actress"

Noel Blanc
702 North Rodeo Drive
Beverly Hills, CA 90210
"Writer"

Nina Blanchard
11288 Ventura Blvd. #615
Studio City, CA 91604
"Talent Agent"

George Blanda
P.O. Box 1153
La Quinta, CA 92253
"Football Player"

Sally Blane
1114 South Roxbury Drive
Los Angeles, CA 90035
"Actress"

Mark Blankfield
141 South El Camino Drive #205
Beverly Hills, CA 90212
"Actor"

Bill Blass
550 - 7th Avenue
New York, NY 10019
"Fashion Designer"

Freddie Blassie
P.O. Box 3859
Stamford, CT 06905
"Wrestler, Manager"

The Blasters
2667 North Beverly Glen
Los Angeles, CA 90077
"Rock & Roll Group"

Richard Blasucci
353 1/2 North Gardner
Los Angeles, CA 90036
"Actor, Writer"

Jeff Blatnick
848 Whitney Drive
Schenectady, NY 12309
"Wrestler"

Drew Bledsoe
Sullivan Stadium-Route 1
Foxboro, MA 02035
"Football Player"

Tempest Bledsoe
P.O. Box 7217
Beverly Hills, CA 90212
"Actress"

Yasmine Bleeth
104-6 Queens Blvd. #10C
Forest Hills, NY 11375
"Actress"

Rocky Bleier
580 Squal Run Road East
Pittsburgh, PA 15238
"Ex-Football Player"

John Bleifer
832 S. Masselin Avenue
Los Angeles, CA 90036
"Actor"

Brian Blessed
82 Broom Park, Teddington
Middlesex TW11 9RR ENGLAND
"Actor"

Mary J. Blige
8942 Wilshire Blvd.
Beverly Hills, CA 90211
"Singer"

Andrew Bloch
718 N. King Road #105
Los Angeles, CA 90069
"Actor"

Herb Block
1150 - 15th Street NW
Washington, DC 20071
"Cartoonist"

Hunt Block
606 N. Larchmont Blvd. #309
Los Angeles, CA 90004
"Actor"

Dirk Blocker
5063 La Ramada Drive
Santa Barbara, CA 93111
"Actor"

Michael Blodgett
10485 National Blvd. #22
Los Angeles, CA 90034
"Actor"

Linda Bloodworth-Thomason
9220 Sunset Blvd. #311
Los Angeles, CA 90069
"Film Producer"

Anne Bloom
11288 Ventura Blvd. #B222
Studio City, CA 91604
"Actress, Comedienne"

Brian Bloom
11 Croydon Court
Dix Hills, NY 11746
"Actor"

Claire Bloom
8428-C Melrose Place
Los Angeles, CA 90069
"Actress"

Lindsay Bloom
8440 Westcliff Drive #2084
Las Vegas, NV 89128
"Actress"

Verna Bloom
327 East 82nd Street
New York, NY 10028
"Actress"

Betsy Bloomingdale
131 Delfern Drive
Los Angeles, CA 90077
"Business Executive"

Lisa Blount
151 El Camino Drive
Beverly Hills, CA 90212
"Actress"

Mel Blount
R.D. 1, Box 91
Claysville, PA 15323
"Ex-Football Player"

Kurtis Blow
P.O. Box 391068
Cleveland, OH 44139
"Singer"

Vida Blue
P.O. Box 1449
Pleasanton, CA 94566
"Ex-Baseball Player"

Judy Blume
54 Riverside Drive
New York, NY 10023
"Writer"

Ann Blyth
P.O. Box 9754
Rancho Santa Fe, CA 92067
"Actress"

True Boardman
2951 Paisano Road
Pebble Beach, CA 93593
"Actor"

Michael Boatman
1571 South Kiowa Crest Drive
Diamond Bar, CA 91765
"Actor"

Lorena Bobbitt
709 Gray Avenue
Durham, NC 27701
"Cut off Husband's Penis"

Steven Bochco
694 Amalfi Drive
Pacific Palisades, CA 90272
"Writer, Producer"

Hart Bochner
1231 Gorham Avenue
Los Angeles, CA 90049
"Actor"

Lloyd Bochner
42 Haldeman Road
Santa Monica, CA 90402
"Actor"

Budd Boetticher
P.O. Box 1137
Ramona, CA 92065
"Film Director"

Sir Dirk Bogarde
76 Oxford Street
London W1N 0AX ENGLAND
"Actor"

Peter Bogdanovich
12451 Mulholland Drive
Beverly Hills, CA 90210
"Film Writer, Director"

Wade Boggs
6006 Windham Place
Tampa, FL 33647
"Baseball Player"

Suzy Bogguss
33 Music Sq. W. #110
Nashville, TN 37203
"Singer"

Heidi Bohay
48 Main Street
South Bound Brook, NJ 08880
"Actress"

Corinne Bohrer
4526 Wilshire Blvd.
Los Angeles, CA 90010
"Actress"

Richard Bohringer
14 Avenue Duquesne
95160 Dewil-la-Barre FRANCE
"Actor"

Brian Boitano
101 First Street #370
Los Altos, CA 94022
"Ice Skater"

Tiffany Bolling
12483 Braddock Drive
Los Angeles, CA 90066
"Actress"

Joseph Bologna
16830 Ventura Blvd. #326
Encino, CA 91436
"Actor, Writer, Director"

Henry Boltinoff
7518A English Ct.
Lake Worth, FL 33467
"Cartoonist"

Michael Bolton
92 Snowberry Lane
New Canaan, CT 06840
"Singer"

Danny Bonaduce
875 N. Michigan Ave. #3750
Chicago, IL 60611
"Actor"

Julian Bond
361 West View Drive
Atlanta, GA 30310
"Politician"

Philip Bond
50 High Street
Abergwynfi
W. Gamorgan SA13 3YW
ENGLAND
"Actor"

Tommy "Butch" Bond
14704 Road 36
Madera, CA 93638
"Actor"

Barry Bonds
42 Robleda Drive
Atherton, CA 94027
"Baseball Player"

Steve Bond
8721 Santa Monica Blvd.
West Hollywood, CA 90069
"Actor"

Gary U.S. Bonds
141 Dunbar Avenue
Fords, NJ 08863
"Singer"

Peter Bonerz
3637 Lowry Road
Los Angeles, CA 90027
"Actor, Director"

Lisa Bonet
1551 Will Geer Road
Topanga, CA 90290
"Actress"

Jon Bon Jovi
250 West 57th Street #603
New York, NY 10107
"Rock & Roll Group"

Rep. David E. Bonior (MI)
House Rayburn Bldg. #2207
Washington, DC 20515
"Politician"

Elayna Bonner
Uliza Tschakalowa 48
Moscow, RUSSIA
"Politician"

Frank Bonner
10100 Santa Monica Blvd. #700
Los Angeles, CA 90067
"Actor, Director"

Chastity Bono
P.O. Box 960
Beverly Hills, CA 90213
"Cher's Daughter"

Rep. Sonny Bono (CA)
32 E. Tahquitz-McCullum Way
Palm Springs, CA 92262
"Singer, Actor, Politician"

Brian Bonsall
11712 Moorpark Street #204
Studio City, CA 91604
"Actor"

Booker T & the MGs
59 Parsons Street
Newtonville, MA 02160
"R&B Group"

Debby Boone
4334 Kester Avenue
Sherman Oaks, CA 91403
"Singer"

Pat Boone
904 North Beverly Drive
Beverly Hills, CA 90210
"Actor, Singer"

Randy Boone
14250 Califa Street
Van Nuys, CA 91401
"Actor"

Charley Boorman
"The Glebe"
Annanoe County Wicklow
IRELAND
"Film Director"

John Boorman
21 Thurlue Square
London W1 ENGLAND
"Film Director"

Elayne Boosler
11061 Wrightwood Lane
North Hollywood, CA 91604
"Comedienne"

Adrian Booth
3922 Glenridge Drive
Sherman Oaks, CA 91423
"Actor"

Connie Booth
Prince of Wales Theatre
Coventry Street
London W1V 7FE ENGLAND
"Actress"

Powers Boothe
23629 Long Valley Road
Hidden Hills, CA 91302
"Actor"

Lynn Borden
6399 Wilshire Blvd. #211
Los Angeles, CA 90048
"Actress"

Carla Borelli
8075 W. 3rd Street #303
Los Angeles, CA 90048
"Actress"

David Boren
211 East Oak
Seminole, OK 74868
"Politician"

Bjorn Borg
One Erieview Plaza #1300
Cleveland, OH 44114
"Tennis Player"

Victor Borge
Fieldpoint Park
Greenwich, CT 06830
"Pianist, Comedian"

Jim Borgman
617 Vine Street
Cincinnati, OH 45201
"Cartoonist"

Ernest Borgnine
3055 Lake Glen Drive
Beverly Hills, CA 90210
"Actor"

Tova Borgnine
3055 Lake Glen Drive
Beverly Hills, CA 90210
"Actress"

Robert Bork
1150-17th Street N.W.
Washington, DC 20036
"Judge"

Matt Borlenghi
8721 Sunset Blvd. #210
Los Angeles, CA 90069
"Actor"

Major Frank Borman
6628 Vista Hermosa
Las Cruces, NM 88005
"Astronaut"

Philip Bosco
337 West 43rd Street #1B
New York, NY 10036
"Actor"

Tom Bosley
2822 Royston Place
Beverly Hills, CA 90210
"Actor"

Barbara Bosson
694 Amalfi Drive
Pacific Palisades, CA 90272
"Actress"

Ralph Boston
3301 Woodbine Avenue
Knoxville, TN 37914
"Track Athlete"

Barry Bostwick
2770 Hutton Drive
Beverly Hills, CA 90210
"Actor"

Brian Bosworth
230 Park Avenue #230
New York, NY 10169
"Actor, Football Player"

Joe Bottoms
1015 Gayley Avenue #300
Los Angeles, CA 90024
"Actor"

Sam Bottoms
4719 Willowcrest Avenue
Toluca Lake, CA 91602
"Actor"

Timothy Bottoms
532 Hot Springs Road
Santa Barbara, CA 93108
"Actor"

Lou Boudreau
15600 Ellis Avenue
Dolton, IL 60419
"Ex-Baseball Player"

Pierre Boulez
Postfach 22
Baden-Baden GERMANY
"Composer, Conductor"

Jim Bouton
P.O. Box 188
North Edremont, MA 01252
"Ex-Baseball Player"

John Bowab
2598 Green Valley
Los Angeles, CA 90046
"TV Director"

Riddick Bowe
1100 New York Ave. NW #814
Washington, DC 20001
"Boxer"

Antoinette Bower
1126 Hollywood Way #203A
Burbank, CA 91505
"Actress"

David Bowie
76 Oxford Street
London W1N OAX ENGLAND
"Singer, Actor"

Judi Bowker
31 Soho Square
London W1V 5DG ENGLAND
"Actress"

Peter Bowles
125 Gloucester Road
London SW7 ENGLAND
"Actor"

Christopher Bowman
5653 Kester Avenue
Van Nuys, CA 91405
"Skater"

Boxcar Willie
1300 Division Street #103
Nashville, TN 37203
"Singer"

Sen. Barbara Boxer (CA)
112 Hart Office Bldg.
Washington, DC 20510
"Politician"

Bruce Boxleitner
24500 Jonh Colter Road
Hidden Hills, CA 91302
"Actor"

Lara Flynn Boyle
12190 1/2 Ventura Blvd. #304
Studio City, CA 91604
"Actress"

Peter Boyle
130 East End Avenue
New York, NY 10024
"Actor"

The Boys
P.O. Box 5482
Carson, CA 90746
"Rock & Roll Group"

Boys II Men
6255 Sunset Blvd. #1700
Los Angeles, CA 90028
"R&B Group"

Lorraine Bracco
130 W. 57th Street #5E
New York, NY 10019
"Actress"

Eddie Bracken
69 Douglas Road
Glen Ridge, NJ 07028
"Actor"

Ray Bradbury
10265 Cheviot Drive
Los Angeles, CA 90064
"Author"

Barbara Taylor Bradford
425 East 58 Street
New York, NY 10022
"Writer"

Richard Bradford
849 S. Broadway #750
Los Angeles, CA 90014
"Actor"

Benjamin Bradlee
1150-15th Street N.W.
Washington, DC 20071
"Journalist"

Bill Bradley
1 Newark Center
Newark, NJ 07102
"Politician"

David Bradley
6310 San Vincente Blvd. #407
Los Angeles, CA 90048
"Actor"

Ed Bradley
285 Central Park West
New York, NY 10024
"Newcaster"

Owen Bradley
P.O. Box 120838
Nashville, TN 37212
"Pianist"

Tom Bradley
555 S. Hope St. #2100
Los Angeles, CA 90071
"Ex-Mayor of Los Angeles"

Terry Bradshaw
8911 Shady Lane Drive
Sherveport, LA 71118
"Ex-Football Player"

James Brady
1255 "I" Street #1100
Washington, DC 20005
"Ex-White House Press Sec."

Eric Braeden
13723 Romany Drive
Pacific Palisades, CA 90272
"Actor"

Sonia Braga
295 Greenwich Street #11B
New York, NY 10007
"Actress"

Don Bragg
P.O. Box 171
New Gretna, NJ 08224
"Track Athlete"

Kenneth Branagh
302-308 Regent Street
London W1R 5AL ENGLAND
"Actor, Director"

Klaus Maria Brandauer
Fischernforf 76
8992 Alta-Ausse, AUSTRIA
"Actress"

Jonathan Brandis
P.O. Box 5617
Beverly Hills, CA 90210
"Actor"

Marlon Brando
13828 Weddington
Van Nuys, CA 91401
"Actor"

Michael Brandon
11664 National Blvd. #108
Los Angeles, CA 90064
"Actor"

Brand X
17171 Roscoe Blvd. #104
Northridge, CA 91325
"Actor"

Benjamin Bratt
8969 Sunset Blvd.
Los Angeles, CA 90069
"Actor"

Andre Braugher
9560 Wilshire Blvd., #500
Beverly Hills, CA 90212
"Actor"

Asher Brauner
190 North Canon Drive #201
Beverly Hills, CA 90210
"Actor"

Bart Braverman
524 North Laurel Avenue
Los Angeles, CA 90048
"Actor"

Toni Braxton
3350 Peachtree Road #1500
Atlanta, GA 30326
"Singer"

Julian Bream
122 Wigmore Street
London W1 ENGLAND
"Guitarist"

Peter Breck
238 East 1st Street
North Vancouver, B.C.
V7L 1B3 CANADA
"Actor"

Buddy Bregman
11288 Ventura Blvd. #700
Studio City, CA 91604
"Director, Producer"

Tracey E. Bregman
7800 Beverly Blvd. #3305
Los Angeles, CA 90036
"Actress"

Eileen Brennan
974 Mission Terrace
Camarillo, CA 91310
"Actress"

Melissa Brennan
6520 Platt Avenue #634
West Hills, CA 90307
"Actress"

Amy Brenneman
9150 Wilshire Blvd. #175
Beverly Hills, CA 90212
"Actress"

David Brenner
42 Downing Street
New York, NY 10014
"Comedian, Talk Show Host"

Dori Brenner
2106 Canyon Drive
Los Angeles, CA 90068
"Actress"

Bobbie Bresee
P.O. Box 1222
Hollywood, CA 90078
"Actress, Model"

Jimmy Breslin
75 Central Park West
New York, NY 10023
"Author, Columnist"

Martin Brest
831 Paseo Miramar
Pacific Palisades, CA 90272
"Film Writer, Director"

George Brett
P.O. Box 419969
Kansas City, MO 64141
"Baseball Player"

Teresa Brewer
384 Pinebrook Blvd.
New Rochelle, NY 10803
"Singer"

Carol Brewster
8721 Sunset Blvd. #203
Los Angeles, CA 90069
"Actress"

Mary Brian
4107 Troost Avenue
North Hollywood, CA 90212
"Actress"

Beth Brickell
P.O. Box 26
Paron, AR 72122
"Writer, Director"

Beau Bridges
5525 North Jed Smith Road
Hidden Hills, CA 91302
"Actor, Director"

Jeff Bridges
985 Hot Springs Road
Montecito, CA 93108
"Actor"

Lloyd Bridges
225 Lorina Avenue
Los Angeles, CA 90077
"Actor"

Todd Bridges
7550 Zombar Avenue #1
Van Nuys, CA 91406
"Actor"

Dee Dee Bridgewater
8 S. Oxford Street
Brooklyn, NY 11217
"Singer, Actress"

Charlie Brill
3635 Wrightwood Drive
Studio City, CA 91604
"Actor"

Bernie Brillstein
9150 Wilshire Blvd. #350
Beverly Hills, CA 90212
"Talent Agent"

Wilfred Brimley
415 North Camden Drive #121
Beverly Hills, CA 90210
"Actor"

Christie Brinkley
2124 Broadway #104
New York, NY 10023
"Model"

David Brinkley
1717 DeSales Street
Washington, DC 20036
"TV Show Host"

May Britt
P.O. Box 525
Zephyr Cove, NV 89448
"Actress"

Morgan Brittany
3434 Cornell Road
Agoura Hills, CA 91301
"Actress, Model"

Tony Britton
76 Oxford Street
London W1N 0AX ENGLAND
"Actor"

Albert "Cubby" Broccoli
809 North Hillcrest Road
Beverly Hills, CA 90210
"Motion Picture Producer"

Lou Brock
11885 Lackland Road
St. Louis, MO 63146
"Ex-Baseball Player"

Beth Broderick
9300 Wilshire Blvd. #555
Beverly Hills, CA 90212
"Actress"

Matthew Broderick
1775 Broadway #701
New York, NY 10019
"Actor"

Kevin Brodie
4292 Elmer Avenue
North Hollywood, CA 91602
"Actor"

Lane Brody
P.O. Box 24775
Nashville, TN 37202
"Singer"

Ronnie Brody
21 Bartle Road
London W11 ENGLAND
"Actor"

Tom Brokaw
941 Park Avenue #14C
New York, NY 10025
"Newscaster"

James Brolin
P.O. Box 56927
Sherman Oaks, CA 91413
"Actor"

Josh Brolin
P.O. Box 56927
Sherman Oaks, CA 91413
"Actor"

John Bromfield
P.O. Box 2655
Lake Havau City, AZ 86405
"Actor"

Edgar M. Bronfman
375 Park Avenue
New York, NY 10152
"Distillery Executive"

Charles Bronson
P.O. Box 2644
Malibu, CA 90265
"Actor"

Hilary Brooke
40 Via Casitas
Bonsall, CA 92003
"Actress"

Gary Brooker
5 Cranley Gardens
London SW7 ENGLAND
"Singer, Composer"

Brooklyn Bridge
P.O. Box 63
Cliffwood, NJ 07721
"Rock & Roll Group"

Brooks & Dunn
P.O. Box 150245
Nashville, TN 37215
"Country Music Duo"

Albert Brooks
1880 Century Park E. #900
Los Angeles, CA 90067
"Actor, Writer, Director"

Avery Brooks
20 Layne Road
Summerset, NJ 08873
"Actor"

Donnie Brooks
8033 Sunset Blvd. #1000
Los Angeles, CA 90046
"Comedian"

Faith Brooks
109 Jermyn Street
London SW1Y 6A5 ENGLAND
"Actress"

Foster Brooks
315 South Beverly Drive #216
Beverly Hills, CA 90212
"Comedian"

Garth Brooks
3322 West End Avenue #1100
Nashville, TN 37203
"Singer"

James L. Brooks
8942 Wilshire Blvd.
Beverly Hills, CA 90211
"TV Writer, Producer"

Mel Brooks
2301 La Mesa Drive
Santa Monica, CA 90405
"Actor, Writer, Director"

Rand Brooks
1701 Capistrano Circle
Glendale, CA 91207
"Actress"

Kevin Brophy
15010 Hamlin Street
Van Nuys, CA 91411
"Actor"

Pierce Brosnan
23715 West Malibu Road
Malibu, CA 90265
"Actor, Model"

Dr. Joyce Brothers
1530 Palisades Avenue
Fort Lee, NJ 07024
"Psychologist"

Louise Brough
1808 Voluntary Road
Vista, CA 92083
"Tennis Player"

Haywood Hale Broun
189 Plochman
Woodstock, NY 12498
"Sportswriter, Sportscaster"

Rebecca Broussard
9911 West Pico Blvd. PH A
Los Angeles, CA 90035
"Actress"

Blair Brown
10 East 44th Street #500
New York, NY 10017
"Actress"

Bobby Brown
1324 Thomas Place
Ft. Worth, TX 76107
"Singer"

Bryan Brown
110 Queen Street
Woollahra NSW 2025
AUSTRALIA
"Actor"

Clarence "Gatemouth" Brown
434 Avenue U.
Bogalusa, LA 70427
"Singer, Guitarist"

Dee Brown
150 Causeway Street
Boston, MA 02114
"Basketball Player"

Denise Brown
P.O. Box 380
Monarch Bay, CA 92629
"Nicole Brown-Simpson's Sister"

Dwier Brown
9200 Sunset Blvd., #710
Los Angeles, CA 90069
"Actor"

Edmund "Jerry" Brown, Jr.
3022 Washington
San Francisco, CA 94115
"Ex-Governor"

Georg Stanford Brown
2565 Greenvalley Road
Los Angeles, CA 90046
"Actor, Director"

Helen Brown
1811 Whitley Avenue #200
Los Angeles, CA 90028
"Actress"

Helen Gurley Brown
1 West 81st Street #22D
New York, NY 10024
"Author, Editor"

Hubie Brown
6 Cobblewood Road
Livingston, NJ 07039
"Basketball Coach"

James Brown
1217 West Medical Park Road
Augusta, GA 30909
"Singer

Jim Brown
1851 Sunset Plaza Drive
Los Angeles, CA 90069
"Ex-Football Player, Actor"

Jim Ed Brown
P.O. Box 121089
Nashville, TN 37212
"Singer"

Johnny Brown
2732 Woodhaven Drive
Los Angeles, CA 90068
"Performer"

Julie Brown
11288 Ventura Blvd. #728
Studio City, CA 91604
"Comedienne"

Kimberlin Brown
4439 Worster Avenue
Studio City, CA 91604
"Singer"

Les Brown
1787 Fernald Point Lane
Montecito, CA 93180
"Orchestra Leader"

Lisa Brown
448 West 44th Street
New York, NY 10036
"Actress"

Nacio Herb Brown, Jr.
1739 DeCamp Drive
Beverly Hills, CA 90210
"Actor"

Peter Brown
854 Cypress Avenue
Hermosa Beach, CA 90254
"Actor"

Reb Brown
5454 Las Virgines Road
Calabasas, CA 91302
"Actor"

Ruth Brown
600 West 165th Street #4-H
New York, NY 10032
"Singer"

Susan Brown
11931 Addison Street
North Hollywood, CA 91607
"Actress"

T. Graham Brown
38 Music Sq. E. #300
Nashville, TN 37203
"Singer"

Thomas Wilson Brown
5918 Van Nuys Blvd.
Van Nuys, CA 91401
"Actor"

Vanessa Brown
5914 Coldwater Canyon Avenue
North Hollywood, CA 91607
"Actress"

Willie L. Brown, Jr.
455 Golden Gate Avenue #2220
San Francisco, CA 94102
"Politician"

Woody Brown
6548 Colbath Avenue
Van Nuys, CA 91401
"Actor"

Jackson Browne
2746 Kling Street
Studio City, CA 91604
"Singer, Composer"

Kathy Browne
P.O. Box 2939
Beverly Hills, CA 90213
"Actress"

Roscoe Lee Browne
3531 Wonderview Drive
Los Angeles, CA 90068
"Actor, Writer, Director

Kurt Browning
11160 River Valley Road #3180
Edmondton, Alberto
T5J 2G7 CANADA
"Ice Skater"

Ricou Browning
5221 SW 196th Lane
Ft. Lauderdale, FL 33332
"Writer, Producer"

Dave Brubeck
221 Millstone Road
Wilton, CT 06807
"Pianist"

Carol Bruce
1361 North Laurel #9
Los Angeles, CA 90046
"Actress"

Kitty Bruce
31 Harrison Street
New York, NY 10019
"Singer"

Bo Brundin
1716 Clybourn Avenue
Burbank, CA 91505
"Actor"

Carla Bruni
10 place de la Concorde
F-75008 Paris FRANCE
"Model"

Frank Bruno
Centurion House,
Birchley Green, Herford
Herfordshire WG14 1AP EN-
GLAND
"Boxer"

Ellen Bry
2800 Neilson Way #1113
Santa Monica, CA 90405
"Actress"

Dora Bryan
11 Marine Parade
Brighton Sussex ENGLAND
"Actress"

Zachary Ty Bryan
4444 Lankershim Blvd. #207
North Hollywood, CA 91602
"Actor"

Anita Bryant
3446 West Highway 76
Branson, MO 65616
"Singer"

Michael Bryant
Willow Cottage
Kington Magna
Dorset SP8 5EW ENGLAND
"Actor"

Scott Bryce
10100 Santa Monica Blvd. #2500
Los Angeles, CA 90067
"Actor"

Peabo Bryson
999 Peachtree Street #2680
Atlanta, GA 30309
"Singer"

Zbigniew Brzezinski
1800 "K" St. NW #400
Washington, DC 20006
"Politician"

Sergei Bubka
Priesterweg 8
D-10829 Berlin GERMANY
"Pole-Vaulter"

Angela "Bay" Buchanan
909 11th Street NE
Washington, D.C. 20002
"Pat Buchanan's Sister"

Ian Buchanan
3500 W. Olive #1400
Burbank, CA 91505
"Actor"

Patrick J. Buchanan
1017 Savile Lane North
McLean, VA 22101
"Politician, Columnist"

Horst Buchholz
232 rue du Fbg. South
St. Honore
F. 75008 Paris FRANCE
"Actor"

Art Buchwald
2000 Pennsylvania Avenue NW
Washington, DC 20006
"Columnist"

Bill Buckner
2425 W. Victory Road
Meridian, ID 83642
"Ex-Baseball Player"

Lindsay Buckingham
900 Airole Way
Los Angleles, CA 90077
"Singer, Songwriter"

The Buckinghams
620 - 16th Avenue South
Hopkins, MN 55343
"Rock & Roll Group"

Betty Buckley
420 Madison Avenue #1400
New York, NY 10017
"Actress"

William F. Buckley, Jr.
150 East 35th Street
New York, NY 10016
"Author, Editor"

Julie Budd
156 West 68th Street
New York, NY 10024
"Actress"

Terence Budd
29 Rylette Road
London W12 ENGLANG
"Actor"

Zola Budd
1 Church Row
Wandsworth Plain
London SW18 ENGLAND
"Runner"

Don Budge
P.O. Box 789
Dingman's Ferry, PA 18328
"Tennis Player"

Maria Bueno
Rua Consolagao 3414 #10
1001 Edificio Augustus
Sao Paulo, BRAZIL
"Tennis Player"

Jimmy Buffet
500 Duval Street #B
Key West, FL 33040
"Singer, Songwriter"

Warren Buffett
1440 Kiewit Plaza
Omana, NE 68131
"Business Executive"

The Buggles
22 St. Peters Square
London W69 NW ENGLAND
"Rock & Roll Group"

Vincent T. Bugliosi
8530 Wilshire Blvd. #404
Beverly Hills, CA 90210
"Attorney, Author"

Genevieve Bujold
27258 Pacific Coast Hwy.
Malibu, CA 90265
"Actress"

Donald Buka
1501 Beacon Street #1802
Brookline, MA 02146
"Actor"

Ray Buktenica
335 N. Maple Drive #360
Beverly Hills, CA 90210
"Actor"

Joyce Bulifant
P.O. Box 6748
Snowmass Village, CO 81615
"Actress"

Richard Bull
750 N. Rush Street #3401
Chicago, IL 60611
"Actor"

Jim J. Bullock
1015 N. Kings Road #215
Los Angeles, CA 90069
"Actor"

Sandra Bullock
9560 Wilshire Blvd. #516
Beverly Hills, CA 90212
"Actress"

Grace Bumbry
165 West 57th Street
New York, NY 10019
"Opera Singer"

Brooke Bundy
1801 Ave. of the Stars #1250
Los Angeles, CA 90067
"Actress"

Jim Bunning
4 Fairway Drive
Southgate, KY 41071
"Politician, Ex-Baseball Player"

Lou Burdette
2019 Beveva Road
Sarasota, FL 34232
"Ex-Baseball Player"

Gregg Burge
420 Madison Avenue #1400
New York, NY 10017
"Singer"

Gary Burghoff
9911 West Pico Blvd. #1200
Los Angeles, CA 90035
"Actor"

Richard Burgi
2423 3/4 Cheremoya Avenue
Los Angeles, CA 90068
"Actor"

David Burke
924 Westwood Blvd., 3900
Los Angeles, CA 90024
"TV Producer"

Delta Burke
427 North Canon Drive #215
Beverly Hills, CA 90210
"Actress"

Paul Burke
2217 Avenida Caballeros
Palm Springs, CA 92262
"Actor"

Robert Burke
151 El Camino Drive
Beverly Hills, CA 90212
"Actor"

Soloman Burke
1048 Tatnall Street
Macon, GA 31201
"Singer"

Dennis Burkley
5145 Costello Avenue
Sherman Oaks, CA 91423
"Actor"

Tom Burleson
c/o General Delivery
Newland, NC 28657
"Actor"

Billy Burnett
1025 - 16th Ave. S. #401
Nashville, TN 37212
"Singer, Guitarist"

Carol Burnett
P.O. Box 1298
Pasadena, CA 91031
"Actress, Comedienne"

Nancy Burnett
7800 Beverity Blvd. #3305
Los Angeles, CA 90036
"Actress"

T-Bone Burnett
211-20th Street
Santa Monica, CA 90402
"Singer"

Eileen Burns
4000 West 43rd Street
New York, NY 10036
"Actress"

Eric Burns
448 1/2 N. Stanley Avenue
Los Angeles, CA 90046
"News Correspondent"

James MacGregor Burns
Bee Hill Road
Williamstown, MA 01267
"Political Scientist, Historian"

Jere Burns
P.O. Box 3596
Mammoth Lakes, CA 93546
"Actor"

Ken Burns
Maple Grove Road
Walpole, NH 03608
"Documentary Producer"

Kenny Burrell
163 Third Avenue #206
New York, NY 10003
"Jazz Musician"

Leroy Burrell
1801 Ocean Park Blvd. #112
Santa Monica, CA 90405
"Track & Field"

James Burrows
5555 Melrose Avenue #D-228
Los Angeles, CA 90038
"Writer, Producer"

Ellen Burstyn
Ferry House, Box 217
Washington Spring Road
Snedens Landing
Palisades, NY 10964
"Actress"

Kate Burton
P.O. Box 5617
Beverly Hills, CA 90210
"Actress"

Levar Burton
13601 Ventura Blvd. #209
Sherman Oaks, CA 91423
"Actor"

Mrs. Sally Burton
Pays de Galles
Coligny, SWITZERLAND
"Widower of Richard Burton"

Tim Burton
5310 Loma Linda Avenue #8
Los Angeles, CA 90027
"Actor, Director, Producer"

Warren Burton
280 S. Beverly Drive #400
Beverly Hills, CA 90212
"Actor"

Wendell Burton
6526 Costello Drive
Van Nuys, CA 91401
"Actor"

Gary Busey
18424 Coastline Drive
Malibu, CA 90265
"Actor"

Timothy Busfield
1901 Avenue of the Stars #1450
Los Angeles, CA 90067
"Actor"

Barbara Bush
9 West Oak Drive
Houston, TX 77056
"Ex-First Lady"

Dick Bush
8 Grande Parade, #16
Plymouth, Devon PL1 3DF EN-
GLAND
"Cinematographer"

George Bush
9 West Oak Drive
Houston, TX 77056
"Ex-President of United States"

George Bush, Jr.
P.O. Box 12404
Austin, TX 78711
"Governor"

Kate Bush
20 Manchester Square
London W1 ENGLAND
"Singer, Songwriter"

Joe Bushkin
435 East 52nd Street
New York, NY 10022
"Pianist, Composer"

Dr. Jerry Buss
P.O. Box 10
Inglewood, CA 90306
"Basketball Team Owner"

Mangosutho Buthelezi
Union Bldg.
Pretoria 0001
South Africa
"Zulu Chief"

Dick Butkus
3500 West Olive #1400
Burbank, CA 91505
"Ex-Football Player"

Brett Butler
P.O. Box 5617
Beverly Hills, CA 90210
"Actress"

Dean Butler
6220 Rogerton Drive
Los Angeles, CA 90068
"Actor"

Jerry Butler
164 Woodstone Drive
Buffalo Grove, IL 60089
"Singer"

Butros Ghali Butros
1 U.N. Plaza
New York, NY 10017
"U.N. Secretary General"

Joey Buttafuoco
1 Adam Road
Massapequa, NY 11158
"Sex with Amy Fisher"

Mary Jo Buttafuoco
1 Adam Road
Massapequa, NY 11158
"Joey's wife"

Dick Button
250 West 57th Street #1818
New York, NY 10107
"TV Producer"

Red Buttons
778 Tortuoso Way
Los Angeles, CA 90077
"Actor"

Ruth Buzzi
2309 Malaga Road
Los Angeles, CA 90068
"Actress"

Gabriel Byrne
76 Oxford Street
London W1N 0AX ENGLAND
"Actor"

John Byner
P.O. Box 232
Woodland Hills, CA 91365
"Comedian, Writer"

Charlie Byrd Trio
11806 North 56th Street #B
Tampa, FL 33617
"Jazz Trio"

Tom Byrd
121 North San Vincente Blvd.
Beverly Hills, CA 90211
"Actor"

Tracy Byrd
P.O. Box 7703
Beaumont, TX 77706
"Singer"

David Byrne
7964 Willow Glen Road
Los Angeles, CA 90046
"Singer, Songwriter"

Edd Byrnes
P.O. Box 1623
Beverly Hills, CA 90213
"Actor"

Jeffrey Byron
9229 Sunset Blvd. #311
Los Angeles, CA 90069
"Actor"

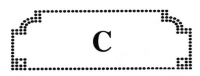

James Caan
1435 Stone Canyon Road
Los Angeles, CA 90077
"Actor"

Montserrat Caballe
Caball, Via Augusta 59
Barcelona, E-08006 SPAIN
"Opera Singer"

Ava Cadell
11130 Huston Street #6
North Hollywood, CA 91601
"Actress, Model"

Herb Caen
901 Mission Street
San Francisco, CA 94119
"Columnist"

Irving Caesar
Hotel Park Sheraton
870 - 7th Avenue
New York, NY 10019
"Lyricist, Composer"

Sid Caesar
1910 Loma Vista
Beverly Hills, CA 90210
"Actor, Comedian"

Nicholas Cage
P.O. Box 69646
Los Angeles, CA 90069
"Actor"

Dean Cain
1019 Chautauqua Blvd.
Pacific Palisades, CA 90272
"Actor"

Michael Caine
Rectory Farm House
North Stoke
Oxfordshire ENGLAND
"Actor"

Rory Calhoun
10637 Burbank Blvd.
North Hollywood, CA 91601
"Actor"

Joseph Cali
247 South Beverly Drive #102
Beverly Hills, CA 90212
"Actor"

Anthony Call
305 Madison Avenue #4419
New York, NY 10165
"Actor"

Brandon Call
5918 Van Nuys Blvd.
Van Nuys, CA 91401
"Actor"

James Callahan
1201 Greenacre Blvd.
Los Angeles, CA 90046
"Actor"

John Callahan
342 North Alfred Street
Los Angeles, CA 90048
"Actor"

K. Callan
4957 Matilija Avenue
Sherman Oaks, CA 91423
"Actress"

Michael (Mickey) Callan
1730 Camden Avenue #201
Los Angeles, CA 90025
"Actor"

Thomas Callaway
10000 Santa Monica Blvd. #305
Los Angeles, CA 90067
"Actor"

Charlie Callas
P.O. Box 67-B-69
Los Angeles, CA 90067
"Comedian, Actor"

Lt. William Calley
V.V. Vicks Jewelry
Cross Country Plaza
Columbus, GA 31906
"Ex-Military"

Simon Callow
60 Finborough Road
London SW10 ENGLAND
"Actor"

Corinne Calvet
1431 Ocean Avenue #109
Santa Monica, CA 90401
"Actress"

John Calvin
8091 Selma Avenue
Los Angeles, CA 90046
"Actor"

Hector Camacho
5151 LeRoy Collins Ave. #522
Miami Beach, FL 33140
"Boxer"

Candace Cameron
4830 Brewster Drive
Tarzana, CA 91356
"Actress"

Dean Cameron
3500 W. Olive Ave. #1400
Burbank, CA 91505
"Actor"

James Cameron
919 Santa Monica Blvd.
Santa Monica, CA 90401
"Director"

Joanna Cameron
P.O. Box 1400
Pebble Beach, CA 93953
"Actress, Director"

John Cameron
35 Ragged Hall Lane
St. Albans
Herts. AL2 3LB ENGLAND
"Composer, Conductor"

Kirk Cameron
P.O. Box 8665
Calabasas, CA 91372
"Actor"

Colleen Camp
2050 Fairburn Avenue
Los Angeles, CA 90025
"Actress"

Joseph Campanella
4647 Arcola Avenue
North Hollywood, CA 91602
"Actor"

Bert Campaneria
P.O. Box 5096
Scottsdale, AZ 85261
"Ex-Baseball Player"

Alan Campbell
2554 Lincoln Blvd. #445
Venice, CA 90291
"Actor"

Bill Campbell
8942 Wilshire Blvd.
Beverly Hills, CA 90211
"Actor"

Bruce Campbell
5314 Alcove Avenue
No. Hollywood, CA 91607
"Actor"

Cheryl Campbell
5 Milner Place
London N1 ENGLAND
"Actress"

Earl Campbell
P.O. Box 909
Austin, TX 78767
"Football Player"

Glen Campbell
5290 Exeter Blvd.
Phoenix, AZ 85018
"Singer, Actor, Composer"

Ken Campbell
74 Watermint Quay
London N16 England
"Actor"

Julia Campbell
2273 Holly Drive
Los Angeles, CA 90068
"Actress"

Kim Campbell
275 Slater Street #600
Ottawa Ontario
K1P 5H9 CANADA
"Ex-Prime Minister"

Luther Campbell
8400 N.E. 2nd Avenue
Miami, FL 33138
"Rap Singer"

Naomi Campbell
107 Greene Street
New York, NY 10012
"Model"

Nicholas Campbell
1825 Benedict Canyon
Beverly Hills, CA 90210
"Actor"

Tevin Campbell
9830 Wilshire Blvd.
Beverly Hills, CA 90212
"Singer"

Tisha Campbell
5750 Wilshire Blvd. #640
Los Angeles, CA 90036
"Actress"

William Campbell
21502 Velicata Street
Woodland Hills, CA 91364
"Actor"

David Canary
903 South Mansfield Avenue
Los Angeles, CA 90036
"Actor"

Vincent Canby
215 West 88th Street
New York, NY 10024
"Film Critic"

Philippe Candeloro
42 rue de Louvre
F-75001 Paris, FRANCE
"Ice Skater"

Stephen Cannell
7083 Hollywood Blvd.
Los Angeles, CA 90028
"TV Writer, Producer"

Billy Cannon
1640 Sherwood Forest Blvd.
Baton Rouge, LA 70815
"Football Player"

Dyan Cannon
8033 Sunset Blvd. #254
Los Angeles, CA 90046
"Actress, Writer"

Freddie Cannon
18641 Cassandra Street
Tarzana, CA 91356
"Singer, Songwriter"

J. D. Cannon
9255 Sunset Blvd. #515
Los Angeles, CA 90069
"Actor"

Katherine Cannon
10100 Santa Monica Blvd. #700
Los Angeles, CA 90067
"Actress"

Diana Canova
1800 Avenue of the Stars #400
Los Angeles, CA 90067
"Actress"

Jose Canseco
4525 Sheridan Avenue
Miami Beach, FL 33140
"Baseball Player"

Lana Cantrell
300 East 71st Street
New York, NY 10021
"Singer, Actress"

Virginia Capers
4317 Canoga Drive
Woodland Hills, CA 91364
"Actress"

John Cappelletti
28791 Brant Lane
Laguna Niguel, CA 92677
"Ex-Football Player"

Ahna Capri
8227 Fountain Avenue #2
Los Angeles, CA 90046
"Actress"

Jennifer Capriatti
80-710 Liberia Place
Indio, CA 92201
"Tennis Player"

Kate Capshaw
P.O. Box 869
Pacific Palisades, CA 90272
"Actress"

Captain & Tennille
(Toni & Daryl Dragon)
3612 Lake View Road
Carson City, NV 89703
"Music Duo"

Irene Cara
8033 Sunset Blvd. #735
Los Angeles, CA 90046
"Actress, Singer"

Roger Caras
22108 Slab Bridge Road
Freeland, MD 21053
"News Correspondent"

Jack Cardiff
Lluca 4, Javea
Provence Alicante SPAIN
"Film Director"

Pierre Cardin
59 rue du Faubourg
St-Honore 8e Paris, FRANCE
"Fashion Designer"

Claudia Cardinale
Via Flaminia KW77
Prima Porta
00188 Rome, ITALY
"Actress"

Rod Carew
5144 East Crescent Drive
Anaheim, CA 92807
"Ex-Baseball Player"

Clare Carey
7632 Hollywood Blvd. #3
Los Angeles, CA 90046
"Actress"

Drew Carey
955 S. Carrillo Drive, #100
Los Angeles, CA 90048
"Actor"

Harry Carey, Jr.
P.O. Box 3256
Durango, CO 81302
"Actor"

Mariah Carey
P.O. Box 4450
New York, NY 10101
"Singer"

Michelle Carey
733 N. Seward Street PH
Los Angeles, CA 90038
"Actress"

Rick Carey
119 Rockland Avenue
Larchmont, NY 10538
"Swimmer"

Len Cariou
100 West 57th Street #149
New York, NY 10019
"Actor"

Frankie Carle
P.O. Box 7415
Mesa, AZ 85216
"Band Leader"

George Carlin
901 Bringham Avenue
Los Angeles, CA 90049
"Comedian"

Lynn Carlin
15301 Ventura Blvd. #345
Sherman Oaks, CA 91403
"Actress"

Belinda Carlisle
3907 West Alameda Avenue #200
Burbank, CA 91505
"Singer, Songwriter"

Kitty Carlisle-Hart
32 East 64th Street
New York, NY 10021
"Actress"

Mary Carlisle
517 North Rodeo Drive
Beverly Hills, CA 90210
"Actress"

King Juan Carlos
Palacio de La Carcuela
Madrid, SPAIN
"Royalty"

Larry Carlton
27815 Lorjen
Canyon Country, CA 91351
"Guitarist"

Steve Carlton
P.O. Box 736
Durango, CO 81302
"Ex-Baseball Player"

Julie Carmen
4526 Wilshire Blvd.
Los Angeles, CA 90010
"Actress"

Ian Carmichael
The Priory, Grosmont
Whitby, Yorks. YO22 SQT
ENGLAND
"Actor, Producer"

Judy Carne
P.O. Box 1442
New York, NY 10274
"Actress"

Kim Carnes
2031 Old Natchez Terrace
Franklin, TN 37064
"Singer, Songwriter"

Art Carney
RR 20, Box 911
Westbrook, CT 06498
"Actor"

Princess Caroline
80 Ave. Foch
F-75016 Paris FRANCE
"Royalty"

Leslie Caron
6 rue de Bellechasse, 7 Dist.
75007 Paris FRANCE
"Actress"

A.J. Carothers
2110 The Terrace
Los Angeles, CA 90049
"Screenwriter"

Carleton Carpenter
R.D. #2 Chardavoyne Road
Warwick, NY 10990
"Actor"

John Carpenter
8532 Hollywood Blvd.
Los Angeles, CA 90046
"Actor, Director"

Mary-Chapin Carpenter
7003 Carroll Avenue
Silver Spring, MD 20912
"Singer"

Richard Capenter
9386 Raviller Drive
Downey, CA 90240
"Pianist, Composer"

Scott Carpenter
P.O. Box 3161
Vail, CO 81658
"Astronaut"

Allan Carr
P.O. Box 691670
Los Angeles, CA 90069
"Film Writer, Producer"

Darlene Carr
1604 North Vista Avenue
Los Angeles, CA 90046
"Actress"

Jane Carr
6200 Mt. Angelus Drive
Los Angeles, CA 90042
"Actress"

Vikki Carr
9901 W. lh 10 #800
San Antonio, TX 78230
"Singer, Songwriter"

David Carradine
9753 La Tuna Canyon Road
Sun Valley, CA 91352
"Actor"

Keith Carradine
P.O. Box 460
Placeville, CO 81430
"Actor, Singer"

Robert Carradine
355 So. Grand Ave. #4150
Los Angeles, CA 90071
"Actor"

Barbara Carrera
15430 Milldale Drive
Los Angeles, CA 90077
"Actress, Model"

Jose Carreras
via Augusta 59
E-08006 Barcelona
SPAIN
"Tenor"

Tia Carrere
8228 Sunset Blvd. #300
Los Angeles, CA 90046
"Actress"

James Carrey
615 Tigertail Road
Los Angeles, CA 90049
"Comedian, Actor"

Mathieu Carriere
26 rue Vavin
Paris 6e FRANCE
"Actor"

Lord Carrington
Manor House
Bledlow, Aylesbury
Buckinghamshire HP17 9PE
ENGLAND
"Politician"

Diahann Carroll
P.O. Box 2999
Beverly Hills, CA 90213
"Actress, Singer"

Pat Carroll
6523 West Olympic Blvd.
Los Angeles, CA 90048
"Actress"

Kitty Carruthers
22 East 71st Street
New York, NY 10021
"Ice Skater"

Peter Carruthers
22 East 71st Street
New York, NY 10021
"Ice Skater"

Marcey Carsey
4024 Radford Ave. #3
Studio City, CA 91604
"TV Producer"

Joanna Carson
400 St. Cloud Road
Los Angeles, CA 90024
"Ex-Wife of Johnny Carson"

Johnny Carson
6962 Wildlife
Malibu, CA 90265
"Ex- TV Show Host, Comedian"

Amy Carter
1 Woodland Drive
Plains, GA 31780
"Ex-President's Daughter"

Benny Carter
8321 Skyline Drive
Los Angeles, CA 90046
"Saxophonist"

Betty Carter
307 Lake Street
San Francisco, CA 94118
"Singer"

Carlene Carter
1114-17th Avenue #101
Nashville, TN 37212
"Singer"

Dixie Carter
P.O. Box 1980
Studio City, CA 91614
"Actress"

Carter Family
P.O. Box 508
Hendersonville, TN 37075
"Music Group"

Helena Carter
1655 Gilcrest
Beverly Hills, CA 90210
"Actress"

Helena Bonham Carter
18/21 Jerrnyn St.
London SW1 ENGLAND
"Actress"

Hodding Carter III
211 South St. Asaph
Alexandria, VA 22314
"News Correspondent"

Jack Carter
1023 Chevy Chase Drive
Beverly Hills, CA 90210
"Comedian, Actor"

Jimmy Carter
1 Woodland Drive
Plains, GA 31780
"Former President of USA"

John Carter
11846 Ventura Blvd. #100
Studio City, CA 91604
"Actor"

Lynda Carter
9200 Harrington Drive
Potomac, MD 20854
"Actress, Singer"

Nell Carter
8484 Wilhire Blvd. #500
Beverly Hills, CA 90211
"Actress, Singer"

Ralph Carter
104-60 Queens Blvd. #1D
Forest Hills, NY 11375
"Actor"

Rosalyn Carter
1 Woodland Drive
Plains, GA 31780
"Former First Lady"

Rubin "Hurricane" Carter
1313 Brookedge Drive
Hamlin, NY 14464
"Boxer, Ex-Convict"

Terry Carter
447-9th Street
Santa Monica, CA 90402
"Actor"

Thomas Carter
10958 Strathmore Drive
Los Angeles, CA 90024
"Actor, Director"

Gabrielle Carteris
5700 Wilshire Blvd. #575
Los Angeles, CA 90036
"Actress"

Barbara Cartland
Camfield Place, Hatfield
Hertfordshire ENGLAND
"Novelist"

Angela Cartwright
10112 Riverside Drive
Toluca Lake, CA 91602
"Actress"

Veronica Cartwright
12754 Sarah Street
Studio City, CA 91604
"Actress"

Anthony Caruso
1706 Mandeville Lane
Los Angeles, CA 90049
"Actor"

David Caruso
3340 Barham Blvd.
Los Angeles, CA 90068
"Actor"

Dana Carvey
17333 Rancho Street
Encino, CA 91316
"Comedian, Actor"

James Carville
1601 Shenandoah Shores Street
Front Royal, VA 22630
"Political Consultant"

Rosie Casals
P.O. Box 537
Sausalito, CA 94966
"Tennis Player"

Harold Case
34 Cunningham Park
Harrow, Middlesex
HA1 4AL ENGLAND
"Cinematographer"

Adriana Caselotti
201 South Larchmont Blvd.
Los Angeles, CA 90004
"Entertainer"

Bernie Casey
6145 Flight Avenue
Los Angeles, CA 90056
"Actor, Ex-Football Player"

Lawrence Casey
4139 Vanette Place
North Hollywood, CA 91604
"Actor"

Johnny Cash
711 Summerfield Drive
Hendersonville, TN 37075
"Singer"

June Carter Cash
711 Summerfield Drive
Hendersonville, TN 37075
"Singer"

Kellye Cash
1400 Oakhill #414
Escondido, CA 92027
"Former Miss America"

Pat Cash
281 Clarence Street
Sydney NSW 2000 AUSTRALIA
"Tennis Player"

Rosalind Cash
P.O. Box 1605
Topanga, CA 90290
"Actress"

Rosanne Cash
1026A 3rd Avenue
New York, NY 10021
"Singer, Songwriter"

Philip Casnoff
3040 Dona Nenita Place
Studio City, CA 91604
"Actor"

Tina Caspary
11350 Ventura Blvd. #206
Studio City, CA 91604
"Actress"

Billy Casper
P.O. Box 1088
Chula Vista, CA 91912
"Golfer"

Dave Casper
4124 Dublin Drive
Minnetonka, MN 55345
"Football Player"

Peggy Cass
200 East 62nd Street
New York, NY 10021
"Actress"

Nick Cassavetes
22223 Buena Ventura Street
Woodland Hills, CA 91364
"Actor"

Jean-Pierre Cassel
76 Oxford Street
London W1N OAX ENGLAND
"Actor"

Seymour Cassell
2800 Neilson Way #1610
Santa Monica, CA 90405
"Actor"

David Cassidy
20501 Ventura Blvd. #392
Woodland Hills, CA 91364
"Actor, Singer"

Joanna Cassidy
2530 Outpost Drive
Los Angeles, CA 90068
"Actress"

Patrick Cassidy
10433 Wilshire Blvd. #605
Los Angeles, CA 90024
"Actor"

Ryan Cassidy
12546 The Vista
Los Angeles, CA 90049
"Actor"

Shaun Cassidy
8484 Wilshire Blvd. #500
Beverly Hills, CA 90212
"Actor, Singer"

Oleg Cassini
3 West 57th Street
New York, NY 10019
"Fashion Designer"

Tricia Cast
20 Georgeff Road
Rolling Hills Estates, CA 90274
"Actress"

John Castle
126 Kennington Park Road
London W1 ENGLAND
"Mezzo-Soprano"

Fidel Castro
Palacio del Gobierno
Havana, CUBA
"Politician"

Gilbert Cates
936 Hilts Avenue
Los Angeles, CA 90024
"Film Director"

Phoebe Cates
9560 Wilshire Blvd. #500
Beverly Hills, CA 90212
"Actress"

Mary Jo Catlett
4375 Farmdale Avenue
Studio City, CA 91604
"Actress"

Kim Cattrell
151 El Camino Drive
Beverly Hills, CA 90212
"Actress"

Maxwell Caufield
4770-B 9th Street
Carpinteria, CA 93013
"Actor"

Steve Cauthen
c/o Cauthen Ranch
Boone County
Walton, KY 41094
"Horse Racer"

Carrie Cavalier
3200 Wyoming Avenue
Burbank, CA 91505
"Actress"

Felix Cavallere
584 N. Larchmont Blvd.
Los Angeles, CA 90004
"Singer, Pianist"

Michael Cavanaugh
9150 Wilshire Blvd., #175
Beverly Hills, CA 90212
"Actor"

Dick Cavett
109 East 79th Street #2C
New York, NY 10021
"TV Show Host, Comedian"

Evonne Goolagong Cawley
1 Erieview Plaza #1300
Cleveland, OH 44114
"Tennis Player"

Christopher Cazenove
9300 Wilshire Blvd. #555
Beverly Hills, CA 90212
"Actor"

Orlando Cepeda
331 Brazelton Court
Suison City, CA 94505
"Ex-Baseball Player"

Eugene Cernan
900 Town & Country Lane #300
Houston, TX 77024
"Astronaut"

Rick Cerrone
63 Eisenhower
Cresskill, NJ 07626
"Ex-Baseball Player"

Don Cervantez
1830 North Mariposa #2
Los Angeles, CA 90027
"Actor"

Peter Cetera
1880 Century Park East #900
Los Angeles, CA 90067
"Singer, Musician"

Ron Cey
22714 Creole Road
Woodland Hills, CA 91364
"Ex-Baseball Player"

Alex Chadwick
c/o National Public Radio
2025 "M" Street N.W.
Washington, DC 20036
"News Correspondent"

Don Chaffey
7020 La Presa Drive
Los Angeles, CA 90068
"TV Director"

Mme. Chaing Kai-Shek
Locust Valley
Lattingtown, NY 11560
"Politician"

Chairman of the Board
2300 East Independence Blvd.
Charlotte, NC 28205
"Music Group"

George Chakiris
7266 Clinton Street
Los Angeles, CA 90036
"Actor"

Richard Chamberlain
3711 Round Top Drive
Honolulu, HI 96822
"Actor, Producer"

Wilt Chamberlain
15216 Antelo Place
Los Angeles, CA 90077
"Ex-Basketball Player"

Marilyn Chambers
4528 West Charleston Blvd. #836
Las Vegas, NV 89102
"Actress"

Tom Chambers
P.O. Box 1369
Phoenix, AZ 85001
"Basketball Player"

Violetta Chamorro
Presidential Palace
Managua, NICARAGUA
"Politician"

Marge Champion
484 West 43rd Street
New York, NY 10036
"Actress, Dancer"

Charles Champlin
2169 Linda Flora Drive
Los Angeles, CA 90024
"Film Critic"

Jackie Chan
Waterloo Road, #145
Kowloon, Hong Kong
"Actor"

Otis Chandler
1421 Emerson
Oxnard, CA 93033
"Publisher"

Patrice Chanel
19216 Andmark Avenue
Carson, CA 90746
"Actress"

Carol Channing
9301 Flicker Way
Los Angeles, CA 90069
"Actress"

Stockard Channing
10390 Santa Monica Blvd. #300
Los Angeles, CA 90025
"Actress"

Rosalind Chao
924 Westwood Blvd. #900
Los Angeles, CA 90024
"Actress"

Doug Chapin
9911 W. Pico Blvd. PH 1
Los Angeles CA 90035
"Film Producer"

Lauren Chapin
P.O. Box 922
Killeen, TX 76541
"Actress"

Tom Chapin
57 Piermont Place
Piermont, NY 10968
"Singer"

Geraldine Chaplin
Caios del Peral 314 Piso
E-28013 Madrid SPAIN
"Actress"

Lita Grey Chaplin
8440 Fountain Ave. #302
Los Angeles, CA 90069
"Actress"

Judith Chapman
247 South Beverly Drive #102
Beverly Hills, CA 90212
"Actress"

Lonny Chapman
3973 Goodland Avenue
Studio City, CA 91604
"Actor"

Marguerite Chapman
11558 Riverside Drive #304
Hollywood, CA 91602
"Actress"

Mark David Chapman
Attica State Prison, Box 149
Attica, NY 14011
"John Lennon's Killer"

Mark Lindsay Chapman
9150 Wilshire Blvd. #175
Beverly Hills, CA 90212
"Actor"

Patricia Charbonneau
10100 Santa Monica Blvd. #700
Los Angeles, CA 90067
"Actress"

Cyd Charisse
10724 Wilshire Blvd. #1406
Los Angeles, CA 90024
"Actress, Dancer"

Josh Charles
8942 Wilshire Blvd.
Beverly Hills, CA 90211
"Actor"

HRH Prince Charles
Highgrove House
Gloucestershire ENGLAND
"Royalty"

Ray Charles
4863 Southridge Avenue
Los Angeles, CA 90008
"Singer, Pianist"

Leslie Charleson
2314 Live Oak Drive East
Los Angeles, CA 90068
"Actress"

Tony Charmoli
1271 Sunset Plaza Drive
Los Angeles, CA 90069
"Director, Choreography"

Charo
P.O. Box 1007
Hanalei, Kaui, HI 96714
"Singer"

Melanie Chartoff
10380 Tennessee Avenue
Los Angeles, CA 90064
"Actress"

David Charvet
8969 Sunset Blvd.
Los Angeles, CA 90069
"Actor"

Julio Ceasar Chavez
539 Telegraph Canyon Road #253
Chula Vista, CA 91910
"Boxer"

Barrie Chase
3750 Beverly Ridge Drive
Sherman Oaks, CA 91423
"Actress, Dancer"

Chevy Chase
17492 Camino de Yatasto
Pacific Palisades, CA 90272
"Actor, Writer"

Lorraine Chase
68 Old Brompton Road
London SW7 ENGLAND
"Actress"

Benjamin Chavis
P.O. Box 1661
Ellicott City, MD 21041
"Ex-N.A.A.C.P. Director"

Cheap Trick
1818 Parmenter St. #202
Middleton, WI 53562
"Rock & Roll Group"

Maree Cheatham
9300 Wilshire Blvd. #555
Beverly Hills, CA 90212
"Actress"

Chubby Checker
1646 Hilltop Road
Birchrunville, PA 19421
"Singer, Songwriter"

Molly Cheek
13038 Landale Street
Studio City, CA 91604
"Actress"

Joan Chen
2601 Filbert Street
San Francisco, CA 94123
"Actress"

Mrs. Anna Chenault
2510 Virgina Avenue NW #1404
Washington, DC 20005
"Author, Journalist"

Dick Cheney
500 North Akard Street #3600
Dallas, TX 75201
"EX-Secretary of Defense"

Cher
P.O. Box 960
Beverly Hills, CA 90213
"Actress, Singer"

Colby Chester
5750 Wilshire Blvd. #512
Burbank, CA 91506
"Actor"

Mark Chestnut
1106 - 16th Avenue South
Nashville, TN 37212
"Singer"

Morris Chestnut
1800 Avenue of the Stars #400
Los Angeles, CA 90067
"Actor"

Sam Chew, Jr.
8075 West 3rd Street #303
Los Angeles, CA 90048
"Actor"

Julia Child
103 Irving Street
Cambridge, MA 02138
"TV Personality"

Linden Chiles
2521 Topanga Skyline
Topanga, CA 90290
"Actor"

Lois Chiles
644 San Lorenzo
Santa Monica, CA 90402
"Actress"

Michael Chiklis
12424 Wilshire Blvd. #840
Los Angeles, CA 90025
"Actor"

Shirley Chisholm
80 Wentworth Lane
Palm Coast, FL 32137
"Politician"

Joey Chitwood
4410 West Alva Street
Tampa, FL 33614
"Race Car Driver"

Anna Chlumsky
70 West Hubbard #200
Chicago, IL 60610
"Actress"

Margaret Cho
151 El Camino Drive
Beverly Hills, CA 90212
"Actress"

Chocolate Milk
P.O. Box 82
Great Neck, NY 11021
"R&B Group"

Rae Dawn Chong
1491 Stone Canyon Road
Los Angeles, CA 90024
"Actress"

Thomas Chong
1625 Casale Road
Pacific Palisades, CA 90272
"Actor, Writer, Director"

Raymond Chow
23 Barker Road
Craigside Mansion #5B
HONG KONG (BCC)
"Film Director"

Todd Christensen
991 Sunburst Lane
Alpine, UT 84004
"Football Player"

Claudia Christian
14431 Ventura Blvd. #260
Sherman Oaks, CA 91423
"Actress"

Julie Christie
23 Linden Gardens
London W2 ENGLAND
"Actress"

Lou Christie
1645 East 50th Street #10H
Chicago, IL 60615
"Singer"

Virginia Christine
12348 Rochedale Lane
Los Angeles, CA 90049
"Actress"

Dennis Christopher
2026 1/2 Argyle
Los Angeles, CA 90028
"Actor"

Sec. Warren Christopher
2201 "C" Street NW
Washington, DC 20520
"Secretary of State"

William Christopher
P.O. Box 50698
Pasadena, CA 91105
"Actor"

Connie Chung
524 West 57th Street
New York, NY 10019
"Newscaster"

Thomas Haden Church
8969 Sunset Blvd.
Los Angeles, CA 90069
"Actor"

"Cicciolina"
Via Cassia 1818
I-00123 Rome ITALY
"Actress"

Joseph Cicippio
25 Gordon Way
Princeton, NJ 08540
"Ex-Hostage"

Michael Cimino
9015 Alta Cedro
Beverly Hills, CA 90210
"Writer, Producer"

Cinderella
P.O. Box 543
Drexel Hill, PA 19026
"Rock & Roll Group"

Charles Cioffi
Glover Avenue
Norwalk, CT 06850
"Actor"

Sec. Henry Cisneros
451-7th Street S.W.
Washington, DC 20401
"Secretary of H.U.D."

Liz Claiborne
650 Fifth Avenue
New York, NY 10019
"Fashion Designer"

Clancy Brothers
11806 N. 56th Street, #B
Tampa, FL 33617
"Folk Group"

Gordon Clapp
9169 Sunset Blvd.
Los Angeles, CA 90069
"Actor"

Eric Clapton
46 Kensington Court
London WE8 5DT ENGLAND
"Singer, Guitarist"

Candy Clark
5 Briarhill Road
Montclair, NJ 07042
"Actress"

Christie Clark
16342 Rockaway
Placentia, CA 92670
"Actress"

Dane Clark
1680 Old Oak Road
Los Angeles, CA 90049
"Actor, Director"

Dick Clark
3003 West Olive Avenue
Burbank, CA 91505
"Ex-TV Show Host, Producer"

Doran Clark
10100 Santa Monica Blvd. #2500
Los Angeles, CA 90067
"Actress"

Lynn Clark
247 South Beverly Drive #102
Beverly Hills, CA 90212
"Actress"

Marcia Clark
210 West Temple Street #1800
Los Angeles, CA 90012
"Attorney"

Marsha Clark
1800 North Vine Street, #120
Los Angeles, CA 90028
"Actress"

Mary Higgins Clark
210 Central Park South
New York, NY 10019
"Writer"

Petula Clark
15 Chemin Rieu Coligny
Geneva SWITZERLAND
"Singer, Actress"

Ramsey Clark
36 East 12th Street
New York, NY 10003
"Politician"

Roy Clark
1800 Forrest Blvd.
Tulsa, OK 74114
"Singer, Guitarist"

Susan Clark
7943 Woodrow Wilson Drive
Los Angeles, CA 90046
"Actress"

Will Clark
1000 Papworth Avenue
Metairie, LA 70005
"Baseball Player"

Angela Clarke
7557 Mulholland Drive
Los Angeles, CA 90046
"Actress"

Arthur C. Clarke
4715 Gregory's Road
Colombo SIR LANKA
"Author"

Brian Patrick Clarke
333-D Kenwood
Burbank, CA 91505
"Actor"

Jordan Clarke
121 N. San Vicente Blvd.
Beverly Hills, CA 90211
"Actor"

Robert Clarke
4841 Gentry Avenue
North Hollywood, CA 91607
"Actor"

Stanley Clarke
1807 Benedict Canyon
Beverly Hills, CA 90210
"Guitarist, Composer"

Robert Clary
10001 Sun Dial Lane
Beverly Hills, CA 90210
"Actor"

The Clash
268 Camden Road
London NW1 ENGLAND
"Rock & Roll Group"

Andrew Dice Clay
836 North La Cienega Blvd. #202
Los Angeles, CA 90069
"Comedian, Actor"

Nicholas Clay
15 Golden Square #315
London W1R 3AG ENGLAND
"Actor"

Jill Clayburgh
P.O. Box 18
Lakeville, CT 06039
"Actress"

John Cleese
82 Ladbroke Road
London W11 3NU ENGLAND
"Actor, Writer"

Roger Clemens
8582 Katy Fwy. #121
Houston, TX 77024
"Baseball Player"

David Clennon
954 - 20th Street #B
Santa Monica, CA 90403
"Actor"

Van Cliburn
455 Wilder Place
Shreveport, LA 71104
"Pianist"

Jimmy Cliff
51 Lady Musgrove Road
Kingston JAMAICA
"Singer"

Clark Clifford
9421 Rockville Pike
Bethesda, MD 20814
"Attorney"

Linda Clifford
402 N. 52nd St. #221
Phoenix, AZ 85008
"Singer"

Eleanor Clift
1750 Pennsylvania Ave. N.W.
Suite #1220
Washington, DC 20001
"News Correspondent"

Debra Clinger
4415 Auckland Avenue
North Hollywood, CA 91602
"Actress"

President Bill Clinton
1600 Pennsylvania Avenue
Washington, DC 20500
"President of United States"

Chelsea Clinton
1600 Pennsylvania Avenue
Washington, DC 20500
"Daughter of the President"

Hillary Rodham-Clinton
1600 Pennsylvania Avenue
Washington, DC 20500
"First Lady, Attorney"

John Clive
4 Court Lodge, Chelsea
London SW3 AJA ENGLAND
"Actor, Writer"

Robert Clohessy
9000 Sunset Blvd. #1200
Los Angeles, CA 90069
"Actor"

George Clooney
151 El Camino Drive
Beverly Hills, CA 90212
"Actor"

Rosemary Clooney
1019 North Roxbury Drive
Beverly Hills, CA 90210
"Singer"

Glenn Close
9830 Wilshire Blvd.
Beverly Hills, CA 90212
"Actress"

Jerry Clower
P.O. Box 121089
Nashville, TN 37212
"Comedian"

The Coasters
4905 S. Atlantic Avenue
Daytona Beach, FL 32127
"Vocal Group"

Phyllis Coates
P.O. Box 1969
Boyes Hot Springs, CA 95416
"Actress"

Sen. Dan Coats
1300 South Harrison Street #3158
Ft. Wayne, IN 46802
"Politician"

Julie Cobb
9744 Wilshire Blvd. #308
Beverly Hills, CA 90212
"Actress"

James Coburn
3550 Wilshire Blvd. #840
Los Angeles, CA 90010
"Actor, Director"

Imogene Coca
200 East 66th Street #1803D
New York, NY 10021
"Actress"

Hank Cochran
Rt. 2, Box 438
Hunter Lane
Hendersonville, TN 37075
"Singer, Songwriter"

Johnnie Cochran, Jr.
2245 West 28th Street
Los Angeles, CA 90018
"Attorney"

Bruce Cockburn
151 John Street #301
Toronto, Ontario M5V 2T2
CANADA
"Singer, Songwriter"

Iron Eyes Cody
2013 Griffith Park Blvd.
Los Angeles, CA 90039
"Actor"

David Allan Coe
P.O. Box 1387
Goodlettsville, TN 37070
"Singer, Songwriter"

Sebastian Coe
16 Upper Woburn Place
London WC1H OOP ENGLAND
"Runner"

Susie Coelho
3500 West Olive Avenue #1440
Burbank, CA 91505
"Actress, Model"

Frank "Junior" Coghlan
12522 Argyle Avenue
Los Alamitos, CA 90720
"Actor"

Alexander Cohen
25 West 54th Street #5-F
New York, NY 10019
"TV/Theater Producer"

Larry Cohen
2111 Coldwater Canyon
Beverly Hills, CA 90210
"Writer, Producer"

Sen. William Cohen (ME)
322 Hart Office Bldg.
Washington, DC 20510
"Politician"

Mindy Cohn
9300 Wilshire Blvd. #400
Beverly Hills, CA 90212
"Actress"

Claudette Colbert
Bellerive St. Peter
Barbados, WEST INDIES
"Actress"

Robert Colbert
10000 Riverside Drive #6
Toluca Lake, CA 91602
"Actor"

Dennis Cole
2160 Century Park East #1712
Los Angeles, CA 90067
"Actor"

Gary Cole
10390 Santa Monica Blvd. #300
Los Angeles, CA 90025
"Actor"

George Cole
Donnelly
Newham Hill Bottom
Nettleford Oxon, ENGLAND
"Actor"

Michael Cole
6332 Costello Avenue
Van Nuys, CA 91401
"Actor"

Mrs. Marie Cole
South House
Tyringham, MA 01264
"Widower of Nat Cole"

Natalie Cole
955 S. Carrillo Drive #200
Los Angeles, CA 90048
"Singer"

Olivia Cole
9744 Wilshire Blvd. #308
Beverly Hills, CA 90212
"Actress"

Dabney Coleman
360 North Kenter Avenue
Los Angeles, CA 90049
"Actor"

Durell Coleman
800 S. Robertson Blvd. #5
Los Angeles, CA 90035
"Actor"

Gary Coleman
4710 Don Miguel Drive
Los Angeles, CA 90008
"Actor"

Jack Coleman
7358 Woodrow Wilson Drive
Los Angeles, CA 90046
"Actor"

Lisa Coleman
3105 Ledgewood
Los Angels, CA 90068
"Actress"

Nancy Coleman
484 West 43rd Street #42-G
New York, NY 10036
"Actress"

Vince Coleman
1864 Hermitage
Imperial, MO 63052
"Baseball Player"

John Colicos
615 Yonge Street #401
Toronto Ontario
M4Y 1Z5 CANADA
"Actor"

Margaret Colin
366 West 11th Street PH C
New York, NY 10014
"Actress"

Mark Collie
P.O. Box 120311
Nashville, TN 37212
"Guitarist"

Rep. Cardiss Collins (IL)
House Rayburn Bldg. #2308.
Washington, DC 20515
"Politician"

Gary Collins
2751 Hutton Drive
Beverly Hills, CA 90210
"Actor, TV Show Host"

Jackie Collins
13701 Riverside Drive #608
Sherman Oaks, CA 91423
"TV Show Host, Author"

Joan Collins
16 Bulbecks Walk
So. Woodham Ferrers
Chelmsford Essex CM3 5ZN
ENGLAND
"Actress, Producer"

Judy Collins
845 West End Avenue
New York, NY 10024
"Singer, Songwriter"

Kate Collins
1410 York Avenue #4-D
New York, NY 10021
"Actress"

Lewis Collins
22 Westbere Road
London NW2 3SR ENGLAND
"Actor"

Marva Collins
4146 West Chicago Avenue
Chicago, IL 60651
"Educator"

Phil Collins
9401 Sunset Blvd.
Beverly Hills, CA 90210
"Singer, Drummer"

Stephen Collins
21 East 90th Street #10A
New York, NY 10128
"Actor"

Scott Colomby
12329 Emelita Street
North Hollywood, CA 91607
"Actor"

Color Me Badd
P.O. Box 552113
Carol City, FL 33055
"Music Group"

Charles Colson
P.O. Box 40562
Washington, DC 20016
"Author"

Marshall Colt
923 Ocean Avenue #5
Santa Monica, CA 90403
"Actor"

Jessie Colter
1117-17th Avenue South
Nashville, TN 37212
"Singer"

Chi Coltrane
5955 Tuxedo Terrace
Los Angeles, CA 90068
"Singer"

Robbie Coltrane
47 Courtfield Road #9
London SW7 4DB ENGLAND
"Actor"

Franco Columbu
2947 South Sepulveda Blvd.
Los Angeles, CA 90064
"Actor, Bodybuilder"

Chris Columbus
847 North Franklin Avenue
River Forest, IL 60305
"Screenwriter"

Jack Colvin
9744 Wilshire Blvd. #308
Beverly Hills, CA 90212
"Actor, Director"

Nadia Comaneci
2325 Westwood Drive
Norman, OK 73069
"Gymnast"

Jeffrey Combs
14006 Morrison Street
Sherman Oaks, CA 91423
"Actor"

Betty Comden
117 East 95th Street
New York, NY 10128
"Writer"

Paul Comi
1665 Oak Knoll Avenue
San Marino, CA 91108
"Actor"

Perry Como
305 Northern Blvd. #3-A
Great Neck, NY 11021
"Singer"

Joyce Compton
23388 Mulholland Drive
Woodland Hills, CA 91364
"Actress"

Cristi Conaway
P.O. Box 46515
Los Angeles CA 90046
"Actress"

Jeff Conaway
3162 Durand Drive
Los Angeles, CA 90068
"Actor"

Gino Conforti
1440 Veteran Avenue #603
Los Angeles, CA 90024
"Actor"

Ray Coniff
2154 Hercules Drive
Los Angeles, CA 90046
"Composer"

John Conlee
38 Music Square East #117
Nashville, TN 37203
"Singer, Songwriter"

Darlene Conley
1840 S. Beverly Glen Blvd. #501
Los Angeles, CA 90025
"Actress"

Earl Thomas Conley
1222-16 Avenue South
Nashville, TN 37212
"Singer, Songwriter"

Didi Conn
14820 Valley Vista Blvd.
Sherman Oaks, CA 91403
"Actress"

Jennifer Connelly
8942 Wilshire Blvd.
Beverly Hills, CA 90211
"Actress"

Bart Conner
2325 Westwood Drive
Norman, OK 73069
"Athlete"

Dennis Conner
720 Gateway Center Drive
San Diego, CA 92102
"Yachstman"

Jason Connery
22 Bishops Road
London SW6 7AB ENGLAND
"Actor"

Sean Connery
15 Portland Place
London W1N 3AA ENGLAND
"Actor"

Harry Connick, Jr.
260 Brookline Street
Cambridge, MA 02139
"Pianist, Singer"

Norma Connolly
4411 Los Feliz Blvd. #1201
Los Angeles, CA 90027
"Actress"

Patrick Connor
3 Spring Bank
New Mills nr. Stockport
SK12 4AS ENGLAND
"Actor"

Carol Connors
1709 Ferrari Drive
Beverly Hills, CA 90210
"Songwriter"

Jimmy Connors
200 South Refugio Road
Santa Ynez, CA 93460
"Tennis Player"

Mike Connors
4810 Louise Avenue
Encino, CA 91316
"Actor"

Barnaby Conrad
3530 Pine Valley Drive
Sarasota, FL 34239
"Author, Painter"

Charles Conrad, Jr.
19411 Merion Circle
Huntington Beach, CA 92648
"Astronaut"

Christian Conrad
15301 Ventura Blvd. #345
Sherman Oaks, CA 91403
"Actor"

Kimberly Conrad
10236 Charing Cross Road
Los Angeles, CA 90077
"Mrs. Hugh Hefner"

Paul Conrad
28649 Crestridge Road
Palos Verdes, CA 90274
"Cartoonist"

Robert Conrad
21355 Pacific Coast Hwy.
Malibu, CA 90265
"Actor, Writer"

Shane Conrad
21355 Pacific Coast Hwy.
Malibu, CA 90125
"Actor"

Kevin Conroy
10100 Santa Monica Blvd. #2500
Los Angeles, CA 90067
"Actor"

John Considine
1930 Century Park West #403
Los Angeles, CA 90067
"Actor, Writer"

Tim Considine
506 North Alpine Drive
Beverly Hills, CA 90210
"Actor, Writer, Director"

Michel Constantin
17 Blvd. Bartole Beauvallon
8321 Sainte Maxime, FRANCE
"Actor"

Ex-King Constantine
4 Linnell Drive
Hampstead Way
London NW11 ENGLAND
"Royalty"

Michael Constantine
1800 Avenue of the Stars #400
Los Angeles, CA 90067
"Actor"

John Conte
75600 Beryl Drive
Indian Wells, CA 92260
"Actor"

Bill Conti
117 Fremont Place
Los Angeles, CA 90005
"Composer, Arranger"

Tom Conti
Chatto & Linnet
Shaftesbury Avenue
London W1 ENGLAND
"Actor"

Peggy Converse
2049 Century Park E. #2500
Los Angeles, CA 90067
"Actress"

Gary Conway
2035 Mandeville Canyon
Los Angeles, CA 90049
"Actor"

Kevin Conway
1999 Ave. of the Stars #2850
Los Angeles, CA 90067
"Actor"

Tim Conway
P.O. Box 17047
Encino, CA 91416
"Actor, Director"

Rep. John Conyers (MI)
House Rayburn Bldg. #2426
Washington, DC 20515
"Politician"

Ry Cooder
326 Entrada Drive
Santa Monica, CA 90402
"Guitarist, Songwriter"

Keith Coogan
1640 S. Sepulveda Blvd. #218
Los Angeles, CA 90025
"Actor"

Carole Cook
8829 Ashcroft Avenue
Los Angeles, CA 90048
"Actress"

Fielder Cook
180 Central Park South
New York, NY 10019
"TV Writer, Producer"

Robin Cook
4601 Gulf Shore Blvd. #P4
Naples, FL 33940
"Screenwriter"

Alistair Cook
Nassau Point
Cutchogue, NY 11935
"Journalist, TV Announcer"

Jack Kent Cooke
Kent Farms
Middleburg, VA 22117
"Attorney, Football Team Owner"

Peter Cookson
30 Norfolk Road
Southfield, MA 01259
"Actor"

Dr. Denton Cooley
3014 Del Monte Drive
Houston, TX 77019
"Heart Surgeon"

Martha Coolidge
2129 Coldwater Canyon
Beverly Hills, CA 90210
"Director"

Rita Coolidge
1330 North Wetherly Drive
Los Angeles, CA 90069
"Singer, Actress"

Alice Cooper
4135 East Keim Drive
Paradise Valley, AZ 85253
"Singer, Songwriter"

Ann Cooper
c/o National Public Radio
2025 "M" Street N.W.
Washington, DC 20036
"News Correspondent"

Ben Cooper
20838 Exhibit Court
Woodland Hills, CA 91367
"Actor"

Camille Cooper
1125 Chantilly Road
Los Angeles, CA 90077
"Actress"

Henry Cooper
36 Brampton Grove
London NW4 ENGLAND
"TV Personality"

Jackie Cooper
9621 Royalton
Beverly Hills, CA 90210
"Actor, Director"

Jeanne Cooper
8401 Edwin Drive
Los Angeles, CA 90046
"Actress"

L. Gordon Cooper
5011 Woodley Avenue
Encino, CA 91436
"Astronaut"

Mark Copage
P.O. Box 461677
Los Angeles, CA 90046
"Actor"

Joan Copeland
88 Central Park West
New York, NY 10023
"Actress"

Teri Copley
18019 San Fernando Mission
Granada Hills, CA 91344
"Actress"

David Copperfield
515 Post Oak Blvd. #300
Houston, TX 77027
"Magician"

Francis Coppola
916 Kearny Street
San Francisco, CA 94133
"Writer, Producer"

Sophia Coppola
781-5th Avenue
New York, NY 10022
"Actress"

Gretchen Corbett
1801 Avenue of the Stars #902
Los Angeles, CA 90067
"Actress"

John Corbett
8969 Sunset Blvd.
Los Angeles, CA 90069
"Actor"

Michael Corbett
1434 North Spalding #A
Los Angeles, CA 90046
"Actor"

Ronnie Corbett
57 Gt. Cumberland Place
London W1H 7LJ ENGLAND
"Comedian"

Barry Corbin
5000 White Oak Avenue
Encino, CA 91316
"Actor"

Ellen Corby
9026 Harratt
Los Angeles, CA 90069
"Actress"

Kevin Corcoran
8617 Balcom
Northridge, CA 91325
"Actor"

Noreen Corcoran
5926 Jamieson Avenue
Encino, CA 91316
"Actress"

Alex Cord
5669 Morella Avenue
North Hollywood, CA 91607
"Actor"

Barbara Corday
532 South Windsor Blvd.
Los Angeles, CA 90020
"TV Writer, Producer"

Mara Corday
P.O. Box 800393
Valencia, CA 91355
"Actress"

Angel Cordero
P.O. Box 90
Jamaica, NY 11411
"Horse Jockey"

Chick Corea
2635 Griffith Park Blvd.
Los Angeles, CA 90039
"Musician"

Prof. Irwin Corey
58 Nassau Drive
Great Neck, NY 11022
"Comedian"

Jeff Corey
29445 Bluewater Road
Malibu, CA 90265
"Actor, Director"

Ann Corio
721 E. Grinnell Drive
Burbank, CA 91501
"Burlesque"

Roger Corman
2501 La Mesa Drive
Santa Monica, CA 90402
"Writer, Producer"

Cornelius Bros. & Sister Rose
2 Professional Drive, #240
Gaithersburg, TN 30879
"R&B Group"

Don Cornelius
1864 N. Commonwealth Ave.
Los Angeles, CA 90027
"TV Show Host"

Don Cornell
100 Bayview Drive #1521
North Miami, FL 33160
"Singer"

Lydia Cornell
142 South Bedford Drive
Beverly Hills, CA 90212
"Actress, Model"

Georges Corraface
1 rue Gueneguard
75006 Paris ENGLAND
"Actor"

Adrienne Corri
2-4 Noel Street
London W1V 3RB ENGLAND
"Actress"

Douglas Corrigan
2828 North Flower
Santa Ana, CA 92706
"Actor"

Bud Cort
955 South Carrillo Drive, #300
Los Angeles, CA 90048
"Actor"

Aneta Corsaut
4312 Agnes Avenue
Studio City, CA 91604
"Actress"

Dan Cortese
1734 Palisades Drive
Pacific Palisades, CA 90272
"Actor"

Joe Cortese
4724 Poe Avenue
Woodland Hills, CA 91364
"Actor"

Valentina Cortese
Pretta S. Erasmo 6
Milan, ITALY
"Actress"

Norman Corwin
1840 Fairburn Avenue #302
Los Angeles, CA 90025
"Writer, Producer"

Bill Cosby
P.O. Box 4049
Santa Monica, CA 90411
"Actor, Comedian"

Pierre Cossette
8899 Beverly Blvd. #100
Los Angeles, CA 90048
"Film Producer"

Mary Costa
3340 Kingston Pike, Unit 1
Knoxville, TN 37919
"Soprano"

Constantin Costa-Gavras
244 rue Saint-Jacques
75005 Paris, FRANCE
"Filmwriter, Director"

Midge Costanza
11811 West Olympic Blvd.
Los Angeles, CA 90264
"Ex-President Aide"

Bob Costas
30 Rockefeller Plaza
New York, NY 10112
"Sportscaster"

Elvis Costello
9028 Great West Road
Middlesex TW8 9EW ENGLAND
"Singer"

Mariclare Costello
8271 Melrose Avenue #110
Los Angeles, CA 90046
"Actress"

Nicholas Coster
1624 North Gardner
Los Angeles, CA 90046
"Actor"

Kevin Costner
2806 Nichols Canyon
Los Angeles, CA 90046
"Actor"

David Coulier
9150 Wilshire Blvd. #350
Beverly Hills, CA 90212
"Actor"

Fred Couples
8251 Greensboro Drive #530
McLean, VA 22102
"Golfer"

Katherine Couric
320 Central Park West #19B
New York, NY 10025
"TV Show Host"

Jim Courier
306 East Southview Avenue
Dade City, FL 33525
"Tennis Player"

Hazel Court
1111 San Vicent Blvd.
Santa Monica, CA 90402
"Actress"

Tom Courtenay
30 Charlywood Road
London SW15 ENGLAND
"Actor"

Jerome Courtland
27354 Landon Place
Valencia, CA 91354
"Film Director"

Robin Cousins
2887 Hollyridge Drive
Los Angeles, CA 90068
"Ice Skater"

Jacques Cousteau
930 West 21st Street
Norfolk, VA 23517
"Oceanographer"

Bob Cousy
459 Salisbury Street
Worchester, MA 01609
"Basketball Player"

Franklin Cover
1422 North Sweetzer #402
Los Angeles, CA 90069
"Actor"

Al "A.C" Cowlings.
777 S. Figueroa Street #813
Los Angeles, CA 90017
"Ex-Football Player"

Archibald Cox
Glesen Lane
Wayland, MA 01778
"Politician"

Courteney Cox
9830 Wilshire Blvd. #500
Beverly Hills, CA 90212
"Actress"

Ronny Cox
13948 Magnolia Blvd.
Sherman Oaks, CA 91423
"Actor, Film Producer"

Peter Coyote
9 Rose Avenue
Mill Valley, CA 94941
"Actor"

Cuffy Crabbe
11216 North 74th Street
Scottsdale, AZ 85260
"Actor"

Billy "Crash" Craddock
P.O. Box 16426
Greensboro, NC 27416
"Singer, Songwriter"

Jenny Craig
445 Marine View Drive #300
Del Mar, CA 92014
"Physical Director"

Jim Craig
15 Jyre Lane
North Easton, MA 02156
"Hockey Player"

Yvonne Craig
P.O. Box 827
Pacific Palisades, CA 90272
"Actress"

Jeanne Crain
354 Hilgard Avenue
Los Angeles, CA 90024
"Actress"

Douglass Cramer
738 Sarbonne Road
Los Angeles, CA 90077
"TV Writer, Producer"

Barbara Crampton
501 South Beverly Drive 3rd Floor
Beverly Hills, CA 90212
"Actress"

Bruce Crampton
7107 Spanky Ranch Drive
Dallas, TX 75248
"Golfer"

Alan Cranston
2024 Camden Avenue
Los Angeles, CA 90025
"Ex-Senator"

Gemma Craven
42 Hazelburg Road
London SW6 ENGLAND
"Actress"

Matt Craven
11553 Zelzah Avenue
Granada Hills, CA 91344
"Actor"

Wes Craven
1000 W. Washington Blvd. #3011
Culver City, CA 90232
"Writer, Producer"

Christina Crawford
7 Springs Farm Sanders Road
Tensed, ID 83870
"Author"

Cindy Crawford
132 South Rodeo Drive #300
Beverly Hills, CA 90212
"Model"

Johnny Crawford
2440 El Contento Drive
Los Angeles, CA 90068
"Actor"

Michael Crawford
76 Oxford Street
London W1N OAX ENGLAND
"Actor"

Randy Crawford
911 Park Street S.W.
Grand Rapids, MI 49504
"Singer"

Bettino Craxi
Palazzo Chigi
Piazza Colonna
1-00100 Rome, ITALY
"Prime Minister"

Robert Cray
P.O. Box 170429
San Francisco, CA 94117
"Band Leader"

Richard Crenna
3951 Valley Meadow Road
Encino, CA 91316
"Actor, Director"

Ben Crenshaw
2905 San Gabriel #213
Austin, TX 78705
"Golfer"

The Crew-Cuts
29 Cedar Street
Creskill, NJ 07626
"Vocal Group"

Michael Crichton
2210 Wilshire Blvd. #433
Santa Monica, CA 90403
"Filmwriter, Director"

The Crickets
7200 France Avenue South #300
Edina, MN 55435
"Rock & Roll Group"

Catherine Crier
77 West 66th Street
New York, NY 10023
"Newscaster"

Quentin Crisp
46 East 3rd Street
New York, NY 10003
"Actor"

Judith Crist
180 Riverside Drive
New York, NY 10024
"Film Critic"

Linda Cristal
9129 Hazen Drive
Beverly Hills, CA 90210
"Actress"

Mary Jane Croft
2160 Century Park East #812
Los Angeles, CA 90067
"Actor"

James Cromwell
10110 Empyrian Way #304
Los Angeles, CA 90067
"Actor"

David Cronenberg
184 Cottingham Street
Toronto, Ontario, CANADA
"Film Writer, Directorr"

Walter Cronkite
519 East 84th Street
New York, NY 10028
"Broadcast Journalist"

Cathy Lee Crosby
1223 Wilshire Blvd. #404
Santa Monica, CA 90403
"Actress"

David Crosby
17351 Rancho Street
Encino, CA 91316
"Singer, Songwriter"

Denise Crosby
345 North Maple Drive #300
Beverly Hills, CA 90210
"Actor"

Mrs. Kathryn Crosby
P.O. Box 85
Genda, NV 89411
"Widower of Bing Crosby"

Norm Crosby
1400 Londonderry Place
Los Angeles, CA 90069
"Comedian, Actor"

Philip Crosby
21801 Providencia
Woodland Hills, CA 91364
"Actor"

Crosby, Stills & Nash
14930 Ventura Blvd. #206
Sherman Oaks, CA 91403
"Rock & Roll Group"

Ben Cross
Contejo la Perdiz
Barriada de Concelada
Esteponda Malaga SPAIN
"Actor"

Christopher Cross
P.O. Box 63
Marble Falls, TX 78654
"Singer, Songwriter"

Marcia Cross
10100 Santa Monica Blvd. #2500
Los Angeles, CA 90067
"Actress"

Lindsay Crouse
9000 Sunset Blvd. #1200
Los Angeles, CA 90069
"Actress"

Sheryl Crow
10345 West Olympic Blvd., #200
Los Angeles, CA 90064
"Singer"

J. D. Crowe
P.O. Box 1210
Hamilton, OH 45012
"Bluegrass"

Tanya Crowe
6620 East Olympic Blvd.
Los Angeles, CA 90022
"Actress"

Rodney Crowell
1111 16th Avenue South #302
Nashville, TN 37212
"Singer, Songwriter"

Mart Crowley
8955 Beverly Blvd.
Los Angeles, CA 90048
"Writer"

Patricia Crowley
1801 Ave. of the Stars #902
Los Angeles, CA 90067
"Actress"

Tom Cruise
14775 Ventura Blvd. #1-710
Sherman Oaks, CA 91403
"Actor"

Denny Crumm
23015 Third Street
Louisville, KY 40292
"Basketball Coach"

Jon Cryer
9560 Wilshire Blvd. #500
Beverly Hills, CA 90212
"Actor"

Billy Crystal
9830 Wilshire Blvd.
Beverly Hills, CA 90212
"Actor, Comedian"

Melinda Culea
5504 Calhoun Avenue
Van Nuys, CA 91401
"Actress"

Kieran Culkin
151 El Camino Drive
Beverly Hills, CA 90212
"Actor"

Macaulay Culkin
124 West 60th Street
New York, NY 10023
"Actor"

Brett Cullen
P.O. Box 5617
Beverly Hills, CA 90210
"Actor"

John Cullum
8942 Wilshire Blvd.
Beverly Hills, CA 90211
"Actor"

Robert Culp
357 Crown Drive
Los Angeles, CA 90049
"Actor, Writer, Director"

Michael Culver
5 Clancarty Road
London SW6 ENGLAND
"Actor"

Constance Cummings
66 Old Church Street
London SW3 ENGLAND
"Actress"

Quinn Cummings
121 North San Vicente Blvd.
Beverly Hills, CA 90211
"Actress"

Randall Cunningham
c/o Veterans Stadium
Philadelphia, PA 19148
"Football Player"

Mario Cuomo
845 - 3rd Avenue
New York, NY 10022
"Ex-Governor"

Mike Curb
3907 West Alameda Avenue
Burbank, CA 91505
"Record Producer"

Kevin Curren
5808 Back Court
Austin, TX 78764
"Tennis Player"

Cherie Currie
3050 North Chandelle Road
Los Angeles, CA 90046
"Singer"

Mark Curry
12540 King Street
North Hollywood, CA 91604
"Actor"

Tim Curry
8942 Wilshire Blvd.
Beverly Hills, CA 90211
"Actor"

Jane Curtin
P.O. Box 1070
Sharon, CT 06069
"Actress"

Valerie Curtin
15622 Meadowgate Road
Encino, CA 91316
"Actress, Writer"

Dan Curtis
10000 W. Washington Blvd. #3014
Culver City, CA 90232
"Actor"

Jamie Lee Curtis
P.O. Box 2358
Running Springs, CA 92382
"Actress"

Keene Curtis
6363 Ivarene Avenue
Los Angeles, CA 90068
"Actor"

Robin Curtis
1234 N. Havenhurst Drive
Los Angeles, CA 90046
"Actress"

Tony Curtis
11831 Folkstone Lane
Los Angeles, CA 90077
"Actor, Director"

Joan Cusack
540 N. Lakeshore Dr. #521
Chicago, IL 60611
"Actress"

John Cusack
151 El Camino Drive
Beverly Hills, CA 90212
"Actor"

Clive Cussier
7731 West 72nd Place
Arvada, CO 80005
"Novelist"

Lise Cutter
4526 Wilshire Blvd.
Beverly Hills, CA 90210
"Actress"

Jon Cypher
424 Manzanita Avenue
Ventura, CA 93003
"Actor"

Billy Ray Cyrus
818 - 18th Avenue South
Nashville, TN 37203
"Singer"

D

Augusta Dabney
North Mountain Road
Dobbs Ferry, NY 10522
"Actress"

Maryan d'Abo
9300 Wilshire Blvd. #555
Beverly Hills, CA 90212
"Actress"

Olivia d'Abo
1122 S. Robertson Blvd. #15
Los Angeles, CA 90035
"Actress"

Mark Dacascos
11684 Ventura Blvd. #476
Studio City, CA 91604
"Actor"

Willem Dafoe
33 Wooster Street #200
New York, NY 10013
"Actor"

Tim Daggett
53 Harmon Street
Long Beach, NY 11561
"Gymnast"

Arlene Dahl
P.O. Box 116
Sparkill, NY 10976
"Actress"

Bill Dailey
1331 Park Avenue SW.
Albuquerque, NM 87104
"Actor"

Janet Dailey
S1947 Lakeshore Drive
Branson, MO 65616
"Author"

John Dalancie
1313 Brunswick Avenue
South Pasadena, CA 91030
"Actor"

Dick Dale
530 Howard Street #200
San Francisco, CA 94105
"Singer, Guitarist"

Jim Dale
555 Fifth Avenue #1900
New York, NY 10017
"Actor"

The Dalai Lama
Thekchen Choling
McLeod Gunji, Hangra Dist.
Himachal Pradesh, INDIA
"Religious Leader"

Richard M. Daley
121 North Main Street
Chicago, IL 60602
"Mayor of Chicago"

Dallas Cowboys Cheerleaders
1 Cowboy Parkway
Irving, TX 75063
"Cheerleading Team"

Abby Dalton
P.O. Box 2423
Mammoth Lakes, CA 93546
"Actress"

Audrey Dalton
15227 Del Gado Drive
Sherman Oaks, CA 91403
"Actress"

Lacy J. Dalton
909 Meadowlark Lane
Goodlettsville, TN 37027
"Singer"

Timothy Dalton
15 Golden Square #315
London W1 ENGLAND
"Actor"

Roger Daltry
48 Harley House
Marylebone Road
London NW1 5HL ENGLAND
"Singer, Actor"

John Daly
P.O. Box 109601
Palm Beach Gardens, FL 33418
"Golfer"

Rad Daly
261 South Robertson Blvd.
Beverly Hills, CA 90211
"Actor"

Timothy Daly
1587 North Bundy Drive
Los Angeles, CA 90049
"Actor"

Tyne Daly
6437 Drexel
Los Angeles, CA 90049
"Actress"

Sen. Alfonse D'Amato (NY)
520 Hart Senate Office Building
Washington, DC 20510
"Politician"

Jacques D'Amboise
244 West 71st Street
New York, NY 10023
"Choreographer"

Leo Damian
25366 Malibu Road
Malibu, CA 90265
"Conductor"

Michael Damian
P.O. Box 25573
Los Angeles, CA 90025
"Actor"

Mark Damon
2781 Benedict Canyon
Beverly Hills, CA 90210
"Actor"

Stuart Damon
367 North Van Ness Avenue
Los Angeles, CA 90004
"Actor"

Vic Damone
P.O. Box 2999
Beverly Hills, CA 90213
"Singer"

Bill Dana
P.O. Box 1792
Santa Monica, CA 90406
"Actor, Comedian"

Justin Dana
16830 Ventura Blvd. #300
Encino, CA 91436
"Actor"

Charles Dance
1311 N. California Street
Burbank, CA 91505
"Actor"

Ruby Dandridge
3737 Don Felipe Drive
Los Angeles, CA 90008
"Actress"

Claire Danes
924 Westwood Blvd. #900
Los Angeles, CA 90024
"Actress"

Beverly D'Angelo
8033 Sunset Blvd. #247
Los Angeles, CA 90046
"Actress"

Rodney Dangerfield
530 East 76th Street
New York, NY 10021
"Comedian, Actor"

Clifton Daniel
830 Park Avenue
New York, NY 10028
"Journalist"

Charlie Daniels Band
17060 Central Pike
Lebanon, TN 37087
"C&W Group"

Jeff Daniels
137 Park Street
Chelsea, MI 48118
"Actor"

William Daniels
10000 Santa Monica Blvd. #305
Los Angeles, CA 90067
"Actor"

Nicholas Daniloff
2400 "N" Street NW
Washington, DC 20037
"News Correspondent"

Alexandra Danilov
100 West 57th Street
New York, NY 10019
"Ballerina"

Blythe Danner
8942 Wilshire Blvd.
Beverly Hills, CA 90211
"Actress"

Sybil Danning
611 South Catalina Street #330
Los Angeles, CA 90005
"Actress"

Danny & The Juniors
P.O. Box 1017
Turnersville, NJ 08012
"Vocal Group"

Ted Danson
1033 Gayley Ave. #208
Los Angeles, CA 90024
"Actor"

Joe Dante
2321 Holly Drive
Los Angeles, CA 90068
"Film Director"

Nikki Dantine
9744 Wilshire Blvd. #308
Beverly Hills, CA 90212
"Actress"

Tony Danza
25000 Malibu Road
Malibu, CA 90265
"Actor"

Patti D'Arbanville-Quinn
9465 Wilshire Blvd. #405
Beverly Hills, CA 90212
"Actress"

Patrika Darbo
346 North Avon Street
Burbank, CA 91505
"Actress"

Kim Darby
4255 Laurel Grove
Studio City, CA 91604
"Actress"

Terence Trent D'Arby
P.O. Box 910-L
London NW1 9AQ ENGLAND
"Singer"

Mireille Darc
78 Blvd. Malesherbes
75008 Paris FRANCE
"Actress"

Christopher Darden
675 South Westmoreland Avenue
Los Angeles, CA 90005
"Attorney"

Alvin Dark
103 Cranberry Way
Easley, SC 29640
"Ex-Baseball Player"

Johnny Dark
1100 North Alta Loma #707
Los Angeles, CA 90069
"Comedian"

Joan Darling
P.O. Box 6700
Tesuque, NM 87574
"Writer, Director"

Ron Darling
19 Woodland Street
Millbury, MA 01527
"Baseball Player"

James Darren
P.O. Box 1088
Beverly Hills, CA 90213
"Actor, Singer"

Danielle Darrieux
1 Rue Alfred de Vingnu
F-75008 Paris, FRANCE
"Actress"

Henry Darrow
9300 Wilshire Blvd. #555
Beverly Hills, CA 90212
"Actor"

Sen Tom Daschle
615 South Main
Aberdeen, SD 57401
"Politician"

Sam Dash
110 Newlands
Chevy Chase, MD 20815
"Watergate Participate"

Jules Dassin
8 Athinalon Efivon St.
Athens 11521 GREECE
"Actor, Director"

Brad Daugherty
2923 Streetsboro Road
Richfield, OH 44286
"Basketball Player"

Elyssa Davalos
2934 1/2 Beverly Glen Circle #53
Los Angeles, CA 90077
"Actress"

Richard Davalos
1958 Vestal Avenue
Los Angeles, CA 90026
"Actor, Director"

Nigel Davenport
5 Annis Close
Kinnerton Street
London SW1 ENGLAND
"Actor"

Robert Davi
6568 Beachview Drive #209
Rancho Palos Verdes, CA 90274
"Actor"

Marty Davich
1044 Armada Drive
Pasadena, CA 91103
"Actor"

Hal David
10430 Wilshire Blvd.
Los Angeles, CA 90024
"Lyricist"

Joanna David
25 Maida Avenue
London W2 ENGLAND
"Actress"

Lolita Davidovich
8942 Wilshire Blvd.
Beverly Hills, CA 90211
"Actress"

Doug Davidson
P.O. Box 5608
Santa Barbara, CA 93150
"Actor"

Eileen Davidson
13340 Galewood Drive
Sherman Oaks, CA 91423
"Actress"

Gordon Davidson
165 Mabery Road
Santa Monica, CA 90406
"Film Director"

Jaye Davidson
8942 Wilshire Blvd.
Beverly Hills, CA 90211
"Actor"

John Davidson
6051 Spring Valley Road
Hidden Hills, CA 91302
"Singer, Actor"

Embeth Davidtz
311-C North Venice Blvd.
Venice, CA 90291
"Actor"

Lane Davies
9200 Sunset Blvd. #625
Los Angeles, CA 90069
"Actor"

Al Davis
332 Center Street
El Segundo, CA 90245
"Football Team Owner"

Altovise Davis
279 South Beverly Drive #1006
Beverly Hills, CA 90212
"Mrs. Sammy Davis, Jr."

Andrew Davis
1800 Ave. of the Stars #400
Los Angeles, CA 90067
"Film Director"

Angela Davis
San Francisco State University
Ehtnic Studies Dept.
1600 Holloway
San Francisco, CA 94132
"Author, Politician"

Ann B. Davis
1427 Beaver Road
Ambridge, PA 15003
"Actress"

Benjamin Davis
1001 Wilson Blvd. #906
Arlington, VA 22209
"Black Military General"

Billy Davis, Jr.
P.O. Box 7905
Beverly Hills, CA 90212
"Singer"

Clifton Davis
14431 Ventura Blvd. #275
Sherman Oaks, CA 91423
"Actor, Clergyman"

Geena Davis
9830 Wilshire Bld.
Beverly Hills, CA 90212
"Actress"

Glenn Davis
47-650 Eisenhower Drive
La Quinta, CA 92253
"Actor"

Jim Davis
3300 Chadam Lane
Muncie, IN 47302
"Cartoonist"

Jimmie Davis
P.O. Box 15826
Baton Rouge, LA 70895
"Ex-Govenor"

Judy Davis
129 Bourke Street
Woollomooloo
Sydney NSW 2011 AUSTRALIA
"Actress"

Mac Davis
10960 Wilshire Blvd.
Los Angeles, CA 90024
"Singer, Actor"

Martha Davis
10513 Cushdon Avenue
Los Angeles, CA 90064
"Singer"

Marvin Davis
1120 Schuyler Road
Beverly Hills, CA 90210
"Film Executive"

Ossie Davis
44 Cortland Avenue
New Rochelle, NY 10801
"Actor, Writer, Director"

Skeeter Davis
508 Seward Road
Brentwood, TN 37027
"Singer"

Todd Davis
245 South Keystone Street
Burbank, CA 91506
"Actor"

Tyrone Davis
1048 Tatnall Street
Macoa, GA 31201
"Singer"

Willie Davis
4419 Buena Vista #203
Dallas, TX 75202
"Ex-Baseball Player"

Bruce Davison
P.O. Box 57593
Sherman Oaks, CA 91403
"Musician"

Pam Dawber
2236-A Encinitas Blvd
Encinitas, CA 92024
"Actress"

Pete Dawkins
178 Rumson Road
Rumson, NJ 07760
"Former Politician"

Andre Dawson
5715 S.W. 130th Street
Miami, FL 33156
"Baseball Player"

Richard Dawson
1117 Angelo Drive
Beverly Hills, CA 90210
"Ex-TV Show Host, Actor"

Doris Day
P.O. Box 223163
Carmel, CA 93922
"Actress"

Laraine Day
10313 Lauriston Avenue
Los Angeles, CA 90025
"Actress"

Linda Day
3335 Coy Drive
Sherman Oaks, CA 91423
"Actress"

Daniel Day-Lewis
46 Albermarle Street
London W1X 4PP ENGLAND
"Actor"

Taylor Dayne
P.O. Box 476
Rockville Centre, NY 11571
"Singer"

Billy Dean
3310 West End Avenue #500
Nashville, TN 37203
"Singer"

Eddie Dean
32161 Sailview Lane
Westlake Village, CA 91360
"Actor, Singer"

Isabel Dean
43-A Princess Road
Regent's Park
London NW1 8JS ENGLAND
"Actress"

Jimmy Dean
28035 Dorothy Drive #210-A
Agoura, CA 91301
"Singer"

John Dean
9496 Rembert Lane
Beverly Hills, CA 90210
"Author"

Robin Deardan
4659 Ethel Avenue
Sherman Oaks, CA 91423
"Actress"

Blossom Dearie
P.O. Box 21
East Durham, NY 12423
"Singer"

Michael K. Deaver
4 Chaparrel Lane
Palos Verdes, CA 90274
"Ex-Government Official"

Dr. Michael De Bakey
Baylor College of Medicine
1200 Moursund Avenue
Houston, TX 77030
"Heart Surgeon"

Burr De Benning
4235 Kingfisher Road
Calabasas, CA 91302
"Actor"

Dorothy DeBorba
1810 Montecito Avenue
Livermore, CA 94550
"Actress"

Chris De Burge
Bargy Castle, Tonhaggard
Wesxord, IRELAND
"Singer, Guitarist"

Rosemary De Camp
317 Camino de Los Colinas
Redondo Beach, CA 90277
"Actress"

Yvonne DeCarlo
PO Box 250070-Y
Glendale, CA 91225
"Actress"

Mary Decker Slaney
2923 Flintlock Street
Eugene, OR 97401
"Track Athlete"

Fred de Cordova
1875 Carla Ridge Drive
Beverly Hills, CA 90210
"Film-TV Director"

Joey Dee
141 Dunbar Avenue
Fords, NJ 08863
"Singer"

Ruby Dee
44 Cortland Avenue
New Rochelle, NY 10801
"Actress"

Sandra Dee
6249 Tapia Drive
Malibu, CA 90265
"Actress"

Dee-Lite
428 Cedar Street NW
Washington, DC 20012
"Singer"

Mickey Deems
13114 Weddington Street
Van Nuys, CA 90401
"Actor, Director"

Deep Pruple
3 East 54th Street #1400
New York, NY 10022
"Rock & Roll Group"

Morris Dees
Rolling Hills Ranch
Route #1
Mathews, AL 36052
"Attorney"

Rick Dees
3400 Riverside Drive #800
Burbank, CA 91505
"Radio-TV Personality"

Eddie Deezen
1570 North Edgemont #603
Los Angeles, CA 90028
"Actor"

Def Leppard
729 7th Avenue #1400
New York, NY 10019
"Rock & Roll Group"

Ellen DeGeneres
1122 S. Roxbury Drive
Los Angeles, CA 90035
"Actress"

Hubert De Givenchy
3 Avenue George V
75008 Paris, FRANCE
"Fashion Designer"

Gloria DeHaven
73 Devonshire Road
Cedar Grove, NJ 07009
"Actress"

Penny DeHaven
P.O. Box 83
Brentwood, TN 37027
"Singer"

Olivia DeHavilland
Boite Postale 156-16
Paris, Cedex 16-75764
FRANCE
"Actress"

Deja Vu
1 Touchstone Lane
Chard, Somerset
TA20 IRF ENGLAND
"Rock & Roll Group"

Frederick deKlerk
Tuyhuys, Capetown 8000
SOUTH AFRICA
"Politician"

Oscar De La Hoya
637 North 1st Street
Montebello, CA 90640
"Boxer"

Kim Delaney
4724 Poe Avenue
Woodland Hills, CA 91364
"Actress"

John deLancie
1313 Brunswick Avenue
South Pasadena, CA 91030
"Actor"

Dana Delany
2522 Beverly Blvd.
Santa Monica, CA 90405
"Actress"

Oscar de la Renta
Brook Hill Farm
Skiff Mountain Road
Kent, CT 06757
"Fashion Designer"

De La Soul
1700 Broadway #500
New York, NY 10019
"Music Group"

Frances De La Tour
15 Golden Square #315
London S1R 3AG ENGLAND
"Actress"

Dino De Laurentis
Via Poutina Ku 23270
Rome, ITALY
"Motion Picture Producer"

Myrna Dell
12958 Valley Heart Drive
Studio City, CA 91604
"Actress"

Rep. Ronald V. Dellums (CA)
House Rayburn Bldg. #2136
Washington, DC 20515
"Politician"

Ken Delo
844 South Masselin
Los Angeles, CA 90048
"Singer"

Alan Delon
Rt. de Malagnous 170
CH-1224 Chene-Bougeries
SWITZERLAND
"Actor"

Nathalie Delon
3 Qual Malaquais
75006 Paris, FRANCE
"Actor"

John Z. DeLorean
567 Larnington Road
Bedminister, NJ 07921
"Automobile Builder"

Michael DeLorenzo
8271 Melrose Avenue, #110
Los Angeles, CA 90046
"Actor"

Daniele Delorme
16 rue de Marignan
75008 Paris, FRANCE
"Actor"

Victoria De Los Angeles
East Magnini, Paseo de Gracia
87-7-D Barcelona SPAIN
"Soprano"

George Deloy
11460 Amanda Drive
Studio City, CA 91604
"Actor"

Vanessa Del Rio
309 Fifth Avenue#234
Brooklyn, NY 11215
"Actress"

Milton De Lugg
2740 Claray Drive
Los Angeles, CA 90024
"Composer, Conductor"

Dom Deluise
1186 Corsica Drive
Pacific Palisades, CA 90272
"Actor, Director"

Michael Deluise
1186 Corsica Drive
Pacific Palisades, CA 90272
"Actor"

Peter Deluise
8899 Beverly Blvd. #102
Los Angeles, CA 90048
"Actor"

The Del Vikings
1001 W. Cypress Creek Road #314
Ft. Lauderdale, FL 33309
"Music Group"

Jonathan Demme
9830 Wilshire Blvd.
Beverly Hills, CA 90212
"Director"

Rebecca De Mornay
760 North La Cienega Blvd. #200
Los Angeles, CA 90069
"Actress"

Patrick Dempsey
431 Lincoln Blvd.
Santa Monica, CA 90402
"Actor"

Nigel Dempster
10 Buckingham Street
London WC2 ENGLAND
"Writer"

Catherine Deneuve
76 rue Bonaparte
F-75006 Paris FRANCE
"Actress"

Maurice Denham
44 Brunswick Gardens #2
London W8 ENGLAND
"Actor"

Lydie Denier
5350 Sepulveda Blvd. #9
Sherman Oaks, CA 91411
"Actress"

Robert DeNiro
110 Hudson Street
New York, NY 10013
"Actor"

Anthony John Denison
7920 Sunset Blvd. #400
Los Angeles, CA 90046
"Actor"

Michael Denison
76 Oxford Street
London W1N OAX ENGLAND
"Actor"

Brian Dennehy
121 North San Vincente Blvd.
Beverly Hills, CA 90211
"Actor"

Martin Denny
4080 Black Point Road
Honolulu, HI 96816
"Composer"

Reginald Denny
844 N. Vernon Avenue
Azusa, CA 91702
"L.A. Riot Beating Victim"

John Densmore
49 Halderman Road
Santa Monica, CA 90402
"Musician"

Bucky Dent
8895 Indian River Run
Boynton Beach, FL 33457
"Baseball Player"

Bob Denver
General Delivery
Princeton, WV 24740
"Actor"

John Denver
P.O. Box 1587
Aspen, CO 81612
"Singer, Songwriter"

James DePaiva
161 W. 61st Street #16B
New York, NY 10023
"Actor"

Brian De Palma
270 North Canyon Drive #1195
Beverly Hills, CA 90210
"Writer, Producer"

Gerard Depardieu
4 Place de la Chapelle
F-75800 Bougival, FRANCE
"Actor"

Suzanne De Passe
1100 North Altal Loma #805
Los Angeles, CA 90069
"TV Writer"

Depeche Mode
P.O. Box 1281
London N1 9UX ENGLAND
"Rock & Roll Group"

Johnny Depp
500 S. Sepulveda Blvd. #500
Los Angeles, CA 90049
"Actor"

Bo Derek
3625 Roblar
Santa Ynez, CA 93460
"Actress, Model"

John Derek
3625 Roblar
Santa Ynez, CA 93460
"Actor, Writer, Director"

Bruce Dern
23430 Malibu Colony Road
Malibu, CA 90265
"Actor"

Laura Dern
760 North La Cienega Blvd.
Los Angeles, CA 90069
"Actress"

Cleavant Derricks
192 Lexington Avenue
New York, NY 10016
"Actor"

✓ **Alan Dershowitz**
1563 Massachusetts Avenue
Cambridge, MA 02138
"Attorney, Professor"

Jean Desailly
53 quai des Grand Augistina
75006 Paris, FRANCE
"Actor"

Jackie DeShannon
7526 Sunnywood Lane
Los Angeles, CA 90069
"Singer"

Robert Desiderio
2934 Beverly Glen Circle #30
Los Angeles, CA 90077
"Actor"

George Deukmejian
555 W. 5th Street
Los Angeles, CA 90013
"Ex-Governor"

William Devane
9000 Sunset Blvd. #1200
Los Angeles, CA 90069
"Actor"

Gail Devers
20214 Leadwell
Canoga Park, CA 91304
"Track & Field"

Danny Devito
P.O. Box 491246
Los Angeles, CA 90049
"Actor"

Devo
P.O. Box 6868
Burbank, CA 91510
"Rock & Roll Group"

Duchess of Devonshire
Chatsworth, Bakewell
Derbyshire ENGLAND
"Royalty"

Duke of Devonshire
Chatsworth, Bakewell
Derbyshire ENGLAND
"Royalty"

William DeVrees
Human Heart Institute
One Audubon Plaza Drive
Louisville, KY 40202
"Heart Surgeon"

Peter DeVries
170 Cross Highway
Westport, CT 06880
"Author, Editor"

Jacqueline Dewit
436 South Alandele Avenue
Los Angeles, CA 90036
"Actress"

Joyce De Witt
11940 San Vicente Blvd.
Los Angeles, CA 90049
"Actress"

Susan Dey
10390 Santa Monica Blvd. #300
Los Angeles, CA 90025
"Actress"

Cliff DeYoung
2143 Colby Avenue
Los Angeles, CA 90025
"Actor"

Diamond Rio
1105-C 16th Avenue South
Nashville, TN 37212
"Music Group"

Bobby Diamond
5309 Comercio Way
Woodland Hills, CA 91364
"Actor"

Neil Diamond
161 South Mapleton Drive
Los Angeles, CA 90077
"Singer, Songwriter"

Don Diamont
8485E Melrose Place
Los Angeles, CA 90069
"Actor"

✓ **HRH Princess Diana**
Kensington Palace
London W8 ENGLAND
"Royalty"

John Diaquino
151 El Camino Drive
Beverly Hills, CA 90212
"Actor"

Cameron Diaz
955 South Carrillo Drive #300
Los Angeles, CA 90048
"Actress"

Rob Dibbie
54 Summit Farms Road
Southington, CT 06489
"Baseball Player"

Vincent Di Bona
1912 Thayer Avenue
Los Angeles, CA 90025
"Director, Producer"

Leonardo DiCaprio
9830 Wilshire Blvd.
Beverly Hills, CA 90212
"Actor"

George Di Cenzo
RD 1, Box 728
Stone Hollow Farm
Pipersville, CA 18947
"Actor"

Douglas Dick
604 Gretna Green Way
Los Angeles, CA 90049
"Actor"

Dick & Dee Dee
9227 Nichols Street
Bellflower, CA 90706
"Vocal Duo"

Jimmy Dickens
510 West Concord
Brentwood, TN 37027
"Singer"

Nancy Dickerson
1811 Karlorama Square N.W.
Washington, DC 20008
"News Correspondent"

James Dickey
4620 Lelias Court
Lake Katherine
Columbia, SC 29206
"Poet, Novelist"

Angie Dickinson
9580 Lime Orchard Road
Beverly Hills, CA 90210
"Actress"

Brenda Dickson
2160 Century Park E. #412
Los Angeles, CA 90067
"Actress"

Bo Diddley
1560 Broadway #1308
New York, NY 10036
"Singer, Guitarist"

John Diehl
15758 Hartland Street
Van Nuys, CA 91405
"Actor"

Dan Dierdorf
c/o ABC Sports
1330 Avenue of the Americas
New York, NY 10019
"Sportscaster"

Charles Dierkop
6300 Lankershim Blvd. #312
North Hollywood, CA 91606
"Actor"

Dena Dietrich
1155 North La Cienega Blvd. #302
Los Angeles, CA 90069
"Actress"

Joe Diffle
27 Music Square East
Nashville, TN 37203
"Singer"

Barry Diller
1365 Enterprise Drive
West Chester, PA 19280
"Business Executive"

Phyllis Diller
163 South Rockingham Avenue
Los Angeles, CA 90049
"Actress, Comedienne"

Bradford Dillman
770 Hot Springs Road
Santa Barbara, CA 93103
"Actor"

C. Douglas Dillon
1270 Ave. of the Americas #2300
New York, NY 10020
"Banker, Diplomat"

Denny Dillon
340 West 57th Street #14C
New York, NY 10019
"Actress"

Kevin Dillon
49 West 9th Street #5B
New York, NY 10010
"Actor"

Matt Dillon
40 West 57th Street
New York, NY 10019
"Actor"

Melinda Dillon
1999 Ave. of the Stars #2850
Los Angeles, CA 90067
"Actress"

Dom DiMaggio
162 Point Road
Marion, MA 02738
"Ex-Baseball Player"

Joe DiMaggio
3233 - 34th Street NE
Ft. Lauderdale, FL 33308
"Ex-Baseball Player"

Dion Di Mucci
P.O. Box 570815
Tarzana, CA 91357
"Singer"

Rep. John D. Dingell (MI)
House Rayburn Bldg. #2328
Washington, DC 20515
"Politician"

Celine Dion
C.P. 65, Repentiguy
PQ J6A 5H7 CANADA
"Singer"

Colleen Dion
10637 Burbank Blvd.
North Hollywood, CA 91601
"Actress"

Christian Dior
St. Anna-Platz 2
80538 Munich, GERMANY
"Fashion Designer"

Dire Straits
509 Hartnell Street
Monterey, CA 93940
"Rock & Roll Group"

The Dirt Band
P.O. Box 1915
Aspen, CO 81611
"Music Group"

Bob Dishy
20 East 9th Street
New York, NY 10003
"Actor, Writer"

Mrs. Lillian Disney
355 Carolwood Drive
Los Angeles, CA 90024
"Mrs. Walt Disney"

Roy Disney
500 South Buena Vista Street
Burbank, CA 91521
"Writer, Producer"

Sacha Distal
3, Quai Malaquais
75006 Paris FRANCE
"Singer"

Mike Ditka
250 N. Washington Road
Lake Forest, IL 60045
"Ex-Football Coach"

Valde Divac
P.O. Box 10
Inglewood, CA 90306
"Basketball Player"

Andrew Divoff
10637 Burbank Blvd.
North Hollywood, CA 91601
"Actor"

Donna Dixon
8955 Norma Place
Los Angeles, CA 90069
"Actress"

Ivan Dixon
2268 Maiden Lane
Altadena, CA 91001
"Actor, Director"

Jeanne Dixon
1225 Connecticut Avenue NW
Suite #411
Washington, DC 20036
"Astrologer"

Jesse Dizon
6427 Gloria Avenue
Van Nuys, CA 91406
"Actor, Writer"

Edward Dmytryk
3945 Westfall Drive
Encino, CA 91436
"Director"

Alan Dobie
Pontus, Molash
Kent CT4 8HW ENGLAND
"Actor"

Lawrence Dobkin
1787 Old Ranch Road
Los Angeles, CA 90049
"Actor, Writer, Director"

Kevin Dobson
P.O. Box 5617
Beverly Hills, CA 90210
"Actor"

Peter Dobson
1351 N. Crescent Heights #318
Los Angeles, CA 90046
"Actor"

Larry Doby
1884 Bellmore Avenue
Bellmore, NY 11710
"Baseball Manager"

Carol Doda
P.O. Box 387
Fremont, CA 94537
"Dancer"

Shannon Doherty
1033 Gayley Ave. #208
Los Angeles, CA 90024
"Actress"

Don Dolan
14228 Emelita Street
Van Nuys, CA 91401
"Actor"

Thomas Dolby
20 Manchester Square
London W1 ENGLAND
"Singer, Songwriter"

Elizabeth Dole
430 17th Street NW
NW Washington, DC 20006
"Ex- Govt. & Red Cross Official"

Robert J. Dole
430-17th street
Washington, DC 20006
"Politician"

Ami Dolenz
6058 St. Clair Avenue
North Hollywood, CA 91607
"Actress"

Mickey Dolenz
2756 N. Green Valley Pkwy #449
Las Vegas, NV 89104
"Musician, Actor"

Arielle Dombasle
201 rue du Faubourg St. Honore
F-75008 Paris FRANCE
"Actress"

Pete Domenici
625 Silver SW #130
Albuquerque, NM 87102
"Politician"

Placido Domingo
150 Central Park South
New York, NY 10019
"Tenor"

Fats Domino
5515 Marais Street
New Orleans, LA 70117
"Singer, Pianist"

Elinor Donahue
4525 Lemp Avenue
North Hollywood, CA 91602
"Actress"

Phil Donahue
420 East 54th St. #22-F
New York, NY 10022
"TV Show Host"

Troy Donahue
1022 Euclid Avenue #1
Santa Monica, CA 90403
"Actor"

Elyse Donaldson
5330 Lankershim Blvd. #210
North Hollywood, CA 91610
"Actress"

Sam Donaldson
1717 DeSales N.W.
Washington, DC 20007
"Broadcast Journalist"

Peter Donat
1030 Broderick Street
San Francisco, CA 94115
"Actor"

Donfeld
2900 Hutton Drive
Beverly Hills, CA 90210
"Costume Designer"

Yolande Donlan
2-4 Noel Street
London W1V 3RB ENGLAND
"Actress, Writer"

Clive Donner
1466 North Kings Road
Los Angeles, CA 90069
"Film Director"

Jorn Donner
Pohjoisranta 12
00170 Helsinki 17
FINLAND
"Film Director"

Richard Donner
4000 Warner Blvd., #102
Burbank, CA 91522
"Film Director"

Robert Donner
3828 Glenridge Drive
Sherman Oaks, CA 91423
"Actor"

Mary Agnes Donoghue
427 Alta Avenue
Santa Monica, CA 90402
"Writer"

Amanda Donohue
151 El Camino Drive
Beverly Hills, CA 90212
"Actress"

Terry Donohue
11918 Laurelwood
Studio City, CA 91604
"Football Coach"

Donovan
P.O. Box 472
London SW1 2QB ENGLAND
"Singer, Songwriter"

Art Donovan
1512 Jeffers Road
Baltimore, MD 21204
"Ex-Football Player"

Tate Donovan
9560 Wilshire Blvd. #500
Beverly Hills, CA 90212
"Actor"

Doobie Brother
15140 Sonoma Highway
Glen Ellen, CA 95442
"Rock & Roll Group"

James Doohan
P.O. Box 2800
Redmond, WA 98073
"Actor"

The Doors
3011 Ledgewood Drive
Los Angeles, CA 90068
"Rock & Roll Group"

Karin Dor
Harthauser Street 54
D-81545 Munich GERMANY
"Actress"

Ann Doran
3939 Walnut Avenue
Carmichael, CA 95608
"Actress"

Stephen Dorff
11333 Moorpark Street, #436
Toluca Lake, CA 91602
"Actor"

Dolores Dorn
7461 Beverly Blvd. #400
Los Angeles, CA 90036
"Actress"

Michael Dorn
3751 Multiview Drive
Los Angeles, CA 90068
"Actor"

Tony Dorsett
1 Cowboy Parkway
Irving, TX 75063
"Ex-Football Player"

David Dortort
133 Udine Way
Los Angeles, CA 90024
"Writer, Producer"

Roy Dotrice
Talbot House
St. Martin Lane
London WC ENGLAND
"Actor"

Jeff Doucette
4311 Coldwater Canyon #3
Studio City, CA 91604
"Actor"

Brandon Douglas
4526 Wilshire Blvd.
Beverly Hills, CA 90210
"Actor"

Donna Douglas
P.O. Box 49455
Los Angeles, CA 90049
"Actress, Singer"

Eric Douglas
9000 Sunset Blvd. #405
Los Angeles, CA 90069
"Actor"

Gordon Douglas
6600 West 6th Street
Los Angeles, CA 90048
"Film Director"

James "Buster" Douglas
700 Ackerman Road #628
Colombus, OH 43202
"Boxer"

Jerry Douglas
8600 Hillside Avenue
Los Angeles, CA 90069
"Actor"

Kirk Douglas
805 North Rexford Drive
Beverly Hills, CA 90210
"Actor, Director"

Michael Douglas
P.O. Box 49054
Los Angeles, CA 90049
"Actor, Producer"

Mike Douglas
1876 Chartley Road
Gates Mill, OH 44040
"TV Show Host, Singer"

Robert Douglas
1810 Parliament Road
Leucadia, CA 92024
"Actor, Director"

Brad Dourif
213 1/2 South Arnaz Drive
Beverly Hills, CA 90211
"Actress"

Billie Dove
P.O. Box 5005
Rancho Mirage, CA 92270
"Actress"

Peggy Dow
2121 S. Yorkstown Avenue
Tulsa, OK 74114
"Actress"

Doris Dowling
9026 Elevado Avenue
Los Angeles, CA 90069
"Actress"

Lesley-Anne Down
9300 Wilshire Blvd. #410
Beverly Hills, CA 90212
"Actress"

Morton Downey, Jr.
8121 Georgia Avenue
Silver Spring, MD 20910
"Ex-TV Show Host"

Robert Downey, Jr.
P.O. Box 6205
Malibu, CA 90264
"Actor"

Roma Downey
P.O. Box 5617
Beverly Hills, CA 90210
"Actress"

Hugh Downs
157 Columbus Avenue
New York, NY 10023
"TV Journalist"

Brian Doyle-Murray
9200 Sunset Blvd. #625
Los Angeles, CA 90067
"Actor"

David Doyle
4731 Noeline Avenue
Encino, CA 91316
"Actor, Director"

Stan Dragoti
755 Stradella Road
Los Angeles, CA 90024
"Writer, Producer"

Victor Drai
1201 Des Resto Drive
Beverly Hills, CA 90210
"Film Producer"

Betsy Drake
10866 Wilshire Blvd. #1000
Los Angeles, CA 90024
"Actress"

Frances Drake
1511 Summit Ridge Drive
Beverly Hills, CA 90210
"Actress"

Larry Drake
1901 Avenue of the Stars #620
Los Angeles, CA 90067
"Actor"

Polly Draper
1324 North Orange Grove
Los Angeles, CA 90046
"Actress"

Dave Dravecky
13840 Gleneagle Drive
Colorado Springs, CO 80921
"Ex-Baseball Player"

Dr. Dre
10900 Wilshire Blvd. #1230
Los Angeles, CA 90024
"Rap Singer"

Tom Dreesen
14570 Benefit Street #201
Sherman Oaks, CA 91403
"Comedian"

Fran Drescher
9336 West Washington Blvd. #R
Culver City, CA 90232
"Actress"

Clyde Drexler
P.O. Box 272349
Houston, TX 77277
"Basketball Player"

Richard Dreyfuss
1717 Crisler Way
Los Angeles, CA 90069
"Actor"

The Drifter
10 Chelsea Court
Neptune, NJ 07753
"Vocal Group"

Joanne Dru
1455 Carla Ridge Drive
Beverly Hills, CA 90210
"Actress"

Allen Drury
P.O. Box 647
Tiburon, CA 94920
"Author"

James Drury
14207 Eventide Drive
Cypress, TX 77429
"Actor"

Roy Drusky
131 Trivett Drive
Portland, TN 37148
"Singer, Songwriter"

Fred Dryer
4117 Radford Avenue
Studio City, CA 91604
"Actor, Football Player"

Ja'Net DuBois
8306 Wilshire Blvd. #189
Beverly Hills, CA 90211
"Actress"

Peter Duchin
305 Madison Avenue #956
New York, NY 10165
"Pianist"

David Duchovny
110-555 Brooks Bank Blvd. #10
North Vancouver BC V7J 3S5
CANADA
"Actor"

Rick Ducommun
7967 Woodrow Wilson Drive
Los Angeles, CA 90046
"Comedian"

Michael Dudikoff
8485 Melrose Place #E
Los Angeles, CA 90069
"Actor"

Peter Duffell
29 Roehampton Gate
London SW15 5JR ENGLAN
"TV Writer, Director"

Julia Duffy
12711 Ventura Blvd #490
Studio City, CA 91604
"Actress, Director"

Patrick Duffy
P.O. Box "D"
Tarzana, CA 91356
"Actor, Director"

Dennis Dugan
2972-1/2 N. Commonwelth Avenue
Los Angeles, CA 90027
"Actor"

Kitty Dukakis
85 Perry Street
Brookline, MA 02146
"Author, Wife of Michael"

Michael Dukakis
85 Perry Street
Brookline, MA 02146
"Ex-Govornor"

Olympia Dukakis
222 Upper Mountain Road
Montclair, NJ 07043
"Actress"

Bill Duke
8306 Wilshire Blvd. #438
Beverly Hills, CA 90211
"Actor"

David Duke
500 North Arnoult
Metairie, LA 70001
"White Supremacist, Politician"

Patty Duke
2950 East Nettleton Gulch Road
Coeur d'Alene, ID 83814
"Actress"

David Dukes
255 South Lorraine Blvd.
Los Angeles, CA 90004
"Actor"

The Dukes
11 Chartfield Square
London SW15 ENGLAND
"Rock & Roll Group"

Keir Dullea
320 Fleming Lane
Fairfield, CT 06430
"Actor"

Melvin Dummar
Dummar's Restaurant
Gabbs, NV 89409
"Alleged in Howard Hughes' Will"

Faye Dunaway
8721 Beverly Blvd. #200
Los Angeles, CA 90048
"Actress"

Sandy Duncan
44 West 77th Street #1B
New York, NY 10024
"Actress"

Angelo Dundee
11264 Pines Blvd.
Hollywood, FL 33026
"Boxing Trainer"

Holly Dunn
209 10th Avenue South #347
Nashville, TN 37203
"C&W Singer"

Dominick Dunne
155 East 49th Street
New York, NY 10017
"Author, Producer"

Griffin Dunne
1501 Broadway #2600
New York, NY 10036
"Actor, Producer"

Murphy Dunne
4400 Encinal Canyon Road
Malibu, CA 90265
"Actor"

Jerry Dunphy
6121 Sunset Blvd.
Los Angeles, CA 90028
"Actor"

Kirsten Dunst
P.O. Box 15036
Beverly Hills, CA 90209
"Actress"

Pierre duPont
Patterns
Rockland, DE 19732
"Ex-Govenor"

Duran Duran
P.O. Box 21
London W10 6XA ENGLAND
"Rock & Roll Group"

Roberto Duran
P.O. Box 157 Arena Colon
Panama City, PANAMA
"Boxer"

Margie Durante
511 North Beverly Drive
Beverly Hills, CA 90210
"Mrs. Jimmy Durante"

Deanna Durbin
B.P. 7677
75123 Paris Cedex 03
FRANCE
"Actress"

Charles Durning
10590 Wilshire Blvd. #506
Los Angeles, CA 90024
"Actor"

Marj Dusay
1964 Westwood Blvd. #400
Los Angeles, CA 90025
"Actress"

Ann Dusenberry
11726 Laurelwood Dr.
Studio City, CA 91604
"Actress"

Nancy Dussault
12211 Iredell Street
Studio City, CA 91604
"Actress"

John Duttine
Pebro House
13 St. Martins Road
London SW9 ENGLAND
"Actor"

Charles Dutton
12312 Viewcrest Road
Studio City, CA 91604
"Actor"

Robert Duvall
P.O. Box 520
The Plains, VA 22171
"Actor"

Shelley Duvall
12725 Ventura Blvd. #J
Studio City, CA 91604
"Actress"

Lenny Dykstra
1031 LaSalle Circle
Corona, CA 91719
"Baseball Player"

Bob Dylan
P.O. Box 870
Cooper Station
New York, NY 10276
"Singer, Songwriter"

Richard Dysart
654 Copeland Court
Santa Monica, CA 90405
"Actor"

Noel Dyson
18 Petherton Road
London N5 ENGLAND
"Actress"

George Dzundza
232 N. Canon Drive
Beverly Hills, CA 90210
"Actor"

Sheila E.
8900 Wilshire Blvd. #300
Beverly Hills, CA 90211
"Singer, Percussionist"

Lawrence Eagleburger
350 Park Avenue #2600
New York, NY 10022
"Ex-Government Official"

The Eagles
8900 Wilshire Blvd. #300
Beverly Hills, CA 90211
"Rock & Roll Group"

Thomas F. Eagleton
1 Mercantitle Center
St. Louis, MO 63101
"Former Senator"

Dale Earnhardt
Box 595-B, Rt. #10
Mooresville, NC 28115
"Race Car Driver"

Earth Wind & Fire
151 El Camino Drive
Beverly Hills, CA 90212
"R&B Group"

Tony Eason
1000 Fulton Road
Hempstead, NY 11550
"Football Player"

Jeff East
5521 Rainbow Crest Drive
Agoura, CA 91301
"Actor"

Leslie Easterbrook
17352 Sunset Blvd. #401-D
Pacific Palisades, CA 90272
"Actress"

Richard Eastham
1529 Oriole Lane
Los Angeles, CA 90069
"Actor"

Michael Easton
8730 Sunset Blvd. #220W
Los Angeles, CA 90069
"Actor"

Robert Easton
9169 Sunset Blvd.
Los Angeles, CA 90069
"Actor"

Sheena Easton
151 El Camino Drive
Beverly Hills, CA 90212
"Singer, Songwriter"

Clint Eastwood
P.O. Box 4366
Carmel, CA 93921
"Actor"

Kyle Eastwood
2628 Larmar Road
Los Angeles, CA 90068
"Actor"

Fred Ebb
146 Central Park West #14D
New York, NY 10023
"Lyricist"

Jose Eber
9465 Santa Monica Blvd. #606
Beverly Hills, CA 90212
"Hair Stylist"

Christine Ebersole
1244-A 11th Street
Santa Monica, CA 90401
"Actress"

Roger Ebert
P.O. Box 146366
Chicago, Il 60614
"Film Critic"

Bonnie Ebsen
P.O. Box 356
Agoura, CA 91301
"Actress"

Buddy Ebsen
P.O. Box 2069
Polos Verdes Estates, CA 90274
"Actor"

Dennis Eckersley
263 Morse Road
Sudbury, MA 01776
"Baseball Player"

Steven Eckholdt
2275 North Gower
Los Angeles, CA 90068
"Actor"

James Eckhouse
4222 Murietta Avenue
Sherman Oaks, CA 91423
"Actor"

Stefan Edberg
Spinnaregaten 6
S-59300 Vastervik SWEDEN
"Tennis Player"

Paul Eddington
388/396 Oxford Street
London W1N 9HE ENGLAND
"Actor"

Duane Eddy
1560 Broad #1308
New York, NY 10036
"Singer, Guitarist"

Herbert Edelman
8730 Sunset Blvd. #480
Los Angeles, CA 90069
"Actor"

Barbara Eden
9816 Denbigh
Beverly Hills, CA 90210
"Actress"

Gertrude Ederle
4465 S.W. 37th Avenue
Ft. Lauderdale, FL 33312
"Swimmer"

Louis Edmonds
250 West 57th Street #2317
New York, NY 10107
"Actor"

HRH The Prince Edward
Buckingham Palace
London SW1 ENGLAND
"Royalty"

Anthony Edwards
3373 Ley Drive
Los Angeles, CA 90027
"Actor"

Blake Edwards
P.O. Box 666
Beverly Hills, CA 90213
"Writer, Producer, Director"

Gov. Edwin Edwards (LA)
P.O. Box 94004
Baton Rouge, LA 70804
"Politician"

Jennifer Edwards
15315 Magnolia Blvd. #429
Sherman Oaks, CA 91403
"Actress"

Luke Edwards
6212 Banner
Los Angeles, CA 90038
"Actor"

Ralph Edwards
610 Arkell Drive
Beverly Hills, CA 90210
"TV Show Host, Producer"

Ronnie Claire Edwards
4900 Los Feliz Blvd.
Los Angeles, CA 90027
"Actress"

Stephanie Edwards
8075 West 3rd Street #303
Los Angeles, CA 90048
"Actress"

Steve Edwards
3980 Royal Oaks Place
Encino, CA 91436
"TV Show Host"

Julie Ege
3300 Hokksund
NORWAY
"Actress, Model"

Samantha Eggar
15430 Mulholland Drive
Los Angeles, CA 90077
"Actress"

Nicole Eggert
20591 Queens Park
Huntington Beach, CA 92646
"Actress"

Marta Eggerth Kiepura
Park Drive North
Rye, NY 10508
"Actress, Singer"

Lisa Eichorn
19 West 44th Street #1000
New York, NY 10036
"Actress"

Jill Eikenberry
2183 Mandeville Canyon
Los Angeles, CA 90049
"Actress"

Cynthia Eilbacher
11051 Ophir Drive
Los Angeles, CA 90024
"Actress"

Lisa Eilbacher
2949 Deep Canyon Drive
Beverly Hills, CA 90210
"Actress"

Bob Einstein
10 Universal City Plaza #3100
Universal City, CA 91608
"Actor, Writer"

Michael Eisner
500 South Buena Vista
Burbank, CA 91521
"Disney Executive"

Britt Ekland
16830 Ventura Blvd. #501
Encino, CA 91436
"Actress"

Jack Elam
P.O. Box 5718
Santa Barbara, CA 93108
"Actor"

Dana Elcar
10000 Santa Monica Blvd. #350
Los Angeles, CA 90067
"Actor, Director"

Lee Elder
1725 "K" Street NW #1202
Washington, DC 20006
"Golfer"

Dr. Joycelyn Elders
800 Marshall Street
Little Rock, AR 72202
"Ex-Surgeon General"

Electric Light Orchestra
9850 Sandalfoot Blvd. #458
Boca Raton, FL 33428
"Rock & Roll Group"

Erika Eleniak
2029 Century Park East #300
Los Angeles, CA 90067
"Actress"

Danny Elfman
3236 Primera
Los Angeles, CA 90068
"Actor"

Larry Elgart
2149 NE 63rd Street
Ft. Lauderdale, FL 33308
"Composer"

Miss Elizabeth
935 Middle Street
Bristol, CT 06010
"Wrestling Valet"

HRH HRH Elizabeth II
Queen
Eliz. II
Buckingham Palace
London SW1 ENGLAND
"Royalty"

HM Queen Elizabeth
Clarence House
London SW1 ENGLAND
"The Queen's Mother"

Hector Elizando
662 North Van Ness Avenue #305
Los Angeles, CA 90004
"Actor"

Robert Ellenstein
5215 Sepulveda Blvd. #23-F
Culver City, CA 90230
"Actor, Director"

Linda Ellerbee
96 Morton Street
New York, NY 10014
"Journalist"

Jane Elliot
606 N. Larchmont Blvd. #309
Los Angeles, CA 90004
"Actress"

Ross Elliott
5702 Graves Avenue
Encino, CA 91316
"Actor"

Sam Elliott
33050 Pacific Coast Hwy.
Malibu, CA 90265
"Actor"

Sean Elliott
P.O. Box 530
San Antonio, TX 78292
"Basketball Player"

Stephen Elliott
3948 Woodfield Drive
Sherman Oaks, CA 91403
"Actor"

Harlan Ellison
P.O. Box 55548
Sherman Oaks, CA 91423
"Actor"

Daniel Ellsberg
90 Norwood Avenue
Kensington, CA 94707
"Author"

Michael Elphick
37 Dennington Park Road
London SW6 ENGLAND
"Actor"

Elvira (Cassandra Peterson)
P.O. Box 38246
Los Angeles, CA 90038
"Actress"

John Elway
13644 E. Dove Valley
Englewood, CO 80112
"Football Player"

Cary Elwes
22611 Vost Street
West Hills, CA 91307
"Actor"

Joe Ely
7101 Hwy. 71 W. #A9
Austin, TX 78735
"Singer, Songwriter"

Ron Ely
4141 Mariposa Drive
Santa Barbara, CA 93110
"Actor"

Kelly Emberg
1608 North Poinsettia
Manhattan Beach, CA 90266
"Model"

Douglas Emerson
1450 Belfast Drive
Los Angeles, CA 90069
"Actor"

Richard Edlund
13335 Maxella Avenue
Marina del Rey, CA 90292
"Actor"

Emir of Bahrain
721 Fifth Avenue, 60th Floor
New York, NY 10022
"Royalty"

Emir of Kuwait
Banyan Palace
Kuwait City Kuwait
"Royalty"

Emmanuel
1406 Georgette Street
Santurce PUERTO RICO 00910
"Fashion Designer"

Dick Enberg
Box 710
Rancho Santa Fe, CA 92067
"Sportscaster"

Michael Ende
via Montegiove 13
00045 Ganzano di Roma
ITALY
"Author"

Georgia Engel
350 West 57th Street #10E
New York, NY 10019
"Actress"

Susan Engel
43A Princess Road
Regent's Park
London NW1 8JS ENGLAND
"Actress"

England Dan
P.O. Box 82
Great Neck, NY 11021
"Singer, Songwriter"

Robert Englund
1616 Santa Cruz Street
Laguna Beach, CA 93651
"Actor"

Brian Eno
330 Harrow Road
London W9 ENGLAND
"Singer, Producer"

Russell Enoch
43A Princess Road
Regent's Park
London NW1 8JS ENGLAND
"Actor"

Philippe Entremont
Schwarzenbergplatz 10/7
A-1040 Vienna, AUSTRIA
"Pianist"

John Entwhistle
1705 Queen Court
Los Angeles, CA 90068
"Musician, Singer"

En Vogue
151 El Camino Drive
Beverly Hills, CA 90212
"Music Group"

Nora Ephron
390 West End Avenue
New York, NY 10024
"Screenwriter"

Richard Erdman
5655 Greenbush Avenue
Van Nuys, CA 91401
"Actor, Director"

John Ericson
RR #3 Box 109JK
Santa Fe, NM 89505
"Actor"

Carl Erskine
6214 South Madison Avenue
Anderson, IN 46013
"Ex-Baseball Player"

Julius Erving
P.O. Box 25040
Southwark Station
Philadelphia, PA 19147
"Ex-Basketball Player"

Bill Erwin
12324 Moorpark Street
Studio City, CA 91604
"Actor"

Christoph Eschenbach
2 Avenue d'Alena
75016 Paris, FRANCE
"Pianist"

"Boomer" Esiason
1000 Fulton Avenue
Hempstead, NY 11550
"Football Player"

Carl Esmond
576 Tigertail Road
Los Angeles, CA 90049
"Actor"

Giancarlo Esposito
484 West 43rd Street #33A
New York, NY 10036
"Actor"

William Grey Espy
205 West 54th Street #3D
New York, NY 10019
"Actor"

David Essex
109 Eastbourne Mews
London W2 ENGLAND
"Singer, Actor"

Gloria Estefan
6205 Bird Road
Miami, FL 33155
"Singer"

Billie Sol Estes
c/o General Delivery
Brady, TX 76825
"Financier, Ex-Convict"

Robert Estes
151 El Camino Drive
Beverly Hills, CA 90212
"Actor"

Simon Estes
Hoschstr. 43
8706 Feldmeilen SWITZERLAND
"Basso-Baritone"

Emilio Estevez
31725 Sea Level Drive
Malibu, CA 90265
"Actor, Writer"

Ramon Estevez
837 Ocean Avenue #101
Santa Monica, CA 90402
"Actor"

Erik Estrada
3768 Eureka Drive
Studio City, CA 91604
"Actor"

Susan Estrich
124 So. Las Palmas Avenue
Los Angeles, CA 90004
"Actress"

Melissa Etheridge
P.O. Box 884563
San Francisc, CA 91488
"Singer"

Bob Eubanks
5900 Highridge Road
Hidden Hills, CA 91302
"TV Show Host"

Wesley Eure
P.O. Box 69405
Los Angeles, CA 90069
"Actor"

Europe
Box 22036, S-104
Stockholm, SWEDEN
"Rock & Roll Group"

Eurythmics
P.O. Box 245
London N8 Q0G ENGLAND
"Rock & Roll Group"

Linda Evangelista
121 rue Legendre
F-75017 Paris, FRANCE
"Model"

Andrea Evans
310 West 72nd Street #7G
New York, NY 10023
"Actress"

Dale Evans Rogers
15650 Seneca Road
Victorville, CA 92392
"Actress"

Evans Evans
3114 Abington Drive
Beverly Hills, CA 90210
"Actress"

Gene Evans
P.O. Box 93
Medon, TN 38356
"Actor"

Janet Evans
424 Brower
Placentia, CA 92670
"Swimmer"

Linda Evans
6714 Villa Madera Drive
Tacoma, WA 98499
"Actress"

Mary Beth Evans
P.O. Box 50105
Pasadena, CA 91115
"Actress"

Mike Evans
12530 Collins Street
North Hollywood, CA 91605
"Actor"

Robert Evans
10033 Woodlawn Drive
Beverly Hills, CA 90210
"Producer, Actor"

Roland Evans
1750 Pennsylvania Avenue NW
Suite #1312
Washington, DC 20006
"Columnist"

Trevor Eve
60 St. James's Street
London W1 ENGLAND
"Actor"

Chad Everett
5472 Island Forest Place
Westlake Village, CA 91362
"Actor"

Rupert Everett
76 Oxford Street
London, W1N 0AX ENGLAND
"Actor"

Nancy Everhard
8899 Beverly Blvd. #102
Los Angeles, CA 90048
"Actress"

Angie Everhart
23 Watts Street #600
New York, NY 10013
"Model"

Don Everly
277 Comroe Road
Nashville, TN 37213
"Singer"

Phil Everly
277 Comroe road
Nashville, TN 37213
"Singer"

Charles Evers
416 W. County Line Road
Tougaloo, MS 39174
"Civil Rights Worker"

Jason Evers
232 North Crescent Drive #101
Beverly Hills, CA 90210
"Actor"

Myrlie Evers-Williams
4805 Mt. Hope Drive
Baltimore, MD 21215
"NAACP ex-Director"

Chris Evert
500 N.E. 25th Street
Wilton Manors, FL 33305
"Tennis Player"

Kellie Everts
P.O. Box 45
Ouaquaga, NY 13826
"Author, Preacher"

Greg Evigan
5472 Winnetka Avenue
Woodland Hills, CA 91364
"Actor, Singer"

Weeb Ewbank
7 Patrick Drive
Oxford, OH 45056
"Football Coach"

Patrick Ewing
5335 Wisconsin Avenue
Washington, DC 20015
"Basketball Player"

Exile
P.O. Box 180763
Utica, MI 48318
"Music Group"

Extreme
189 Carlton Street
Toronto, Ontario
M5A 2K7 Canada
"Music Group"

Richard Eyer
2739 Underwood Lane
Bishop, CA 93514
"Actor"

F

Shelley Fabaras
P.O. Box 6010-909
Sherman Oaks, CA 91413
"Actress"

Ava Fabian
2112 Broadway
Santa Monica, CA 90404
"Actress, Model"

Fabio
P.O. Box 4
Inwood, NY 11696
"Male Model"

Nanette Fabray
14360 Sunset Blvd.
Pacific Palisades, CA 90272
"Actress"

Max Factor III
1875 Century Park East #1760
Los Angeles, CA 90067
"Attorney, Finance"

HM King Fahd
Royal Palace
Riyadh, SAUDI ARABIA
"Royalty"

Jeff Fahey
250 N. Robertson Blvd. #518
Beverly Hills, CA 90211
"Actor"

Bruce Fairbairn
9744 Wilshire Blvd. #308
Beverly Hills, CA 90212
"Actor"

Douglas Fairbanks, Jr.
575 Park Avenue
New York, NY 10021
"Actor"

Morgan Fairchild
3480 Blair Drive
Los Angeles, CA 90068
"Actress"

Adam Faith
Crockham Hill
Edenbridge Kent, ENGLAND
"Singer, Actor"

Marianne Faithfull
Yew Tree Cottage
Aldworth, Berks. ENGLAND
"Singer, Songwriter"

Falco
Franz-Josef Str. 14
D-(W) 8000 Munich 40
GERMANY
"Singer, Actress"

Lee Falk
P.O. Box Z
Truro, MA 02666
"Cartoonist"

Peter Falk
1004 North Roxbury Drive
Beverly Hills, CA 90210
"Actor, Director"

Jinx Falkenburg
10 Shelter Rock Road
Manhasset, NY 11030
"Actress, Model"

Rev. Jerry Falwell
3765 Candlers Mountain Road
Lynchburg, VA 24502
"Evangelist"

Hampton Fancher III
115 S. Topanga Canyon Blvd. #180
Topanga, CA 90290
"Screenwriter"

Stephanie Faracy
8765 Lookout Mountain Road
Los Angeles, CA 90046
"Actress"

Debrah Farentino
10390 Santa Monica Blvd. #300
Los Angeles, CA 90025
"Actress"

James Farentino
1340 Londonderry Place
Los Angeles, CA 90069
"Actor"

Linda Farentino
10683 Santa Monica Blvd.
Los Angeles, CA 90025
"Actress"

Antonio Fargas
1930 Century Park West #403
Los Angeles, CA 90067
"Actor"

Donna Fargo
P.O. Box 150527
Nashville, TN 37215
"Singer"

Dennis Farina
1201 Greenacre Avenue
Los Angeles, CA 90046
"Actor"

Chris Farley
9150 Wilshire Blvd., #350
Beverly Hills, CA 90212
"Actor"

Lillian Farley
84 Kenneth Avenue
Huntington, NY 11743
"Model"

Shannon Farnon
12743 Milbank Street
Studio City, CA 91604
"Actress"

Richard Farnsworth
c/o Diamond D Ranch, Box 123
Lincoln, NM 88338
"Actor"

Felica Farr
141 South El Camino Drive #201
Beverly Hills, CA 90212
"Actress"

Jamie Farr
53 Ranchero
Bell Canyon, CA 91307
"Actor, Director"

Louis Farrakhan
4855 So. Woodlawn Ave.
Chicago, IL 60615
"Religious Leader"

Mike Farrell
14011 Ventura Blvd.
Sherman Oaks, CA 91423
"Actor, Writer, Director"

Sharon Farrell
10637 Burbank Blvd
North Hollywood, CA 91601
"Actress"

Shea Farrell
1930 Century Park West #403
Los Angeles, CA 90067
"Actor"

Mia Farrow
124 Henry Sanford Road
Bridgewater, CT 06752
"Actress"

Howard Fast
222 Berkeley Street
Boston, MA 02116
"Writer"

Fat Boys
250 W. 57th Street #1723
New York, NY 10107
"Rap Group"

David Faustino
11350 Ventura Blvd. #206
Studio City CA 91604
"Actor"

Brett Favre
P.O. Box 10628
Green Bay, WI 54307
"Football Player"

Allen Fawcett
8091 Selma Avenue
Los Angeles, CA 90046
"Actor, TV Show Host"

Farrah Fawcett
9507 Heather Road
Beverly Hills, CA 90210
"Actress, Model"

Alice Faye
49400 JFK Trail
Palm Desert, CA 92260
"Actress, Singer"

Tom Fears
41470 Woodhaven Drive W.
Palm Desert, CA 92260
"Ex-Football Player"

Dr. Feelgood
3 East 54th Street
New York, NY 10022
"Singer"

Jules Feiffner
RR #1 Box 440
Vineyard Haven, MA 02568
"Writer"

Alan Feinstein
9229 Sunset Blvd. #311
Los Angeles, CA 90069
"Actor"

Sen. Dianne Feinstein (CA)
331 Hart Office Bldg.
Washington, DC 20510
"Politician"

Michael Feinstein
2233 Cheremoya Avenue
Los Angeles, CA 90068
"Actor"

Don Felder
30600 Sicamoro Drive
Malibu, CA 90265
"Singer, Songwriter"

Corey Feldman
1101 1/2 Victoria Avenue
Venice, CA 90291
"Actor"

Barbara Feldon
22 West 19th Street
New York, NY 10019
"Actress, Model"

Tovah Feldshuh
322 Central Park West #118
New York, NY 10025
"Actor"

Martin Feldstein
147 Clifton Street
Belmont, MA 02178
"Economist"

Jose Feliciano
266 Lyons Plain Road
Weston, CT 06883
"Singer, Guitarist"

Maria Felix
Hegel 610 Col. Polanco
Mexico D.F. MEXICO
"Actress"

Norman Fell
4335 Marina City Drive
Marina del Rey, CA 90292
"Actor"

Bob Feller
P.O. Box 157
Gates Mills, OH 44040
"Ex-Baseball Player"

Edith Fellows
2016 1/2 North Vista Del Mar
Los Angeles, CA 90068
"Actress"

Narvel Felts
2005 Narvel Felts Avenue
Malden, MO 63863
"Singer"

John Femia
1650 Boradway #714
New York, NY 10019
"Singer"

Sherilyn Fenn
9830 Wilshire Blvd.
Beverly Hills, CA 90212
"Actress"

George Fenneman
4461 Stern Avenue
Sherman Oaks, CA 91423
"TV Show Host"

Jay Ferguson
4465 Stern Avenue
Sherman Oaks, CA 91423
"Singer"

Maynard Ferguson
P.O. Box 716
Ojai, CA 93023
"Trumpeter"

Mary Jo Fernandez
133 1st Street Northeast
St. Petersburg, FL 33701
"Tennis Player"

Ferrante & Teicher
12224 Avila Drive
Kansas City, MO 64145
"Piano Duo"

Cristina Ferrare
1280 Stone Canyon
Los Angeles, CA 90077
"Actress, Model"

Geraldine Ferraro
22 Deepdene Road
Forest Hills, NY 11375
"Ex-Congresswoman"

Conchata Ferrell
1347 North Seward Street
Los Angeles, CA 90028
"Actress"

Lupita Ferrer
861 Stone Canyon Road
Los Angeles, CA 90077
"Actress"

Mel Ferrer
6590 Camino Carreta
Carpenteria, CA 93013
"Actor"

Miguel Ferrer
4334 Kester Avenue
Sherman Oaks, CA 91403
"Actor"

Lou Ferrrigno
621-17th Street
Santa Monica, CA 90402
"Actor, Bodybuilder"

Brian Ferry
8380 Melrose Avenue #310
Los Angeles, CA 90069
"Singer, Songwriter"

Debra Feuer
9560 Wilshire Blvd. #500
Beverly Hills, CA 90212
"Actress"

Mark Fidrych
260 West Street
Northboro, MA 01532
"Ex-Baseball Player"

John Fiedler
225 Adams Street #10B
Brooklyn, NY 11201
"Actor"

Chelsea Field
P.O. Box 5617
Beverly Hills, CA 90210
"Actress"

Sally Field
P.O. Box 492417
Los Angeles, CA 90049
"Actress"

Shirley Anne Field
68 St. James's Street
London SW1 ENGLAND
"Actress"

Sylvia Field
3263 Via Alta Mira
Fallbrook, CA 92028
"Actress"

Cecil Fielder
c/o Tiger Stadium
Detroit, MI 48216
"Baseball Player"

Freddie Fields
8899 Beverly Blvd. #918
Los Angeles, CA 90048
"Motion Picture Producer"

Mrs. Fields
333 Main Street
Park City, UT 84060
"Cookie Executive"

Kim Fields
9034 Sunset Blvd. #250
Los Angeles, CA 90069
"Actress"

Ralph Fiennes
955 S. Carrillo Drive #200
Los Angeles, CA 90048
"Actor"

Harvey Fierstein
1479 Carla Ridge Drive
Beverly Hills, CA 90210
"Dramatist, Actor"

Dennis Fimple
6736 Laurel Canyon Blvd. #369
N. Hollywood, CA 91606
"Actor"

Jon Finch
135 New Kings Road
London SW6 ENGLAND
"Actor"

Travis Fine
200 N. Robertson Blvd. #219
Beverly Hills, CA 90211
"Actor"

Fyvush Finkel
8730 Sunset Blvd. #480
Los Angeles, CA 90069
"Actor"

Frank Finlay
55 Park Lane
London W1 ENGLAND
"Actor"

Albert Finney
76 Oxford Street
London W1R 1RB ENGLAND
"Actor"

Linda Fiorentino
9830 Wilshire Blvd.
Beverly Hills, CA 90212
"Actress"

Eddie Firestone
303 South Crescent Heights
Los Angeles, CA 90048
"Actor"

The Firm
57A Great Titchfield Street
London W1P 7FL ENGLAND
"Rock & Roll Group"

Colin Firth
68 St. James's Street
London SW1A 1LE ENGLAND
"Actor"

Peter Firth
4 Windmill Street
London W1 England
"Actor"

Bobby Fischer
186 Route 9-W
New Windsor, NY 12550
"Chess Player"

Dietrich Fischer-Diskau
Lindenalle 22
D-14050 Berlin 19 GERMANY
"Baritone"

Larry Fishburne
5200 Lankershim Blvd. #260
North Hollywood, CA 91601
"Actor"

Amy Fisher
3595 State School Road
Albion, NY 14411
"Statutory Rape Victim"

Carrie Fisher
c/o Kaufman Eisenberg
1201 Alta Loma Road
West Hollywood, CA 90069
"Actress"

Eddie Fisher
10000 North Point Street #1802
San Francisco, CA 94109
"Actor, Singer"

Frances Fisher
8730 Sunset Blvd. #490
Los Angeles, CA 90069
"Actress"

Mary Fisher
3075 Hampton Place
Boco Raton, FL 33434
"AIDS Advocate"

Terry Louise Fisher
5314 Pacific Avenue
Marina del Rey, CA 90292
"TV Writer, Producer"

Todd Fisher
3435 Ocean Park Blvd. #206
Santa Monica, CA 90405
"Actress"

Michael Fishman
1530 Bainum Drive
Topanga, CA 90290
"Actor"

Carlton Fisk
16612 Catawba Road
Lockport, IL 60441
"Ex-Baseball Player"

Christian Fittipaldi
282 Alphaville Baruei, 064500
Sao Paulo BRAZIL
"Race Car Driver"

Emerson Fittipaldi
950 South Miami Avenue
Miami, FL 33130
"Race Car Driver"

Ella Fitzgerald
908 North Whittier Drive
Beverly Hills, CA 90210
"Singer"

Geraldine Fitzgerald
50 East 79th Street
New York, NY 10019
"Actress"

Cotton Fitzsimmons
2910 North Central
Phoenix, AZ 85012
"Basketball Coach"

Marlin Fitzwater
2001 Swan Terrace
Alexandria, VA 22307
"Ex Press Secretary"

Roberta Flack
1 West 72nd Street
New York, NY 10023
"Singer, Songwriter"

Fanny Flagg
1520 Willina Lane
Montecito, CA 93108
"Actress"

The Flamingos
141 Dunbar Avenue
Fords, NJ 08863
"Vocal Group"

Fionnula Flanagan
13438 Java Drive
Beverly Hills, CA 90210
"Actress"

Susan Flannery
789 River Rock Road
Santa Barbara, CA 93108
"Actress"

Flash Cadillac
P.O. Box 6588
San Antonio, TX 78209
"Rock & Roll Group"

Jennifer Flavin
7271 Angela Avenue
Canoga Park, CA 91307
"Model"

Fleetwood Mac
4905 South Atlantic Avenue
Daytona Beach, FL 32127
"Rock & Roll Group"

Mick Fleetwood
4905 South Atlantic Avenue
Daytona Beach, FL 32127
"Drummer, Songwriter"

Charles Fleischer
749 North Crescent Heights Blvd.
Los Angeles, CA 90038
"Actor"

Heidi Fleiss
1247 Third St. Prom
Santa Monic, CA 90401
"Convicted Hollywood Madam"

Peggy Fleming
16387 Aztec Ridge
Los Gatos, CA 95030
"Ice Skater"

Rhonda Fleming
2129 Century Woods Way
Los Angeles, CA 90067
"Actress"

Louise Fletcher
1520 Camden Avenue #105
Los Angeles, CA 90025
"Actress"

Lucy Lee Flippin
1753 Canfield Avenue
Los Angeles, CA 90035
"Actress"

Flock of Seagulls
526 Nicollett Mall
Minneapolis, MN 55402
"Rock & Roll Group"

Curt Flood
4149 Cloverdale Avenue
Los Angeles, CA 90008
"Ex-Baseball Player"

Myron Floran
26 Georgeff Road
Rolling Hills, CA 90274
"Composer"

Tom Flores
11220 N.E. 53rd Street
Kirkland, WA 98033
"Football Executive"

Gennifer Flowers
7500 Devista Drive
Los Angeles, CA 90046
"Personality"

Ray Floyd
1 Erieview Plaza #1300
Cleveland, OH 44114
"Golfer"

Darlanne Fluegel
11333 Darling Road
Aqua Dulce, CA 91350
"Actress"

Larry Flynt
9211 Robin Drive
Los Angeles, CA 90069
"Publisher"

Nina Foch
P.O. Box 1884
Beverly Hills, CA 90213
"Actress"

Dan Fogelberg
P.O. Box 2399
Pagosa Springs, CO 81147
"Singer, Songwriter"

John Fogerty
P.O. Box 3513
Granada Hills, CA 91364
"Singer, Songwriter"

Tom Foley
601 West 1st Ave. #2W
Spokane, WA 99204
"Ex-Congressman"

Ken Follett
P.O. Box 708
London SW10 0DH ENGLAND
"Author"

Meg Follows
121 North San Vicente Blvd.
Beverly Hills, CA 90211
"Actress"

Bridget Fonda
8730 Sunset Blvd #490
Los Angeles, CA 90069
"Actress"

Jane Fonda
1050 Techwood Drive N.W.
Atlanta, GA 30318
"Actress, Writer"

Peter Fonda
RR#38
Livingston, MT 59047
"Actor, Writer, Director"

Shirlee Fonda
110 East 57th Street
New York, NY 10022
"Mrs. Henry Fonda"

Joan Fontaine
P.O. Box 222600
Carmel, CA 93922
"Actress"

Wayne Fontana
Box 81, Ruyton, Oldham
Manchester OL2 5DG
ENGLAND
"Rock & Roll"

Horton Foote
95 Horatio Street #332
New York, NY 10014
"Screenwriter"

Shelby Foote
542 East Parkway South
Memphis, TN 38104
"Historian"

June Foray
22745 Erwin Street
Woodland Hills, CA 91367
"Actress"

Brenda Forbes
430 East 57th Street
New York, NY 10022
"Actress"

Brian Forbes
Seven Pines
Wentworth, Surrey, ENGLAND
"Writer, Director"

Steve Forbes
60 Fifth Avenue
New York, NY 10011
"Magazine Publisher"

Bette Ford
1999 Avenue of the Stars
Suite #2850
Los Angeles, CA 90067
"Actress"

Mrs. Betty Ford
40365 San Dune Road
Rancho Mirage, CA 92270
"Ex-First Lady, Author"

Charlotte Ford
25 Sutton Place
New York, NY 10023
"Daughter of Henry Ford II"

Doug Ford
100 Avenue of the Champions
Palm Beach Gardens, FL 33418
"Golfer"

Eileen Ford
344 East 59th Street
New York, NY 10022
"Talent Agent"

Faith Ford
7920 Sunset Blvd. #350
Los Angeles, CA 90046
"Actress, Model"

Frankie Ford
7200 France Avenue #330
Edina, MN 55435
"Singer, Songwriter"

Gerald R. Ford
40365 San Dune Road
Rancho Mirage, CA 92270
"Former President"

Glenn Ford
911 Oxford Way
Beverly Hills, CA 90210
"Actor"

Harrison Ford
3555 North Moose Wilson Road
Jackson, WY 83001
"Actor"

Ruth Ford
1 West 72nd Street
New York, NY 10023
"Actress"

Whitey Ford
38 Schoolhouse Lane
Lake Success, NY 11020
"Ex-Baseball Player"

Foreigner
640 Lee Road #106
Wayne, PA 19087
"Rock & Roll Group"

Deborah Foreman
1341 Ocean Avenue #213
Santa Monica, CA 90401
"Actress"

George Foreman
7639 Pine Oak Drive
Humble, TX 77397
"Boxer"

Forester Sisters
P.O. Box 1456
Trenton, GA 30752
"C&W Group"

Milos Forman
Hampshire House
150 Central Park South
New York, NY 10019
"Film Director"

Frederick Forrest
4121 Wilshire Blvd. #405
Los Angeles, CA 90010
"Actor"

Helen Forrest
1870 Caminito del Cielo
Glendale, CA 91208
"Singer"

Sally Forrest
1125 Angelo Drive
Beverly Hills, CA 90210
"Actress"

Steve Forrest
1605 Michael Lane
Pacific Palisades, CA 90272
"Actor"

Constance Forslund
165 West 46th Street #1214
New York, NY 10036
"Actress"

Brian Forster
16172 Flamstead Drive
Hacienda Heights, CA 91745
"Actor"

Robert Forster
8550 Hollywood Drive #402
Los Angeles, CA 90069
"Actor"

Bruce Forsyth
Kent House
Upper Ground
London SE1 ENGLAND
"TV Personality"

Frederick Forsyth
61-63 Oxbridge Rd., Ealing
London W5 5SA ENGLAND
"Writer"

Bill Forsythe
20 Winton Drive
Glasgow G12 SCOTLAND
"Guitarist"

John Forsythe
3849 Roblar Avenue
Santa Ynez, CA 93460
"Actor"

Henderson Forsythe
204 Elm Street
Tenafly, NJ 07670
"Actor"

Rosemary Forsythe
1591 Benedict Canyon
Beverly Hills, CA 90210
"Actress"

Fabian Forte
1800 North Argyle Avenue #201
Los Angeles, CA 90028
"Actor, Singer"

Dick Fosbury
P.O. Box 2311
Ketchum, ID 83340
"Track Athlete"

Gen. Joe Foss
P.O. Box 566
Scottsdale, AZ 85252
"Firearms Assoc. Executive"

Brigitte Fossey
18 rue Troyon
75017 Paris, FRANCE
"Actress"

Jodie Foster
10900 Wilshire Blvd. #511
Los Angeles, CA 90024
"Actress"

Kimberly Foster
957 North Cole Avenue
Los Angeles, CA 90038
"Actress"

Meg Foster
10100 Santa Monica Blvd. #2500
Los Angeles, CA 90067
"Actress"

Radney Foster
50 West Main Street
Ventura, CA 93001
"Singer"

Pete Fountain
237 North Peters Street #400
New Orleans, LA 71030
"Clarienetist"

Four Aces
12 Marshall Street #8Q
Irvington, NJ 07111
"Vocal Group"

Four Lads
32500 Concord Drive #221
Madison Heights, MI 49071
"Vocal Group"

The Four Seasons
P.O. Box 262
Carteret, NJ 07008
"Rock & Roll Group"

Gene Fowler, Jr.
7261 Outpost Cove
Los Angeles, CA 90068
"Film Director"

John Fowles
52 Floral Street
London WC2 ENGLAND
"Author"

Douglas V. Fowley
38510 Glen Abbey Lane
Murietta, CA 92362
"Actor"

Fox Brothers
Rt. 6, Bending Chestnut
Franklin, TN 37064
"Gospel Group"

Bernard Fox
1624 South Crescent Heights Blvd.
Los Angeles, CA 90035
"Actor"

Edward Fox
25 Maida Avenue
London W2 ENGLAND
"Actor"

James Fox
125 Gloucester Road
London SW7 ENGLAND
"Actor"

Michael J. Fox
100 Universal City Plaza #74
Universal City, CA 91608
"Actor, Director"

Samantha Fox
110-112 Disraeli Road
London SW1S 2DX ENGLAND
"Singer, Model"

Vivica Fox
250 W. 57 Street #2223
New York, NY 10019
"Actress"

Robert Foxworth
1230 Benedict Canyon Drive
Beverly Hills, CA 90210
"Actor"

A.J. Foyt
6415 Toledo
Houston, TX 77008
"Race Car Driver"

Don Frabotta
5036 Riverton Avenue #2
N. Hollywood, CA 91601
"Actor"

Jonathan Frakes
9033 Briarcrest Drive
Beverly Hills, CA 90210
"Actor"

Peter Frampton
234 S. Tower Drive #1
Beverly Hills, CA 90211
"Singer, Guitarist"

Anne Francine
24 West 40th Street #1700
New York, NY 10018
"Actress"

Tony Franciosa
567 Tigertail Road
Los Angeles, CA 90049
"Actor"

Anne Francis
P.O. Box 5417
Santa Barbara, CA 93103
"Actress"

Connie Francis
7305 W. Sample Road #101
Coral Springs, FL 33065
"Singer, Actress"

Dick Francis
5100 North Ocean Avenue
Ft. Lauderdale, FL 33308
"Author"

Freddie Francis
12 Ashley Drive
Jersey Road, Osterley
Middlesex TW7 5QA ENGLAND
"TV Director"

Genie Francis
9033 Briarcrest Drive
Beverly Hills, CA 90210
"Actress"

Nancy Frangione
280 S. Beverly Drive #400
Beverly Hills, CA 90210
"Actress"

Rep. Barney Frank (MA)
House Rayburn Bldg. #2404
Washington, DC 20515
"Politician"

Charles Frank
9744 Wilshire Blvd. #308
Beverly Hills, CA 90212
"Actor"

Gary Frank
11401 Ayrshire Road
Los Angeles, CA 90049
"Actor"

Joanna Frank
1274 Capri Drive
Pacific Palisades, CA 90272
"Actress"

Mark Frankel
151 El Camino Drive
Beverly Hills, CA 90212
"Actor"

John Frankenheimer
3114 Abington Drive
Beverly Hills, CA 90210
"Director, Producer"

Frankie Goes To Hollywood
153 George Street
London W1 ENGLAND
"Rock & Roll Group"

Aretha Franklin
P.O. Box 12137
Birmingham, MI 49012
"Singer, Songwriter"

Bonnie Franklin
448 West 44th Street
New York, NY 10036
"Actress"

Joe Franklin
P.O. Box 1
Lynbrook, NY 11563
"TV Swow Host"

Mary Frann
250 North Robertson Blvd. #518
Beverly Hills, CA 90211
"Actress"

Arthur Franz
32960 Pacific Coast Hwy.
Malibu, CA 90265
"Actor"

Dennis Franz
11805 Bellagio Road
Los Angeles, CA 90049
"Actor"

Brendan Fraser
2210 Wilshire Blvd. #513
Santa Monica, CA 90403
"Actor"

Douglas Fraser
800 East Jefferson Street
Detroit, MI 48214
"Ex-Union Leader"

Ronald Fraser
52 Shaftesbury Avenue
London W1V 7DE ENGLAND
"Actor"

Linda Fratianne
1177 North Vista Vespero
Palm Springs, CA 92262
"Skater"

Liz Frazer
29 King's Road
London SW3 ENGLAND
"Actress"

Joe Frazier
2917 North Broad Street
Philadelphia, PA 19132
"Ex-Boxer Champion"

Walt Frazier
675 Flamingo Drive
Atlanta, GA 30311
"Basketball Player"

Stan Freberg
10450 Wilshire Blvd. #1A
Los Angeles, CA 90024
"Actor, Director"

Peter Frechette
233 East 12th Street #2B
New York, NY 10003
"Actor"

Al Freeman, Jr.
1 Executive Blvd.
Suffern, NY 10901
Los Angeles, CA 90067
"Actor"

Kathleen Freeman
6247 Orion Avenue
Van Nuys, CA 91406
"Actress"

Mona Freeman
608 North Alpine Drive
Beverly Hills, CA 90210
"Actor"

Morgan Freeman
2472 Broadway #227
New York, NY 10025
"Actor"

Phyllis Frelich
8485-E Melrose Place
Los Angeles, CA 90069
"Actress"

Leigh French
1850 North Vista Avenue
Los Angeles, CA 90046
"Actor"

Susan French
110 East 9th Street #C-1005
Los Angeles, CA 90079
"Actress"

Matt Frewer
6670 Wildlife Road
Malibu, CA 90265
"Actor"

Glen Frey
29623 Louis Avenue
Santa Clarita, CA 91351
"Singer, Guitarist"

Janie Fricke
P.O. Box 798
Lancaster, TX 75146
"Singer"

Brenda Fricker
68 Old Brompton Road
London SW7 3LQ ENGLAND
"Actress"

Squire Fridell
7080 Hollywood Blvd. #704
Los Angeles, CA 90028
"Actor"

William Friedkin
1363 Angelo Drive
Beverly Hills, CA 90210
"Film Director"

Milton Friedman
Quadrangle Office
Hoover Institute
Stanford University
Palo Alto, CA 94305
"Econominist"

Sonya Friedman
208 Harriston Road
Glen Rock, NJ 07452
"TV Show Host"

Chuck Fries
6922 Hollywood Blvd.
Los Angeles, CA 90028
"TV Executive"

Lynette "Squeaky" Fromme
#06075180
F.C.I. Road
Marianna, FL 32446
"Prisnor"

Georgia Frontiere
2327 West Lincoln Avenue
Anaheim, CA 92801
"Football Team Owner"

Sir David Frost
130 West 57th Street
New York, NY 10019
"TV Show Host"

Lindsay Frost
310 Madison Avenue #232
New York, NY 10017
"Actress"

Ed Fry
10100 Santa Monica Blvd. #2500
Los Angeles, CA 90067
"Actor"

Soleil Moon Frye
2713 North Keystone
Burbank, CA 91504
"Actress"

Alan Fudge
355 South Rexford Drive
Beverly Hills, CA 90212
"Actor"

Daisy Fuentes
2200 Fletcher Avenue
Fort Lee, NJ 07024
"MTV Host"

Robert Fulghum
1713 Cedar Street #A
Alhambra, CA 91801
"Author, Clergyman"

Penny Fuller
12428 Hesby Street
North Hollywood, CA 91607
"Actress"

Samuel Fuller
7628 Woodrow Wilson Drive
Los Angeles, CA 90046
"Film Writer, Producer"

Eileen Fulton
301 West 57th Street
New York, NY 10019
"Actress"

Wendy Fulton
9169 Sunset Blvd.
Los Angeles, CA 90069
"Actor"

✓ **Annette Funicello**
16102 Sandy Lane
Encino, CA 91316
"Actress"

Allen Funt
2359 Nichols Canyon
Los Angeles, CA 90068
"TV Show Host, Director"

John Furey
9911 West Pico Blvd. #1060
Los Angeles, CA 90035
"Actor"

Edward Furlong
10573 W. Pico Blvd. #853
Los Angeles, CA 90064
"Actor"

Stephen Furst
3900 Huntercrest Court
Moopark, CA 93021
"Actor"

George Furth
3030 Durand Drive
Los Angeles, CA 90068
"Actor, Writer"

G

Kenny G ✓
2600 Benedict Canyon
Beverly Hills, CA 90210
"Singer"

Christopher Gable
60 St. James's Street
London SW1 ENGLAND
"Actor"

Princess Zsa Zsa Gabor
1001 Bel Air Road
Los Angeles, CA 90024
"Actress"

John Gabriel
100 West 57th Street #5-Q
New York, NY 10019
"Actor"

Peter Gabriel
Box Mill
Wiltshire SN14 9PL ENGLAND
"Singer, Songwriter"

Roman Gabriel
5601-77 Center Drive #250
Charlotte, NC 28217
"Ex-Football Player"

Col. Moammar Gaddafi
State Office
Tripoli, LIBYA
"Politician"

Max Gail
P.O. Box 4160
Malibu, CA 90265
"Actor"

Boyd Gaines
1999 Avenue of the Stars #2850
Los Angeles, CA 90067
"Actor"

John Kenneth Galbraith
30 Francis Avenue
Cambridge, MA 02138
"Economist"

Dr. Robert Gale
UCLA Medical Center
Dept. of Medicine, Rm. 42-121
Los Angeles, CA 90024
"Medical Doctor"

Helen Gallagher
260 West End Avenue
New York, NY 10023
"Actress"

Megan Gallagher
P.O. Box 5617
Beverly Hills, CA 90210
"Actress"

Peter Gallagher
151 El Camino Drive
Beverly Hills, CA 90212
"Actor"

Silvana Gallardo
10637 Burbank Blvd.
No. Hollywood, CA 91601
"Actress"

Gina Gallego
6550 Murietta Avenue
Van Nuys, CA 91401
"Actress"

Zack Galligan
924 Westwood Blvd. #900
Los Angeles, CA 90024
"Actor"

Joe Gallison
13515 Magnolia Blvd. #429
Sherman Oaks, CA 91403
"Actor"

Don Galloway
P.O. Box 786
Cedar Glen, CA 92321
"Actor"

Rita Gam
180 West 58th Street #8
New York, NY 10019
"Actress"

Bruno Ganz
Glattalstrasse 83
8052 Zurich SWITZERLAND
"Actor"

Teresa Ganzel
9300 Wilshire Blvd. #410
Beverly Hills, CA 90212
"Actress"

Joe Garagiola
6221 East Huntress Drive
Paradise Valley, AZ 85253
"TV Show Host, Sportscaster"

Kaz Garas
31276 Bailard Road
Malibu, CA 90265
"Actor, Director"

Terri Garber
851 Euclid Street
Santa Monica, CA 90403
"Actress"

Victor Garber
40 West 57th Street
New York, NY 10019
"Actor"

Gil Garcetti
139 North Cliffwood
Los Angeles, CA 90049
"District Attorney"

Andy Garcia
4323 Forman Avenue
Toulca Lake, CA 91602
"Actor"

Randy Gardner
4640 Glencove Avenue #6
Marina Del Rey, CA 90291
"Ice Skater"

Allen Garfield
289 S. Robertson Blvd. #462
Beverly Hills, CA 90211
"Actor"

Art Garfunkel
9 East 79th Street
New York, NY 10021
"Singer, Songwriter"

Beverly Garland
8014 Briar Summit Drive
Los Angeles, CA 90046
"Actress"

Jake Garn
2000 Eagle Gate Tower
Salt Lakes City, UT 84111
"Ex-Senator"

James Garner
33 Oakmont Drive
Los Angeles, CA 90049
"Actor, Director"

Janeane Garofalo
9560 Wilshire Blvd., #500
Beverly Hills, CA 90212
"Actress"

Teri Garr
145 South Fairfax Avenue #310
Los Angeles, CA 90036
"Actress"

Anne Garrels
c/o National Public Radio
2025 "M" Street N.W.
Washington, DC 20036
"News Correspondent"

Betty Garrett-Parks
3231 Oakdell Road
Studio City, CA 91604
"Actress"

Leif Garrett
11524 Amanda Drive
Studio City, CA 91604
"Actor, Singer"

Snuff Garrett
6255 Sunset Blvd. #1019
Los Angeles, CA 90028
"Talent Agent"

David Garrison
9229 Sunset Blvd. #710
Los Angeles, CA 90069
"Actor"

Greg Garrison
1655 Hidden Valley Road
Thousand Oaks, CA 91361
"Director"

Zina Garrison
P.O. Box 272305
Houston, TX 77277
"Tennis Player"

Jennie Garth
3500 West Olive #920
Burbank, CA 91505
"Actress"

Kathy Garver
170 Woodbridge Road
Hillsborough, CA 94010
"Actress"

Steve Garvey
11718 Barrington Court #6
Los Angeles, CA 90049
"Ex-Baseball Player"

John Gary
32500 Concord Drive #221
Madison Heights, MI 48071
"Singer"

Lorraine Gary
1158 Tower Drive
Beverly Hills, CA 90210
"Actress"

Vittorio Gassman
Giuseppe Broja
Piazza Alvania 10
I-00193 Rome ITALY
"Actor"

Bill Gates
16011 NE 36th Way
Redmond, WA 98052
"Microsoft Owner"

Daryl Gates
756 Portola Terrace
Los Angeles, CA 90042
"Ex-Police Chief"

Larry Gates
1015 Gayley Avenue #300
Los Angeles, CA 90024
"Actor"

Larry Gatlin
Fantacy Harbour, Waccamaw
Myrtle Beach, SC 29577
"Singer, Songwriter"

Willie Gault
332 Center Street
El Segundo, CA 90245
"Football Player"

Dan Gauthier
151 El Camino Drive
Beverly Hills, CA 90212
"Actor"

Dick Gautier
11333 Moorpark Street #59
North Hollywood, CA 91602
"Actor, Writer"

John Gavin
10263 Century Woods Drive
Los Angeles, CA 90067
"Actor"

Crystal Gayle
51 Music Square East
Nashville, TN 37203
"Singer"

Jackie Gayle
13109 Chandler Blvd.
Van Nuys, CA 91401
"Comedian"

Mitch Gaylord
P.O. Box 15001
Beverly Hills, CA 90209
"Actor"

George Gaynes
3344 Campanil Drive
Santa Barbara, CA 93109
"Actor, Director"

Gloria Gaynor
15 Atherton Place Southall
Middlesex UB1 3QT ENGLAND
"Singer"

Mitzi Gaynor
610 North Arden Drive
Beverly Hills, CA 90210
"Actor, Dancer"

Ben Gazzara
1080 Madison Avenue
New York, NY 10028
"Actor"

Tony Geary
7010 Pacific View Drive
Los Angeles, CA 90068
"Actor"

Nicolei Gedda
Valhavagen 128
S-11441 Stockholm, SWEDEN
"Tenor"

Jason Gedrick
8730 Sunset Blvd. #490
Los Angeles, CA 90069
"Actor"

Ellen Geer
21418 West Entrada Road
Topanga, CA 90290
"Actress"

Judy Geeson
Guild House
Upper St. Martin Lane
London WC2H 9EG ENGLAND
"Actress"

David Geffen
9130 Sunset Blvd.
Los Angeles, CA 90069
"Record Executive"

Martha Gehman
2488 Cheremoya Avenue
Los Angeles, CA 90068
"Actress"

Larry Gelbart
807 North Alpine Drive
Beverly Hills, CA 90210
"Writer, Producer"

Sir Bob Geldof, KBE
Davington Priory
Faversham Kent, ENGLAND
"Singer"

Daniel Gelin
92 Blvd. Murat
75015 Paris, FRANCE
"Film Director"

Uri Geller
Sonning-on-Thames
Berkshire, ENGLAND
"Psychic"

The X Generation
184 Glochester Place
London NW1 ENGLAND
"Rock & Roll Group"

Bryan Genesse
9000 Sunset Blvd. #1200
Los Angeles, CA 90069
"Actor"

Genesis
25 Ives Street
London SW3 ENGLAND
"Rock & Roll Group"

Peter Gennaro
115 Central Park West
New York, NY 10024
"Choreographer"

Hans-Dietrich Genscher
Am Kottenforst 16
D-53343 Wachtberg-Pech
GERMANY
"Diplomat"

Bobbie Gentry
8 Tidewater Way
Savannah, GA 31411
"Singer"

Race Gentry
2379 Mountain View Drive
Escondido, CA 92116
"Actress"

Boy George (O'Dowd)
7 Pepy's Court
84 The Chase, Clapham
London SW4 0NF ENGLAND
"Singer, Composer"

Lynda Day George
10310 Riverside Drive #104
Toluca Lake, CA 91602
"Actress"

Phyllis George
Cave Hill, Box 4308
Lexington, KY 40503
"TV Personality"

Susan George
520 Washington Blvd. #187
Marina del Rey, CA 90292
"Actress"

Wally George
14155 Magnolia Blvd. #127
Sherman Oaks, CA 91423
"TV Show Host"

Rep. Richard Gephardt (MO)
House Longworth Bldg. #1432
Washington, DC 20515
"Politician"

✓ **Geraldo** Rivera
29012 Delphine Drive
Walnut, CA 91789
"TV Show Host"

Gil Gerard
16947 Adlon Road
Encino, CA 91436
"Actor"

Richard Gere
9696 Culver Blvd. #203
Culver City, CA 90232
"Actor"

David Gergen
1600 Pennsylvania Avenue
Washington, DC 20500
"Advisor to the President"

Jack Germond
1627 "K" Street NW #1100
Washington, DC 20006
"News Correspondent"

Gerry & The Pacemakers
38A Manor Road
Bradford, BDL 4QU England
"Music Group"

Jami Gertz
8942 Wilshire Blvd.
Beverly Hills, CA 90211
"Actress"

Balthazar Getty
151 El Camino Drive
Beverly Hills, CA 90212
"Actor"

Estelle Getty
8730 Sunset Blvd. #470
Los Angeles, CA 90069
"Actress"

Gordon Getty
2880 Broadway
San Francisco, CA 94115
"Executive, Composer"

Mrs. J. Paul Getty
1535 North Beverly Drive
Beverly Hills, CA 90210
"Philanthropist"

John Getz
402 - 21st Place
Santa Monica, CA 90402
"Actor"

Alice Ghostley
3800 Reklaw Drive
North Hollywood, CA 91604
"Actress"

Giancarlo Giannini
Via della Giuliana 101
1-00195 Rome ITALY
"Actor"

Barry Gibb
3088 South Mann
Las Vegas, NV 89102
"Singer"

Cynthia Gibb
1139 South Hill Street #177
Los Angeles, CA 90015
"Actress"

Maurice Gibb
P.O. Box 2429
Miami Beach, FL 33140
"Singer, Songwriter"

Robin Gibb
P.O. Box 2429
Miami Beach, FL 33140
"Singer, Songwriter"

Leeza Gibbons
1760 Courtney Avenue
Los Angeles, CA 90046
"TV Show Host"

Georgia Gibbs
965 Fifth Avenue
New York, NY 10021
"Singer"

Marla Gibbs
2323 West M. L. King, Jr. Blvd.
Los Angeles, CA 90008
"Actress"

Terri Gibbs
414 Gibbs Circle
Grovertown, GA 30813
"Singer, Songwriter"

Althea Gibson-Darbeu
275 Prospect Street #768
East Orange, NJ 07017
"Tennis Player"

Bob Gibson
215 Belleview Road South
Belleview, NE 68005
"Ex-Baseball Player"

Charles Gibson
1965 Broadway #500
New York, NY 10023
"TV Show Host"

Debbie Gibson
300 Main Street #201
Huntington, NY 11743
"Singer"

Don Gibson
P.O. Box 50474
Nashville, TN 37205
"Singer, Songwriter"

Henry Gibson
26740 Latigo Shore Drive
Malibu, CA 90265
"Actress"

Kirk Gibson
1082 Oak Pointe Drive
Waterford, MI 48327
"Baseball Player"

Mel Gibson
4000 Warner Blvd. #P3-17
Burbank, CA 91522
"Actor, Writer"

Sir John Gielgud
South Pavillion, Wotten
Underwood Aylesbury
Buckinghamshire, ENGLAND
"Actor"

Frank Gifford
625 Madison Avenue #1200
New York, NY 10022
"Sportscaster"

Kathie Lee Gifford
625 Madison Avenue #1200
New York, NY 10022
"TV Show Host"

Elaine Giftos
1800 Avenue of the Stars #400
Los Angeles, CA 90067
"Actress"

Elsie Gilbert
1016 North Orange Grove #4
Los Angeles, CA 90046
"Actress"

Herschel Burke Gilbert
2451 Nichols Canyon
Los Angeles, CA 90046
"Composer, Conductor"

Melissa Gilbert
P.O. Box 57593
Sherman Oaks, CA 91413
"Actress"

Sara Gilbert
16254 High Valley Drive
Encino, CA 91346
"Actress"

Johnny Gill
17539 Corinthian Drive
Encino, CA 91316
"Singer, Songwriter"

Vince Gill
2325 Crestmoor Road
Nashville, TN 37215
"Singer, Songwriter"

Robert Gillespie
10 Irving Road
London W14 0JS ENGLAND
"Actor, Director"

Mickey Gilley
P.O. Box 1242
Pasadena, TX 77501
"Singer, Songwriter"

Terry Gilliam
The Old Hall
South Grove Highgate
London W6 ENGLAND
"Actor, Writer, Director"

Richard Gilliland
4545 Noeline Avenue
Encino, CA 91436
"Actor"

David Gilmore
43 Portland Road
London, W11 4LJ ENGLAND
"Guitarist"

Peri Gilpin
15760 Ventura Blvd., #1730
Encino, CA 91436
"Actress"

Frank Gilroy
6 Magnin Road
Monroe, NY 10950
"Dramatist"

Erica Gimpel
10100 Santa Monica Blvd., #2500
Los Angeles, CA 90067
"Actress"

Jack Ging
10000 Santa Monica Blvd. #305
Los Angeles, CA 90067
"Actor"

Candace Gingrich
26 Stephen Road #8C
Camp Hill, PA 17011
"Newt's Sister"

Rep. Newt Gingrich (GA)
House Rayburn Bldg. #2438
Washington, DC 20515
"Politician"

Allen Ginsberg
P.O. Box 582
Stuyvesant Station
New York, NY 10009
"Poet"

Ruth Bader Ginsbury
1-1st Street N.E.
Washington, DC 20543
"Supreme Court Justice"

Robert Ginty
16133 Ventura Blvd. #800
Encino, CA 91436
"Actor"

Annie Girardot
6 pl. St.-Sulpice,
F-75006 Paris FRANCE
"Actress"

Annabeth Gish
8942 Wilshire Blvd.
Beverly Hills, CA 90211
"Actress"

Carlo Giuffre
via Massimi 45
00132 Rome, ITALY
"Conductor"

Rudy Giuliani
City Hall
New York, NY 10007
"Mayor"

Hubert Givenchy
3 Avenue George V
75008 Paris, FRANCE
"Fashion Designer"

Robin Givens
885 - 3rd Avenue #2900
New York, NY 10022
"Actress"

Glaser Brothers
916-19th Avenue South
Nashville, TN 37212
"Music Group"

Paul Michael Glaser
317 Georgina Avenue
Santa Monica, CA 90402
"Actor, Director"

Philip Glass
231-2nd Avenue
New York, NY 10003
"Composer"

Ron Glass
2485 Wild Oak Drive
Los Angeles, CA 90068
"Actor"

Glass Tiger
238 Davenport #126
Toronto, Ontario M5R 1J6
CANADA
"Rock & Roll Group"

Paul Gleason
10100 Santa Monica Blvd. #700
Los Angeles, CA 90067
"Actor"

Sen. John Glenn (OH)
Senate Hart Bldg. #503
Washington, DC 20210
"Politician, Astronaut"

Scott Glenn
P.O. Box 1018
Ketchum, ID 83340
"Actor"

Sharon Gless
4709 Teesdale Avenue
Studio City, CA 91604
"Actress"

Yoram Globus
640 San Vicente Blvd.
Los Angeles, CA 90048
"Producer, Executive"

Bruce Glover
11449 Woodbine Street
Los Angeles, CA 90066
"Actor"

Crispin Glover
3573 Carnation Avenue
Los Angeles, CA 90026
"Actor"

Danny Glover
41 Sutter Street #1648
San Francisco, CA 94104
"Actor"

John Glover
2517 Micheltorena Street
Los Angeles, CA 90039
"Actor"

Julian Glover
19 Ullswater Road
London SW13 ENGLAND
"Actor"

Jean-Luc Godard
15 rue du Nord
CH-1180 Rolle
SWITZERLAND
"Film Director"

Alexander Goehr
11 West Road
Cambridge, ENGLAND
"Composer"

Bob Goen
21767 Plainwood Drive
Woodland Hills, CA 91364
"TV Performer"

Bernhard Goetz
55 West 14th Street
New York, NY 10011
"Subway Shooter"

Joanna Going
233 Park Ave. So., 10th Flr.
New York, NY 10022
"Actress"

Missy Gold
3500 West Olive Ave. #1400
Burbank, CA 91505
"Actress"

Tracey Gold
4619 Goodland Avenue
Studio City, CA 91604
"Actress"

Gary David Goldberg
25 Oakmont Drive
Los Angeles, CA 90049
"Writer, Producer"

Leonard Goldberg
235 Ladera Drive
Beverly Hills, CA 90210
"TV-Film, Producer"

Whoopi Golberg
5555 Melrose Avenue #114
Los Angeles, CA 90038
"Actress, Comedienne"

Jeff Goldblum
8033 Sunset Blvd. #367
Los Angeles, CA 90046
"Actor"

William Lee Golden
Rt. 2, Saundersville Road
Hendersonville, TN 37075
"Singer, Songwriter"

Ricky Paull Golin
9320 Wilshire Blvd. #300
Beverly Hills, CA 90212
"Actor"

William Goldman
50 East 77th Street #30
New York, NY 10021
"Screenwriter"

Lelia Goldoni
15459 Wyandotte Street
Van Nuys, CA 91405
"Actress"

Bobby Goldsboro
P.O. Box 5250
Ocala, FL 32678
"Singer, Songwriter"

Bob Goldthwait
3950 Fredonia Drive
Los Angeles, CA 90068
"Actor, Comedian"

Barry Goldwater
6250 Hogahn
Paradise Valley, AZ 85253
"Ex-Senator"

Sam Goldwyn, Jr.
10203 Santa Monica Blvd. #500
Los Angeles, CA 90067
"Director, Producer"

Tony Goldwyn
9830 Wilshire Blvd.
Beverly Hills, CA 90212
"Actor"

Valeria Golino
8036 Woodrow Wilson Drive
Los Angeles, CA 90046
"Actress"

Arlene Golonka
17849 Duncan Street
Reseda, CA 91335
"Actress"

Richard Golub
42 East 64th Street
New York, NY 10021
"Attorney"

Panchito Gomez
P.O. Box 7016
Burbank, CA 91510
"Actor"

Pedro Gonzalez-Gonzalez
4154 Charles Avenue
Culver City, CA 90203
"Wrestler"

Dwight Gooden
c/o Yankee Stadium
Bronx, NY 10451
"Baseball Player"

Grant Goodeve
21416 N.E. 68th Court
Redmond, WA 98053
"Actor"

Linda Goodfriend
5700 Etiwanda #150
Tarzana, CA 91365
"Actress"

Cuba Gooding, Jr.
8942 Wilshire Blvd.
Beverly Hills, CA 90211
"Actor"

Dody Goodman
10144 Culver Blvd. #21
Culver City, CA 90232
"Actress"

John Goodman
5180 Louise Avenue
Encino, CA 91316
"Actor"

Gail Goodrich
601-26th Street
Santa Monica, CA 90402
"Ex-Basketball Player"

Ron Goodwin
70 Charlotte Street
London W1 ENGLAND
"Actor"

Michael Goorjian
9000 Sunset Blvd., #1200
Los Angels, CA 90069
"Actor"

Lecy Goranson
1201 Greenacre Blvd.
West Hollywood, CA 90046
"Actress"

Mikhail S. Gorbachev
Leningradsky Prospekt 49
Moscow, RUSSIA
"Former U.S.S.R. Chairman"

Barry Gordon
18140 Supreior Street
Northridge, CA 91325
"Actor"

Bruce Gordon
231-C Tano Road
Santa Fe, NM 87501
"Actor"

Don Gordon
8899 Beverly Blvd. #808
Los Angeles, CA 90048
"Actor"

Richard Gordon
1 Craven Hill
London W2 3EP ENGLAND
"Writer"

Robby Gordon
1463 Kennymead Avenue
Orange, CA 92669
"Race Car Driver"

Berry Gordy
878 Stradella Road
Los Angeles, CA 90077
"Record Executive"

V.P. Albert Gore, Jr.
Admiral House
34th & Massachusetts
Washington, DC 20005
"Vice President U.S.A."

Lesley Gore
170 East 77th Street #2-A
New York, NY 10021
"Actress, Singer"

Michael Gore
310 West End Avenue #12C
New York, NY 10023
"Composer"

Tipper Gore
Admiral House
34th & Massachusetts
Washington, DC 20005
"Wife of V.P. Albert Gore, Jr."

Marius Goring
Middlecourt, The Green
Hampton Court
Surrey ENGLAND
"Actor"

Cliff Gorman
333 West 57th Street
New York, NY 10019
"Actor"

Eydie Gorme
820 Greenway Drive
Beverly Hills, CA 90210
"Singer"

Karen Lynn Gorney
853-7th Avenue #7-C
New York, NY 10019
"Actress"

Frank Gorshin
1740 El Camino Parocela
Palm Springs, CA 92264
"Actor, Comedian"

Vern Gosdin
2509 Marquette Avenue
Tampa, FL 33614
"Singer, Songwriter"

Mark Paul Gosselaar
27512 Wellsley Way
Valencia, CA 91354
"Actor"

Louis Gossett, Jr.
P.O. Box 57018
Sherman Oaks, CA 91413
"Actor, Director"

John Gotti #18261-053
Rt. 5, Box 2000
Marion, IL 62959
"Convicted Mafia Boss"

Elliott Gould
21250 Califa #201
Woodland Hills, CA 91367
"Actor"

Harold Gould
603 Ocean Avenue, 4 East
Santa Monica, CA 90402
"Actor"

Jason Gould
446 North Orlando Avenue
Los Angeles, CA 90048
"Financier"

Sandra Gould
3219 Oakdell Lane
Studio City, CA 91604
"Actress"

Robert Goulet
3110 Monte Rosa
Las Vegas, NV 89120
"Singer"

Curt Gowdy
300 Boylston Street #506
Boston, MA 02116
"Sportscaster"

Lord Lew Grade
8 Queen Street
Embassy House
London W1X 7PH ENGLAND
"Film Executive"

Don Grady
4444 Lankershim Blvd. #207
North Hollywood, CA 91602
"Actor"

Steffi Graff
Luftschiffring 8
D-6835 Bruhl, GERMANY
"Tennis Player"

Ilene Graff
11455 Sunshine Terrace
Studio City, CA 91604
"Actress"

Sue Grafton
P.O. Box 41446
Santa Barbara, CA 93140
"Novilist"

Rev. Billy Graham
1300 Harmon Place
Minneapolis, MN 55408
"Evangelist"

Sen. Bob Graham (FL)
Senate Dirksen Bldg. #241
Washington, DC 20510
"Politician"

Gerrit Graham
5601 Park Oak Place
Los Angeles, CA 90068
"Actor, Writer"

Katherine Graham
2920 "R" Street N.W.
Washington, DC 20007
"Publishing Executive"

Otto Graham
2216 Riviera Drive
Saratoga, FL 34232
"Ex-Football Player"

Ronny Graham
863 Castac Place
Pacific Palisades, CA 90272
"TV Writer"

Virginia Graham
211 East 70th Street
New York, NY 10021
"TV Show Host"

Nancy Grahn
4910 Agnes Avenue
North Hollywood, CA 91607
"Actress"

Sen. Phil Gramm (TX)
Senate Russell Bldg. #370
Washington, DC 20510
"Politician"

Kelsey Grammer
3266 Cornell Road
Agoura Hills, CA 91301
"Actor"

Fred Grandy
2506 West Soway St.
Sioux City, IA 51104
"Actor, Politician"

Farley Granger
18 West 72nd Street #25D
New York, NY 10023
"Actor"

Amy Grant
9 Music Square S. #214
Nashville, TN 37203
"Singer"

Mrs. Barbara Grant
9966 Beverly Grove Drive
Beverly Hills, CA 90210
"Cary Grant's Widower"

Eddy Grant
155-D Holland Park Drive
London W11 4UX ENGLAND
"Singer, Writer"

Faye Grant
P.O. Box 5617
Beverly Hills, CA 90213
"Actress"

Gogi Grant
10323 Alamo Avenue #202
Los Angeles, CA 90064
"Singer"

Horace Grant
One Magic Place
Orlando, FL 32801
"Basketball Player"

Hugh Grant
76 Oxford Street
London W1N OAX ENGLAND
"Actor"

Johnny Grant
5800 Sunset Blvd.
Los Angeles, CA 90028
"TV Show Host"

Lee Grant
610 West End Avenue #7B
New York, NY 10024
"Actress, Director"

Dr. Tony Grant
610 South Ardmore Avenue
Los Angeles, CA 90005
"Radio Personality"

Guenther Grass
Niedstrasse 13
12159 Berlin 41 GERMANY
"Author"

Karen Grassle
9744 Wilshire Blvd. #308
Los Angeles, CA 90012
"Actress"

Grateful Dead
P.O. Box 1073-C
San Rafael, CA 94915
"Rock & Roll Group"

Peter Graves
660 East Channel Road
Santa Monica, CA 90402
"Actor"

Teresa Graves
3437 West 78th Place
Los Angeles, CA 90043
"Actress"

Billy Gray
19612 Grandview Drive
Topanga, CA 90290
"Actor"

Colleen Gray
1432 North Kenwood Street
Burbank, CA 91505
"Actress"

Dulcie Gray
44 Brunswick Gardens
Flat #2
London W8 ENGLAND
"Actress, Author"

Erin Gray
10921 Alta View
Studio City, CA 91604
"Actress"

Linda Gray
P.O. Box 5064
Sherman Oaks, CA 91403
"Actress, Director"

William H. Gray III
500 East 62nd Street
New York, NY 10021
"U.N.C.F. President"

Kathryn Grayson
2009 La Mesa Drive
Santa Monica, CA 90402
"Actress, Singer"

Adolph Green
211 Central Park W. #19E
New York, NY 10024
"Actor, Writer"

Al Green
P.O. Box 456
Memphis, TN 38053
"Singer, Clergy"

Dennis Green
9520 Viking Drive
Eden Prairie, MN 55344
"Football Coach"

Ellen Greene
151 South El Camino Drive
Beverly Hills, CA 90212
"Actress, Singer"

Graham Greene
121 N. San Vicente Blvd.
Beverly Hills, CA 90211
"Author"

James Greene
60 Pope's Grove, Twickenham
Middlesex ENGLAND
"Actor"

Melanie Greene
8904 Wonderland Avenue
Los Angeles, CA 90046
"Actress"

Michele Greene
2281 Holly Drive
Los Angeles, CA 90068
"Actress"

Shecky Greene
612 S. Lorraine Blvd.
Los Angeles, CA 90004
"Comedian"

David Greenlee
1811 North Whitley #800
Los Angeles, CA 90028
"Actor"

Bud Greenspan
33 East 68th Street
New York, NY 10021
"Writer, Producer"

Bruce Greenwood
12414 Cascade Canyon Drive
Granada Hills, CA 91344
"Actor"

Lee Greenwood
1311 Elm Hill Pike
Nashville, TN 37214
"Singer, Songwriter"

Michael Greenwood
14 Kingston House Prince Gate
London SW7 1LJ ENGLAND
"Actor"

Brodie Greer
5840 Shirley Avenue
Tarzana, CA 91356
"Actor"

Dabs Greer
284 South Madison #102
Pasadena, CA 91101
"Actor"

Germaine Greer
29 Frenshaw Road
London SW10 0TG ENGLAND
"Feminist, Author"

(Betty) Jane Greer
966 Moraga Drive
Los Angeles, CA 90049
"Actress"

Dick Gregory
P.O. Box 3270
Plymouth, MA 02361
"Activist, Comedian"

James Gregory
55 Cathedral Rock Drive #33
Sedona, AZ 86336
"Actor"

Mary Gregory
1350 N. Highland Avenue #24
Los Angeles, CA 90028
"Actress"

Paul Gregory
P.O. Box 38
Palm Springs, CA 92262
"Film Producer"

Bob Greise
3250 Mary Street
Miami, FL 33133
"Football Player"

Kim Greist
1776 Broadway #1810
New York, NY 10019
"Actress"

Wayne Gretzky
401 S. Prairie Avenue
Inglewood, CA 90301
"Hockey Player"

Jennifer Grey
500 South Sepulveda Blvd. #500
Los Angeles, CA 90049
"Actress"

Joel Grey
7515 Clinton Street
Los Angeles, CA 90036
"Actor, Singer"

Virginia Grey
15101 Magnolia Blvd. #54
Sherman Oaks, CA 91403
"Actress"

Richard Grieco
2934 1/2 N. Beverly Glen Circle
Suite #252
Los Angeles, CA 90077
"Actor"

Helmut Griem
Klugstr. 36
D-80638 Munich GERMANY
"Actor"

David Alan Grier
148 S. Gramercy Place #18
Los Angeles, CA 90004
"Actor"

Pam Grier
P.O. Box 370958
Denver, CO 80237
"Actress"

Rosey Grier
11656 Montana #301
Los Angeles, CA 90049
"Actor, Football Player"

Ken Griffey, Jr.
P.O. Box 4100
Seattle, WA 98104
"Baseball Player"

Ken Griffey, Sr.
5385 Cross Bridge Road
Westchester, OH 45069
"Ex-Baseball Player"

Archie Griffin
410 Woody Hayes Drive #237
Columbus, OH 43210
"Ex-Football Player"

Merv Griffin
9876 Wilshire Blvd.
Beverly Hills, CA 90210
"Singer, Producer"

Andy Griffith
P.O. Box 1968
Manteo, NC 27954
"Actor"

Melanie Griffith
201 South Rockingham Avenue
Los Angeles, CA 90049
"Actress"

Nanci Griffith
72-74 Brewer Street
London W1 ENGLAND
"Singer, Songwriter"

Thomas Ian Griffith
5444 Agnes Avenue
North Hollywood, CA 91607
"Actor"

Florence Griffith-Joyner
27758 Santa Margarita #385
Mission Viejo, CA 92691
"Track Athlete"

Gary Grimes
4578 West 165th Street
Lawndale, CA 90260
"Actor"

Tammy Grimes
10 East 44th Street #700
New York, NY 10017
"Actress"

John Grisham
114-A South Lamar Street
Oxford, MS 38655
"Author"

George Grizzard
400 East 54th Street
New York, NY 10022
"Actor"

Dick Groat
320 Beach Street
Pittsburgh, PA 15218
"Ex-Baseball Player"

Charles Grodin
2200 Fletcher Avenue
Ft. Lee, NJ 07024
"Actor"

Ferde Grofe, Jr.
18139 West Coastline
Malibu, CA 90265
"Writer"

Steve Grogan
8 Country Club Drive
Foxboro, MA 02035
"Ex-Football Player"

David Groh
8485-E Melrose Place
Los Angeles, CA 90069
"Actor"

Sam Groom
10000 Santa Monica Blvd. #305
Los Angeles, CA 90067
"Actor"

Arye Gross
151 El Camino Drive
Beverly Hills, CA 90212
"Actor"

Michael Gross
Paul Ehlich Strasse 6
D-6000 Frankfurt 70
GERMANY
"Swimmer"

Michael Gross
P.O. Box 522
La Canada, CA 91012
"Actor"

Sir Charles Groves
12 Camden Square
London NW1 9UY ENGLAND
"Conductor"

Lou Groza
5287 Parkway Drive
Berea, OH 44017
"Ex-Football Player"

Gary Grubbs
9744 Wilshire Blvd. #308
Beverly Hills, CA 90212
"Actor"

Dave Grushin
1282 Route 376
Wappingers Falls, NY 12590
"Composer"

Christopher Guard
2 Geraldine Road
London W4 ENGLAND
"Actor"

Peter Guber
10202 W. Washington Blvd.
Suite #1070
Culver City, CA 90232
"Film Producer"

Bob Guccione
1965 Broadway
New York, NY 10023
"Publisher"

Christopher Guest
P.O. Box 2358
Running Springs, CA 92382
"Actor, Writer"

Lance Guest
9229 Sunset Blvd. #311
Los Angeles, CA 90069
"Actor"

Ron Guirdy
109 Conway
Lafayette, LA 70507
"Ex-Baseball Player"

Ann Morgan Guilbert
5750 Wilshire Blvd. #512
Los Angeles, CA 90036
"Actress"

Robert Guillaume
11963 Crest Place
Beverly Hills, CA 90210
"Actor"

Sir Alec Guiness
Kettle Brook Meadows
Petersfield, Hampshire
ENGLAND
"Actor, Director"

Professor Lani Guinier
3400 Chestnut Street
Philadelphia, PA 19104
"Attorney, Educator"

Cathy Guisewite
4039 Camellia Avenue
Studio City, CA 91604
"Cartoonist"

Tito Guizar
Sierra Madre
640 Lomas Drive Chaupultepec
Mexico City 10 09999 MEXICO
"Actor, Guitarist"

Clu Gulager
2118 South Atlanta Place
Tulsa, OK 74114
"Actor'

Dorothy Gulliver
28792 Lajos Lane
Valley Center, CA 92082
"Actress"

Bryant Gumbel
30 Rockefeller Plaza #1508
New York, NY 10020
"Morning TV Show Host"

Greg Gumbel
347 West 57th Street
New York, NY 10019
"Sports Anchor"

Guns & Roses
83 Riverside Drive
New York, NY 10024
"Rock & Roll Group"

Dan Gurney
2334 South Broadway
Santa Ana, CA 92707
"Race Car Drive"

HM King Carl Gustav XVI
Kungliga Slottet
11130 Stockholm SWEDEN
"Royalty"

Arlo Guthrie
The Farm
Washington, MA 01223
"Singer, Songwriter"

Steve Guttenburg
15237 Sunset Blvd. #48
Pacific Palisades, CA 90272
"Actor"

Lucy Gutteridge
76 Oxford Street
London W1N 0AX ENGLAND
"Actress"

Jasmine Guy
21243 Ventura Blvd. #101
Woodland Hills, CA 91364
"Actress, Singer"

James "Gypsy" Haake
1256 North Flores #1
Los Angeles, CA 90069
"Actor"

Lukas Haas
9 Niles Road
Austin, TX 78703
"Actor"

Shelley Hack
1208 Georgina
Santa Monica, CA 90402
"Actress, Model"

Joseph Hacker
211 South Beverly Drive #107
Beverly Hills, CA 90212
"Actor"

Buddy Hackett
800 North Whittier Drive
Beverly Hills, CA 90210
"Comedian, Actor"

Taylor Hackford
2003 La Brea Terrace
Los Angeles, CA 90046
"Actor"

Gene Hackman
118 South Beverly Drive #201
Beverly Hills, CA 90212
"Actor"

Pat Haden
8525 Wilson Avenue
San Marion, CA 91108
"Sportscaster"

Brett Hadley
5070 Woodley Avenue
Encino, CA 91436
"Actor"

Molly Hagan
1800 Avenue of the Stars #400
Los Angeles, CA 90067
"Actress"

Sammy Hagar
8502 Fathom Drive
Baldwinsville, NY 13027
"Singer"

Kevin Hagen
1539 Sawtelle Blvd. #10
Los Angeles, CA 90025
"Actor"

Uta Hagen
27 Washington Square N.
New York, NY 10011
"Actress"

Merle Hager
P.O. Box 536
Palo Cedro, CA 96073
"Singer"

Marvin Hagler
112 Island Street
Stoughton, MA 02702
"Boxer"

Larry Hagman
23730 Malibu Colony Road
Malibu, CA 90265
"Actor, Director"

Albert Hague
9107 Wilshire Blvd. #602
Beverly Hills, CA 90210
"Actor, Composer"

Jessica Hahn
6345 Balboa Blvd. #375
Encino, CA 91316
"Radio Personality"

Charles Haid
4376 Forman Avenue
North Hollywood, CA 91602
"Actor, Producer"

Gen. Alexander Haig, Jr.
1155 15th St. NW #800
Washington, DC 20005
"Ex-Military Leader, Politician"

Arthur Hailey
P.O. Box N-7776
Lyford Cay
Nassau, BAHAMAS
"Writer"

Oliver Hailey
11747 Canton Place
Studio City, CA 91604
"Screenwriter"

Corey Haim
233 S. St. Andrews Place
Los Angeles, CA 90004
"Actor"

Connie Haines
880 Mandalay Shores
Cleanwater Beach, FL 34630
"Singer"

Randa Haines
1033 Gayley Avenue #208
Los Angeles, CA 90024
"TV Director"

Jester Hairston
5047 Valley Ridge Avenue
Los Angeles, CA 90043
"Actor"

Ron Hajak
17420 Ventura Blvd. #4
Encino, CA 91316
"Actor"

Khrystyne Haje
P.O. Box 8750
Universal City, CA 91608
"Actress"

Barbara Hale
P.O. Box 1980
North Hollywood, CA 91604
"Actress"

Georgina Hale
74A St. John's Wood
High Street
London NW8 ENGLAND
"Actress"

Jack Haley, Jr.
1443 Devlin Drive
Los Angeles, CA 90069
"Writer, Producer"

Jackie Earle Haley
10000 Riverside Drive #6
Toluca Lake, CA 91602
"Actor"

Bill Haley's Comets
2011 Ferry Avenue #U19
Camden, NJ 08104
"Rock & Roll Group"

Charles Haley
1 Cowboy Parkway
Irving, TX 78063
"Football Player"

Anthony Michael Hall
574 West End Avenue #4
New York, NY 10024
"Actor"

Arsenio Hall
8560 Wilshire Blvd. #516
Beverly Hills, CA 90212
"TV Show Host, Actor"

Hall & Oates
130 West 57th Street #2A
New York, NY 10019
"Music Duo"

Deidre Hall
215 Strada Corta Road
Los Angeles, CA 90077
"Actress"

Fawn Hall
1319 Bishop Lane
Alexanderia, VA 22302
"Secretary, Model"

Gus Hall
235 West 23rd Street
New York, NY 10011
"Politician"

Huntz Hall
12512 Chandler Blvd. #307
North Hollywood, CA 91607
"Actor"

Jerry Hall
304 West 81st Street
New York, NY 10024
"Model"

Lani Hall
31930 Pacific Coast Highway
Malibu, CA 90265
"Singer, Songwriter"

Monty Hall
519 North Arden Drive
Beverly Hills, CA 90210
"TV Show Host"

Rich Hall
P.O. Box 2350
Los Angeles, CA 90078
"Actor, Comedian, Writer"

Tom T. Hall
P.O. Box 1246
Franklin, TN 37065
"Singer, Songwriter"

Johnny Halladay
10 Avenue George V
F-75008 Paris, FRANCE
"Singer"

Charles Hallahan
1975 West Siverlake Drive
Los Angeles, CA 90039
"Actor"

Tom Hallick
13900 Tahiti Way #108
Marina del Rey, CA 90292
"Actor"

Holly Hallstrom
5750 Wilshire Blvd. #475-W
Los Angeles, CA 90036
"Model"

Brett Halsey
141 North Grand Avenue
Pasadena, CA 91103
"Actor"

Alan Hamel
8899 Beverly Blvd. #713
Los Angeles, CA 90048
"TV Personality"

Veronica Hamel
129 North Woodburn
Los Angeles, CA 90049
"Actress"

Dorothy Hamill
75490 Fairway Drive
Indian Wells, CA 92210
"Ice Skater"

Mark Hamill
P.O. Box 124
Malibu, CA 90265
"Actor"

Ashley Hamilton
12824 Evanston Street
Los Angeles, CA 90049
"Actor"

Carrie Hamilton
415 N. Camden Dr. #121
Beverly Hills, CA 90210
"Carol Burnett's Daughter"

Donald Hamilton
984 Acequia Madre #1045
Santa Fe, NM 87501
"Author"

George Hamilton
9255 Doheny Drive #2302
Los Angeles, CA 90069
"Actor"

George Hamilton IV
P.O. Box 1558
Gainesville, FL 32602
"Singer"

Guy Hamilton
22 Mont Port
E-07157 Port d'Andratx
Mallorca, SPAIN
"Film Director"

Josh Hamilton
151 El Camino Drive
Beverly Hills, CA 90212
"Actor"

Kim Hamilton
1229 North Horn Avenue
Los Angeles, CA 90069
"Actress"

Linda Hamilton
8955 Norman Place
West Hollywood, CA 90069
"Actress"

Scott Hamilton
1 Erieview Plaza
Cleveland, OH 44114
"Ice Skater"

Harry Hamlin
612 North Sepulveda Blvd. #10
Los Angeles, CA 90049
"Actor"

Marvin Hamlisch
970 Park Avenue #65
New York, NY 10028
"Composer, Pianist"

Hammer
44896 Vista del Sol
Fremont, CA 94539
"Rap Singer"

John Hammond
9229 Sunset Blvd. #607
Los Angeles, CA 90069
"Singer, Guitarist"

Earl Hamner
11575 Amanda Drive
Studio City, CA 91604
"TV Writer, Producer"

Susan Hampshire
Billing Road
London SW10 ENGLAND
"Actress"

James Hampton
5155 Valjean Avenue
Encino, CA 91436
"Actor, Writer"

Lionel Hampton
575 Laramie Lane
Mahwah, NJ 07430
"Musician"

Maggie Han
9200 Sunset Blvd. #710
Los Angeles, CA 90069
"Actress"

Herbie Hancock
1250 North Doheny Drive
Los Angeles, CA 90069
"Pianist, Composer"

Tom Hanks
23414 Malibu Colony Drive
Malibu, CA 90265
"Actor"

Bridget Hanley
16671 Oak View Drive
Encino, CA 91316
"Actress"

Daryl Hannah
8306 Wilshire Blvd. #535
Beverly Hills, CA 90211
"Actress"

Page Hannah
P.O. Box 5617
Beverly Hills, CA 90210
"Actress"

Sir James Hanson
180 Brompton Road
London SW3 1HF ENGLAND
"Film Director"

Otto Harbach
3455 Congress Street
Fairfield, CT 06430
"Lyricist"

Jim Harbaugh
100 South Capital Avenue
Indiana Polis, IN 46225
"Football Player"

Anfernee Hardaway
One Magic Place
Orlando, FL 32801
"Basketball Player"

Ernest Harden, Jr.
10653 Riverside Drive
Toluca Lake, CA 91602
"Actor"

Marcia Gay Harden
1358 Woodbrook Lane
Southlake, TX 76092
"Actress"

Melora Hardin
3033 Vista Crest Drive
Los Angeles, CA 90068
"Actress"

Jerry Hardin
3033 Vista Crest Drive
Los Angeles, CA 90068
"Actor"

Tonya Harding
13610 Tarleton S.W.
Tigard, OR 97224
"Ex-Ice Skater"

Kadeem Hardison
19743 Valleyview Drive
Topanga, CA 90290
"Actor"

Billy Hardwick
1576 South White Station
Memphis, TN 38117
"Bowler"

Robert Hardy
Newhall House, Carlops
Midlothian, SCOTLAND
"Actor"

Dorian Harewood
9300 Wilshire Blvd. #555
Beverly Hills, CA 90212
"Actress"

Billy James Hargis
Rose of Sharon Farm
Neosho, MO 64840
"Evangelist"

Mariska Hargitay
270 North Canon Drive #1064
Beverly Hills, CA 90210
"Actress"

Mickey Hargitay
1255 North Sycamore Avenue
Los Angeles, CA 90038
"Actor"

Dean Hargrove
474 Halvern Drive
Los Angeles, CA 90049
"TV Writer, Producer"

Marion Hargrove
401 Monica Avenue #6
Santa Monica, CA 90403
"TV Writer"

Sen. Tom Harkin (IA)
Senate Hart Bldg. #531
Washington, DC 20510
"Politician"

John Harkins
121 N. San Vicente Blvd.
Beverly Hills, CA 90211
"Actor"

Harlem Globetrotters
1000 South Fremont Avenue
Alhambra, CA 91803
"Comedy Basketball Team"

Renny Harlin
1033 Gayley Avenue #208
Los Angeles, CA 90024
"Director"

Debbie Harmon
13243 Valley Heart
Sherman Oaks, CA 91423
"Actress"

Kelly Harmon
13224 Old Oak Lane
Los Angeles, CA 90049
"Actress"

Manny Harmon
8350 Santa Monica Blvd.
Los Angeles, CA 90069
"Conductor"

Mark Harmon
2236 Encinitas Blvd. #A
Encinitas, CA 92024
"Actor"

Magda Harout
13452 Vose Street
Van Nuys, CA 91405
"Actress"

Heather Harper
20 Milverton Road
London NW67AS ENGLAND
"Actress"

Jessica Harper
3454 Glorietta Place
Sherman Oaks, CA 91423
"Actress"

Ron Harper
6767 Forest Lawn Dr. #101
Los Angeles, CA 90068
"Actor"

Tess Harper
151 El Camino Drive
Beverly Hills, CA 90212
"Actress"

Valerie Harper
14 East 4th Street
New York, NY 10012
"Actress"

The Harptones
55 West 119th Street
New York, NY 10026
"Vocal Group"

Woody Harrelson
2387 Kimridge Road
Beverly Hills 90210
"Actor"

Pamela Harriman
3038 "N" Street N.W.
Washington, DC 20007
"Averell Harriman's Widower"

Curtis Harrington
6286 Vine Way
Los Angeles, CA 90028
"Film Director"

Pat Harrington
730 Marzella Avenue
Los Angeles, CA 90049
"Actor, Writer"

Bishop Barbara Harris
138 Tremont Street
Boston, MA 02111
"Clergy"

Ed Harris
9434 East Champagne Drive
Sun Lakes, AZ 85248
"Actor"

Emmylou Harris
P.O. Box 158568
Nashville, TN 37215
"Singer, Songwriter"

Franco Harris
400 West North Avenue
Old Allegheny, CA 15212
"Football Player"

Mrs. Jean Harris
c/o General Delivery
Monroe, NH 03771
"Killed Scarsdale Diet Doctor"

Jonathan Harris
16830 Marmaduke Place
Encino, CA 91316
"Actor"

Julie Harris
132 Barn Hill Road #1267
West Chatham, MA 02669
"Actress"

Mel Harris
9250 Wilshire Blvd. #208
Beverly Hills, CA 90212
"Actress"

Neil Patrick Harris
13351 Riverside Drive #D-420
Sherman Oaks, CA 91423
"Actor"

Richard Harris
1325 Avenue of the Americas
New York, NY 10019
"Actor"

Sam Harris
2001 Wayne Avenue #103
San Leandro, CA 94577
"Singer"

Susan Harris
11828 La Grange #200
Los Angeles, CA 90025
"TV Producer"

George Harrison
Friar Park Road
Henley-On-Thames ENGLAND
"Singer, Songwriter"

Gregory Harrison
11750H Moorpark
Studio City, CA 91604
"Singer, Songwriter"

Jenilee Harrison
15315 Magnolia Blvd. #429
Sherman Oaks, CA 91403
"Actress, Model"

Linda Harrison
211 North Main Street #A
Berlin, MD 21811
"Actress"

Kathryn Harrold
151 El Camino Drive
Beverly Hills, CA 90212
"Actress"

Donald Harron
P.O. Box 4700
Vancouver B.C. V6B 4A3
CANADA
"TV Show Host"

Lisa Harrow
200 Fulham Road
London SW10 ENGLAND
"Actress"

Deborah Harry
156 W. 56th Street, 5th Floor
New York, NY 10019
"Singer"

Ray Harryhausen
2 Ilchester Place
West Kesington
London ENGLAND
"Special Effect Technician"

Bret "Hit Man" Hart
435 Patina Place S.W.
Calgary Alberto
T3H 2P5 CANADA
"Wrestler"

Cecilia Hart
5750 Wilshire Blvd. #512
Los Angeles, CA 90036
"Actress"

Christopher Hart
8520 Ridpath Drive
Los Angeles, CA 90046
"Actor"

Corey Hart
81 Hymus Blvd.
Montreal, Que. H9R 1E2
CANADA
"Singer, Songwriter"

Mother Dolores
(Dolores Hart)
Regina Laudis Convent
Bethlehem, CT 06751
"Actress, Nun"

Dorothy Hart
430 Haywood Road
Asheville, NC 28806
"Actress"

Freddie Hart
505 Canton Place
Madison, TN 37115
"Singer"

Gary Hart
9785 Maroon Circle #210
Englewood, CO 80112
"Ex-Senator"

Jim Hart
113 Kenick Plaza
Webster Grove, MD 63119
"Ex-Football Player"

John Hart
35109 Highway 79 #134
Warner Springs, CA 92086
"Actor"

Mary Hart
150 South El Camino Drive #303
Beverly Hills, CA 90212
"TV Show Host"

Mariette Hartley
10110 Empyrean Way #304
Los Angeles, CA 90067
"Actress"

Lisa Hartman-Black
8489 West Third Street #200
Los Angeles, CA 90048
"Actress, Model"

Phil Hartman
9150 Wilshire Blvd. #350
Beverly Hills, CA 90212
"Actor"

Jim Hartz
475 L'Enfant Plaza
Washington, DC 20024
"TV Show Host"

Paul Harvey
1035 Park Avenue
River Forest, IL 60305
"News Analyst"

Rodney Harvey
1608 N. Las Palmas Avenue
Los Angeles, CA 90028
"Actor"

Ernie Harwell
2121 Trumbull Avenue
Detroit, MI 48216
"Sportscaster"

Eugene Hasenfus
c/o General Delivery
Marinette, WI 54143
"Ex-Flight Master"

Peter Haskell
19924 Acre Street
Northridge, CA 91324
"Actor"

Dennis Haskins
1735 Peyton Avenue #303
Burbank, CA 91504
"Actor"

King Hassan II
Royal Palace
Rabat, MOROCCO
"Royalty"

David Hasselhoff
11342 Dona Lisa
Studio City, CA 91604
"Actor"

Marilyn Hassett
8485 Brier Drive
Los Angeles, CA 90046
"Actress"

Signe Hasso
582 S. Orange Grove Avenue
Los Angeles, CA 90036
"Actress"

Bob Hastings
620 S. Sparks Street
Burbank, CA 91505
"Actor"

Sen. Orrin G. Hatch (UT)
Senate Russell Bldg. #135
Washington, DC 20510
"Politician"

Richard Hatch
1604 N. Courtney Avenue
Los Angeles, CA 90046
"Actor"

Teri Hatcher
P.O. Box 1101
Sunland, CA 91040
"Actress"

Bobby Hatfield
599 Camillo Street
Sierra Madre, CA 90124
"Singer"

Hurd Hatfield
Ballinterry House
Rathcormac, County Cork
IRELAND
"Actor"

Juliana Hatfield
1 Camp Street, #2
Cambridge, MA 02140
"Singer"

Sen. Mark Hatfield (OR)
Senate Hart Bldg. #711
Washington, DC 20510
"Politician"

Noah Hathaway
455 South Maple Drive #1
Beverly Hills, CA 90212
"Actor"

Rutger Hauer
Singel 440, NL-1017 Av.
Amsterdam HOLLAND
"Actor"

Wings Hauser
14126 Marquesas Way
Marina del Rey, CA 90292
"Actor"

President Vaclav Havel
Hradecek
CR-11908 Prague 1
CZECHOLOVAKIA REPUBLIC
"Politician"

Richie Havens
123 West 44th Street #11A
New York, NY 10036
"Singer, Guitarist"

John Havlicek
24 Beech Road
Weston, CT 02193
"Ex-Basketball Player"

June Haver
485 Halvern Drive
Los Angeles, CA 90049
"Actress"

Nigel Havers
125 Gloucester Road
London SW7 ENGLAND
"Actor"

June Havoc
405 Old Long Ridge Road
Stamford, CT 06903
"Actress"

Ethan Hawke
9830 Wilshire Blvd.
Beverly Hills, CA 90212
"Actor"

Sophie B. Hawkins
550 Madison Avenue, #2500
New York, NY 10022
"Singer"

John Hawksworth
24 Cottersmore Gardens #2
London W8 ENGLAND
"TV Writer, Producer"

Goldie Hawn
955 South Carrillo Drive #200
Los Angeles, CA 90048
"Actress"

Jill Haworth
300 East 51st Street
New York, NY 10019
"Actress"

Nigel Hawthorne
Radwell Grange, Baldock
Hertfordshire SG7 5EU ENGLAND
"Actor"

Tom Hayden
10951 W. Pico Blvd. #202
Los Angeles, CA 90064
"Politician"

Julie Hayek
5645 Burning Tree Drive
La Canada, CA 91011
"Actress, Model"

Salma Hayek
151 El Camino Drive
Beverly Hills, CA 90212
"Actress"

Bill Hayes
4528 Beck Avenue
North Hollywood, CA 91602
"Actor"

Isaac Hayes
504 West 168th Street
New York, NY 10032
"Singer, Songwriter"

Patricia Hayes
20 West Hill Road
London SW18 ENGLAND
"Actress"

Peter Lind Hayes
3538 Pueblo Way
Las Vegas, NV 89109
"Actor, Comedian"

Susan Seaforth Hayes
4528 Beck Avenue
North Hollywood, CA 91602
"Actress"

Jim Haynie
10519 Troon Avenue
Los Angeles, CA 90064
"Actor"

Robert Hays
6310 San Vicente Blvd. #310
Los Angeles, CA 90048
"Actor"

Dennis Haysbert
3624 Canyon Crest Road
Altadena, CA 91001
"Actor"

Brooke Hayward
305 Madison Avenue #956
New York, NY 10165
"Author, Actress"

Jonathan Haze
3636 Woodhill Canyon
Studio City, CA 91604
"Actor"

Glenne Headley
8942 Wilshire Blvd.
Beverly Hills, CA 90211
"Actress"

Mary Healy
3538 Pueblo Way
Las Vegas, NV 89109
"Actress"

John Heard
347 West 84th Street #5
New York, NY 10024
"Actor"

George Hearn
200 West 57th Street #900
New York, NY 10019
"Actor"

Tommy Hearns
19785 West 12 Mile Road
Southfield, MI 48076
"Boxer"

Patricia Hearst
110-5th Street
San Francisco, CA 94103
"Author"

Mrs. Victoria Hearst
865 Comstock Avenue #168
Los Angeles, CA 90024
"Wife of William Hearst"

Heart
9220 Sunset Blvd. #320
Los Angeles, CA 90069
"Rock & Roll Group"

David Heavener
6442 Coldwater Canyon #211
North Hollywood, CA 90068
"Actor"

Ann Heche
6063 Scenic Avenue
Los Angeles, CA 90068
"Actress"

Jessica Hecht
280 South Beverly Drive, #400
Beverly Hills, CA 90212
"Actress"

Gina Hecht-Herskowitz
5930 Foothill Drive
Los Angeles, CA 90068
"Actress"

Eileen Heckart
1223 Foxboro Drive
Norwalk, CT 06851
"Actress"

David (Al) Hedison
280 South Beverly Drive #400
Beverly Hills, CA 90212
"Actor"

Tippi Hedren
P.O. Box 189
Acton, CA 93510
"Actress"

Hee Haw
P.O. Box 140400
Nashville, TN 37214
"Comedy Show"

Howell Heflin
311 East 6th Street
Tuscumbia, AL 35674
"Politician"

Christie Hefner
680 North Lake Avenue
Chicago IL 60611
"Hugh Hefner's Daughter"

Hugh Hefner
10236 Charing Cross Road
Los Angeles, CA 90077
"Publishing Executive"

Robert Hegyes
10323 Llona Avenue
Los Angeles, CA 90064
"Actor"

Beth Heiden
3505 Blackhawk Drive
Madison, WI 53704
"Skater"

Eric Heiden
3505 Blackhawk Drive
Madison, WI 53704
"Skater"

Katherine Heigl
8942 Wilshire Blvd.
Beverly Hills, CA 90211
"Actress"

Carol Heiss
809 Lafayette Drive
Akron, OH 44303
"Actress"

Marg Helgenberger
8942 Wilshire Blvd.
Beverly Hills, CA 90211
"Actress"

Levon Helm
192 Lexington Ave. #1204
New York, NY 10016
"Actor"

Katherine Helmond
2035 Davies Way
Los Angeles, CA 90046
"Actress, Director"

Sen. Jesse Helms (NC)
403 Everett Dirksen Bldg.
Washington, DC 20510
"Politician"

Harry Helmsley
Park Lane Hotel
36 Central Park South
New York, NY 10019
"Real Estate Executive"

Leona Helmsley
Park Lane Hotel
36 Central Park South
New York, NY 10019
"Hotel Executive"

Mariel Hemingway
P.O. Box 2249
Ketchum, ID 83340
"Actress"

David Hemmings
P.O. Box 5836
Sun Valley, ID 83340
"Actor, Director"

Shirley Hemphill
539 Trona Avenue
West Covina, CA 91790
"Actress"

Sherman Hemsley
15043 Valley Heart Drive
Sherman Oaks, CA 91403
"Actor"

Florence Henderson
P.O. Box 11295
Marina del Rey, CA 90295
"Singer, Actor"

Rickey Henderson
10561 Englewood Drive
Oakland, CA 94621
"Baseball Player"

Skitch Henderson
Hunt Hill Farm
RFD #3 Upland Road
New Milford, CT 06776
"Composer, Conductor"

Thomas "Hollywood" Henderson
7 Seafield Lane
Westhampton Beach, NY 11978
"Ex-Football Player"

Lauri Hendler
4034 Stone Canyon Avenue
Sherman Oaks, CA 91403
"Actress"

Don Henley
13601 Ventura Blvd. #99
Sherman Oaks, CA 91423
"Singer, Songwriter"

Marilu Henner
2101 Castilian
Los Angeles, CA 90068
"Actress"

Linda Kaye Henning
843 N. Sycamore Avenue
Los Angeles, CA 90038
"Actress"

Lance Henriksen
9540 Dale Avenue
Sunland, CA 91040
"Actor"

Clarence "Frogman" Henry
6808 Argonne Blvd.
New Orleans, LA 70124
"Singer, Guitarist"

Buck Henry
117 East 57th Street
New York, NY 10019
"Writer, Producer"

Gregg Henry
121 N. San Vicente Blvd.
Beverly Hills, CA 90211
"Actor"

Justin Henry
3 Clark Lane
Rye, NY 10580
"Child Actor"

Lenny Henry
294 Earl's Court Road
London SW5 9BB ENGLAND
"Actor"

Pamela Hensley
9526 Dalegrove Drive
Beverly Hills, CA 90210
"Actress"

Hans Werner Henze
La Leprara
via Del Fontonile
00047 Marino ITALY
"Composer, Conductor"

Richard Herd
4610 Worsten Avenue
Sherman Oaks, CA 91423
"Actor"

Jerry Herman
10847 Bellagio Road
Los Angeles, CA 90077
"Composer, Lyricist"

Herman's Hermits
2455 East Sunrise Blvd.
Ft. Lauderdale, FL 33304
"Rock & Roll Group"

Pee Wee Herman
P.O. Box 29373
Los Angeles, CA 90029
"Actor"

Keith Hernandez
255 East 49th Street #28-D
New York, NY 10017
"Ex-Baseball Player"

Lynn Herring
3500 West Olive #1400
Burbank, CA 91505
"Actress"

Barbara Hershey
9830 Wilshire Blvd.
Beverly Hills, CA 90211
"Actress"

Orel Hershiser
1585 Orlando Road
Pasadena, CA 91106
"Baseball Player"

Irene Hervey
7432 Sylvia Avenue
Reseda, CA 91335
"Actress"

Jason Hervey
1755 Seaview Trail
Los Angeles, CA 90046
"Actor"

Pres. Chaim Herzog
The Knesset
Hakiria Jerusalem, ISRAEL
"Politician"

Werner Herzog
Turkenstr. 91
D-80799 Munich 40 GERMANY
"Film Director"

Howard Hesseman
7146 La Presa
Los Angeles, CA 90068
"Actor, Director"

Charlton Heston
2859 Coldwater Canyon
Beverly Hills, CA 90210
"Actor, Director"

Christopher Hewett
1422 North Sweetzer #110
Los Angeles, CA 90069
"Actor, Director"

Don Hewitt
555 West 57th Street
New York, NY 10019
"Writer, Producer"

Martin Hewitt
8942 Wilshire Blvd.
Beverly Hills, CA 90211
"Actor"

Arthur Hewlett
10 Heath Drive
London NW3 ENGLAND
"Actor"

Donald Hewlett
Old King's Head
Whitstable, Kent ENGLAND
"Actor"

Tor Heyerdahl
Guimar
Tenerife CANARY ISLANDS
"Ethnologist, Explorer"

Anne Heywood
9966 Liebe Drive
Beverly Hills, CA 90210
"Actress"

William Hickey
69 West 12th Street
New York, NY 10011
"Actor"

Gov. Walter J. Hickel (AK)
P.O. Box A
Juneau, AK 99811
"Governor"

Catherine Hickland
247 S. Beverly Drive #102
Beverly Hills, CA 90212
"Actress"

Dwayne Hickman
812-16th Street #1
Santa Monica, CA 91403
"Actor"

Catherine Hicks
15422 Brownwood Place
Los Angeles, CA 90077
"Actress"

Dan Hicks
P.O. Box 5481
Mill Valley, CA 94942
"Singer, Songwriter"

Jack Higgins
Septembertide
Mont De La Rocqque
Jersey Channel Islands
ENGLAND
"Writer"

Joel Higgins
24 Old Hill Road
Westport, CT 06880
"Actor"

Gerald Hiken
910 Moreno Avenue
Palo Alto, CA 94303
"Actor"

Hildegarde
230 East 48th Street
New York, NY 10017
"Singer"

Anita Hill
300 Timberdell Road
Norman, OK 73019
"Professor of Law"

Arthur Hill
1515 Clubview Drive
Los Angeles, CA 90024
"Actor"

Carla Hills
3125 Chain Bridge Rd. NW
Washington, DC 20018
"Ex-Government Official"

Dana Hill
11763 Canton Place
Studio City, CA 91604
"Actress"

Faith Hill
7021 Mayflower Circle
Brentwood, TN 37027
"Singer"

Grant Hill
3777 Lapeer Road
Auburn Hills, MI 48057
"Basketball Player"

Steven Hill
18 Jill Lane
Monsey, NY 10952
"Actor"

Terrence Hill
P.O. Box 818
Stockbridge, MA 01262
"Actor"

Sir Edmund Hillary
278A Remuera Road
Auckland SE2 NEW ZEALAND
"Mountaineer"

Arthur Hiller
1218 Benedict Canyon
Beverly Hills, CA 90210
"Film Director"

Dame Wendy Hiller
Beaconsfield
Stratton Road
Buckinghamshire ENGLAND
"Actress"

John Hillerman
P.O. Box 218
Blue Jay, CA 92317
"Actor"

Barron Hilton
28775 Sea Ranch Way
Malibu, CA 90265
"Hotel Executive"

John Hinckley, Jr.
St. Elizabeth's Hospital
2700 Martin Luther King Avenue
Washington, DC 20005
"Attempted to kill Ronald Reagan"

Art Hindle
3500 West Olive Avenue #1400
Burbank, CA 91505
"Actor"

Gregory Hines
377 West 11th Street, PH. 4-A
New York, NY 10014
"Actor"

Mimi Hines
1605 South 11th Street
Las Vegas, NV 89109
"Actress"

Pat Hingle
P.O. Box 2228
Carolina Beach, NC 28428
"Actor"

Jurgen Hingsen
655 Circle Dr.
Santa Barbara, CA 93108
"Decathlon Athlete"

Darby Hinton
1234 Bel Air Road
Los Angeles, CA 90024
"Actor"

James David Hinton
2808 Oak Point Drive
Los Angeles, CA 90068
"Actor"

S.E. Hinton
8955 Beverly Blvd.
Los Angeles, CA 90048
"Screenwriter"

Thora Hird
21 Leinster Mews
Lancaster Gate
London W2 3EX ENGLAND
"Actress"

Hiroshima
1460 4th Street #205
Santa Monica, CA 90401
"Jazz Group"

Elroy Hirsch
1440 Monroe Street
Madison, WI 53711
"Actor"

Judd Hirsch
11 East 44th Street
New York, NY 10017
"Actor"

Al Hirschfield
122 East 95th Street
New York, NY 10028
"Caricaturist"

Al Hirt
6808 Argonne Blvd.
New Orleans, LA 70124
"Trumpeter"

Don Ho
277 Lewers
Honolulu, HI 96814
"Singer, Songwriter"

Tony Hoare
430 Edgware Road
London W2 1EH ENGLAND
"Playwright"

Rose Hobart
23388 Mulholland Drive
Woodland Hills, CA 91364
"Actress"

Valerie Hobson
Old Barn Cottage
Upton Gey
Hampshire RG25 2RM
ENGLAND
"Actress"

David Hockney
2907 Mt. Calm Avenue
Los Angeles, CA 90046
"Artist"

Patricia Hodge
76 Oxford Street
London W1N OAX ENGLAND
"Actress"

Stephanie Hodge
141 El Camino Drive #205
Beverly Hills, CA 90212
"Actress"

Joy Hodges
P.O. Box 1252
Cathedral City, CA 92235
"Actress"

James Hoffa, Jr.
5890 Lawndale Street
North Branch, MI 48461
"Union Official"

Alice Hoffman
3 Hurlbut Street
Cambridge, MA 02138
"Screenwriter"

Basil Hoffman
4456 Cromwell
Los Angeles, CA 90027
"Actor"

Dustin Hoffman
145 Central Park West #16B
New York, NY 10023
"Actor"

Isabella Hoffmann
121 N. San Vicente Blvd.
Beverly Hills, CA 90211
"Actress"

Syd Hoff
P.O. Box 2463
Miami Beach, FL 33140
"Cartoonist"

James Hoffa, Jr.
5890 Lawndale Street
North Branch, MI 48461
"Union Leader"

Susanna Hoffs
9720 Wilshire Blvd. #400
Beverly Hills, CA 90212
"Singer"

Ben Hogan
P.O. Box 15006
Richmond, VA 23227
"Golfer"

Hulk Hogan
4505 Morella Avenue
Valley Village, CA 91607
"Wrestler"

Paul Hogan
55 Lavender Place
Milson's Point
Sydney NSW 2060 AUSTRALIA
"Actor"

Robert Hogan
344 West 89th Street #1B
New York, NY 10024
"Actor"

Drake Hogestyn
3625 Sierra Road
Malibu, CA 90265
"Actor"

Hal Holbrook
P.O. Box 1980
Studio City, CA 91614
"Actor"

Rebecca Holden
1105-16th Avenue South #C
Nashville, TN 37212
"Actress, Singer"

Christopher Holden
113 N. San Vicente Blvd. #202
Beverly Hills, CA 90211
"Actor"

Sue Holderness
10 Rectory Close, Windsor
Berks. SL4 5ER ENGLAND
"Actress"

Jonathan Hole
5024 Balboa Blvd.
Encino, CA 91316
"Actor"

Hope Holiday
8538 Eastwood Road
Los Angeles, CA 90046
"Actress"

Xaviera Hollander
Stadionweg 17
1077 RU Amsterdam HOLLAND
"Author"

Lauren Holley
13601 Ventura Blvd. #99
Sherman Oaks, CA 91423
"Actress"

Polly Holliday
888-7th Avenue #2500
New York, NY 10106
"Actress"

Earl Holliman
4249 Bellingham Avenue
Studio City, CA 91604
"Actor"

Sen. Ernest F. Hollings (SC)
125 Russell Senator Office Bldg.
Washington, DC 20510
"Politician"

Julian Holloway
5344 Orrville Avenue
Woodland Hills, CA 91364
"Actor, Producer"

Celeste Holm
88 Central Park West
New York, NY 10023
"Actress"

Ian Holm
46 Albermarle Street
London W1X 4PP ENGLAND
"Actor"

Clint Holmes
697 Middle Neck Road
Great Neck, NY 11023
"Actor"

Jennifer Holmes
P.O. Box 6303
Carmel, CA 93921
"Actress"

Larry Holmes
101 Larry Holmes Drive #500
Easton, PA 18042
"Ex-Boxing Champion"

Charlene Holt-Hiara
151 El Camino Drive
Beverly Hills, CA 90212
"Actress"

Jack Holt, Jr.
504 Temple Drive
Harrah, OK 73045
"Actor"

Lou Holtz
P.O. Box 518
Nortre Dame, IN 46556
"Football Coach"

Evander Holyfield
310 Madison Avenue #804
New York, NY 10017
"Ex-Boxing Champion"

Honeymoon Suite
Box 70 - Station C
Queens St. West
Toronto, Ontario
M6J 3M7 CANADA
"Rock & Roll Group"

Dr. Hook
P.O. Box 121017
Nashville, TN 37212
"Rock & Roll Group"

Benjamin Hooks
260 Fifth Avenue
New York, NY 10001
"Ex-N.A.A.C.P. President"

Jan Hooks
151 El Camino Drive
Beverly Hills, CA 90212
"Actress"

Kevin Hooks
15534 Morrison Street
Sherman Oaks, CA 91403
"Actor, Director"

Robert Hooks
145 North Valley Street
Burbank, CA 91505
"Actor"

Tobe Hooper
1875 Century Park E. #1300
Los Angeles, CA 90067
"Film Director"

Burt Hooten
3619 Grandby Court
San Antonio, TX 78217
"Ex-Baseball Player"

Hootie & The Blowfish
46 Kensington Court
London, W8 5DP ENGLAND
"Music Group"

William Hootkins
16 Berners Street
London W1 ENGLAND
"Actor"

Bob Hope
10346 Moopark
North Hollywood, CA 91602
"Actor, Comedian"

Dolores Hope
10346 Moopark
North Hollywood, CA 91602
"Mrs. Bob Hope"

Leslie Hope
151 El Camino Drive
Beverly Hills, CA 90212
"Actress"

Anthony Hopkins
7 High Park Road
Kew, Surrey TW9 3BL ENGLAND
"Actor"

Bo Hopkins
6620 Ethel Avenue
North Hollywood, CA 91606
"Actor"

Linda Hopkins
382 North Lemon
Walnut, CA 91789
"Singer"

Telma Hopkins
4122 Don Luis Drive
Los Angeles, CA 90008
"Actress, Singer"

Dennis Hopper
9830 Wilshire Blvd.
Beverly Hills, CA 90212
"Actor, Director"

Lena Horne
23 East 74th Street
New York, NY 10021
"Singer"

Marilyn Horne
165 West 57th Street
New York, NY 10019
"Mezzo-Soprano"

Harry Horner
728 Brooktree Road
Pacific Palisades, CA 90272
"Film Director"

Paul Horning
133 S. 3rd Street #301
Louisville, KY 40202
"Ex-Football Player"

Bruce Hornsby
P.O. Box 3545
Williamburg, VA 23187
"Rock & Roll Group"

David Horowitz
P.O. Box 49915
Los Angeles, CA 90049
"TV Show Host"

Anna Maria Horsford
6402 Lindenhurst Ave.
Los Angeles, CA 90048
"Actress"

Lee Horsley
15054 East Dartmouth
Aurora, CO 80014
"Actor"

Peter Horton
9560 Wilshire Blvd. #500
Beverly Hills, CA 90212
"Actor"

Robert Horton
5317 Anadsol Avenue
Encino, CA 91316
"Actor"

Bob Hoskins
200 Fulham Road
London SW10 9PN ENGLAND
"Actor"

Robert Hossein
33 rue Galilee
75116 Paris, FRANCE
"Actor"

Ricard C. Hottelet
120 Chestnut Hill Road
Wilton, CT 06897
"News Correspondent"

Dee Hoty
333 West 56th Street
New York, NY 10019
"Actress"

Charlie Hough
2266 Shade Tree Circle
Brea, CA 92621
"Baseball Manager"

John Hough
8 Queen Street
London W1X 7PH ENGLAND
"Film Director"

James Houghton
8585 Walnut Drive
Los Angeles, CA 90046
"Actor, Writer"

Katharine Houghton
345 East 68 Street #11J
New York, NY 10021
"Actress"

Jerry Houser
3236 Brenda Street
Los Angeles, CA 90068
"Actor"

Cissy Houston
2160 North Central Road
Ft. Lee, NJ 07024
"Singer"

Thelma Houston
4296 Mount Vernon
Los Angeles, CA 90008
"Singer"

Whitney Houston
2160 North Central Road
Ft. Lee, NJ 07024
"Singer"

Clint Howard
346 East Tujunga Avenue
Burbank, CA 91505
"Actor"

Ken Howard
59 East 54th Street
New York, NY 10022
"Actor"

Rance Howard
4286 Clybourn Avenue
Burbank, CA 91505
"Actor, Writer"

Ron Howard
1925 Century Park E. #2300
Los Angeles, CA 90067
"Actor, Director"

Susan Howard
P.O. Box 1456
Boern, TX 78006
"Actress"

Gordie Howe
6645 Peninsula Drive
Traverse City, MI 49684
"Ex-Hockey Player"

Michael Howe
7 Floral Street
London WC2 ENGLAND
"Actor, Singer, Dancer"

Steve Howe
318 West 6th Street
Whitefish, MT 59937
"Guitarist"

C. Thomas Howell
151 El Camino Drive
Beverly Hills, CA 90212
"Actor"

Anne Howells
Milestone, Broomclose
Esher, Surrey, ENGLAND
"Opera Singer"

Sally Ann Howes
222 Central Park South
New York, NY 10019
"Actress"

Freddie Hubbard
17609 Ventura Blvd. #212
Encino, CA 91316
"Musician"

Hubcaps
P.O. Box 1388
Dover, DE 19003
"Rock & Roll Group"

Season Hubley
121 N. San Vicente Blvd.
Beverly Hills, CA 90211
"Actress"

Whip Hubley
9000 Sunset Blvd #1200
Los Angeles, CA 90069
"Actor"

Cooper Huckabee
1800 East Cerrito Place #34
Los Angeles, CA 90068
"Actor"

David Huddleston
9200 Sunset Blvd. #625
Los Angeles, CA 90069
"Actor"

Bill Hudson
6712 Portshead Road
Malibu, CA 90265
"Singer, Actor"

Hudson Brothers
151 El Camino Drive
Beverly Hills, CA 90212
"Vocal Group"

Ernie Hudson
3500 West Olive Avenue #1400
Burbank, CA 91505
"Actor"

Hues Corporation
P.O. Box 5295
Santa Monica, CA 90405
"Vocal Trio"

Brent Huff
2203 Ridgemont Drive
Los Angeles, CA 90046
"Actor"

Billy Hufsey
19134 Gayle Place
Tarzana, CA 91356
"Actor"

Daniel Hugh-Kelly
130 West 42nd Street #2400
New York, NY 10036
"Actor"

Barnard Hughes
250 West 94th Street
New York, NY 10025
"Actor"

Finola Hughes
270 North Canon Drive #1084
Beverly Hills, CA 90210
"Actress"

Irene Hughes
500 N. Michigan Avenue #1039
Chicago, IL 60611
"Journalist"

John Hughes
9830 Wilshire Blvd.
Beverly Hills, CA 90212
"Film Director, Producer"

Kathleen Hughes
8818 Rising Glen Place
Los Angeles, CA 90069
"Actress"

Wayne H. Huizenga
One Blockbuster Plaza
Ft. Lauderdale, FL 33301
"Blockbuster Video Owner"

Thomas Hulce
175 - 5th Avenue #2409
New York, NY 10010
"Actor"

Bobby Hull
15-1430 Maroons Road
Winnipeg, Manitoba R3G OL5
CANADA
"Hockey Player"

Human League
P.O. Box 153
Sheffield SL 1DR ENGLAND
"Rock & Roll Group"

Mary Margaret Humes
P.O. Box 1168-714
Studio City, CA 91604
"Actress, Model"

Englebert Humperdinck
10100 Sunset Blvd.
Los Angeles, CA 90077
"Singer"

Leann Hunley
1888 North Crescent Heights
Los Angeles, CA 90069
"Actress, Model"

Gayle Hunnicutt
174 Regents Park Road
London NW1 ENGLAND
"Actress"

Bonnie Hunt
9830 Wilshire Blvd.
Beverly Hills, CA 90212
"Actress"

E. Howard Hunt
1149 NE 101st Street
Miami Shores, FL 33138
"Author"

Helen Hunt
9830 Wilshire Blvd.
Beverly Hills, CA 90212
"Actress"

Lamar Hunt
1601 Elm #2800
Dallas, TX 75021
"Football Team Owner"

Linda Hunt
233 Park Avenue S. 10th Flr.
New York, NY 10017
"Actress"

Marsha Hunt
13131 Magnolia Blvd.
Sherman Oaks, CA 91423
"Actress"

Holly Hunter
8423 Densmore Avenue
North Hills, CA 91343
"Actress"

Jim "Catfish" Hunter
RR #1, Box 895
Hertford, NC 27944
"Ex-Baseball Player"

Kim Hunter
42 Commerce Street
New York, NY 10014
"Actress"

Rachel Hunter
23 Beverly Park
Beverly Hills, CA 90210
"Model"

Tab Hunter
223 North Guadalupe Street #292
Santa Fe, NM 87501
"Actor"

Isabelle Huppert
40 rue Francois
75008 Paris, FRANCE
"Actress"

Douglas Hurd
5 Mitford Cottages, Westwell
Burford Oxon ENGLAND
"Government Official"

Gale Ann Hurd
270 North Canon Drive #1195
Beverly Hills, CA 90210
"Film Producer"

Bobby Hurley
1 Sports Parkway
Sacramento, CA 95834
"Basketball Player"

Elizabeth Hurley
3 Cromwell Place
London SW 2JE ENGLAND
"Model"

Rick Hurst
1230 North Horn #401
Los Angeles, CA 90069
"Actor"

John Hurt
46 Albermarle Street
London W1X 4PP ENGLAND
"Actor"

Mary Beth Hurt
1619 Broadway #900
New York, NY 90019
"Actress"

William Hurt
370 Lexington Ave. #808
New York, NY 10017
"Actor"

Ferlin Husky
38 Music Square East #300
Nashville, CA 37203
"Singer, Songwriter"

Rick Husky
13565 Lucca Dive
Pacific Palisades, CA 90272
"Actor, Writer, Producer"

King Hussein I
P.O. Box 1055
Amman, JORDAN
"Royalty"

Saddam Hussein
Al-Sijoud Palace
Baghdad, IRAQ
"Politician"

Olivia Hussey
4872 Topanga Canyon Blvd. #301
Woodland Hills, CA 91364
"Actress"

Ruth Hussey
3361 Don Pablo Drive
Carlsbad, CA 92008
"Actress"

Angelica Huston
2771 Hutton Drive
Beverly Hills, CA 90210
"Actress"

Will Hutchins
3461 Waverly Drive #108
Los Angeles, CA 90027
"Actor"

Josephine Hutchinson
360 East 55th Street
New York, NY 10022
"Actress"

Betty Hutton
Harrison Avenue
Newport, RI 02840
"Actress"

Danny Hutton
2437 Horseshoe Canyon Road
Los Angeles, CA 90046
"Singer, Songwriter"

Lauren Hutton
382 Lafayette Street #6
New York, NY10003
"Actress, Model"

Timothy Hutton
RR 2, Box 3318
Cushman Road
Patterson, NY 12563
"Actor"

Laura Huxley
6233 Mulholland Drive
Los Angeles, CA 90068
"Author"

Joe Hyams
10375 Wilshire Blvd. #4D
Los Angeles, CA 90024
"Author"

Peter Hyams
932 Hills Avenue
Los Angeles, CA 90024
"Writer, Producer"

Alex Hyde-White
8271 Melrose Avenue #110
Los Angeles, CA 90046
"Actor"

Scott Hylands
12831 Mulholland Drive
Beverly Hills, CA 90210
"Actor"

Earle Hyman
484 West 43rd Street #33E
New York, NY 10036
"Actor"

Kenneth Hyman
Sherwood House
Tilehouse Lane
Denham, Bucks. ENGLAND
"Film Executive"

Joyce Hyser
10100 Santa Monica Blvd. #2500
Los Angeles, CA 90067
"Actress"

I

Lee Iacocca
30 Scenic Oaks
Bloomfield Hills, MI 48304
"Automobile Executive"

Carl Icahn
100 South Bedford Drive
Mt. Kisco, NY 10549
"Business Executive"

Ice Cube
(Oshea Jackson)
6809 Victoria Avenue
Los Angeles, CA 90043
"Rap Singer, Actor"

Ice Tea
2287 Sunset Plaza Drive
Los Angeles, CA 90069
"Rap Singer, Actor"

Eric Idle
3131 Floye Drive
Los Angeles, CA 90046
"Actor, Director"

Billy Idol
8209 Melrose Avenue
Los Angeles, CA 90046
"Singer, Songwriter"

Julio Iglesias
4770 Biscayne Blvd. #1420
Miami Beach, FL 33137
"Singer"

Rev. Ike
4140 Broadway
New York, NY 10004
"Evangelist"

Iman
111 East 22nd Street #200
New York, NY 10010
"Model"

Gary Imhoff
3500 West Olive Avenue #1400
Burbank, CA 91505
"Actor"

Don Imus
34-12 36th Street
Astoria, NY 11106
"Radio Talk Show Host"

Indigo Girls
315 Ponce De Leon Ave., #755
Decatur, GA 30030
"Music Group"

Marty Ingels
701 North Oakhurst Drive
Beverly Hills, CA 90210
"Actor"

James Ingram
867 Muirfield Road
Los Angeles, CA 90005
"Singer"

John Inman
51A Oakwood Road
London NW11 6RJ ENGLAND
"Actor"

The Ink Spots
P.O. Box 70218
Ft. Lauderdale, FL 33307
"Vocal Group"

Roy Innis
800 Riverside Drive #6E
New York, NY 10032
"Activist"

Sen. Daniel Inouye (HI)
Senate Hart Bldg. #722
Washington, DC 20510
"Politician"

INXS
8 Hayes St.
#1 Neutray Bay
NSW 20891 AUSTRALIA
"Rock & Roll Group"

Kathy Ireland
1900 Avenue of the Stars #1640
Los Angeles, CA 90069
"Model"

Donnie Iris
807 Darlington Road
Beaver Falls, PA 15010
"Singer"

Iron Butterfly
6400 Pleasant Park Drive
Chanhassen, MN 55317
"Rock & Roll Group"

Iron Maiden
82 Bishop's Bridge Road
London W2 ENGLAND
"Rock & Roll Group"

Jeremy Irons
194 Old Brompton Street
London SW5 ENGLAND
"Actor"

Michael Ironside
3500 West Olive #1400
Burbank, CA 91505
"Actor"

Monte Irvin
11 Douglas Court South
Homosassa, FL 32646
"Ex-Baseball Player"

Amy Irving
11693 San Vicente Blvd. #335
Los Angeles, CA 90049
"Actress"

Michael Irving
1 Cowboy Parkway
Irving, TX 78063
"Football Player"

Hale Irwin
12444 Powerscourt Drive #284
St. Louis, MO 63131
"Golfer"

James B. Irwin
P.O. Box 1387
Colorado Springs, CO 80901
"Astronaut"

Peter Isaacksen
4635 Placidia Avenue
North Hollywood, CA 91602
"Actor"

Chris Isaak
P.O. Box 547
Larkspur, CA 94939
"Singer"

Isley Brothers
1211 Sunset Plaza Dr. #110
Los Angeles, CA 90069
"R&B Group"

Ragib Ismail
332 Center Street
El Segundo, CA 90245
"Football Player"

Lance A. Ito
210 West Temple
Los Angeles, CA 90012
"Judge"

Robert Ito
825 South Madison Avenue
Pasadena, CA 91106
"Actor"

Zeljko Ivanek
145 West 45th Street #1204
New York, NY 10036
"Actor"

Dana Ivey
10100 Santa Monica Blvd. #2500
Los Angeles, CA 90067
"Actress"

Judith Ivey
15760 Ventura Blvd. #1730
Encino, CA 91436
"Actress"

James Ivory
9830 Wilshire Blvd.
Beverly Hills, CA 90212
"Actor"

Jackee
8649 Metz Place
Los Angeles, CA 90069
"Actress"

Alan Jackson
33 Music Square W. #102-B
Nashville, TN 37203
"Singer"

Anne Jackson
90 Riverside Drive
New York, NY 10024
"Actress"

Barry Jackson
29 Rathcoole Avenue
London N8 9LY ENGLAND
"Actor"

Donald Jackson
1080 Brocks
South Pickering
Ontario, CANADA

Freddie Jackson
231 West 58th Street
New York, NY 10019
"Singer"

Glenda Jackson
59 Fifth Street
London W1 ENGLAND
"Actress"

Janet Jackson
14755 Ventura Blvd. #1-170
Sherman Oaks, CA 91403
"Singer, Songwriter"

Jeremy Jackson
4444 Lankershim Blvd., #207
North Hollywood, CA 91602
"Singer"

Jermaine Jackson
4641 Hayvenhurst Avenue
Encino, CA 91316
"Singer, Songwriter"

Rev. Jesse Jackson
400 "T" Street N.W.
Washington, DC 20001
"Politician, Evangelist"

Jesse Jackson, Jr.
House Office Bldg.
Washington, DC 20515
"Son of Jesse Jackson"

Joe Jackson
6 Pembridge Road
Trinity House #200
London W11 ENGLAND
"Singer, Songwriter"

Kate Jackson
1628 Marlay Drive
Los Angeles, CA 90069
"Actress"

LaToya Jackson
301 Park Ave. #1970
New York, NY 10022
"Singer, TV Show Host"

Marlon Jackson
4641 Hayvenhurst Avenue
Encino, CA 91316
"Singer"

Mary Jackson
2055 Grace Avenue
Los Angeles, CA 90068
"Actress"

Mary Ann Jackson
1242 Alessandro Drive
Newbury Park, CA 91320
"Actress"

Maynard Jackson
68 Mitchell
Atlanta, GA 30303
"ex-Mayor of Atlanta, GA"

Melody Jackson
6269 Selma Avenue #15
Los Angeles, CA 90028
"Actress"

Michael Jackson
Neverland Ranch
Los Olivos, CA 93441
"Singer, Songwriter"

Michael Jackson
1420 Moraga Drive
Los Angeles, CA 90049
"Talk Show Host"

Paul Jackson, Jr.
40 West 57th Street
New York, NY 10019
"Actor"

Phil Jackson
980 N. Michigan Avenue #1600
Chicago, IL 60611
"Basketball Coach"

Randy Jackson
4641 Hayvenhurst Drive
Encino, CA 91316
"Singer"

Rebbie Jackson
4641 Hayvenhurst Drive
Encino, CA 91316
"Singer"

Reggie Jackson
325 Elder Avenue
Seaside, CA 93955
"Ex-Baseball Player"

Samuel L. Jackson
955 S. Carrillo Drive #300
Los Angeles, CA 90048
"Actor"

Sherry Jackson
4933 Encino Avenue
Encino, CA 91316
"Actress"

Stonewall Jackson
6007 Cloverland Drive
Brentwood, TN 37027
"Singer, Songwriter

Stoney Jackson
1602 North Fuller Avenue #102
Los Angeles, CA 90046
"Actor"

Tito Jackson
15255 Del Gado Drive
Sherman Oaks, CA 91403
"Singer"

Victoria Jackson
8330 Lookout Mountain Drive
Los Angeles, CA 90046
"Actress"

Wanda Jackson
725 N. Broadway Avenue
Oklahoma City, OK 73102
"Singer"

Sir Derek Jacobi
76 Oxford Street
London W1N OAX ENGLAND
"Actor"

Lou Jacobi
240 Central Park South
New York, NY 10019
"Actor"

Helen Hull Jacobs
26 Joanne Lane
Weston, CT 06883
"Tennis Player, Author"

Lawrence-Hilton Jacobs
3804 Evans #2
Los Angeles, CA 90027
"Actor"

Billy Jacoby
P.O. Box 46324
Los Angeles, CA 90046
"Actor"

Laura Jacoby
P.O. Box 46324
Los Angeles, CA 90046
"Actress"

Scott Jacoby
P.O. Box 461100
Los Angeles, CA 90046
"Actor"

Richard Jaeckel
23388 Mulholland Drive
Woodland Hills, CA 91364
"Actor"

Henry Jaffe
7920 Sunset Blvd. #400
Los Angeles, CA 90046
"Film Producer"

Bianca Jagger
530 Park Avenue #18-D
New York, NY 10021
"Actress, Model"

Mick Jagger
304 West 81st Street
New York, NY 10024
"Singer"

Henry Jaglom
9165 Sunset Blvd. PH
Los Angeles, CA 90069
"Actor"

John Jakes
19 West 44th Street
New York, NY 10036
"Author"

Ahmad Jamal
223 1/2 East 48th Street
New York, NY 10017
"Musician"

Clifton James
95 Buttonwood Drive
Dix Hills, NY 11746
"Actor"

Dalton James
178 S. Victory Blvd. #208
Burbank, CA 91502
"Actor"

Dennis James
3581 Caribeth Drive
Encino, CA 91316
"TV Personality"

Etta James
4031 Panama Court
Piedmont, CA 94611
"Singer"

Godfrey James
The Shack, Western Road
Pevensey Bay
East Sussex ENGLAND
"Actor"

John James
P.O. Box #9
Cambridge, NY 12816
"Actor"

Joni James
P.O. Box 7027
Westchester, IL 60154
"Singer"

Sheila James-Kuehl
3201 Pearl Street
Santa Monica, CA 90405
"Actress"

Sonny James
818 - 18th Avenue
Nashville, TN 37203
"Singer, Songwriter"

Paulene Jameson
7 Warrington Gardens
London W9 ENGLAND
"Actress"

Jan & Dean
1720 North Ross Street
Santa Ana, CA 92706
"Vocal Duo"

Jane's Addiction
8800 Sunset Blvd. #401
Los Angeles, CA 90069
"Rock & Roll Group"

Conrad Janis
29169 Heathercliff Road #216
Malibu, CA 90265
"Actor"

Dan Jansen
c/o General Delivery
Greenfield, WI 53220
"Ice Skater"

Famke Janssen
9560 Wilshire Blvd., #500
Beverly Hills, CA 90212
"Actress"

Don January
P.O. Box 109601
Palm Beach Garden, FL 33410
"Golfer"

Lois January
225 North Crescent Drive #103
Beverly Hills, CA 90210
"Actress"

Al Jardine
P.O. Box 36
Big Sur, CA 93920
"Singer, Musician"

Claude Jarman, Jr.
11 Dos Encinas
Orinda, CA 94563
"Actor"

Maurice Jarre
27011 Sea Vista Drive
Malibu, CA 90265
"Composer"

Al Jarreau
8942 Wilshire Blvd.
Beverly Hills, CA 90211
"Musician"

Tom Jarrell
77 West 66th Street
New York, NY 10023
"News Correspondent"

Gen.Wojciech Jaruzelski
ul Klonowa 1
009909 Warsaw, POLAND
"Military, Politician"

Graham Jarvis
15351 Via De Las Olas
Pacific Palisades, CA 90272
"Actor"

Lucy Jarvis
171 West 57th Street
New York, NY 10019
"TV Executive, Producer"

Jason & The Scorchers
P.O. Box 1200235
Nashville, TN 37212
"Rock & Roll Group"

Harvey Jason
1280 Sunset Plaza Drive
Los Angeles, CA 90069
"Writer"

Sybil Jason
P.O. Box 40024
Studio City, CA 91604
"Actress"

Terry Jastrow
13201 Old Oak Lane
Los Angeles, CA 90049
"Director, Producer"

Jay & The Americans
360 Central Avenue
Lawrence, NY 11559
"Rock & Roll Group"

Michael Jayston
60 St. James's Street
London SW1 ENGLAND
"Actor"

D.J. Jazzy Jeff &
The Fresh Prince
298 Elizabeth Street #100
New York, NY 10012
"Rap Duo"

Gloria Jean
20309 Leadwell
Canoga Park, CA 91303
"Actress"

ZiZi Jeanmaire
22 rue de la Paix
75002 Paris, FRANCE
"Actress"

Sen. Jim Jeffords (VT)
Senate Hart Bldg. #530
Washington, DC 20510
"Politician"

Anne Jeffreys
121 South Bentley Avenue
Los Angeles, CA 90049
"Actress"

Herb Jeffries
P.O. Box C
River Edge, NJ 07601
"Singer"

Lionel Jeffries
Guild House
Upper St. Martin's Lane
London WC2H 9EG ENGLAND
"Actor, Director"

Richard Jeni
9454 Wilshire Blvd. #405
Beverly Hills, CA 90212
"Comedian"

Carol Mayo Jenkins
606 North Larchmont Blvd. #309
Los Angeles, CA 90004
"Actress"

Ferguson Jenkins
P.O. Box 275
Flenheim, Ontario CANADA
"Ex-Baseball Player"

Hayes Alan Jenkins
809 Lafayette Drive
Akron, OH 44303
"Skater"

Jackie "Butch" Jenkins
Rt. #6, Box 541-G
Fairview, NC 28730
"Actor"

Bruce Jenner
P.O. Box 11137
Beverly Hills, CA 90213
"Athlete, Actor"

Peter Jennings
77 West 66th Street
New York, NY 10023
"News Anchor"

Waylon Jennings
824 Old Hickory Blvd.
Brentwood, TN 37027
"Singer, Songwriter"

Salome Jens
9400 Readcrest Drive
Beverly Hills, CA 90210
"Actress"

Adele Jergens Langan
32108 Village 32
Camarillo, CA 93010
"Actress"

Michael Jeter
4571 North Figueroa #20
Los Angeles, CA 90065
"Actor"

Jethro Tull
2 Wansdown Place, Fulham
London SW6 ENGLAND
"Rock & Roll Goup"

Joan Jett
155 East 55th Street #6H
New York, NY 10022
"Rock & Roll Group"

Norman Jewison
23752 Malibu Road
Malibu, CA 90265
"Director, Producer"

Ann Jillian
4241 Woodcliff Road
Sherman Oaks, CA 91403
"Actress, Singer"

Joyce Jillson
64 East Concord Street
Orlando, FL 32801
"Astrologer, Columnist"

Jim & Jesse
P.O. Box 27
Gallatin, TN 37066
"C&W Group"

Marlene Jobert
8-10 Blvd. de Courcelles
75008 Paris, FRANCE
"Actress"

Steve Jobs
900 Chesapeake Drive
Redwood City, CA 94063
"Computer Executive"

Billy Joel
200 W. 57th Street #308
New York, NY 10019
"Singer, Songwriter"

David Johanssen
200 West 58th Street
New York, NY 10019
"Actor"

Elton John
3660 Peachtree Street NW
Atlanta, GA 30305
"Singer, Songwriter"

Pope John Paul II
Palazzo Apostolico Vaticano
Vatican City, ITALY
"Pope"

Johnny Hates Jazz
321 Fulham Road
London ZW10 9QL ENGLAND
"Rock & Roll Group"

Glynis Johns
121 North San Vicente Blvd.
Beverly Hills, CA 90211
"Actress"

Anne-Marie Johnson
2606 Ivan Hill Terrace
Los Angeles, CA 90026
"Actress"

Arte Johnson
2725 Bottlebrush Drive
Los Angeles, CA 90024
"Actor, Comedian"

Ben Johnson
2 St. Clair Avenue E. #1400
Toronto, Ont. W4T 2R1 CANADA
"Runner"

Beverly Johnson
250 West 40th Street #400
New York, NY 10018
"Actress"

Brad Johnson
9830 Wilshire Blvd.
Beverly Hills, CA 90212
"Actor"

Don Johnson
9555 Heather Road
Beverly Hills, CA 90210
"Actor"

Earvin "Magic" Johnson
13100 Mulholland Drive
Beverly Hills, CA 90210
"Ex-Basketball Player"

Georgann Johnson
218 North Glenroy Place
Los Angeles, CA 90049
"Actress"

Jill Johnson
43 Matheson Road
London W14 ENGLAND
"Actress"

Jimmy Johnson
2269 N.W. 199th Street
Miami, FL 33056
"Football Coach"

John Dennis Johnson
9744 Wilshire Blvd. #308
Beverly Hills, CA 90212
"Actor"

Kevin Johnson
201 East Jefferson Street
Phoenix, AZ 85004
"Basketball Player"

Lamont Johnson
601 Paseo Miramar
Pacific Palisades, CA 90272
"Director, Producer"

Laura Johnson
1917 Weepah Way
Los Angeles, CA 90046
"Actress"

Mrs. Lady Bird Johnson
LBJ Ranch Stonewall
Austin, TX 78701
"Ex-First Lady"

Lucie Baines Johnson
170 Crescent Road
Torontom Ont. M4W 1V2
CANADA
"Ex-President's Daughter"

Lynn-Holly Johnson
6605 Hollywood Blvd. #220
Los Angeles, CA 90028
"Actress"

Michael Johnson
Gold Medal Management
1350 Pine Street, #3
Boulder, CO 80302
"Track & Field"

Michelle Johnson
1322 Shady Brook Drvie
Beverly Hills, CA 90028
"Actress"

Rafer Johnson
501 Colorado Ave. #200
Santa Monica, CA 90401
"Actor"

Richard Johnson
2 Stoken Church Street
London SW6 3TR ENGLAND
"Actor"

Russell Johnson
P.O. Box 3135
La Jolla, CA 92038
"Actor"

Van Johnson
405 East 54th Street
New York, NY 10022
"Actor"

Sen. J. Bennett Johnston (LA)
Senate Hart Bldg. #136
Washington, DC 20510
"Politician"

Tom Johnston Band
P.O. Box 878
Sonoma, CA 95476
"Rock & Roll Group"

Christopher Jones
7936 Santa Monica Blvd.
Los Angeles, CA 90046
"Actor"

Chuck Jones
P.O. Box 2319
Costa Mesa, CA 92628
"Animated Cartoon Producer"

Davey Jones
P.O. Box 400
Beavertown, PA 17813
"Singer, Actor"

Dean Jones
500 N. Buena Vista
Burbank, CA 91521
"Actor"

Dub Jones
223 Glendale
Rusten, LA 71270
"Actor"

Gemma Jones
3 Goodwins Court
London WC2 ENGLAND
"Actor"

George Jones
1005-A Lavergne Circle
Hendersonville, TN 37075
"Singer, Songwriter"

The Jones Girls
P.O. Box 6010, #761
Sherman Oaks, CA 91413
"Vocal Group"

Grace Jones
P.O. Box 82
Great Neck, NY 10014
"Model, Actress"

Grandpa Jones
P.O. Box 853
Goodlettsville, TN 37070
"Singer, Guitarist"

Dame Gwyneth Jones
P.O. Box 380
8040 Zurich SWITZERLAND
"Soprano"

Henry Jones
502 - 9th Street
Santa Monica, CA 90402
"Actor"

Howard Jones
Box 185, High Wycom.
Bucks. HP11 2E2 ENGLAND
"Singer, Songwriter"

Jack Jones
78-825 Osage Trail
Indian Wells, CA 92210
"Singer, Actor"

James Earl Jones
P.O. Box 610
Pawling, NY 12564
"Actor"

Janet Jones
14135 Beresford Drive
Beverly Hills, CA 90210
"Actress"

Jennifer Jones-Simon
P.O. Box 50067
Pasadena, CA 91115
"Actress"

Jenny Jones
454 North Columbus Drive
Chicago, IL 60611
"Talk Show Host"

Jesus Jones
193 Joralemon Street #300
Brooklyn, NY 11201
"Singer"

L.Q. Jones
2144 1/2 N. Cahuenga Blvd.
Los Angeles, CA 90068
"Actor, Director"

Marcia Mae Jones
4541 Hazeltine Avenue #4
Sherman Oaks, CA 91423
"Actress"

Mick Jones
279 Central Park W. #19A
New York, NY 10024
"Actor"

Parnelli Jones
P.O. Box "W"
Torrance, CA 90507
"Race Car Driver"

Paula Jones
2159 Elm Street #1
Long Beach, CA 90806
"Sexual Harrassment Accuser"

Quincy Jones
3800 Barham Blvd. #503
Los Angeles, CA 90068
"Composer, Producer"

Rickie Lee Jones
476 Broome Street, #6A
New York, NY 10013
"Singer, Songwriter"

Sam J. Jones
15250 Ventura Blvd. #720
Sherman Oaks, CA 91403
"Actor"

Shirley Jones
701 North Oakhurst Drive
Beverly Hills, CA 90210
"Actress"

Terry Jones
25 Newman Street
London W1 ENGLAND
"Actor, Writer, Director"

Tom Jones
363 Copa de Oro Drive
Los Angeles, CA 90077
"Singer"

Tommy Lee Jones
P.O. Box 966
San Saba, TX 76877
"Actor"

Trevor Jones
46 Avenue Road
Highgate,
London N6 5DR England
"Actor"

Erica Jong
121 Davis Hills Road
Weston, CT 06883
"Poet, Author"

The Jordanaires
3814 Cleghorn Avenue
Nashville, TN 37215
"Music Group"

Hamilton Jordan
333 Main Avenue West
Nashville, TN 37902
"Former Government Offical"

James Carroll Jordan
8333 Lookout Mountain Avenue
Los Angeles, CA 90046
"Actor"

Lee Roy Jordan
2425 Burbank
Dallas, TX 75235
"Ex-Football Player"

Michael Jordan
980 N. Michigan Avenue #1600
Chicago, IL 60611
"Basketball Player"

Stanley Jordan
9000 Sunset Blvd. #1200
Los Angeles, CA 90069
"Guitarist"

Vernon E. Jordan, Jr.
1333 New Hampshire Avenue NW
Suite #400
Washington, DC 20036
"Politician"

Will Jordan
435 West 57th Street #10-F
New York, NY 10019
"Comedian"

William Jordan
10806 Lindbrook Avenue #4
Los Angeles, CA 90024
"Actor"

Jackie Joseph
111 North Valley
Burbank, CA 91505
"Actress, Writer"

Jeffrey Joseph
121 North San Vicente Blvd.
Beverly Hills, CA 90211
"Actor"

Erland Josephson
Valhallavagen 10
11-422 Stockholm, SWEDEN
"Actor"

Louis Jourdan
1139 Maybrook
Beverly Hills, CA 90210
"Actor"

Journey
2051 Third Street
San Francisco, CA 94107
"Rock & Roll Group"

Milla Jovovich
933 North LaBrea Avenue
Los Angeles, CA 90038
"Model, Actress"

Elaine Joyce
724 North Roxbury Drive
Beverly Hills, CA 90210
"Actress"

Odette Joueux
1 rue Seguier
75006 Paris, FRANCE
"Writer"

Jackie Joyner-Kersee
20214 Leadwell
Canoga Park, CA 91304
"Track & Field Athlete"

Judas Priest
3 East 54th, #1400
New York, NY 10022
"Music Group"

Ashley Judd
P.O. Box 680339
Franklin, TN 37068
"Actress"

Naomi Judd
P.O. Box 17087
Nashville, TN 37217
"Singer"

Wynonna Judd
P.O. Box 681828
Franklin, TN 37068
"Singer"

Gordon Jump
1631 Hillcrest
Glendale, CA 91202
"Actor, Director"

Katy Jurado
Apartado Postal 209
Cuernavaca, Moro. MEXICO
"Actress"

Sonny Jurgensen
P.O. Box 53
Mt. Vernon, VA 22121
"Ex-Football Player"

Charlie Justice
P.O. Box 819
Cherryville, NC 28021
"Violinist"

David Justice
40 Point Ridge
Atlanta, GA 30328
"Baseball Player"

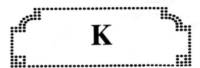

K.C. & The Sunshine Band
5215 Madison St.
Hollywood, FL 33021
"Rock & Roll Group"

Pauline Kael
2 Berkshire Heights Raod
Great Barrington, MA 02130
"Film Critic, Author"

Brian "Kato" Kaelin
100 Wilshire Blvd. #1000
Santa Monica, CA 90401
"OJ's House Guest"

David Kagen
6457 Firmament Avenue
Van Nuys, CA 91406
"Actor"

Madeline Kahn
975 Park Avenue #9A
New York, NY 10028
"Actress, Singer"

Marvin Kalb
79 John F. Kennedy Street
Cambridge, MA 01238
"Journalist"

Patricia Kalember
324 W. 83rd St. #3B
New York, NY 10024
"Actress"

Al Kaline
945 Timberlake Drive
Bloomfield Hills, MI 48013
"Ex-Baseball Player"

Helena Kallianides
12830 Mulholland Drive
Beverly Hills, CA 90210
"Actress, Writer, Director"

Herbert Kalmbach
1056 Santiago Drive
Newport Beach, CA 92660
"Watergate Participant"

Stanley Kamel
9300 Wilshire Blvd. #410
Beverly Hills, CA 90210
"Actor"

Steve Kampmann
801 Alma Real
Pacific Palisades, CA 90272
"Actor, Writer"

Steven Kanaly
828 Foothill Lane
Ojai, CA 93023
"Actor"

Sean Kanan
1999 Avenue of the Stars #2850
Los Angeles, CA 90067
"Actor, Karate Expert"

Big Daddy Kane
151 El Camino Drive
Beverly Hills, CA 90212
"Rap Singer"

Carol Kane
1416 North Havenhurst #1-C
Los Angeles, CA 90046
"Actress"

Fay Kanin
653 Ocean Front
Santa Monica, CA 90402
"Screenwriter"

Garson Kanin
210 Central Park South
New York, NY 10019
"Writer, Producer"

Stan Kann
570 North Rossmore Avenue
Los Angeles, CA 90004
"Actor"

Hal Kanter
15941 Woodvale Road
Encino, CA 91316
"Writer, Producer"

Mickey Kanter
600 - 17th Street N.W.
Washington, DC 20506
"U.S. Trade Representative"

Gabriel Kaplan
9551 Hidden Valley Road
Beverly Hills, CA 90210
"Comedian, Actor"

Jonathan Kaplan
2413 Canyon Oak Dr.
Los Angeles, CA 90069
"Director"

Marvin Kaplan
7600 Claybeck Avenue
Burbank, CA 91505
"Actor"

Valerie Kapriski
10 Avenue George V
F-75008 Paris FRANCE
"Actress"

Mitzi Kapture
8281 Melrose Avenue #200
Los Angeles, CA 90046
"Actress"

Donna Karan
240 West 41st Street
New York, NY 10018
"Fashion Designer"

Kym Karath
2267 Roscomare Road
Los Angeles, CA 90077
"Actress"

James Karen
4455 Los Feliz Blvd. #807
Los Angeles, CA 90027
"Actor"

John Karlen
911 - 2nd Street #16
Santa Monica, CA 90403
"Actor"

Phil Karlson
3094 Patricia Avenue
Los Angeles, CA 90064
"Director"

Richard Karn
1427 3rd Street #205
Santa Monica, CA 90401
"Actor"

Bela Karolyi
17203 Bamwood
Houston, TX 77090
"Gymnastic Coach"

Anatoly Karpov
Luzhnetskaya 8
Moscow 119270 RUSSIA
"Chess Champion"

Alex Karras
7943 Woodrow Wilson Drive
Los Angeles, CA 90046
"Ex-Football Player, Actor"

Yousuf Karsh
Chateau Laurier
Ottawa Ontario
K1N 8S7 CANADA
"Photographer"

Lawrence Kasdan
10345 West Olympic Blvd.
Los Angeles, CA 90064
"Director, Producer"

Casey Kasem
138 North Mapleton Drive
Los Angeles, CA 90077
"Radio-TV Personality"

Jean Kasem
138 North Mapleton Drive
Los Angeles, CA 90077
"Radio-TV Personality"

Sen. Nancy Kassebaum (KS)
302 Russell Office Bldg.
Washington, DC 20510
"Politician"

John Kassir
1201 Larrabee Street #207
Los Angeles, CA 90069
"Comedian"

Dr. Irene Kassorla
10231 Charing Cross Road
Los Angeles, CA 90077
"Psychologist, Author"

William Katt
26608 Sunflower Court
Calabasas, CA 91302
"Actor"

Julie Kavner
25154 Malibu Road #2
Malibu, CA 90265
"Actress"

Charles Kay
18 Epple Road
London SW6 ENGLAND
"Actor"

Dianne Kay
1559 Palisades Drive
Pacific Palisades, CA 90272
"Actress"

Caren Kaye
16835 Edgar Street
Pacific Pallisades, CA 90272
"Actress"

Lila Kaye
47 Courtfield Road #9
London SW7 4DB ENGLAND
"Actress"

Melvina Kaye
P.O. Box 6085
Burbank, CA 90510
"Singer"

Beau Kayzer
2906 Seabreeze Drive
Malibu, CA 90265
"Actor"

Elia Kazan
174 East 95th Street
New York, NY 10128
"Director, Producer"

Lainie Kazan
9903 Santa Monica Blvd #283
Beverly Hills, CA 90212
"Singer, Actress"

James Keach
P.O. Box 548
Agoura, CA 91376
"Actor"

Stacy Keach, Jr.
27525 Winding Way
Malibu, CA 90265
"Actor"

Stacy Keach, Sr.
8749 Sunset Blvd.
Los Angeles, CA 90069
"Actor"

Jean Kean
28128 West Pacific Coast Hwy.
Malibu, CA 90265
"Actress"

Bill Keane
5815 E. Joshua Tree Lane
Paradise Valley, AZ 85253
"Cartoonist"

Diane Keane
23 Primrose Hill
Charleton Mackrell
Summerset ENGLAND
"Actress"

James Keane
10206 Camarillo Place #6
North Hollywood, CA 91602
"Actor"

Diane Keaton
2255 Verde Oak Drive
Los Angeles, CA 90068
"Actress, Director"

Michael Keaton
11901 Santa Monica Blvd. #547
Los Angeles, CA 90025
"Actor"

Lila Kedrova
50 Forest Manor Road #3
Willowdale Ontario
M2J 1M1 CANADA
"Actress"

Don Keefer
4146 Allot Avenue
Sherman Oaks, CA 91423
"Actor"

Howard Keel
394 Red River Road
Palm Desert, CA 92211
"Actor, Singer"

William Keene
435 29th Street
Manhattan Beach, CA 90266
"Actor"

Bob Keeshan
(Capt. Kangaroo)
40 West 57th Street #1600
New York, NY 10019
"TV Show Host"

Garrison Keillor
N7613 1250th Street
River Falls, WI 54022
"Author, Radio Personality"

Betty Lou Keim
10642 Arnel Place
Chatsworth, CA 91311
"Actress"

Andrew Keir
Grafton House #44
2-3 Golden Square
London W1R 3AD ENGLAND
"Actor"

Harvey Keitel
110 Hudson Street #9A
New York, NY 10013
"Actor"

Brian Keith
23449 Malibu Colony Road
Malibu, CA 90265
"Actor"

David Keith
449 South Beverly Drive #212
Beverly Hills, CA 90212
"Actor"

Penelope Keith
66 Berkeley House
Hay Hill
London SW3 ENGLAND
"Actress"

Robert Kelker-Kelly
606 N. Larchmont Blvd. #309
Los Angeles, CA 90004
"Actor"

George Kell
P.O. Box 70
Swifton, AR 72471
"Ex-Baseball Player"

Marthe Keller
5 rue St. Dominique
75007 Paris, FRANCE
"Actress"

Mary Page Keller
151 El Camino Drive
Beverly Hills, CA 90212
"Actress"

Sally Kellerman
7944 Woodrow Wilson Drive
Los Angeles, CA 90046
"Actress"

DeForrest Kelley
14710 Arminta Street
Van Nuys, CA 91402
"Actor"

Kitty Kelley
3037 Dunbarton Avenue NW
Washington, DC 20007
"Author"

Sheila Kelley
10540 Cushdon Avenue
Los Angeles, CA 90064
"Actress"

Barbara Kelly
5 Kidderpore Avenue
London NW3 7SX ENGLAND
"Actress"

David Patrick Kelly
211 E. 89th Street
New York, NY 10128
"Actor"

Jim Kelly
One Bill Drive
Orchard Park, NY 14127
"Football Player"

Moira Kelly
106 So. Orange Drive
Los Angeles, CA 90036
"Actress"

Paula Kelly
1801 Avenue of Stars #1250
Los Angeles, CA 90067
"Actress, Dancer"

Roz Kelly
5614 Lemp Avenue
North Hollywood, CA 91601
"Actress"

Linda Kelsey
9200 Sunset Blvd. #625
Los Angeles, CA 90069
"Actress"

Ed Kemmer
11 Riverside Drive #17PE
New York, NY 10022
"Actor"

Jack Kemp
1776 "I" Street NW #800
Washington, DC 20006
"Ex-Football Player, Politician"

Jeremy Kemp
Danbury Street #6A
London N18 JJ ENGLAND
"Actor"

Shawn Kemp
190 Queen Anne Avenue N.
Suite #200
Seattle, WA 98109
"Basketball Player"

Suzy Kendall
Dentham House #4
Hampstead
NW 3 ENGLAND
"Actress"

Adams Kennedy
P.O. Box 679
Kent, CT 06757
"Screenwriter"

Justice Anthony Kennedy
1-1st Street N.E.
Washington, DC 20543
"Supreme Court Justice"

Burt Kennedy
13138 Magnolia Blvd.
Sherman Oaks, CA 91423
"Film Writer, Director"

Caroline Kennedy-Schlosseberg
641 6th Avenue
New York, NY 10011
"Ex-President's Daughter"

Sen. Edward Kennedy (MA)
315 Russell Office Bldg.
Washington, DC 20510
"Politician"

Ethel Kennedy
1147 Chain Bridge Road
McLean, VA 22101
"Mrs. Robert Kennedy"

George Kennedy
10100 Santa Monica Blvd. #2500
Los Angeles, CA 90067
"Actor"

Jayne Kennedy-Overton
230 Sunridge Street
Playa del Rey, CA 90293
"Actress, Model"

Joan Kennedy
Squaw Island
Hyannisport, MA 02647
"Ted Kennedy's Ex-Wife"

John F. Kennedy, Jr.
20 North Moore Street
New York, NY 10013
"Ex-President's Son"

Rep. Joseph Kennedy II (MA)
1210 Longworth House Bldg.
Washington, DC 20510
"Politician"

Leon Isaac Kennedy
9427 Via Monique
Burbank, CA 91504
"Actor, Producer"

Mimi Kennedy
9000 Sunset Blvd. #1200
Los Angeles, CA 90069
"Actress"

Nigel Kennedy
9A Penzance Place
London W11 4PE ENGLAND
"Violinist"

Robert F. Kennedy, Jr.
78 North Broadway
White Plains, NY 10603
"Robert Kennedy's Son"

Ted Kennedy, Jr.
636 Chain Bridge Road
McLean, VA 22101
"Sen. Ted Kennedy's Son"

Mr. Kenneth
19 East 54th Street
New York, NY 10022
"Hairstylist"

Patsy Kensit
14 Lambton Place
Nottinghill
London W11 2SH ENGLAND
"Actress"

Arthur Kent
19-22 Rathbone Place
London, W1P 1DF England
"Broadcast Journalist"

Jean Kent
22-23 Marlybone High
Flat #80
London W1 ENGLAND
"Actress"

Lord Philip Kentner
1 Mallord Street
London SW3 ENGLAND
"Musician"

Kentucky Headhunters
212 Third Avenue North #301
Nashville, TN 37201
"Music Group"

Shell Kepler
3123 Belden Drive
Los Angeles, CA 90068
"Actress"

Ken Kercheval
P.O. Box 325
Goshen, KY 40026
"Actor"

Kirk Kerkorian
4045 S. Spencer Street #A57
Las Vegas, NV 89119
"Business Executive"

Joanna Kerns
P.O. Box 49216
Los Angeles, CA 90049
"Actress"

Sandra Kerns
620 Resolano Drive
Pacific Palisades, CA 90272
"Actress"

Deborah Kerr
Los Monteras
E-29600 Marbella
Malaga, SPAIN
"Actress"

Jean Kerr
1 Beach Avenue
Larchmont, NY 10538
"Dramatist"

John Kerr
1570 Abajo Drive
Monterey Park, CA 91754
"Actor"

Sen. Robert Kerrey (NE)
Senate Hart Bldg. #316
Washington, DC 20510
"Politician"

Linda Kerridge
9812 West Olympic Blvd.
Beverly Hills, CA 90212
"Actress, Model"

Nancy Kerrigan
7 Cedar Avenue
Stoneham, MA 02180
"Ice Skater"

Sen. John Kerry (MA)
Senate Russell Bldg. #421
Washington, DC 20510
"Politician"

Sammy Kershaw
817 18th Avenue South
Nashville, TN 37203
"Singer"

Irwin Kershner
424 Sycamore Road
Santa Monica, CA 90402
"Director"

Brian Kerwin
304 W. 81st Street #2
New York, NY 10024
"Actor"

Hank Ketcham
P.O. Box 800
Pebble Beach, CA 93953
"Cartoonist"

Dave Ketchum
2318 Waterby Street
Westlake Village, CA 91361
"Writer, Producer"

Dr. Jack Kevorkian
327 East 4th Street
Royal Oaks, MI 48067
"Assist with Suicide Dr."

Ted Key
1694 Glenhardie Road
Wayne, PA 19087
"Cartoonist"

Dr. Alan Keyes
1030 - 15th Street NW #700
Washington, DC 20005
"Talk Show Host"

Evelyn Keyes
999 North Doheny Drive #509
Los Angeles, CA 90069
"Actress"

Mark Keyloun
3500 West Olive Avenue #1400
Burbank, CA 91505
"Actor"

Persis Khambatta
P.O. Box 46539
Los Angeles, CA 90046
"Actress, Model"

Chaka Khan
P.O. Box 16680
Beverly Hills, CA 90209
"Singer"

Princess Yasmin Khan
146 Central Park West
New York, NY 10023
"Royalty"

Adnan Khashoggi
P.O. Box 6
Riyadh SAUDIA-ARABIA
"Arms Dealer"

Victor Kiam II
60 Main Street
Bridgeport, CT 06602
"Business Executive"

Sidney Kibrick
711 North Oakhurst Drive
Beverly Hills, CA 90210
"Actor"

Jason Kidd
777 Sports Street
Dallas, TX 75207
"Basketball Player"

Michael Kidd
1614 Old Oak Road
Los Angeles, CA 90049
"Actor, Dancer"

Margot Kidder
P.O. Box 829
Los Angeles, CA 90078
"Actress"

Nicole Kidman
335 North Maple Drive #135
Beverly Hills, CA 90210
"Actress"

Richard Kiel
40356-T Oak Park Way
Oakhurst, CA 93644
"Actor"

Kaleena Kiff
1800 North Vine Street #120
Los Angeles, CA 90028
"Actress"

Richard Kiley
Ryerson Road
Warwick, NY 10990
"Actor"

Merle Kilgore
P.O. Box 850
Paris, TN 38242
"Singer, Songwriter"

Harmon Killebrew
P.O. Box 14550
Scottsdale, AZ 85267
"Ex-Baseball Player"

Jean-Claude Killey
13 Chemin Bellefontaine
1223 Cologny GE SWITZERLAND
"Skier"

Val Kilmer
P.O. Box 362
Tesuque, NM 87574
"Actor"

Eric Kilpatrick
6330 Simpson Avenue #3
North Hollywood, CA 91606
"Actor"

James L. Kilpatrick
White Walnut Hill
Woodville, VA 22749
"Columnist, Journalist"

Lincoln Kilpatrick
6330 Simpson Avenue #8
N. Hollywood, CA 91606
"Actor"

Ward Kimball
8910 Ardendale Avenue
San Gabriel, CA 91775
"Animation Director"

Bruce Kimmel
12230 Otsego Street
North Hollywood, CA 91607
"Writer, Director"

Aaron Kincaid
12307-C Ventura Blvd.
North Hollywood, CA 91601
"Actor"

Roslyn Kind
8871 Burton Way, #303
Los Angeles, CA 90048
"Actress"

Alan King
888-7th Avenue, 38th Floor
New York, NY 10106
"Comedian, Actor"

Andrea King
1225 Sunset Plaza Drive #3
Los Angeles, CA 90069
"Actress"

B.B. King
P.O. Box 4396
Las Vegas, NV 89107
"Singer, Guitarist"

Ben E. King
P.O. Box 1094
Teaneck, NJ 07666
"Singer, Songwriter"

Billie Jean King
445 N. Wells #404
Chicago, IL 60610
"Tennis Player"

Cammie Conlon King
511 Cypress Street, #2
Ft. Bragg, CA 95437
"Actress"

Carole King
P.O. Box 7308
Carmel, CA 93921
"Singer, Songwriter"

Coretta Scott King
234 Sunset Avenue N.W.
Atlanta, GA 30314
"Mrs. Martin Luther King, Jr."

Don King
871 W. Oakland Blvd.
Ft. Lauderdale, FL 33311
"Fight Promoter"

Evelyn "Champagne" King
2746 N. Green Valley Pkwy., #499
Las Vegas, NV 89014
"Singer"

Larry King
10801 Lockwood Drive #230
Silver Springs, MD 20901
"TV Talk Show Host"

Mabel King
P.O. Box 022115
Brooklyn, NY 10202
"Actress"

Perry King
3647 Wrightwood Drive
Studio City, CA 91604
"Actor"

Regina King
3814 Dunford Lane
Inglewood, CA 90305
"Actress"

Rodney King
9100 Wilshire Blvd. #250-W
Beverly Hills, CA 90212
"Beaten Motorist"

Stephen King
47 West Broadway
Bangor, ME 04401
"Novelist"

Zalman King
1393 Rose Avenue
Venice, CA 90291
"Writer"

Roger Kingdom
322 Mall Blvd. #303
Monroeville, PA 15146
"Track & Field Athlete"

Ben Kingsley
Stratford Upon Avon
New Penworth House
Warwickshire 0V3 7QX
ENGLAND
"Actor"

The Kingsmen
1720 North Ross Avenue
Santa Ana, CA 92706
"Rock & Roll Group"

The Kingston Trio
P.O. Box 34397
San Diego, CA 92103
"Vocal Trio"

The Kinks
29 Rushton Mews
London W11 1RB ENGLAND
"Rock & Roll Group"

Kathleen Kinmont
641 Mariposa Drive
Burbank, CA 91506
"Actress"

Greg Kinnear
3000 W. Alameda Ave., #2908
Burbank CA 91523
"Actor"

Leonid Kinskey
15009 N. Tarmarack Lane
Fountain Hills, AZ 85268
"Actor"

Michael Kinsley
5602 Lakeview Drive #J
Kirkland, WA 98033
"Political Commentator"

Nastassja Kinski
151 El Camino Drive
Beverly Hills, CA 90212
"Actress, Model"

Durward Kirby
P.O. Box 400
Sherman, CT 06784
"Screenwriter"

Phyllis Kirk
321-M South Beverly Drive
Beverly Hills, CA 90212
"Actress"

Tommy Kirk
833 South Beacon Avenue
Los Angeles, CA 90017
"Actor"

Clare Kirkconnell
515 South Irving Blvd.
Los Angeles, CA 90020
"Actress"

Gelsey Kirkland
191 Silver Moss Drive
Vero Beach, FL 32963
"Dancer"

Lane Kirkland
815-16th Street N.W.
Washington, DC 20006
"Union Executive"

Sally Kirkland
9229 Sunset Blvd. #710
Los Angeles, CA 90069
"Actress"

Jeane Kirkpatrick
6812 Granby Street
Bethesda, MD 20817
"Politician"

Terry Kiser
9911 West Pico Blvd. #1060
Los Angeles, CA 90035
"Actor, Comedian"

KISS
6363 Sunset Blvd. #417
Los Angeles, CA 90028
"Rock & Roll Group"

Dr. Henry Kissinger
435 East 52nd Street
New York, NY 10022
"Politician"

Tawny Kitaen
P.O. Box 16693
Beverly Hills, CA 90209
"Actress"

Michael Kitchen
4 Windmill Street
London W1P 1HF ENGLAND
"Actor"

Eartha Kitt
125 Boulder Ridge Road
Scarsdale, NY 10583
"Singer, Actress"

Franz Klammer
Mooswald 22
A-9712 Friesach, AUSTRIA
"Skier"

Calvin Klein
205 West 39th Street
New York, NY 10018
"Fashion Designer"

Robert Klein
67 Ridge Crest Road
Briarcliff, NY 10510
"Comedian, Actor"

Werner Klemperer
44 West 62nd Street, 10th Floor.
New York, NY 10023
"Actor"

Kevin Kline
9830 Wilshire Blvd
Beverly Hills, CA 90212
"Actor"

Richard Kline
14322 Mulholland Drive
Los Angeles, CA 9007
"Actor"

Don Klosterman
2220 Avenue of the Stars #2502
Los Angeles, CA 90067
"Ex-Football Player"

Patricia Klous
18095 Karen Drive
Encino, CA 91316
"Actress"

Jack Klugman
22548 Pacific Coast Hwy. #8
Malibu, CA 90265
"Actor, Writer"

Hildegard Knef
Maria-Theresia-Street
800 Munich Bogenhausen
GERMANY
"Actress, Singer"

Evel Knievel
160 East Flamingo Road
Las Vegas, NV 89109
"Daredevil"

Bobby Knight
Indiana University Basketball
Bloomington, IN 47405
"Basketball Coach"

Christopher Knight
7738 Chandelle Place
Los Angeles, CA 90046
"Actor"

Gladys Knight
2700 E. Sunset Road #31D
Las Vegas, NV 89120
"Singer"

Holly Knight
1585 Stone Canyon Road
Los Angeles, CA 90077
"Singer, Songwriter"

Michael E. Knight
10100 Santa Monica Blvd.
Suite #2500
Los Angeles, CA 90067
"Actor"

Shirley Knight
2130 N. Beachwood Drive #8
Los Angeles, CA 90068
"Actress"

Wayne Knight
PO Box 5617
Beverly Hills, CA 90210
"Actor"

Mark Knopfler
10 Southwick Mews
London SW2 ENGLAND
"Rock Musician"

Don Knotts
1854 South Beverly Glen #402
Los Angeles, CA 90025
"Actor"

Patric Knowles
6243 Randi Avenue
Woodland Hills, CA 91367
"Actor"

Buddy Knox
RR 3, C-10
Evans Armstrong B.C.
V0E 1B0 CANADA
"Singer, Songwriter"

Chuck Knox
11220 N.E. 53rd Street
Kirkland, WA 98033
"Football Coach"

Elyse Knox-Harmon
320 North Gunston
Los Angeles, CA 90049
"Actress"

Terence Knox
1440 South Sepulvede Blvd. #200
Los Angeles, CA 90025
"Actor"

Mayor Edward I. Koch
1290 Avenue of the Stars
30th Floor
New York, NY 10104
"Ex-Mayor"

Howard W. Koch
704 North Crescent Drive
Beverly Hills, CA 90210
"Director, Producer"

Fanny Blankers Koen
"Nachtegaal"
Strat. NO.67
Utrecht HOLLAND
"Track Athlete"

Walter Koenig
P.O. Box 4395
North Hollywood, CA 91607
"Actor, Writer"

Helmut Kohl
Marbacher Str. 11
D-6700 Ludwigshafen/Rhein
GERMANY
"Politician"

Sen. Herbert Kohl (WI)
Senate Hart Bldg. #330
Washington, DC 20510
"Politician"

Susan Kohner
710 Park Avenue #14-E
New York, NY 10021
"Actress"

Mayor Teddy Kollek
22 Jaffa Road
Jerusalem, ISRAEL
"Politician"

James Komack
617 North Beverly Drive
Beverly Hills, CA 90210
"Actor, Writer, Director"

Dorothy Konrad
10650 Missouri Avenue #2
Los Angeles, CA 90025
"Actress"

Kool & The Gang
89 Fifth Avenue #700
New York, NY 10003
"R&B Group""

Kool Moe Dee
151 El Camino Drive
Beverly Hills, CA 90212
"Rap Singer"

Dean R. Koontz
P.O. Box 9529
Newport Beach, CA 92658
"Writer"

Dr. C. Everett Koop
111 Michigan Avenue NW
Washington, DC 20010
"Ex-Surgeon General"

Bernie Kopel
19413 Olivos
Tarzana, CA 91356
"Actor, Writer"

Ted Koppel
1717 DeSales N.W. #300
Washington, DC 20036
"TV Show Host"

Olga Korbut
4705 Masters Court
Duluth, MN 30136
"Gymnast"

Marla Korda
304 N. Screenland Drive
Burbank, CA 91505
"Actress"

Michael Korda
1230 Avenue of the Americas
New York, NY 10019
"Writer"

Harvey Korman
1136 Stradella
Los Angeles, CA 90077
"Actor, Director"

Bernie Kosar
2269 NW 199th Street
Miami, FL 33056
"Football Player"

Lauren Koslow
17520 Mayall Street
Northridge, CA 91325
"Actress"

David Kossoff
45 Roe Green Close
College Lane
Hatfield, Herts. ENGLAND
"Actor, Writer"

Yaphet Kotto
10100 Santa Monica Blvd. #2490
Los Angeles, CA 90067
"Actor"

Martin Kove
8091 Selma Avenue
Los Angeles, CA 90046
"Actor"

Harley Jane Kozak
9560 Sunset Blvd. #500
Beverly Hills, CA 90212
"Actor"

Linda Kozlowski
151 El Camino Drive
Beverly Hills, CA 90212
"Actress"

Jeroen Krabbe
107 Van Eeghenstraat
1071 EZ Amsterdam, HOLLAND
"Actor"

Ken Kragen
240 Baroda
Los Angeles, CA 90077
"Talent Agent"

Jack Kramer
231 North Glenroy Place
Los Angeles, CA 90049
"Tennis Player"

Stanley Kramer
2530 Shira Drive
Valley Village, CA 91607
"Film Director"

Stephanie Kramer
8455 Beverly Blvd. #505
Los Angeles, CA 90048
"Actress, Director"

Judith Krantz
166 Groverton Place
Los Angeles, CA 90077
"Author"

Peter Kraus
Kaiserplatz 7
8000 Munich 40 GERMANY
"Actor"

Brian Krause
10683 Santa Monica Blvd.
Los Angeles, CA 90025
"Actor"

Alison Krauss
59 Music Square West
Nashville, TN 37203
"Singer"

Lenny Kravitz
14681 Harrison Street
Miami, FL 33176
"Singer"

Paul Kreppel
14300 Killion Street
Van Nuys, CA 91401
"Actor"

Kreskin
P.O. Box 1383
West Caldwell, NJ 07006
"Psychic"

Robbie Krieger
8033 Sunset Blvd. #76
Los Angeles, CA 90046
"Actress'

Alice Krige
10816 Lindbrook Drive
Los Angeles, CA 90024
"Actress'

Wortham Krimmer
1642 Redesdale Avenue
Los Angeles, CA 90026
"Actor"

Kris Kross
9380 SW 72nd Street #B-220
Miami, FL 33173
"R&B Duo"

Sylvia Kristal
8955 Norma Place
Los Angeles, CA 90069
"Actress"

Marta Kristen
11766 Wilshire Blvd. #1580
Los Angeles, CA 90025
"Actress"

Kris Kristofferson
P.O. Box 2147
Malibu, CA 90265
"Singer, Actor, Writer"

Joan Kroc
8939 Villa La Jolla Drive #201
La Jolla, CA 92037
"Ray Kroc's Widower"

Marty Krofft
7710 Woodrow Wilson Drive
Los Angeles, CA 90046
"Puppeteer, Producer"

Sid Krofft
7710 Woodrow Wilson Drive
Los Angeles, CA 90046
"Puppeteer, Producer"

Hardy Kruger
P.O. Box 726
Crestline, CA 92325
"Actor"

Jack Kruschen
8733 Farralone Avenue
Canoga Park, CA 91304
"Actor"

Mike Krzyzewski
Duke University Basketball
Durham, NC 27706
"Basketball Coach"

Tony Kubek
8323 North Shore Road
Menosha, WI 43952
"Sportscaster"

Stanley Kubrick
P.O. Box 123
Borehamwood, Herts.
ENGLAND
"Film Director"

Lisa Kudrow
8722 Burton Way, #402
Los Angeles, CA 90048
"Actress"

Toni Kukoc
980 North Michigan Ave. #1600
Chicago, IL 60611
"Basketball Player"

Mitch Kupchak
1686 Justin Drive
Crofton, MD 21114
"Ex-Basketball Player"

Akira Kurosawa
Seijo 2-21-6
Setagaya-Ku
Tokyo, JAPAN
"Film Director"

Swoosie Kurtz
320 Central Park West
New York, NY 10025
"Actress"

Kay Kuter
6207 Satsuma Avenue
North Hollywood, CA 91606
"Actress"

Nancy Kwan
4154 Woodman Avenue
Sherman Oaks, CA 91403
"Actress"

Burt Kwouk
2-4 Noel Street
London W1V 3RB ENGLAND
"Actor"

Patti LaBelle
1212 Grennox Road
Wynnewood, PA 19096
"Singer, Actress

Matthew Laborteaux
4555 Mariota Avenue
Toluca Lake, CA 91602
"Actor"

Patrick Laborteaux
1450 Belfast Drive
Los Angeles, CA 90069
"Actor"

Jerry Lacy
10100 Santa Monica Blvd. #2500
Los Angeles, CA 90067
"Actor, Writer, Director"

Alan Ladd, Jr.
312 N. Faring Road
Los Angeles, CA 90077
"Film Executive"

Alana Ladd
1420 Moraga Drive
Los Angeles, CA 90049
"Actress"

Cheryl Ladd
P.O. Box 1329
Santa Ynez, CA 93460
"Actress, Singer"

David Ladd
9212 Hazen Drive
Beverly Hills, CA 90210
"Actor"

Diane Ladd
P.O. Box 17111
Beverly Hills, CA 90209
"Actress"

Margaret Ladd
444-21st Street
Santa Monica, CA 90402
"Actress"

Dr. Arthur Laffer
5375 Executive Square #330
La Jolla, CA 92037
"Economist"

Perry Lafferty
335 South Bristol Avenue
Los Angeles, CA 90049
"TV Executive"

Guy LaFleur
3400 Chemin Ste-Foy
St. Foy, Que. G1X 1X6 CANADA
"Hockey Player"

Christine Lahti
927 Berkeley Street
Santa Monica, CA 90403
"Actress"

Francis Lai
4146 Lankershim Blvd. #401
North Hollywood, CA 91602
"Composer"

Cleo Laine
Wavendon (Old Rectory)
Milton Keynes
MK17 8LT ENGLAND
"Singer"

Frankie Laine
P.O. Box 6910
San Diego, CA 92166
"Singer, Actor"

Melvin Laird
1730 Rhode Island Avenue
Washington, DC 20036
"Ex-Government Official"

Ricki Lake
401 Fifth Avenue
New York, NY 10016
"Actress"

Sir Freddie Laker
138 Cheapside
London EC2V 6BL ENGLAND
"Business Executive"

Jack LaLanne
P.O. Box 1023
San Luis Obispo, CA 93406
"Exercise Instructor"

Donny Lalonde
33 Howard Street
Toronto, Ont. M4X 1J6
CANADA
"Boxer"

Hedy Lamarr
568 Orange Drive #47
Altamonte Springs, FL 32701
"Actress"

Lorenzo Lamas
P.O. Box 500907
San Diego, CA 92150
"Actor"

Gil Lamb
755 Madrid Circle
Palm Springs, CA 92262
"Actor"

Jack Lambert
222 Highland Drive
Carmel, CA 93921
"Football Player"

Jerry Lambert
P.O. Box 25371
Charlotte, NC 28212
"Singer"

L.W. Lambert
Route #1
Olin, NC 28860
"C&W Singer"

Robert Lamm
1113 Sutton Way
Beverly Hills, CA 90210
"Musician, Songwriter"

Jake Lamotta
400 East 57th Street
New York, NY 10022
"Boxer"

Zohra Lampert
10 East 44th St. #500
New York, NY 10017
"Actress"

Jim Lampley
3347 Tareco Drive
Los Angeles, CA 90068
"Sportscaster"

Mark LaMura
10100 Santa Monica Blvd. #2500
Los Angeles, CA 90067
"Actor"

Bert Lance
P.O. Box 637
Calhoun, GA 30701
"Politician"

Martin Landau
7455 Palo Vista Drive
Los Angeles, CA 90046
"Actor"

David L. Lander
7009 West Senalda Drive
Los Angeles, CA 90069
"Actor, Writer"

Ann Landers
435 North Michigan Avenue
Chicago, IL 60611
"Columnist"

Audrey Landers
3112 Nicka Drive
Los Angeles, CA 90077
"Actress, Singer"

Judy Landers
9849 Denbigh
Beverly Hills, CA 90210
"Actress, Model"

Steve Landesburg
355 North Genesee Avenue
Los Angeles, CA 90036
"Actor"

John Landis
9369 Lloydcrest Drive
Beverly Hills, CA 90210
"Film Writer, Director"

Joe Lando
151 El Camino Drive
Beverly Hills, CA 90212
"Actor"

Michael Landon, Jr
9595 Wilshire Blvd. #711
Beverly Hills, CA 90211
"Actor"

Paul Landres
5343 Amestoy Avenue
Encino, CA 91316
"TV Director"

Moon Landrieu
4301 South Prieur
New Orleans, LA 70125
"Ex-Mayor"

Tom Landry
8411 Preston Road #720
Dallas, TX 75225
"Ex-Football Coach"

Vytatis Landsbergis
Parliment House
Vilnius, LITHUANIA
"Politician"

Valerie Landsburg
22745 Chamera Lane
Topanga, CA 90290
"Actress"

Andre Landzaat
7500 Devista Drive
Los Angeles, CA 90046
"Actor"

Abby Lane
444 North Faring Road
Los Angeles, CA 90077
"Actress, Singer"

Charles Lane
321 Gretna Green Way
Los Angeles, CA 90049
"Actor"

Christy Lane
1225 Apache Lane
Madison, TN 37115
"Singer"

Diane Lane
151 El Camino Drive
Beverly Hills, CA 90212
"Actress"

Dick "Night Train" Lane
18100 Meyer
Detroit, MI 48235
"Ex-Football Player"

Nathan Lane
1325 Avenue of the Americas
New York, NY 10019
"Actor"

Eric Laneuville
5138 W. Slauson Avenue
Los Angeles, CA 90056
"Actor"

June Lang-Morgan
12756 Kahlenberg Lane
North Hollywood , CA 91607
"Actress"

Katherine Kelly Lang
317 South Carmelina Avenue
Los Angeles, CA 90049
"Actress"

K.D. Lang
P.O. Box 33800, Station D
Vancouver B.C.
V6J 5C7 CANADA
"Singer"

SueAnne Langdon
12429 Laurel Terrace Drive
Studio City, CA 91604
"Actress"

Robert Lang
68 St. James's Street
London SW1A 1PH ENGLAND
"Actor"

Hope Lange
803 Bramble
Los Angeles, CA 90049
"Actress"

Jessica Lange
9830 Wilshire Blvd.
Beverly Hills, CA 90212
"Actress"

Ted Lange
7420 Carlin Avenue #17
Reseda CA 91335
"Actor, Writer, Director"

Frank Langella
21114 Lighthill Drive
Topanga, CA 90290
"Actor"

Heather Langenkamp
1800 Avenue of the Stars #400
Los Angeles, CA 90067
"Actress"

Bernhard Langer
1120 S.W. 21st Lane
Boca Raton, FL 33486
"Golfer"

Frances Langford
P.O. Box 96
Jensen Beach, FL 33457
"Singer"

Murray Langston
RR #3, Box 4630-31
Tehachapi, CA 93561
"Comedian, Actor"

Lester Lanin
157 West 57th Street
New York, NY 10019
"Band Leader"

Kim Lankford
9911 W. Pico Blvd. #1060
Los Angeles, CA 90035
"Actress"

Angela Lansbury
635 Bonhill Road
Los Angeles, CA 90049
"Actress"

Sherry Lansing
1363 Angelo Drive
Beverly Hills, CA 90210
"Film Executive"

Anthony LaPaglia
8942 Wilshire Blvd.
Beverly Hills, CA 90211
"Actor"

Alison La Placa
8380 Melrose Avenue #207
Los Angeles, CA 90069
"Actress"

Laura La Plante
Motion Picture Country Home
23388 Mulholland Drive
Woodland Hills, CA 91364
"Actress"

Guy LaPointe
2313 West St. Catherine Street
Montreal PQ H3H 1N2 CANADA
"Hockey Player"

Joe Lara
8383 Wilshire Blvd. #954
Beverly Hills, CA 90211
"Actor"

John Larch
4506 Varna Avenue
Sherman Oaks, CA 91403
"Actor"

Ring Lardner, Jr.
55 Central Park West
New York, NY 10023
"Writer"

Rep. Steve Largent (OK)
Cannon House Office Bldg. #410
Washington, DC 20515
"Politician"

Sheila Larkin
1626 North Orange Grove
Los Angeles, CA 90046
"Actress"

Julius LaRosa
67 Sycamore Lane
Irvington, NY 10533
"Actor, Singer"

Lyndon La Rouche
2110 Center Street East
Rochester, MN 55904
"Politician, Cult Leader"

John Larroquette
5874 Dearhead Road
Malibu, CA 90265
"Actor"

Don Larsen
P.O. Box 2863
Hayden Lake, ID 83835
"Ex-Baseball Player"

Darrell Larson
8380 Melrose Avenue #207
Los Angeles, CA 90069
"Actor"

Gary Larson
4900 Main Street #900
Kansas City, MO 62114
"Cartoonist"

Glen Larson
351 Delfern Drive
Los Angeles, CA 90077
"TV Writer, Producer"

Jack Larson
449 Skyway Road North
Los Angeles, CA 90049
"Actor"

Nicolette Larson
3818 Abbot Martin Rd.
Nashville, TN 37215
"Singer, Songwriter"

Wolf Larson
10600 Holman Avenue, #1
Los Angeles, CA 90024
"Actor"

Danny LaRue
57 Gr. Cumberland Place
London W1M 7LJ ENGLAND
"Actor"

Florence La Rue
4300 Louis Avenue
Encino, CA 91316
"Singer"

Eriq LaSalle
P.O. Box 5617
Beverly Hills, CA 90210
"Actor"

Tommy Lasorda
1473 West Maxzim Avenue
Fullerton, CA 92633
"Baseball Manager"

Louise Lasser
200 East 71st Street #20C
New York, NY 10021
"Actor, Writer"

Sydney Lassick
2734 Bellevue
Los Angeles, CA 90026
"Actor"

Fred Lasswell
1111 N. Westshore Blvd. #604
Tampa, FL 33607
"Cartoonist"

Louise Latham
2125 Piedras
Santa Barbara, CA 93108
"Actress"

Queen Latifah
151 El Camino Drive
Beverly Hills, CA 90212
"Rap Singer"

Matt Lattanzi
P.O. Box 2710
Malibu, CA 90265
"Actor"

Niki Lauda
San Costa de Baix
Santa Eucalia IBIZA
SPAIN
"Race Car Driver, Author"

Estee Lauder
767 Fifth Avenue
New York, NY 10153
"Fashion Designer"

John Laughlin
11815 Magnolia Blvd., #2
North Hollywood, CA 91607
"Actor"

Cyndi Lauper
1325 Avenue of the Americas
New York, NY 10019
"Singer, Songwriter"

Matthew Laurance
1951 Hillcrest Road
Los Angeles, CA 90068
"Actor"

Mitchell Laurance
2250 Malcolm Avenue
Los Angeles, CA 90064
"Actor"

Ralph Lauren
1107-5th Avenue
New York, NY 10028
"Fashion Designer"

Tammy Lauren
8899 Beverly Blvd., #700
Los Angeles, CA 90048
"Actress"

Arthur Laurents
P.O. Box 582
Quoque, NY 11959
"Writer"

Dan Lauria
601 North Cherokee Avenue
Los Angeles, CA 90004
"Actor"

Piper Laurie
2210 Wilshire Blvd. #931
Santa Monica, CA 90403
"Actress"

Ed Lauter
1800 Avenue of the Stars #400
Los Angeles, CA 90067
"Actor"

Rod Laver
P.O. Box 4798
Hilton Head, SC 29928
"Tennis Player"

Linda Lavin
20781 Big Rock Road
Malibu, CA 90265
"Actress, Director"

John Phillip Law
1339 Miller Drive
Los Angeles, CA 90069
"Actor"

Patricia Kennedy Lawford
1 Sutton Place South
New York, NY 10021
"Widower of Peter Lawford"

Lucy Lawless
P.O. Box 49859
Los Angeles, CA 90049
"Actress"

Carol Lawrence
12337 Ridge Circle
Los Angeles, CA 90049
"Actress, Singer"

Joey Lawrence
9255 Sunset Blvd. #710
Los Angeles, CA 90069
"Actor"

Linda Lawrence
4926 Commonwealth
La Canada, CA 91011
"Actress"

Marc Lawrence
2200 N. Vista Grande Avenue
Palm Springs, CA 92262
"Actor, Director"

Martin Lawrence
6310 San Vicente Blvd. #407
Los Angeles, CA 90048
"Actor"

Patricia Lawrence
33 St. Luke's Street
London SW3 ENGLAND
"Actress"

Tracy Lawrence
38 Music Square East, #300
Nashville, TN 37203
"Singer"

Vicki Lawrence-Schultz
6000 Lido Avenue
Long Beach, CA 90803
"Actress, Singer"

Hubert Laws
1078 South Ogden Drive
Los Angeles, CA 90019
"Flutist"

Leigh Lawson
162-170 Wardour Street
London W1V 3AT ENGLAND
"Actress"

Paul Laxalt
1455 Pennsylvania Avenue NW
Washington, DC 20004
"Ex-Senator"

George Lazenby
1127-21st Street
Santa Monica, CA 90403
"Actor"

Buddy Lazier
8135 West Crawfordsville
Indianapolis, IN 46224
"Race Car Driver"

Rep. Jim Leach (IA)
Rayburn House Office Bldg. #2186
Washington, DC 20515
"Politician"

Robin Leach
1 Dag Hammarskjold Plaza
21st Floor
New York, NY 10017
"TV Personality"

Cloris Leachman
77 Avenue Road 416
Toronto, Ont. M3R 5R8 CANADA
"Actress"

Sen. Patrick J. Leahy (VT)
Senate Russell Bldg. #433
Washington, DC 20510
"Politician"

Amanda Lear
Postfach 800149
D-81601 Munich GERMANY
"Singer, Actress"

Norman Lear
1999 Avenue of the Stars #500
Los Angeles, CA 90067
"TV Writer, Producer"

Michael Learned
1600 N. Beverly Drive
Beverly Hills, CA 90210
"Actress"

Brianne Leary
9229 Sunset Blvd. #311
Los Angeles, CA 90069
"Actress"

Denis Leary
9560 Wilshire Blvd. #516
Beverly Hills, CA 90212
"Commedian"

Sabrina LeBeauf
15 Wavecrest Avenue
Venice, CA 90291
"Actress"

Matt LeBlanc
11766 Wilshire Blvd. #1470
Los Angeles, CA 90025
"Actor"

Kelly LeBrock
2282 Mandeville Canyon
Los Angeles, CA 90049
"Actress, Model"

John Le Carre
9 Gainsborough Gardens
London NW3 1BJ ENGLAND
"Writer"

Francis Lederer
23134 Sherman Way
Canoga Park, CA 91307
"Actor, Director"

Chris Ledoux
4205 Hillsboro Road #208
Nashville, TN 37215
"Singer, Songwriter"

Anna Lee
4031 Hollyline Avenue
Sherman Oaks, CA 91423
"Actress"

Billy Lee
P.O. Box 3217
Beaumont, CA 92223
"Actor"

Brenda Lee
2175 Carson Street
Nashville, TN 37210
"Singer"

Christopher Lee
21 Golden Square #200
London W1R 3PA ENGLAND
"Actor"

Dorothy Lee
434 Santa Dominga
Solana Beach, CA 92075
"Actress"

Hyapatia Lee
15127 Califa Street
Van Nuys, CA 91411
"Actress, Model"

Jason Scott Lee
P.O. Box 1083
Pearl City, HI 96782
"Actor"

Johnny Lee
1851 Gulf Freeway South #3
League City, TX 77573
"Singer, Songwriter"

Kathy Lee
204 River Edge Lane
Seiverville, TN 37862
"Singer"

Michelle Lee
830 Birchwood
Los Angeles, CA 90024
"Actress, Singer"

Peggy Lee
11404 Bellagio Road
Los Angeles, CA 90024
"Singer, Actress"

Ruta Lee
2623 Laurel Canyon Road
Los Angeles, CA 90046
"Actress"

Dr. Sammy Lee
16537 Harbour Lane
Huntington Beach, CA 92649
"Physician, Athlete"

Sheryl Lee
331 North Martel
Los Angeles, CA 90036
"Actress"

Spike Lee
40 Acres & A Mule Film Works
124 De Kalb Avenue #2
Brooklyn, NY 11217
"Actor, Film Director"

Stan Lee
1440 S. Sepulveda Blvd. #114
Los Angeles, CA 90025
"Cartoonist"

Beverly Leech
9150 Wilshire Blvd. #175
Beverly Hills, CA 90212
"Actress"

Richard Leech
27 Clayland's Road
London SW8 1NX ENGLAND
"Actor"

Peter Leeds
626 North Screenland Drive
Burbank, CA 91505
"Actor"

Jane Leeves
9560 Wilshire Blvd. #516
Beverly Hills, CA 90212
"Actress"

Jim Lefebvre
1060 West Addison Street
Chicago, IL 60613
"Actor"

John Leguizamo
151 El Camino Dr.
Beverly Hills, CA 90212
"Actor"

Jim Lehrer
1775 Broadway #608
New York, NY 10019
"Broadcast Journalist"

Ron Leibman
10530 Strathmore Drive
Los Angeles, CA 90024
"Actor, Writer"

Annie Leibovitz
55 Vandam Street
New York, NY 10013
"Photographer"

Janet Leigh
1625 Summitridge Drive
Beverly Hills, CA 90210
"Actress"

Jennifer Jason Leigh
2400 Whitman Place
Los Angeles, CA 90068
"Actress"

Mike Leigh
8 Earlham Grove
London N22 ENGLAND
"Film Writer, Director"

Laura Leighton
8033 Sunset Blvd., #4048
Los Angeles, CA 90046
"Actress"

Roberta Leighton
20700 Ventura Blvd. #240
Woodland Hills, CA 91364
"Actress"

David Leisure
8428-C Melrose Place
Los Angeles, CA 90069
"Actor"

Donovan Leitch
8528 Walnut Drive
Los Angeles, CA 90046
"Actor"

Claude LeLouch
15 Avenue Foch
F-75016 Paris, FRANCE
"Director, Producer"

Paul Le Mat
1100 North Alta Loma #805
Los Angeles, CA 90069
"Actor"

Michael Lembeck
13530 Erwin Street
Van Nuys, CA 91401
"Actor"

Christopher Lemmon
80 Murray Drive
South Glastonbury, CT 06073
"Actor"

Jack Lemmon
141 South El Camino Drive #201
Beverly Hills, CA 90212
"Actor, Director"

Bob Lemon
95 Fairway Lakes
Myrtle Beach, SC 29577
"Baseball Manager"

Greg Lemond
1101 Wilson Blvd. #1800
Arlington, VA 22209
"Bicyclist"

Mark Lenard
6767 Forest Lawn Drive #115
Los Angeles, CA 90068
"Actor"

Ivan Lendl
60 Arch Street
Greenwich, CT 06830
"Tennis Player"

Julian Lennon
12721 Mulholland Drive
Beverly Hills, CA 90210
"Singer, Composer"

Sean Lennon
1 West 72nd Street
New York, NY 10023
"Singer, Composer"

Lennon Sisters
1984 State Highway 165
Branson, MO 65616
"Vocal Group"

Annie Lennox
31/32 Soho Square
London W1V 5DG ENGLAND
"Singer"

Jay Leno
P.O. Box 7885
Burbank, CA 91510
"TV Show Host, Comedian"

Rula Lenska
306-16 Euston Road
London NW13 ENGLAND
"Actress"

Kay Lenz
9255 Sunset Blvd. #515
Los Angeles, CA 90069
"Actress"

Rick Lenz
12955 Calvert Street
Van Nuys, CA 91401
"Actor"

Michael Leon
P.O. Box 241609
Los Angeles, CA 90024
"Actor"

Buck Leonard
605 Atlantic Ave.
Rocky Mount, NC 27807
"Ex-Baseball Player"

Elmore Leonard
2192 Yarmouth Road
Bloomfield Village, MI 48301
"Author, Screenwriter"

Lu Leonard
12245 Chandler Blvd.
North Hollywood, CA 91607
"Actress"

Robert Sean Leonard
P.O. Box 454
Sea Isle City, NJ 08243
"Actor"

Sheldon Leonard
1141 Loma Vista Drive
Beverly Hills, CA 90210
"Actor, Director"

Sugar Ray Leonard
4922 Fairmont Avenue #200
Bethesda, MD 20814
"Boxer"

Tea Leoni
248 Horizon #1
Venice, CA 90291
"Actress"

Michael Lerner
8347 Sunset View
Los Angeles, CA 90069
"Actress"

Gloria LeRoy
3500 West Olive Avenue #1400
Burbank, CA 91505
"Actress"

Aleen Leslie
1700 Lexington Road
Beverly Hills, CA 90210
"Writer"

Bethel Leslie
393 West End Avenue #11C
New York, NY 10024
"Actress, Writer"

Joan Leslie
2228 North Catilina Avenue
Los Angeles, CA 90027
"Actress"

Lenn Lesser
934 N. Evergreen St.
Burbank, CA 91505
"Actor"

Doris Lessing
11 Kingscroft Road #3
London NW2 3QE ENGLAND
"Author"

Ketty Lester
5931 Comey Avenue
Los Angeles, CA 90034
"Actress"

Mark Lester
Carlton Clinic
Cheltenham ENGLAND
"Singer, Actor"

Richard Lester
River Land
Petersham Surrey, ENGLAND
"Film Director, Composer"

Terry Lester
15760 Ventura Blvd. #1730
Encino, CA 91436
"Actor"

Tom Lester
P.O. Box 1854
Beverly Hills, CA 90213
"Actor"

Jared Leto
1999 Ave. of the Stars #2850
Los Angeles, CA 90067
"Actor"

David Letterman
1697 Broadway
New York, NY 10019
"TV Show Host"

Shelby Leverington
1801 Avenue of the Stars #1250
Los Angeles, CA 90067
"Actress"

Le Vert
110-112 Lantoga Road #D
Wayne, PA 19087
"Singer, Songwriter"

Sen. Carl Levin (MI)
Senate Russell Bldg. #459
Washington, DC 20510
"Politician"

Ira Levin
40 East 49th Street
New York, NY 10017
"Author"

Rep. Sander Levin (MI)
House Cannon Bldg. #106
Washington, DC 20515
"Politician"

Ted Levine
1999 Ave. of the Stars #2850
Los Angeles, CA 90067
"Actor"

Barry Levinson
9830 Wilshire Blvd.
Beverly Hills, CA 90212
"Film Writer, Director"

Gene Levitt
9200 Sunset Blvd., PH. 25
Los Angeles, CA 90069
"TV Writer, Director"

Al Lewis
P.O. Box 277
New York, NY 10044
"Actor"

Carl Lewis
P.O. Box 571990
Houston, TX 77082
"Track & Field Athlete"

Clea Lewis
1999 Avenue of the Stars, #2850
Los Angeles, CA 90067
"Actress"

Dawnn Lewis
9229 Sunset Blvd. #607
Los Angeles, CA 90069
"Actress"

Geoffrey Lewis
19756 Collier
Woodland Hills, CA 91364
"Actor"

Huey Lewis
P.O. Box 819
Mill Valley, CA 94942
"Singer"

Jennifer Lewis
8730 Sunset Blvd., #480
Los Angeles, CA 90069
"Actress"

Jerry Lewis
1701 Waldman Avenue
Las Vegas, NV 89102
"Comedian, Actor"

Jerry Lee Lewis
P.O. Box 3864
Memphis, TN 38173
"Singer, Composer"

Rep. John Lewis (GA)
Cannon House Office Bldg. #329
Washington, DC 20515
"Politician"

Juliette Lewis
151 El Camino Drive
Beverly Hills, CA 90212
"Actress"

Lennox Lewis
811 Totowa Road #100
Totowa, NJ 07512
"Boxer"

Ramsey Lewis
370 Harrison Avenue
Harrison, NY 10528
"Pianist, Composer"

Richard Lewis
8170 Beverly Blvd. #305
Los Angeles, CA 90048
"Actor"

Shari Lewis
603 North Alta Drive
Beverly Hills, CA 90210
"Ventriloquist"

John Leyton
53 Keyes House, Dophin Sq.
London SW1V 3NA ENGLAND
"Actor"

Richard Libertini
2313 McKinley Avenue
Venice, CA 90291
"Actor"

Jeremy Licht
2029 Century Park E. #600
Los Angeles, CA 90067
"Actor"

G. Gordon Liddy
9112 Riverside Drive
Ft. Washington, MD 20744
"Talk Show Host"

Sen. Joseph I Lieberman (CT)
Senate Hart Bldg. #502
Washington, DC 20510
"Politician"

Judith Light
2934 Beverly Glen Circle #30
Los Angeles, CA 90077
"Actress"

Gordon Lightfoot
1365 Yonge Street #207
Toronto, Ontario
M4T 2P7 CANADA
"Singer, Songwriter"

Leonard Lightfoot
446 South Orchard Drive
Burbank, CA 91506
"Actor"

Tom Ligon
227 Waverly Place
New York, NY 10014
"Actor"

Arthur L. Liman
1285 Avenue of the Americas
New York, NY 10019
"Musician"

Rush Limbaugh
366 Madison Avenue #700
New York, NY 10117
"Radio & TV Talk Show Host"

Scott Lincoln
1305 N. Laurel #111
Los Angeles, CA 90046
"Actor"

Ann Morrow Lindbergh
Scotts Cove
Darien, CT 06820
"Aviatrix, Author"

Hal Linden
151 El Camino Drive
Beverly Hills, CA 90212
"Actor, Director"

Kate Linden
9111 Wonderland Avenue
Los Angeles, CA 90046
"Actress"

Vivica Lindfors
172 East 95th Street
New York, NY 10028
"Actress"

Astrid Lindgren
Dalagatan 46
11314 Stockholm, SWEDEN
"Author"

Audra Lindley
317 S. Carmelina Avenue
Los Angeles, CA 90049
"Actress"

Delroy Lindo
151 El Camino Drive
Beverly Hills, CA 90212
"Actor"

Eric Lindros
1 Pattison Place
Philadelphia, PA 19148
"Hockey Player"

Mark Lindsay
P.O. Box 544
Grangeville, ID 83530
"Singer, Composer"

Robert Lindsay
1 Robert Street
London WC2N 6BH ENGLAND
"Actor"

Pia Lindstrom
30 Rockefeller Plaza
7th Floor
New York, NY 10020
"Film Critic"

Art Linkletter
1100 Bel Air Road
Los Angeles, CA 90077
"TV Personality"

Jack Linkletter
765 Baker Street
Costa Mesa, CA 92626
"TV Personality"

Mark Linn-Baker
7102 La Presa Drive
Los Angeles, CA 90068
"Actor"

Teri Ann Linn
4267 Marina City Drive #312
Marina del Rey, CA 90292
"Actress"

Joanne Linville
3148 Fryman Road
Studio City, CA 91604
"Actress"

Ray Liotta
955 South Carrillo Drive #300
Los Angeles, CA 90048
"Actor"

Peggy Lipton
15250 Ventura Blvd. #900
Sherman Oaks, CA 91403
"Actress"

Robert Lipton
9300 Wilshire Blvd. #410
Beverly Hills, CA 90212
"Actor"

Lisa Lisa
747-10th Avenue
New York, NY 10019
"R&B Group"

Verna Lisi
Via di Filomarino 4
Rome, ITALY
"Actress"

John Lithgow
1319 Warnall Avenue
Los Angeles, CA 90024
"Actor"

Little River Band
87-91 Palmerstin Cres.
Albert Park
Melbourne, Vic 3206
AUSTRALIA
"Rock & Roll Group"

Rich Little
8916 Canyon Spring Road
Las Vegas, NV 89117
"Actor, Comedian"

Little Richard
Hyatt Sunset Hotel
8401 Sunset Blvd.
Los Angeles, CA 90069
"Singer, Songwriter"

Tawny Little
5515 Melrose Avenue
Los Angeles, CA 90038
"TV Show Host"

Big Tiny Little
West 3985 Taft Drive
Spokane, WA 98208
"Singer, Songwriter"

Gene Littler
P.O. Box 1919
Rancho Santa Fe, CA 92067
"Golfer"

Robyn Lively
9200 Sunset Blvd., #625
Los Angeles, CA 90069
"Actress"

Barry Livingston
8271 Melrose Avenue #202
Los Angeles, CA 90046
"Actor"

Stanley Livingston
P.O. Box 1782
Studio City, CA 91604
"Actor"

LL Cool J
298 Elizabeth Street
New York, NY 10012
"Rap Singer"

Doug Llewelyn
8075 West Third Street #303
Los Angeles, CA 90048
"Actor"

Christopher Lloyd
P.O. Box 491264
Los Angeles, CA 90049
"Actor"

Emily Lloyd
9560 wilshire Blvd. #500
Beverly Hills, CA 90212
"Actress"

Norman Lloyd
1813 Old Ranch Road
Los Angeles, CA 90049
"Actor, Director"

Tony Lo Bianco
15301 Ventura Blvd. #345
Sherman Oaks, CA 91403
"Actor, Writer, Director"

Amy Locane
8942 Wilshire Blvd.
Beverly Hills, CA 90211
"Actress"

Dick Locher
435 N. Michigan Avenue
Chicago, IL 60611
"Cartoonist"

Sondra Locke
P.O. Box 69865
Los Angeles, CA 90069
"Actress"

Brad Lockerman
1800 Avenue of the Stars #400
Los Angeles, CA 90067
"Actor"

Anne Lockhart
28245 Driver Avenue
Agoura Hills, CA 91301
"Actress"

June Lockhart
404 San Vicente Blvd. #208
Santa Monica, CA 90402
"Actress"

Heather Locklear
4970 Summit View Drive
Westlake Village, CA 91362
"Actress, Model"

Gary Lockwood
3083 1/2 Rambla Pacifica
Malibu, CA 90265
"Actor"

David Lodge
8 Sydney Road
Richmond, Surrey, ENGLAND
"Actor"

Phyllis Logan
47 Courtfield Road #9
London SW7 4DB ENGLAND
"Actress"

Robert Logan
10637 Burbank Blvd.
North Hollywood, CA 91601
"Actor"

Robert Loggia
12659 Promontory Road
Los Angeles, CA 90049
"Actor, Director"

Kenny Loggins
3281 Padaro Lane
Carpinteria, CA 93013
"Singer, Songwriter"

Gina Lollobrigida
Via Appino Antica 223
I-00179 Rome, ITALY
"Actress"

Herbert Lom
76 Oxford Street
London W1N 0AX ENGLAND
"Actor"

Jeremy London
9200 Sunset Blvd., #625
Los Angeles, CA 90069
"Actor"

Julie London
16074 Royal Oaks
Encino, CA 91436
"Actress, Singer"

John Lone
9560 Wilshire Blvd. #500
Beverly Hills, CA 90212
"Actor"

Howie Long
514 South Juanita Avenue
Redondo Beach, CA 90277
"Football Player"

Shelley Long
15237 Sunset Blvd.
Pacific Palisades, CA 90272
"Actress"

Johnny Longdon
5401 Palmer Drive
Banning, CA 92220
"Actor"

Tony Longo
24 Westwind Street
Marina del Rey, CA 90292
"Actor"

Mike Lookinland
2839 East 2960 South
Salt Lake City, UT 84109
"Actor"

Rod Loomis
12600 Miranda Street
No. Hollywood, CA 91607
"Actor"

Al Lopez
3601 Beach Street
Tampa, FL 33609
"Ex-Baseball Player"

Mario Lopez
4526 Wilshire Blvd.
Los Angeles, CA 90010
"Actor"

Nancy Lopez
1 Erieview Plaza #1300
Cleveland, OH 44114
"Golfer"

Trini Lopez
1139 Abrigo Road
Palm Springs, CA 92762
"Singer, Actress"

John Loprieno
924 Westwood Blvd. #900
Los Angeles, CA 90024
"Actor"

Stefan Lorant
215 West Mountain Road
Lenox, MA 01240
"Photojournalist, Author"

Jack Lord
4999 Kahala Avenue
Honolulu, HI 96816
"Actor"

Marjorie Lord
1110 Maytor Place
Beverly Hills, CA 90210
"Actress"

Traci Lords
9150 Wilshire Blvd. #175
Beverly Hills, CA 90212
"Actress"

Sophia Loren
1151 Hidden Valley Road
Thousand Oaks, CA 91360
"Actress"

Gloria Loring
4125 Parva Avenue
Los Angeles, CA 90027
"Singer, Actress"

Lisa Loring
4706 Ketherine Avenue
Sherman Oaks, CA 91423
"Actress"

Joan Lorring
345 East 68th Street
New York, NY 10021
"Actress"

Sen. Trent Lott (MS)
Senate Russell Bldg. #487
Washington, DC 20510
"Politician"

Dorothy Loudon
101 Central Park West
New York, NY 10023
"Actress"

Greg Louganis
P.O. Box 4068
Malibu, CA 90265
"Diver"

Lori Loughlin
9279 Sierra Mar Drive
Los Angeles, CA 90069
"Actress"

Julia Louis-Dreyfus
9150 Wilshire Blvd. #205
Beverly Hills, CA 90212
"Actress"

Tina Louise
310 East 46th Street #18T
New York, NY 10017
"Actress"

Col. Jack R. Lousma
2722 Roseland Street
Ann Arbor, MI 48103
"Astronaut"

Courtney Love
955 South Carrillo Drive #200
Los Angeles, CA 90048
"Singer"

Peter Love
P.O. Box 4826
Valley Village, CA 91617
"Actor"

Love & Rockets
4, The Lakes
Bushey, Hertsfordshire
WD2 1HS ENGLAND
"Rock & Roll Group"

Linda Lovelace
120 Enterprise
Secaucus, NJ 07094
"Actress"

Patty Loveless
1908 Wedgewood Avenue
Nashville, TN 37212
"Singer"

James Lovell
5725 East River Road
Chicago, IL 60611
"Astronaut"

Loverboy
406-68 Water Street
Gastown, Vancouver B.C.
VGB 1AY CANADA
"Rock & Roll Group"

Lyle Lovett
c/o General Delivery
Klein, TX 77391
"Singer"

Jon Lovitz
4735 Vivinana Drive
Tarzana, CA 91356
"Actor"

Dale Lowdermilk
P.O. Box 5743
Montecito, CA 93150
"Actor"

Barry Lowe
31 South Audley Street
London W1 ENGLAND
"Actor"

Chad Lowe
7920 Sunset Blvd. 4th Flr.
Los Angeles, CA 90046
"Actor"

Rob Lowe
270 N. Canon Drive #1072
Beverly Hills, CA 902120
"Actor"

Carey Lowell
8942 Wilshire Blvd.
Beverly Hills, CA 90211
"Model, Actress"

George Lucas
P.O. Box 2009
San Rafael, CA 94912
"Writer, Producer, Director"

Susan Lucci
P.O. Box 621
Quogue, NY 11959
"Actress"

Gloria Luchenbill
415 South Shirley Place
Beverly Hills, CA 90212
"Actress"

Laurance Luckenbill
RR #3 Flintlock Ridge Road
Katonah, NY 10536
"Actor"

William Lucking
10100 Santa Monica Blvd. #700
Los Angeles, CA 90067
"Actor"

Sid Luckman
5303 St. Charles Road
Bellwood, IL 60104
"Ex-Football Player"

Lorna Luft
9100 Wilshire Blvd. #455
Beverly Hills, CA 90212
"Actress"

Sen. Richard Lugar (IN)
306 Hart Office Bldg.
Washington, DC 20510
"Politician"

Bela Lugosi, Jr.
1029 Flintridge Avenue #1
La Canada, CA 91011
"Actor"

James Luisi
14315 Riverside Drive #1
Sherman Oaks, CA 91423
"Actor"

Johnny Lujack
6321 Crow Valley Drive
Bettendorf, IA 52722
"Ex-Football Player"

Lulu
22 D'Arblay Street #100
London W1V 3FP ENGLAND
"Singer, Actress"

Lulabel & Scottie
P.O. Box 171132
Nashville, TN 37217
"Vocal Group"

Carl Lumbly
924 Westwood Blvd. #900
Los Angeles, CA 90024
"Actor"

Sidney Lumet
1 West 81st Street
New York, NY 10024
"Film Writer, Director"

Joanna Lumley
23 Crescent Lane
London SW4 9PT ENGLAND
"Actress"

Robert Ludlum
P.O. Box 235
Bedford Hills, NY 10507
"Novelist"

Barbara Luna
18026 Rodarte Way
Encino, CA 91316
"Actress"

Deanna Lund
545 Howard Street
Salem, VA 24153
"Actress"

Lucille Lund
3424 Shore Heights Drive
Malibu, CA 90265
"Actress"

Joan Lunden
1965 Broadway #400
New York, NY 10023
"TV Show Host"

Dolph Lundgren
151 El Camino Drive
Beverly Hills, CA 90212
"Bodybuilder, Actor"

Steve Lundquist
3448 Southbay Drive
Jonesboro, GA 30236
"Swimmer"

Jessica Lundy
3500 W. Olive Ave. #1400
Burbank, CA 91505
"Actress"

Ida Lupino
12116 Hesby Street
North Hollywood, CA 91607
"Actress, Writer"

Patti LuPone
40 West 57th Street
New York, NY 10019
"Singer"

Peter Lupus
11375 Dona Lisa Drive
Studio City, CA 91604
"Actor"

Nellie Lutcher
1524 La Baig Avenue
Los Angeles, CA 90028
"Pianist, Vocalist"

Frank Luz
606 North Larchmont Blvd. #309
Los Angeles, CA 90004
"Actor"

Greg Luzinski
620 Jackson Road
Medford, NJ 08055
"Ex-Baseball Player"

Jacki Lyden
c/o National Public Radio
2025 "M" Street NW
Washington, DC 20036
"News Correspondent"

Jimmy Lydon
1317 Los Arboles Avenue N.W.
Albuquerque, NM 87107
"Actor"

A.C. Lyles
2115 Linda Flora
Los Angeles, CA 90024
"Writer, Producer"

Dorothy Lyman
1930 Century Park West #403
Los Angeles, CA 90067
"Actress"

David Lynch
P.O. Box 93624
Los Angeles, CA 90093
"TV Writer"

Kelly Lynch
1970 Mandeville Canyon Road
Los Angeles, CA 90049
"Actress"

Richard Lynch
8271 Melrose Avenue #202
Los Angeles, CA 90046
"Actor"

Carol Lynley
P.O. Box 2190
Malibu, CA 90265
"Actress"

Betty Lynn
10424 Tennessee Avenue
Los Angeles, CA 90064
"Actress"

Fred Lynn
24 Haykey Way
Boston, MA 02115
"Ex-Baseball Player"

Jeffrey Lynn
2621 Deep Canyon Drive
Beverly Hills, CA 90210
"Actor"

Loretta Lynn
P.O. Box 120369
Nashville, TN 37212
"Singer"

Dame Vera Lynn
Ditchling
Sussex ENGLAND
"Singer, Actress"

Jeff Lynne
2621 Deep Canyon Drive
Beverly Hills, CA 90210
"Musician, Composer"

Lynyrd Skynyrd
3423 Piedmont Road NE #220
Atlanta, GA 30305
"Music Group"

Sue Lyon
1244 North Havenhurst Drive
Los Angeles, CA 90046
"Actress"

Jeffrey Lyons
205 W. 57th Street
New York, NY 10019
"Film Critic"

Phyllis Lyons
8949 Sunset Blvd. #202
Los Angeles, CA 90069
"Actress"

Robert F. Lyons
1801 Avenue of the Stars #1250
Los Angeles, CA 90067
"Actor"

M

Andrea McArdle
713 Disaton Street
Philadelphia, PA 19111
"Actress"

Alex McArthur
10435 Wheatland Avenue
Sunland, CA 91040
"Actor"

Diane McBain
27533 Cherry Creek Drive
Valencia, CA 91355
"Actress"

Martina McBride
406-68 Water Street
Vancouver BC V6B 1A4
CANADA
"Singer"

Amanda McBroom
9150 Wilshire Blvd. #175
Beverly Hills, CA 90212
"Singer, Songwriter"

Frances Lee McCain
8075 West 3rd Street #303
Los Angeles, CA 90048
"Actress"

Sen. John McCain (AZ)
Senate Russell Bldg. #111
Washington, DC 20510
"Politician"

Mitzi McCall
3635 Wrightwood Drive
Studio City, CA 91604
"Actress"

Irish McCalla
920 Oak Terrace
Prescott, AZ 86301
"Actress"

Lon McCallister
P.O. Box 6030
Stateline, NV 89449
"Actor"

David McCallum
91 The Grove
London N13 5JS ENGLAND
"Actor"

Napoleon McCallum
332 Center Street
El Segundo, CA 90245
"Football Player"

Mercedes McCambridge
2500 Torrey Pines Road #1203
La Jolla, CA 92037
"Actress"

Chuck McCann
2941 Briar Knoll Drive
Los Angeles, CA 90046
"Actor, Comedian"

Les McCann
4031 Panama Court
Piedmont, CA 94611
"Musician, Composer"

Fred McCarren
9200 Sunset Blvd. #710
Los Angeles, CA 90069
"Actor"

Chris McCarron
3328 Clarendon Drive #216
Beverly Hills, CA 90210
"Jockey"

Andrew McCarthy
4708 Vesper Avenue
Sherman Oaks, CA 91403
"Actor"

Eugene McCarthy
271 Hawlin Road
Woodville, VA 22749
"Ex-Senator"

Jenny McCarthy
2112 Broadway
Santa Monica, CA 90404
"MTV Host/Model"

Kevin McCarthy
14854 Sutton Street
Sherman Oaks, CA 91403
"Actor"

Lin McCarthy
233 North Swall Drive
Beverly Hills, CA 90210
"Actor"

Nobu McCarthy
9229 Sunset Blvd., #311
Los Angeles, CA 90069
"Actor"

Paul McCartney
Waterfall Estate
Peamarsh, St. Leonard-on-Sea
Sussex ENGLAND
"Singer, Composer"

Tim McCarver
1518 Youngford Road
Gladwynne, PA 19035
"Ex-Baseball Player"

Constance McCashin
2037 Desford Drive
Beverly Hills, CA 90210
"Actress"

Peggy McCay
8811 Wonderland Avenue
Los Angeles, CA 90046
"Actress"

Rue McClanahan
9454 Wilshire Blvd. #405
Beverly Hills, CA 90212
"Actress"

Sarah McClendon
2933-28th Street N.W.
Washington, DC 20006
"News Correspondent"

Leigh McCloskey
8730 Sunset Blvd. #220W
Los Angeles, CA 90069
"Actor"

Paul McCloskey
2200 Gengo Road
Palo Alto, CA 94304
"Ex-Congressman"

Marc McClure
1420 Beaudry Blvd.
Glendale, CA 91208
"Actor"

Edie McClurg
145 S. Fairfax Avenue #310
Los Angeles, CA 90036
"Actress"

Rep. Bill McCollum (FL)
House Rayburn Bldg. #266
Washington, DC 20515
"Politician"

Judith McConnell
3300 Bennett Drive
Los Angeles, CA 90068
"Actress"

Sen. Mitch McConnell (KY)
Senate Russell Bldg. #120
Washington, DC 20510
"Politician"

Marilyn McCoo-Davis
P.O. Box 7905
Beverly Hills, CA 90212
"Singer"

John McCook
7800 Beverly Blvd. #3371
Los Angeles, CA 90036
"Actor, Writer, Director"

Patty McCormack
14723 Magnolia Blvd.
Sherman Oaks, CA 91403
"Actress"

Maureen McCormick
151 El Camino Drive
Beverly Hills, CA 90212
"Actress"

Pat McCormick
P.O. Box 250
Seal Beach, CA 90740
"Swimmer"

Alec McCowen
3 Goodwins Court
St. Martin's Lane
London WG2 ENGLAND
"Actor"

Charlie McCoy
P.O. Box 158558
Nashville, TN 37215
"Singer, Guitarist"

Matt McCoy
4526 Wilshire Blvd.
Los Angeles, CA 90010
"Actor"

George McCrae
495 S.E. 10th Court
Hialeah, FL 33010
"Singer, Songwriter"

Gwen McCrae
495 S.E. 10th Court
Hialeah, FL 33010
"Singer, Songwriter"

Jody McCrea
Rt#1, Box 575
Camarillo, CA 93010
"Actor"

Julie McCullough
8033 Sunset Blvd. #353
Los Angeles, CA 90046
"Model"

Kimberly McCullough
9200 Sunset Blvd. #625
Los Angeles, CA 90069
"Actress"

Shanna McCullough
7920 Alabama Avenue
Canoga Park, CA 91304
"Actress"

James McDaniel
8730 Sunset Blvd., #480
Los Angeles, CA 90069
"Actor"

Mel McDaniel
191 Dickerson Bay Road
Gallatin, TN 37066
"Singer"

Brian McDermott
27 Upper Berkeley Street
London W1 ENGLAND
"Actor"

Dylan McDermott
2700 Neilson Way #1133
Santa Monica, CA 90405
"Actor"

James McDivitt
P.O. Box 3105
Anaheim, CA 92803
"Astrouaut"

Christopher McDonald
8033 Sunset Blvd. #4011
Los Angeles, CA 90046
"Actor"

"Country" Joe McDonald
17337 Ventura Blvd. #208
Encino, CA 91316
"Singer"

Grace McDonald
6115 Lincoln Drive
Minneapolis, MN 55436
"Singer, Dancer"

Mary McDonnell
P.O. Box 6010-540
Sherman Oaks, CA 91413
"Actress"

Mary McDonough
6858 Cantelope Avenue
Van Nuys, CA 91405
"Actress"

Frances McDormand
333 West End Avenue #12C
New York, NY 10023
"Actress"

Malcolm McDowall
76 Oxford Street
London W1N OAX ENGLAND
"Actor"

Roddy McDowall
3110 Brookdale Road
Studio City, CA 91604
"Actor"

Ronnie McDowell
P.O. Box 53
Portland, TN 37148
"Singer"

Peter McEnery
9 Cork Street
London W1 ENGLAND
"Actor"

John McEnroe
23712 Malibu Colony Road
Malibu, CA 90265
"Tennis Player"

Reba McEntire
511 Fairground Court
Nashville, TN 37204
"Singer"

Geraldine McEwan
308 Regent Street
London W1 ENGLAND
"Actress"

Gates McFadden
1999 Avenue of the Stars
Suite #2850
Los Angeles, CA 90067
"Actor"

Robert C. McFarlane
3414 Prospect Street N.W.
Washington, DC 20007
"Politician"

Bobby McFerrin
853 Broadway #1901
New York, NY 10003
"Singer"

Paul McGann
7 Windmill Street
London W1 ENGLAND
"Actor"

Darren McGavin
P.O. Box 2939
Beverly Hills, CA 90213
"Actor"

Henry McGee
47 Courtfield Road #20
London SW7 4DB ENGLAND
"Actor"

Kirk McGee
P.O Box 626
Franklin, TN 37064
"Singer"

Vonetta McGee
1801 Avenue of the Stars #902
Los Angeles, CA 90067
"Actress"

Howard McGinnin
151 El Camino Drive
Beverly Hills, CA 90212
"Actor, Singer"

Kelly McGillis
303 Whitehead Street
Key West, FL 33040
"Actress"

Ted McGinley
14951 Alva Drive
Pacific Palisades, CA 90272
"Actor"

Patrick McGoohan
16808 Bollinger Drive
Pacific Palisades, CA 90272
"Actor, Writer, Producer"

Elizabeth McGovern
17319 Magnolia Blvd.
Encino, CA 91316
"Actress"

George McGovern
Box 5591, Friendship Station
Washington, DC 20016
"Ex-Senator"

Maureen McGovern
163 Amsterdam Avenue #174
New York, NY 10023
"Singer"

Tim McGraw
47 Music Square East
Nashville, TN 37201
"Singer"

Tug McGraw
1518 Grace Lake Circle
Longwood, FL 32750
"Ex-Baseball Player"

Dorothy McGuire
121 Copley Place
Beverly Hills, CA 90210
"Actress"

Phyllis McGuire
100 Rancho Circle
Las Vegas, NV 89119
"Singer"

McGuire Sisters
100 Rancho Circle
Las Vegas, NV 89119
"Vocal Group"

Mark McGwire
2329 Siena Court
Claremont, CA 91711
"Baseball Player"

Stephen McHattie
9229 Sunset Blvd. #710
Los Angeles, CA 90069
"Actor"

Gardner McKay
252 Lumahai Place
Honolulu, HI 96825
"Actor"

Jim McKay
2805 Sheppard Road
Monkton, MD 21111
"Sportscaster"

John McKay
1 Buccaneer Road
Tampa, FL 33607
"Football Coach"

Wanda McKay
P.O. Box "Y"
Rancho Mirage, CA 92270
"Actress"

Michael McKean
833 Thornhill Road
Calabasas, CA 91302
"Actor"

Lonette McKee
130 West 57th Street, #5B
New York, NY 10019
"Actress"

Todd McKee
32362 Lake Pleasant Drive
Westlake Village, CA 91361
"Actor"

Danica McKellar
6212 Banner
Los Angeles, CA 90068
"Actress"

Sir Ian McKellen
25 Earl's Terrace
London W8 ENGLAND
"Actor"

Virginia McKenna
67 Glebe Place
London SW3 5JB ENGLAND
"Actress"

Julia McKenzie
Richmond Park
Kingston Surrey, ENGLAND
"Actress"

Doug McKeon
818-6th Street #202
Santa Monica, CA 90403
"Actor"

Nancy McKeon
P.O. Box 6778
Burbank, CA 91510
"Actress"

Philip McKeon
P.O. Box 1272
Studio City, CA 91604
"Actor"

Leo McKern
29 Roehampton Gate
London SW15 5JR ENGLAND
"Actor"

Gov. John McKernan (ME)
Executive Department
State House Station #1
Augusta, ME 04333
"Governor"

Tamara McKinney
4935 Parkers Mill Road
Lexington, KY 40502
"Skier"

Rod McKuen
1155 Angelo Drive
Beverly Hills, CA 90210
"Singer, Poet"

Andrew McLaglen
P.O. Box 1056
Friday Harbor, WA 98250
"Film Director"

Denny McLain
11994 Hyne Road
Brighton, MI 48116
"Ex-Baseball Player"

John McLaughlin
1211 Connecticut Avenue N.W.
Washington, DC 20036
"News Correspondent"

Don McLean
1282 Route 376
Wappinger's Falls, NY 12590
"Singer, Songwriter"

Catherine McLeod
4146 Allott Avenue
Van Nuys, CA 91423
"Actress"

Allyn Ann McLerie
3344 Campanil Drive
Santa Barbara, CA 93109
"Actress"

Rachel McLish
120 S. El Camino Drive #116
Beverly Hills, CA 90212
"Actress"

Ed McMahon
12000 Crest Court
Beverly Hills, CA 90210
"TV Show Host"

Jenna McMahon
435 Palisades Ave.
Santa Monica, CA 90402
"Writer, Producer"

Jim McMahon
8701 S. Hardy
Tempe, AZ 85284
"Football Player"

Jim McMullen
515 Mt. Holyoke Avenue
Pacific Palisades, CA 90272
"Actor"

Sam McMurray
4728 1/2 Forman Lane
North Hollywood, CA 91602
"Actor"

Larry McMurtry
P.O. Box 552
Archer City, TX 76351
"Screenwriter"

Steve McNair
c/o Houston Oilers
Houston, TX 77054
"Football Player"

Terrence McNally
218 West 10th Street
New York, NY 10014
"Dramatist"

Brian McNamara
P.O. Box 5617
Beverly Hills, CA 90210
"Actor"

Robert McNamara
2412 Tracy Place N.W.
Washington, DC 20008
"Banker, Government"

William McNamara
9830 Wilshire Blvd.
Beverly Hills, CA 90212
"Actor"

Kate McNeil
9229 Sunset Blvd. #710
Los Angeles, CA 90069
"Actress"

Robert Duncan McNeill
121 N. San Vicente Blvd.
Beverly Hills, CA 90211
"Actor"

James McNichol
4022 Willow Crest Ave.
Studio City, CA 91604
"Actor"

Kristy McNichol
1800 Avenue of the Stars #400
Los Angeles, CA 90067
"Actress"

Chad McQueen
8306 Wilshire Blvd. #438
Beverly Hills, CA 90211
"Actor"

Niele McQueen
2323 Bowmont Drive
Beverly Hills, CA 90210
"Actress"

Gerald McRaney
329 North Wetherly Drive #101
Beverly Hills, CA 90211
"Actor, Director"

Jim McReynolds
P.O. Box 304
Gallatin, TN 37066
"Singer, Guitarist"

Jesse McReynolds
P.O. Box 304
Gallatin, TN 37066
"Singer, Guitarist"

Ian McShane
11620 Wilshire Blvd. #700
Los Angeles, CA 90025
"Actor"

Timothy Mcveigh-
#12076-064
9595 West Quincy Avenue
Littleton, CO 80123
"Bombing Convict"

Tyler McVey
14130 Weddington Street
Van Nuys, CA 91401
"Actor"

Christine McVie
9830 Wilshire Blvd.
Beverly Hills, CA 90212
"Singer, Songwriter"

Gov. Ned McWherter (TN)
State Capitol
Nashville, TN 37219
"Governor"

Caroline McWilliams
4919 Mandeville Canyon
Los Angeles, CA 90049
"Actress"

Yo-Yo Ma
40 West 57th Street
New York, NY 10019
"Cellist"

James MacArthur
P.O. Box 230
Crested Butte, CO 81224
"Actor"

Mrs. Jean MacArthur
Waldorf Towers
100 East 50th Street
New York, NY 10022
"Widower of Douglas MacArthur"

Ralph Macchio
451 Deerpark Avenue
Dix Hills, NY 11746
"Actor"

Simon MacCorkindale
520 Washington Blvd. #187
Marina del Rey, CA 90292
"Actor"

Dr. Jeffrey MacDonald
#00131-177
Federal Correctional Institute
27072 Ballston
Sheridan, OR 97378
"Accused of Killing His Family"

Andie MacDowell
8942 Wilshire Blvd.
Beverly Hills, CA 90211
"Actress"

Ali MacGraw
10345 West Olympic Blvd. #200
Los Angeles, CA 90064
"Actress, Model"

Jeff MacGregor
151 El Camino Drive
Beverly Hills, CA 90212
"TV Personality"

Mario Machado
5750 Briarcliff Road
Los Angeles, CA 90068
"Actor"

Stephen Macht
248 South Rodeo Drive
Beverly Hills, CA 90212
"Actor"

Sen. Connie Mack (FL)
Senate Hart Bldg. #517
Washington, DC 20510
"Politician"

Warner Mack
1136 Sunnymeade Drive
Nashville, TN 37216
"Singer, Guitarist"

Gisele MacKenzie
11014 Blix Street
North Hollywood, CA 91602
"Actress"

Patch MacKenzie
3500 West Olive Avenue #1400
Burbank, CA 91505
"Actress"

Janet MacLachlan
1919 North Taft Avenue
Los Angeles, CA 90068
"Actress"

Kyle MacLachlan
1033 Gayley Avenue #208
Los Angeles, CA 90024
"Actor"

Shirley MacLaine
25200 Old Malibu Road
Malibu, CA 90265
"Actress"

Gavin MacLeod
1025 Fifth Avenue
New York, NY 10028
"Actor"

Patrick Macnee
P.O. Box 1685
Palm Springs, CA 92263
"Actor"

Robert Macneil
356 West 58th Street
New York, NY 10019
"News Correspondent"

Jeff MacNelly
64 E. Concord St.
Orlando, FL 32801
"Cartoonist"

Elle MacPherson
107 Greene Street
New York, NY 10012
"Model"

Heather MacRae
4430 Hayvenhurst Avenue
Encino, CA 91436
"Actress"

Meredith MacRae
518 Pacific Avenue
Manhattan Beach, CA 90266
"Actress"

Sheila Macrea
301 North Canon Drive #305
Beverly Hills, CA 90210
"Singer, Actress"

Bill Macy
10130 Angelo Circle
Beverly Hills, CA 90210
"Actor"

Dave Madden
13034 Delano
Van Nuys, CA 91406
"Actor"

John Madden
c/o Fox Sports
10201 West Pico Blvd.
Los Angeles, CA 90035
"Sportscaster"

Lester Maddox
3155 Johnson Ferry Road N.E.
Marietta, GA 30062
"Ex-Governor"

Amy Madigan
151 El Camino Drive
Beverly Hills, CA 90212
"Actress"

Guy Madison
P.O. Box 1281
Morongo Valley, CA 92256
"Actor"

Bill Madlock
453 East Decatur Street
Decatur, IL 62521
"Ex-Baseball Player"

Madonna
8000 Beverly Blvd.
Los Angeles, CA 90048
"Singer, Actress"

Michael Madsen
1331 Jonesboro Drive
Los Angeles, CA 90049
"Actor"

Virginia Madsen
9830 Wilshire Blvd.
Beverly Hills, CA 90212
"Actress"

Debra Sue Maffett
1525 McGavock Street
Nashville, TN 37203
"Actress, Model"

Brandon Maggart
9200 Sunset Blvd. #710
Los Angeles, CA 90069
"Actor"

Ann Magnuson
1317 Maltman Avenue
Los Angeles, CA 90026
"Proformance Artist"

Jeb Struart Magruder
4814 Ft. Sumner Drive
Washington, DC 20016
"Former Government Official"

John Mahaffey
3100 Richmond Avenue #500
Houston, TX 77098
"Golfer"

Valerie Mahaffey
121 North San Vicente Blvd.
Beverly Hills, CA 90211
"Actress"

George Maharis
13150 Mulholland Drive
Beverly Hills, CA 90210
"Actor"

Bill Maher
120 East 23rd Street
New York, NY 10010
"Actor"

Cardinal Roger Mahony
1531 West 9th Street
Los Angeles, CA 90012
"Clergy"

Phil Mahre
White Pass Drive
Naches, WA 98937
"Skier"

Steve Mahre
2408 North 52nd Avenue
Yakima, WA 98908
"Skier"

Norman Mailer
142 Columbia Heights
Brooklyn, NY 11201
"Author"

Beth Maitland
23555 Neargate
Santa Clarita, CA 91321
"Actress"

Taj Majal
1671 Appian Way
Santa Monica, CA 90401
"Singer, Songwriter"

John Major
8 Stuckley Road, Huntingdon
Cambs, ENGLAND
"Prime Minister"

Lee Majors
625 San Marco Drive
Ft. Lauderdale, FL 33301
"Actor"

Tommy Makem
2 Longmeadow Road
Dover, NH 03820
"Singer"

Chris Makepeace
Box 1095, Station "Q"
Toronto, Ontario
M4T 2P2 CANADA
"Actor"

Mako
6310 San Vicente Blvd. #407
Los Angeles, CA 90048
"Actor"

Kristina Malandro
P.O. Box 491035
Los Angeles, CA 90049
"Actress"

Karl Malden
1845 Mandeville Canyon
Los Angeles, CA 90049
"Actor"

Wendy Malick
822 S. Robertson Blvd. #200
Los Angeles, CA 90035
"Actress"

Art Malik
47 Courtfield Rd. #20
London SW7 4DB ENGLAND
"Actor"

Ross Malinger
6212 Banner Aveune
Los Angeles, CA 90038
"Actor"

John Malkovich
1322 S. Genesee Avenue
Los Angeles, CA 90019
"Actor"

Louis Malle
222 Central Park South
New York, NY 10019
"Film Director"

Carole Mallory
2300-5th Avenue
New York, NY 10037
"Model, Actress, Author"

Bruce Malmuty
9981 Robin Drive
Beverly Hills, CA 90210
"Screenwriter, Director"

Dorothy Malone
P.O. Box 7287
Dallas, TX 75209
"Actress"

Karl Malone
301 W. South Temple
Salt Lake City, UT 84101
"Basketball Player"

Nancy Malone
4507 Auckland Avenue
North Hollywood, CA 91602
"Actress, Director"

Patty Maloney
6767 Forest Lawn Dr. #101
Los Angeles, CA 90068
"Actress"

Leonard Maltin
10424 Whipple Street
Toluca Lake, CA 91602
"Film Critic, Author"

The Mamas & The Papas
805-3rd Avenue #2900
New York, NY 10022
"Rock & Roll Group"

David Mamet
P.O. Box 381589
Cambridge, MA 02238
"Writer"

Charles T. Manatt
4814 Woodway Lane N.W.
Washington, DC 20016
"Politician"

Melissa Manchester
15822 High Knoll Road
Encino, CA 91436
"Singer, Songwriter"

William Manchester
P.O. Box 329 Wesleyan Station
Middletown, CT 06457
"Author"

Ray "Boom Boom" Mancini
2611 - 25th Street
Santa Monica, CA 90405
"Boxer"

Nick Mancuso
822 S. Robertson Blvd. #200
Los Angeles, CA 90035
"Actor"

Robert Mandan
1800 Avenue of the Stars #400
Los Angeles, CA 90067
"Actor"

Babaloo Mandel
5121 Van Alden
Tarzana, CA 91356
"Screenwriter"

Howie Mandel
8942 Wilshire Blvd.
Beverly Hills, CA 90211
"Actor, Comedian"

Johnny Mandel
28946 Cliffside Drive
Malibu, CA 90265
"Composer, Conductor"

Loring Mandel
555 West 57th Street #1230
New York, NY 10019
"Screenwriter"

Nelson Mandela
51 Plain Street
Johannesburg 2001
SOUTH AFRICA
"Social Activist, Politician"

Winnie Mandela
Orlando West, Soweto
Johannesburg SOUTH AFRICA
"Social Activist"

Barbara Mandrell
P.O. Box 800
Hendersonville, TN 37075
"Singer, Singwriter"

Erline Mandrell
P.O. Box 800
Hendersonville, TN 37077
"Actress, Drummer"

Louise Mandrell
P.O. Box 800
Hendersonville, TN 37077
"Singer, Musician"

Costas Mandylor
151 El Camino Drive
Beverly Hills, CA 90212
"Actor"

Larry Maneti
4615 Winnetka
Woodland Hills, CA 91364
"Actor"

Manhattan Transfer
3575 Cahuenga Blvd. West #450
Los Angeles, CA 90068
"Vocal Group"

Barry Manilow
5443 Beethoven Street
Los Angeles, CA 90066
"Singer, Composer"

Tom Mankiewicz
1609 Magnetic Terrace
Los Angeles, CA 90069
"Writer, Producer"

Wolf Mankowitz
Bridge House
Ahakista, County Cork
Kilcrohane 11 IRELAND
"Author, Producer, Dramatist"

Abby Mann
1240 La Collina Drive
Beverly Hills, CA 90210
"Writer, Producer"

Delbert Mann
401 South Burnside Avenue
Suite #11D
Los Angeles, CA 90036
"Director, Producer"

Johnny Mann
78516 Gorham Lane
Indio, CA 92203
"Composer, Conductor"

Michael Mann
13746 Sunset Blvd.
Pacific Palisades, CA 90272
"Writer, Producer"

David Manners
717 Santeclto Street
Santa Barbara, CA 93105
"Actor"

Dorothy Manners
744 North Dohney Drive
Los Angeles, CA 90069
"Actress"

Miss Manners
1651 Harvard Street N.W.
Washington, DC 20009
"Etiquette Expert"

Irene Manning
3165 La Mesa Drive
Santa Carlos, CA 94070
"Actress, Singer, Author"

Dinah Manoff
21244 Ventura Blvd. #101
Woodland Hills, CA 91364
"Actress"

Nigel Mansell
Station Road Box 1
Ballasalle
Isle of Man ENGLAND
"Race Car Driver"

Charles Manson #B33920
Corcoran State Prison
Corcoran, CA 93212
"Convicted Serial Killer"

Paul Mantee
9057A Nemo Street
West Hollywood, CA 90069
"Actor"

Joe Mantegna
10415 Sarah Street
Toluca Lake, CA 91602
"Actor"

John Mantley
4121 Longridge Avenue
Sherman Oaks, CA 91423
"Screenwriter"

Randolph Mantooth
300 W. 55th Street #9C
New York, NY 10019
"Actor"

Martin Manulis
242 Copa de Oro Road
Los Angeles, CA 90077
"TV Producer"

Ralph Manza
550 Hygeia Avenue
Leucadia, CA 92024
"Actor"

Ray Manzarek
232 South Rodeo Drive
Beverly Hills, CA 90212
"Keyboardist"

Marla Maples-Trump
721 Fifth Avenue
New York, NY 10022
"Actress"

Adela Mara
1928 Mandeville Canyon
Los Angeles, CA 90049
"Dancer, Actress"

Diego Maradona
Avertida Eduardo Dato
E-41005 Seville SPAIN
"Soccer Player"

Sophie Marceau
13 rue Madeleine Michelle
F-92200 Neuilly-sur-Seine
FRANCE

Mario Marcelino
1418 North Highland Avenue #102
Los Angeles, CA 90028
"Actress, Writer"

Muzzy Marcellino
14633 Round Valley Drive
Sherman Oaks, CA 91403
"Composer"

Jane March
5 Jubilee Place #100
London SW3 3TD ENGLAND
"Actress"

Guy Marchand
40 rue Francois ler
F-75008 Paris, FRANCE
"Actor"

Nancy Marchand
250 West 89th Street
New York, NY 10024
"Actress"

Vanessa Marcil
9000 Sunset Blvd. #1200
Los Angeles, CA 90069
"Actress"

Adrea Marcovicci
8273 West Norton Avenue
Los Angeles, CA 90046
"Actress, Singer"

HRH The Princess Margaret
Kensington Palace
London N5 ENGLAND
"Royalty"

Stuart Margolin
9401 Wilshire Blvd. #700
Beverly Hills, CA 90212
"Actor, Director"

Miriam Margolyes
121 North San Vicente Blvd.
Beverly Hills, CA 90211
"Actress"

Julianne Margulies
P.O. Box 5617
Beverly Hills, CA 90210
"Actress"

Juan Marichal
3178 NW 19th Street
Miami, FL 33125
"Ex-Baseball Player"

Anne Marie
120 Hickory Street
Madison, TN 37115
"Actress, Model"

Teena Marie
1000 Laguna Road
Pasadena, CA 91105
"Actress"

Marilyn
33-34 Cleveland Street
London W1 ENGLAND
"Singer"

Richard Marin
(Cheech & Chong)
32020 Pacific Coast Hwy.
Malibu, CA 90265
"Actor, Comedian"

Ed Marinaro
1466 North Doheny Drive
Los Angeles, CA 90069
"Ex-Football Player, Actor"

Dan Marino
#13, 7500 NW 30th Street
Davie, FL 33314
"Football Player"

Monte Markhan
P.O. Box 607
Malibu, CA 90265
"Actor"

Marky Mark
63 Pilgrim Road
Braintree, MA 02184
"Rap Singer"

Ziggy Marley
Jack's Hill
Kingston, JAMAICA
"Raggae Singer"

Jean Marlow
32 Exeter Road
London NW2 ENGLAND
"Actress"

Christian Marquand
45 rue de Belle Chasse
75007 Paris FRANCE
"Actor"

Gabriel Garcia Marques
Fuego 144
Pedregal de San Angel
Mexico DF MEXICO
"Author"

Forrest Mars
6885 Elm Street
McLean, VA 22101
"Candy Executive"

Kenneth Mars
9911 West Pico Blvd. #1060
Los Angeles, CA 90035
"Actor"

Branford Marsalis
3 Hastings Square
Cambridge, MA 02139
"Saxophonist"

Wynton Marsalis
3 Lincoln Center #2911
New York, NY 10023
"Trumpeter"

Jean Marsh
Guild House
Upper St. Martin's Lane
London WC2H 9EG ENGLAND
"Actress"

Marian Marsh
P.O. Box 1
Palm Desert, CA 92260
"Actress"

Marshall Tucker Band
100 West Putnam
Greenwich, CT 06830
"Music Group"

E.G. Marshall
RFD #2, Oregon Road
Mt. Kisco, NY 10549
"Actor"

Garry Marshall
10459 Sarah Street
Toluca Lake, CA 91602
"Writer, Producer"

James Marshall
30710 Monte Lado Drive
Malibu, CA 90265
"Author"

Ken Marshall
10100 Santa Monica Blvd.
Suite #2500
Los Angeles, CA 90067
"Actor"

Penny Marshall
7150 La Presa Drive
Los Angeles, CA 90068
"Actress"

Peter Marshall
16714 Oakview Drive
Encino, CA 91316
"Actor, TV Show Host"

Trudy Marshall
1852 Marcheeta Place
Los Angeles, CA 90069
"Actress"

William Marshall
P.O. Box 331212
Pacoima, CA 91331
"Actor"

Frank Marth
8538 Eastwood Road
Los Angeles, CA 90046
"Actor, Singer"

Andrea Martin
575 South Barrington Avenue
Los Angeles, CA 90049
"Actress"

Ann-Marie Martin
144 S. Beverly Drive #405
Beverly Hills, CA 90212
"Actress"

Barney Martin
12838 Milbank Street
Studio City, CA 91604
"Actor"

Dean Martin
511 North Maple Drive
Beverly Hills, CA 90210
"Actor, Singer"

Dick Martin
11030 Chalon Road
Los Angeles, CA 90077
"Actor, Writer, Comedian"

Eric Martin Band
P.O. Box 5952
San Francisco, CA 94101
"Rock & Roll Group"

Helen Martin
1440 North Fairfax #109
Los Angeles, CA 90046
"Actress"

Jared Martin
15060 Ventura Blvd. #350
Sherman Oaks, CA 91403
"Actor"

Kellie Martin
5918 Van Nuys Blvd.
Van Nuys, CA 91401
"Actress"

Millicent Martin
P.O. Box 101
Redding, CT 06875
"Singer, Actresss"

Nan Martin
33604 Pacific Coast Hwy.
Malibu, CA 90265
"Actress"

Pamela Sue Martin
P.O. Box 1684
Studio City, CA 91604
"Actress, Producer"

Steve Martin
P.O. Box 929
Beverly Hills, CA 90213
"Actor"

Tony Martin
10724 Wilshire Blvd. #1406
Los Angeles, CA 90024
"Actor, Singer"

Wink Martindale
5744 Newcastle
Calabasas, CA 91302
"Game Show Host"

A. Martinez
6835 Wild Life Road
Malibu, CA 90265
"Actor"

Al Martino
927 North Rexford Drive
Beverly Hills, CA 90210
"Singer'

Leslie Martinson
2288 Coldwater Canyon
Beverly Hills, CA 90210
"TV Director"

The Marvelettes
9936 Majorca Place
Boca Raton, FL 33434
"R & B Group"

Greg Marx
606 N. Larchmont Blvd. #309
Los Angeles, CA 90004
"Actor"

Mrs. Harpo Marx
37631 Palm View Road
Rancho Mirage, CA 92270
"Harpo Marx's Widower"

Richard Marx
15250 Ventura Blvd. #900
Sherman Oaks, CA 91403
"Conductor"

Ron Masak
5440 Shirley Avenue
Tarzana, CA 91356
"Actor"

Hugh Masekela
230 Park Avenue #1512
New York, NY 10169
"Trumpeter"

Jackie Mason
30 Park Avenue
New York, NY 10016
"Comedian"

Marlyn Mason
8242 Hillside Avenue
Los Angeles, CA 90069
"Actress, Singer"

Marsha Mason
RR #2 - Box 269
Santa Fe, NM 87505
"Actress"

Tom Mason
853-7th Avenue #9A
New York, NY 10019
"Actor"

Osa Massen
10501 Wilshire Blvd. #704
Los Angeles, CA 90024
"Actress"

Andrew Masset
11635 Huston
No. Hollywood, CA 91607
"Actor"

Anna Massey
76 Oxford Street
London W1N 0AX ENGLAND
"Actress"

Daniel Massey
35 Tynehan Road
London SW11 ENGLAND
"Actor"

Ben Masters
9255 Sunset Blvd. #710
Los Angeles, CA 90069
"Actor"

Mary Stuart Masterson
9830 Wilshire Blvd.
Beverly Hills, CA 90212
"Actress"

Mary Elizabeth Masttrantonio
8942 Wilshire Blvd.
Beverly Hills, CA 90211
"Actress"

Marcello Mastroianni
Via Pompeo Magno 11A
Rome ITALY
"Actor"

Richard Masur
121 North San Vicente Blvd.
Beverly Hills, CA 90211
"Actor, Writer"

Mary Matalin
1601 Shenandoah Shores Street
Front Royal, VA 22630
"Political Consultant"

Jerry Mathers
23965 Via Aranda
Valencia, CA 91355
"Actor"

Don Matheson
10275 1/2 Missouri Ave.
Los Angeles, CA 90025
"Actor"

Tim Matheson
250 North Robertson Blvd. #518
Beverly Hills, CA 90211
"Actor"

Kerwin Mathews
67-A Buena Vista Terrace
San Francisco, CA 94117
"Actor"

Bob Mathias
7469 East Pine Avenue
Fresno, CA 93727
"Athlete, Actor"

Mirielle Mathieu
12 rue du Boise de Blulogne
F-92200 Neuilly FRANCE
"Singer"

Johnny Mathis
3500 West Olive Avenue
Suite #750
Burbank, CA 91505
"Singer"

Samantha Mathis
P.O. Box 480137
Los Angeles, CA 90048
"Orchestra Leader"

Melissa Mathison
655 MacCulloch Drive
Los Angeles, CA 90049
"Screenwriter"

Marlee Matlin
7920 Sunset Blvd. #400
Los Angeles, CA 90046
"Actress"

Walter Matthau
1999 Avenue of the Stars #2100
Los Angeles, CA 90067
"Actor"

Kathy Mattea
P.O. Box 158482
Nashville, TN 37215
"Singer"

Roland Matthes
Storkower Street 118
1055 Berlin GERMANY
"Swimmer"

Eddie Matthews
13744 Recuerdo Dr.
Del Mar, CA 92014
"Ex-Baseball Player"

Don Mattingly
RR #5, Box 74
Evansville, IN 47711
"Baseball Player"

Robin Mattson
77 West 66th Street
New York, NY 10023
"Actress"

Victor Mature
P.O. Box 706
Rancho Santa Fe, CA 92067
"Actor"

Billy Mauch
23427 Canzonet Street
Woodland Hills, CA 91364
"Actor"

Bobby Mauch
23427 Canzonet Street
Woodland Hills, CA 91364
"Actor"

Gene Mauch
71 Princeton
Rancho Mirage, CA 92270
"Baseball Manager"

Bill Mauldin
112 8th Street
Seal Beach, CA 90740
"Cartoonist

Brad Maule
4136 Dixie Canyon
Sherman Oaks, CA 91423
"Actor"

Nicole Maurey
21 Chemin Vauillons
78160 Marly-le-roi FRANCE
"Actress"

Claire Maurier
11 rue de la Montague-le-Breuil
91360 Epinay sur Orge, FRANCE
"Actress"

Max Maven
1746 North Orange Drive #1106
Los Angeles, CA 90028
"Mind Reader"

The Mavericks
P.O. Box 23329
Nashville, TN 37202
"Music Group"

Peter Max
118 Riverside Drive
New York, NY 10024
"Artist, Designer"

Frank Maxwell
447 San Vicente Blvd. #301
Santa Monica, CA 90401
"Actor"

Lois Maxwell
150 Carlton Street #200
Toronto, Ontario CANADA
"Actress"

Billy May
4 San Remo
San Clemente, CA 92672
"Composer"

Brian May
83 Riverside Drive
New York, NY 10024
"Composer"

Donald May
4616 Los Feliz Blvd. #2
Los Angeles, CA 90027
"Actor"

Elaine May
2017 California Avenue
Santa Monica, CA 90403
"Actress, Writer, Director"

Curtis Mayfield
1650 Broadway #508
New York, NY 10019
"Singer"

Don Maynard
6545 Butterfield Drive
El Paso, TX 79932
"Football Player"

Ferdianand Mayne
100 South Doheny Drive #620
Los Angeles, CA 90048
"Actor"

Asa Maynor
P.O. Box 1641
Beverly Hills, CA 90213
"Actress, Producer"

Virginia Mayo
109 East Avenue De Los Arboles
Thousand Oaks, CA 91360
"Actress"

Whitman Mayo
10100 Santa Monica Blvd. #2500
Los Angeles, CA 90067
"Actor"

Melanie Mayron
7510 Sunset Blvd.
Los Angeles, CA 90046
"Actress, Writer"

Willie Mays
P.O. Box 2410
Menlo Park, CA 94026
"Ex-Baseball Player"

Debi Mazar
8942 Wilshire Blvd.
Beverly Hills, CA 90211
"Actress"

Bill Mazeroski
RR 6, Box 130
Greensburg, PA 15601
"Ex-Baseball Player"

Julia Meade
1010 Fifth Avenue
New York, NY 10021
"Actress"

Jayne Meadows
16185 Woodvale
Encino, CA 91316
"Actress"

Kristen Meadows
8383 Wilshire Blvd. #954
Beverly Hills, CA 90211
"Actress"

Mary T. Meagher
4100 Ormond Drive
Louisville, KY 40207
"Swimmer"

Colm Meaney
9255 Sunset Blvd. #515
Los Angeles, CA 90069
"Actor"

Natrone Means
9449 Friars Road
San Diego, CA 92108
"Football Player"

Anne Meara
1999 Avenue of the Stars #2850
Los Angeles, CA 90067
"Actress, Comedienne"

Meatloaf
Box 68, Stockport
Cheshire SK3 0JY ENGLAND
"Singer, Composer"

Peter Medak
1712 Stanley Avenue
Los Angeles, CA 90046
"Film Director"

Mike Medavoy
7920 Sunset Blvd. #400
Los Angeles, CA 90046
"Film Executive"

Patricia Medina
10590 Wilshire Blvd. #1202
Los Angeles, CA 90024
"Actress"

Michael Medved
1224 Ashland Avenue
Santa Monica, CA 90405
"Writer, Film Critic"

Thomas Meehan
Brook House
Obtuse Road
Newtown, CT 06470
"Screenwriter"

Edwin Meese
1075 Springhill Road
McLean, VA 22102
"Ex-Government Official"

Zubin Mehta
27 Oakmont Drive
Los Angeles, CA 90049
"Violinist"

Gunter Meisner
Schildhornstrasse 74
D-1000 Berlin 41
GERMANY
"Actor"

Randy Meisner
11846 Balboa Blvd. #204
Granada Hills, CA 91344
"Singer, Songwriter"

Melanie
2000 South Dixie Highway
West Palm Beach, FL 33401
"Singer"

John Mellencamp
Rt. 1, Box 361
Nashville, IN 47448
"Singer, Songwriter"

Daniel Melnick
1123 Sunset Hills Drive
Los Angeles, CA 90069
"Film Producer"

Sid Melton
5347 Cedros Avenue
Van Nuys, CA 91410
"Actor"

Allen Melvin
271 North Bowling Green Way
Los Angeles, CA 90049
"Actor"

Harold Melvin
P.O. Box 82
Great Neck, NY 11021
"Singer, Songwriter"

Murray Melvin
535 Kings Road
19 Plaza #2
London SW10 OSZ ENGLAND
"Actor"

Men At Work
15 Blue Street
North Sydney NSW 2060 AUS-
TRALIA
"Rock & Roll Group"

Erik Menedez #1878449
Los Angeles County Men's Jail
441 Bauchet St.
Los Angeles, CA 90012
"Charged for Killing Parents"

Lyle Menedez #1887106
Los Angeles County Men's Jail
441 Bauchet St.
Los Angeles, CA 90012
"Charged for Killing Parents"

Sergio Mendez
4849 Encino Avenue
Encino, CA 91316
"Pianist, Songwriter"

John Mengatti
4424 Colfax Avenue #3
North Hollywood, CA 91602
"Actor"

Gian Carlo Menotti
Gilford Haddington
East Lothian
EH41 4JF SCOTLAND
"Composer"

Menudo
2895 Biscayne Blvd. #455
Miami, FL 33137
"Rock & Roll Group"

Sir Yehudi Menuhin
Buhlstr
CH-3780 Gstaad-Neuret
SWITZERLAND
"Violinist"

Heather Menzies
P.O. Box 5973-1006
Sherman Oaks, CA 91403
"Actress"

Marian Mercer
25901 Pluma
Calabasas, CA 91302
"Actress"

Paul Mercurio
61 Wetherill Street
Leichhardt NSW 2040
AUSTRALIA
"Actor"

Burgess Meredith
P.O. Box 757
Malibu, CA 90265
"Actress, Writer, Director"

Don Meredith
P.O. Box 597
Santa Fe, NM 87504
"Ex-Football Player"

James Meredith
427 Eastview Street
Jackson, MS 39206
"First Black Attend U of MS"

Lee Ann Meriwether
P.O. Box 260402
Encino, CA 91326
"Actress"

Jan Merlin
9016 Wonderland Avenue
Los Angeles, CA 90046
"Actor, Director"

Dina Merrill
405 E. 54th Street #12A
New York, NY 10022
"Actress"

Robert Merrill
79 Oxford Drive
New Rochelle, NY 10801
"Baritone"

Teresa Merritt
192-06 110th Road
St. Albans, NY 11412
"Actress"

Dale Messick
64 East Concord Street
Orlando, FL 32801
"Cartoonist"

Don Messick
P.O. Box 5426
Santa Barbara, CA 93150
"Actor"

Jim Messina
RD #1 Box 214
High Falls, NY 10801
"Singer, Songwriter"

Reinhold Messner
139040 Villnoss
St. Magdalena 52 ITALY
"Mountaineer, Author"

Laurie Metcalf
11845 Kling Street
North Hollywood, CA 91607
"Actress"

Burt Metcalfe
11800 Brookdale Lane
Studio City, CA 91604
"TV Writer, Producer"

Pat Metheny
173 Brighton Avenue
Boston, MA 02134
"Jazz Musician"

Sophie Metral
20 rue Sauffrey
75017 Paris, FRANCE
"Actress"

Art Metrano
9300 Wilshire Blvd. #410
Beverly Hills, CA 90212
"Actor"

Howard Metzenbaum
1240 East 9th Street #2915
Cleveland, OH 44199
"Ex-Senator"

Nicholas Meyer
2109 Stanley Hills Drive
Los Angeles, CA 90046
"Writer, Producer"

Russ Meyer
3121 Arrowhead Drive
Los Angeles, CA 90068
"Film Writer, Producer"

Ari Meyers
875 Comstock #11C
Los Angeles, CA 90024
"Actress"

Kweisi Mfume
3000 Druld Park Drive
Baltimore, MD 21215
"N.A.A.C.P. Director"

Miami Sound Machine
6205 Bird Road
Miami, FL 33155
"Rock & Roll Group"

Rep. Bob Michael (IL)
House Rayburn Bldg. #2112
Washington, DC 20515
"Politician"

George Michael
2222 Mt. Calvary Road
Santa Barbara, CA 93105
"Singer, Composer"

Prince Michael of Kent
Kensington Palace
London N5 ENGLAND
"Royalty"

Princess Michael of Kent
Kensington Palace
London N5 ENGLAND
"Royalty"

Al Michaels
c/o ABC Sports
47 West 66th Street
New York, NY 10023
"Sports Announcer"

Lorne Michaels
88 Central Park West
New York, NY 10023
"TV Writer, Producer"

Marilyn Michaels
185 West End Avenue
New York, NY 10023
"Comedienne"

Kari Michaelson
1717 North Highland Avenue #414
Los Angeles, CA 90028
"News Correspondent, Actress"

Keith Michell
130 West 57th Street #10-A
New York, NY 10019
"Actor"

Guy Michelmore
72 Goldsmith Avenue
London, W3 6HN England
"Actor"

James Michener
2706 Mountain Laurel Lane
Austin, TX 78703
"Writer"

Gov. George Mickelson (SD)
State Capitol, 2nd Floor
Pierre, SD 57501
"Governor"

Bette Midler
820 N. San Vicente Blvd. #690
Los Angeles, CA 90069
"Singer, Actress, Comedy"

Toshiro Mifune
9-30-7 Siejko, Setagaysku
Tokyo JAPAN
"Actor"

Mighty Morphin Power Rangers
26020-A Avenue Hall
Valencia, CA 91355
"Martial Arts Fighting Characters"

Mike & The Mechanics
P.O. Box 107
London N65 ARU ENGLAND
"Rock & Roll Group

George Mikell
23 Shuttleworth Road
London SW11 ENGLAND
"Actor"

Sen. Barbara A. Mikulski (MD)
Senate Hart Bldg. #320
Washington, DC 20510
"Politician"

Alyssa Milano
151 El Camino Drive
Beverly Hills, CA 90212
"Actress"

Joanna Miles
2062 North Vine Street
Los Angeles, CA 90068
"Actress"

Sarah Miles
Chithurst Manor
Trotton, nr. Petersfield
Hampshire GU31 5EU ENGLAND
"Actor, Singer"

Sylvia Miles
240 Central Park South
New York, NY 10019
"Actress"

Vera Miles
P.O. Box 1704
Big Bear Lake, CA 92315
"Actress"

John Milford
334 South Bentley Avenue
Los Angeles, CA 90049
"Actor"

Tomas Milian
Via Virgilo Orsini 27
00100 Rome ITALY
"Actor"

Michael Milken
4543 Tara Drive
Encino, CA 91436
"Stock Broker"

Ann Miller
618 North Alta Drive
Beverly Hills, CA 90210
"Actress, Dancer"

Arthur Miller
Box 320 RR #1 Tophet Road
Roxbury, CT 06783
"Author, Dramatist"

Cheryl Miller
6767 Forest Lawn Drive #115
Los Angeles, CA 90068
"Sports Analyst"

Denise Miller
9560 Wilshire Blvd. #516
Beverly Hills, CA 90212
"Actress"

Dennis Miller
9560 Wilshire Blvd. #511
Beverly Hills, CA 90212
"TV Show Host"

Denny Miller
733 N. Seward Street, PH
Los Angeles, CA 90038
"Actor"

Jason Miller
436 Spruce Street #600
Scranton, PA 18503
"Actor, Writer, Director"

Jeremy Miller
6057 Rhodes Avenue
North Hollywood, CA 91606
"Actor"

Jody Miller
Rt. #3
Blanchard, OK 73010
"Singer"

Johnny Miller
P.O. Box 2260
Napa, CA 94558
"Golfer"

Jonathan Miller
63 Gloucester Crescent
London NW1 ENGLAND
"Film Director"

Larry Miller
9000 Sunset Blvd. #1200
Los Angeles, CA 90069
"Writer"

Linda G. Miller
1325 Centinela Ave. #1
Santa Monica, CA 90404
"Actress"

Mitch Miller
345 West 58th Street
New York, NY 10019
"Musician, Composer"

Nolan Miller
816 North Whittier Drive
Beverly Hills, CA 90210
"Fashion Designer"

Patsy Ruth Miller
425 Sierra Madre North
Palm Desert, CA 92260
"Actress"

Penelope Ann Miller
43-B Navy Street
Venice, CA 90291
"Actress"

Reggie Miller
300 East Market Street
Indianapolis, IN 46204
"Basketball Player"

Gov. Robert J. Miller (NV)
State Capitol
Carson City, NV 89710
"Governor"

Shannon Miller
715 South Kelley Avenue
Edmond, OK 73034
"Gymnast"

Sidney Miller
2724 Bottlebrush Drive
Los Angeles, CA 90077
"Actor, Director"

Spike Milligan
9 Orme Court
London W2 ENGLAND
"Actor, Director"

Alley Mills
444 Carol Canal
Venice, CA 90291
"Actress"

Donna Mills
2660 Benedict Canyon
Beverly Hills, CA 90210
"Actress, Model"

Hayley Mills
81 High Street
Hampton, Middlesex, ENGLAND
"Actress"

Sir John Mills
Hill House
Denham Village
Buckinghamshire ENGLAND
"Actor"

Juliet Mills
4770-B 9th Street
Carpinteria, CA 93013
"Actress"

Martin Milner
1930 Century Park W. #403
Los Angeles, CA 90067
"Actor, Radio Personality"

Ronnie Milsap
12 Music Circle South
Nashville, TN 37203
"Singer, Songwriter"

Yvette Mimieux
500 Perugia Way
Los Angeles, CA 90077
"Actress, Writer"

Jan Miner
P.O. Box 293
Southbury, CT 06488
"Actress"

Steve Miner
1137-2nd Street #103
Santa Monica, CA 90403
"Film Director"

Charles Mingus
484 W. 43rd Street #43-S
New York, NY 10036
"Bassist"

Liza Minnelli
P.O. Box 790039
Middle Village, NY 11379
"Actress, Singer"

Kylie Minogue
P.O. Box 292, Watford
Herfordshire, ENGLAND
"Singer"

Minnie Minoso
805 Main Road
Independence, MO 64056
"Ex-Baseball Player"

Miou-Miou
10 Avenue George V
75008 Paris, FRANCE
"Actress"

Walter Mirisch
647 Warner Avenue
Los Angeles, CA 90024
"Film Executive, Producer"

Helen Mirren
2003 La Brea Terrace
Los Angeles, CA 90046
"Actress"

Missing Persons
11935 Laurel Hills Road
Studio City, CA 91604
"Rock & Roll Group"

Mr. Mister
P.O. Box 69343
Los Angeles, CA 90069
"Rock & Roll Group"

Don Mitchell
1930 South Marvin
Los Angeles, CA 90016
"Actor"

Edgar Mitchell
P.O. Box 812127
Boca Rotan, FL 33481
"Astronuat"

Sen. George Mitchell (ME)
Senate Russell Bldg. #176
Washington, DC 20510
"Politician"

James Mitchell
330 West 72nd Street #12C
New York, NY 10023
"Actor"

Joni Mitchell
10960 Wilshire Blvd. #938
Los Angeles, CA 90024
"Singer, Songwriter"

Kim Mitchell
41 Britain Street #305
Toronto, Ont. M5A 1R7 CANADA
"Singer, Guitarist"

Sasha Mitchell
9057-A Nemo Street
W. Hollywood, CA 90069
"Actor"

Shirley Mitchell
133 South Oakhurst Drive
Beverly Hills, CA 90212
"Actress"

Warren Mitchell
28 Sheldon Avenue
London N6 ENGLAND
"Actor"

Marvin Mitchelson
1486 N. Sweetzer Avenue
Los Angeles, CA 90069
"Talent Agent"

Jim Mitchum
8942 Wilshire Blvd.
Beverly Hills, CA 90211
"Actor"

Robert Mitchum
P.O. Box 5216
Montecito, CA 93108
"Actor"

Rosi Mittermaier
Winkelmoosalm
D-83242 Reit im Winkel
GERMANY
"Skier"

Kim Miyori
121 North San Vicente Blvd.
Beverly Hills, CA 90211
"Actress"

Larry Mize
P.O. Box 109601
Palm Beach Gardens, FL 33410
"Golfer"

Mary Ann Mobley
2751 Hutton Drive
Beverly Hills, CA 90210
"Actress"

Jayne Modean
10000 Santa Monica Blvd.
Suite #305
Los Angeles, CA 90025
"Actress"

The Modernaires
RD #1, Box 91
Tannersville, PA 18372
"Vocal Group"

Matthew Modine
9696 Culver Blvd. #203
Culver City, CA 90232
"Actor"

John Moffatt
59A Warrington Street
London W9 ENGLAND
"Actor"

Katy Moffatt
PO Box 334
O'Fallon, IL 62269
"Singer, Songwriter"

D.W. Moffett
450 N. Rossmore Avenue #401
Los Angeles, CA 90004
"Actor"

Al Molinaro
P.O. Box 9218
Glendale, CA 91226
"Actor"

Richard Moll
1119 N. Amalfi Drive
Pacific Palisades, CA 90272
"Actor"

Thomas L. Monaghan
3001 Earhart
Ann Arbor, MI 48106
"Domino Pizza Owner"

Paul Monash
912 Alto Cedro Drive
Beverly Hills, CA 90210
"Writer, Producer"

Walter Mondale
Unit 45005, P.O. Box 258
APO AP Tokyo
96334-0001 JAPAN
"Ambassador"

Rick Monday
149 42nd Ave.
San Mateo, CA 94403
"EX-Baseball Player"

Eddie Money
P.O. Box 429094
San Francisco, CA 94142
"Singer"

Corbett Monica
PO Box 801406
Miami, FL 33280
"Comedian, Actor"

The Monkees
8369A Sausalito Avenue
West Hills, CA 91304
"Rock & Roll Group"

Bob Monkhouse
118 Beaufort Street
London SW3 6BU ENGLAND
"Actor, Writer"

Bill Monroe
2804 Opryland Drive
Nashville, TN 37214
"Singer, Guitarist"

Marilyn Monroe, Int. Fan Club
PO Box 7544
Northridge, CA 91327
"Fan Club"

Joe Montagna
10415 Sarah Street
Toluca Lake, CA 91602
"Actor"

Ashley Montague
321 Cherry Hill Road
Princeton, NJ 08540
"Model"

Lee Montague
5 Keats Close
London NW3 ENGLAND
"Actor"

Ricardo Montalban
1423 Oriole Drive
Los Angeles, CA 90069
"Actor, Director"

Joe Montana
292 Valpariso Avenue
Atherton, CA 94027
"Football Player"

Monte Montana
10326 Montana Lane
Agua Dulce, CA 91350
"Actor"

Patsy Montana
P.O. Box 147
21100 Highway 79
San Jacinto, CA 93483
"Singer"

Kelly Monteith
1539 Sawtelle Blvd. #10
Los Angeles, CA 90025
"Comedian, Writer"

Belinda Montgomery
335 North Maple Drive #361
Beverly Hills, CA 90210
"Actress"

George Montgomery
P.O. Box 2187
Rancho Mirage, CA 92270
"Actor"

John Michael Montgomery
1819 Broadway
Nashville, TN 37203
"Singer"

Julia Montgomery
10100 Santa Monica Blvd.
Suite #2500
Los Angeles, CA 90067
"Actress"

Gloria Monty
10500 Rocca Place
Los Angeles, CA 90077
"TV Writer, Producer"

Ron Moody
Ingleside
41 The Green, Southgate
London N14 ENGLAND
"Actor"

Donn Moomaw
3124 Corda Drive
Los Angeles, CA 90049
"Clergy"

Rev. Sun Myung Moon
4 West 43rd Street
New York, NY 10010
"Cult Leader"

Warren Moon
500-11th Avenue South
Minneapolis, MN 55415
"Football Player"

Alvy Moore
8546 Amestov Avenue
Northridge, CA 91324
"Actor"

Clayton Moore
4720 Parkolivo
Calabasas, CA 91302
"Actor"

Constance Moore
10450 Wilshire Blvd. #1-B
Los Angeles, CA 90024
"Actress"

Demi Moore
1453-3rd Street #420
Santa Monica, CA 90401
"Actress"

Dickie Moore
150 West End Avenue #26C
New York, NY 10023
"Actor"

Dudley Moore
73 Market Street
Venice, CA 90291
"Actor, Writer, Pianist"

Juanita Moore
3802-L Dunsford Lane
Inglewood, CA 90305
"Actress"

Julianne Moore
1724 North Vista Street
Los Angeles, CA 90046
"Actress"

Mary Tyler Moore
510 East 86th Street #21A
New York, NY 10028
"Actress"

Melba Moore
200 Central Park South #8R
New York, NY 10019
"Singer"

Roger Moore
Chalet Fenil
Grund bei Gstaad
SWITZERLAND
"Actor"

Terry Moore
833 Ocean Avenue #104
Santa Monica, CA 90403
"Actress"

Jim Mora
6928 Saints Drive
Metairie, LA 70003
"Football Coach"

Esai Morales
1147 South Wooster Street
Los Angeles, CA 90035
"Actor"

Erin Moran
1800 Avenue of the Stars, #400
Los Angeles, CA 90067
"Actress"

Peggy Moran
3101 Village #3
Camarillo, CA 93010
"Actress"

Rick Moranis
101 Central Park West #128
New York, NY 10023
"Actor"

Tony Mordente
4541 Comber
Encino, CA 91316
"Film Director"

Jeanne Moreau
103 Blvd. Haussman
F-75008 Paris, FRANCE
"Actress"

Rita Moreno
1620 Amalfi Drive
Pacific Palisades, CA 90272
"Actress"

Cindy Morgan
280 South Beverly Drive #400
Beverly Hills, CA 90212
"Actress"

Debbie Morgan
12312 Viewcrest Road
Studio City, CA 91604
"Actress"

Elaine Morgan
24 Aberfford Road
Mountain Ash
Glamorgan ENGLAND

"Playwright"

Harry Morgan
13172 Boca De Canon Lane
Los Angeles, CA 90049
"Actor, Director"

Jane Morgan
27740 Pacific Coast Highway
Malibu, CA 90265
"Actress"

Jaye P. Morgan
1717 N. Highland Avenue #414
Hollywood, CA 90028
"Actress"

Lorrie Morgan
1209 - 16th Avenue South
Nashville, TN 37212
"Singer"

Michelle Morgan
5 rue Jacques Dulud
92200 Neuily, FRANCE
"Actress"

Robert M. Morganthau
1085 Park Avenue
New York, NY 10028
"Attorney"

Cathy Moriarity
930 Doheny Drive #308
West Hollywood, CA 90069
"Actress"

Michael Moriarty
200 West 58th Street #3B
New York, NY 10019
"Actor"

Patricia Morison
400 South Hauser Blvd.
Los Angeles, CA 90036
"Actress, Singer"

Noriyuki "Pat" Morita
P.O. Box 491278
Los Angeles, CA 90049
"Actor, Comedian"

Karen Morley
5320 Ben Avenue #3
North Hollywood, CA 91607
"Actress"

Alonzo Morning
701 Areana Blvd.
Miami, FL 33136
"Basketball Player"

Giorgio Moroder
9348 Civic Center Drive #101
Beverly Hills, CA 90210
"Composer, Conductor"

David Morphet
101 Honor Oak Road
London SE23 3LB ENGLAND
"Writer, Producer"

Dr. Desmond Morris
78 Danbury Road
Oxford, ENGLAND
"Zoologist, Author"

Garret Morris
3740 Barham Blvd. #E116
Los Angeles, CA 90068
"Actor"

Gary Morris
6027 Church Drive
Sugarland, TX 77478
"Actor, Singer"

Greg Morris
1930 Century Park West #403
Los Angeles, CA 90067
"Actor"

Howard Morris
2723 Carmar Drive
Los Angeles, CA 90046
"Actor, Director"

Phil Morris
704 Strand
Manhattan Beach, CA 90266
"Actor"

Toni Morrison
201 E. 50th St.
New York, NY 10022
"Writer"

Van Morrison
12304 Santa Monica Blvd. #300
Los Angeles, CA 90025
"Singer, Songwriter"

Karen Morrow
9400 Readcrest Drive
Beverly Hills, CA 90210
"Actress"

Rob Morrow
151 El Camino Drive
Beverly Hills, CA 90212
"Actor"

David Morse
13937 Valley Vista Blvd.
Sherman Oaks, CA 91423
"Actor"

Robert Morse
13830 Davana Terrace
Sherman Oaks, CA 91403
"Actor"

Gary Morton
40241 Clubview Drive
Rancho Mirage, CA 92270
"Comedian"

Howard Morton
12311 Cantura Street
Studio City, CA 91604
"Actor"

Joe Morton
606 North Larchmont Blvd.
Suite #309
Los Angeles, CA 90004
"Actor"

John Moschitta, Jr.
8033 Sunset Blvd. #41
Los Angeles, CA 90046
"Actor"

Sen. Carol Moseley-Braun
Senate Hart Building #708
Washington, DC 20510
"Politician"

Mark Mosley
P.O. Box 17247
Washington, DC 20041
"Ex-Football Player"

Albert Moses
12 Pickering Court
Granville Road
London N22 4EL ENGLAND
"Actor"

Billy Moses
405 Sycamore Road
Santa Monica, CA 90402
"Actor"

Edwin Moses
P.O. Box 3807
Laguna Hills, CA 92654
"Track & Field Athlete"

Roger E. Moseley
3756 Prestwick Drive
Los Angeles, CA 90027
"Actor"

Kate Moss
205 West 39th Street
New York, NY 10018
"Model"

Ronn Moss
7800 Beverly Blvd. #3371
Los Angeles, CA 90036
"Actor"

Sterling Moss
46 Shepherd Street, Mayfair
London W1Y 8JN ENGLAND
"Actor"

Donny Most
280 South Beverly Drive #400
Beverly Hills, CA 90212
"Actor"

Manny Mota
3926 Los Olivos Lane
La Crescenta, CA 91214
"Ex-Baseball Player"

Mark Mothersbaugh
2164 Sunset Plaza Drive
Los Angeles, CA 90046
"Writer"

Motley Crue
40/42 Newman Street
London W1P 3PA ENGLAND
"Rock & Roll Group"

Stewart Mott
515 Madison Avenue
New York, NY 10022
"Philanthropist"

Mickey Mouse Club
P.O. Box 10200
Lake Buena Vista, FL 32830
"Fan Club"

Movita
2766 Motor Avenue
Los Angeles, CA 90064
"Actress"

Bill Moyers
524 West 57th Street
New York, NY 10019
"News Correspondent"

Sen. Daniel Moynihan (NY)
Senate Russell Bldg. #464
Washington, DC 20510
"Politician"

Pres. Hosni Mubarak
Royal Palace
Cairo, EGYPT
"President of Egypt"

Roger Mudd
7167 Old Dominion Drive
McLean, VA 22101
"News Correspondent"

Armin Mueller-Stahl
Ordensmeisterstr. 15-16
1000 Berlin GERMANY
"Actor"

Diana Muldaur
1930 Century Park West #403
Los Angeles, CA 90067
"Actress"

Maria Muldaur
1222 Kenilworth Avenue
Charlotte, NC 28204
"Singer, Songwriter"

Patrick Muldoon
9300 Wilshire Blvd., #400
Beverly Hills, CA 90212
"Actor"

Shirley Muldowney
79559 North Avenue
Armada, MI 48005
"Race Car Driver"

Kate Mulgrew
11938 Foxboro Drive
Los Angeles, CA 90049
"Actress"

Edward Mulhare
6045 Sunnyslope Avenue
Van Nuys, CA 91401
"Actor"

Chris Mulkey
918 Zenizia Avenue
Venice, CA 90291
"Actor"

Martin Mull
338 Chadbourne Avenue
Los Angeles, CA 90049
"Actor, Comedian, Writer"

Richard Mulligan
145 South Beachwood Drive
Los Angeles, CA 90004
"Actor"

Gardner Mulloy
1 Fisher Island Drive
Fisher Island, FL 33109
"Tennis Player"

Dermot Mulroney
439 North Gower
Los Angeles, CA 90004
"Actor"

Billy Mumy
8271 Melrose Avenue #202
Los Angeles, CA 90046
"Actor"

Caroline Munro
1348 Fern Avenue
Reading, PA 19607
"Actress, Model"

The Muppets
P.O. Box 20750
New York, NY 10023
"Puppets"

Bobby Murcer
P.O. Box 75089
Oklahoma City, OK 73147
"Ex-Baseball Player"

George Murdock
5733 Sunfield Avenue
Lakewood, CA 90712
"Actor"

Rupert Murdoch
210 South Street
New York, NY 10002
"Publisher"

Sen. Frank Murkowski (AK)
Senate Hart Bldg. #709
Washington, DC 20510
"Politician"

Ben Murphy
3601 Vista Pacifica #17
Malibu, CA 90265
"Actor"

Brian Murphy
22 Gilden Road
London NW5 ENGLAND
"Actor"

Dale Murphy
P.O. Box 4064
Atlanta, GA 30302
"Ex-Baseball Player"

Eddie Murphy
P.O. Box 1028
Englewood Cliffs, NY 07632
"Actor, Comedian"

Michael Martin Murphy
207K Paseo Del Pueble Sur
Taos, NM 87571
"Singer, Guitarist"

Rosemary Murphy
220 East 73rd Street
New York, NY 10021
"Actress"

Anne Murray
4950 Yonge Street #2400
Toronto, Ontario
M2N 6KL CANADA
"Singer"

Bill Murray
RFD 1, Box 573
Palisades, NY 10964
"Actor"

Don Murray
1215-F De La Vina Street
Santa Barbara, CA 93101
"Actor, Writer, Director"

Jan Murray
1157 Calle Vista
Beverly Hills, CA 90210
"Actor, Comedian"

Katherine Murray
2877 Kalakaua Avenue
Honolulu, HI 96815
"Dance Instructor"

Ruby Murray
10A Victoria Parade, Torquay
Devon ENGLAND
"Singer"

Kate Murtagh
15146 Moorpark Street
Sherman Oaks, CA 91403
"Actress"

Tony Musante
38 Bedford Street
New York, NY 10014
"Actor, Writer"

Brent Musburger
47 West 66th Street
New York, NY 10023
"Sportscaster"

Stan Musial
1655 Des Peres Rd. #125
St. Louis, MO 63131
"Ex-Baseball Player, Manager"

Marjorie Ann Mutchie
1169 Mary Circle
La Verne, CA 91750
"Actress"

Ornella Muti
Via Giovanni Bettolo 3
I-00195 Rome ITALY
"Actress"

Michael Murphy
P.O. Box FFF
Taos, NM 87571
"Actor"

Dee Dee Myers
2200 Fletcher Avenue
Fort Lee, NJ 07024
"Ex-Press Secretary"

Mike Myers
9150 Wilshire Blvd. #350
Beverly Hills, CA 90212
"Actor"

Bess Myerson
3 East 71st Street
New York, NY 10021
"Columnist"

The Mystics
88 Anador Street
Staten Island, NY 10303
"Vocal Group"

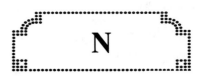

John Naber
P.O. Box 50107
Pasadena, CA 91105
"Swimmer"

Jim Nabors
P.O. Box 10364
Honolulu, HI 96816
"Actor, Singer"

George Nader
893 Camino del Sur
Palm Springs, CA 92662
"Actor"

Michael Nader
10100 Santa Monica Blvd. #2500
Los Angeles, CA 90067
"Actor"

Ralph Nader
P.O. Box 19367
Washington, DC 20036
"Consumer Advocate"

Kathy Najimy
120 W. 45th Street #3601
New York, NY 10036
"Actress"

Joe Namath
300 East 51st Street #11-A
New York, NY 10022
"Football Player"

Nantucket
3924 Browning Place #200
Raleigh, NC 27609
"Rock & Roll Group"

Charles Napier
Star Rt. Box 60-H
Caliente, CA 93518
"Actor"

Jack Narz
1906 Beverly Place
Beverly Hills, CA 90210
"TV Show Host"

Grahan Nash
584 North Lachmont Blvd.
Hollywood, CA 90004
"Singer, Songwriter"

Ille Nastase
15 East 69th Street
New York, NY 100021
"Tennis Player"

Marie-Jose Nat
10 rue Royale
75008 Paris, FRANCE
"Actress"

Kitten Natividad
5917 Oak Avenue, #148
Temple, City, CA 91780
"Actress, Model"

Melinda Naud
12330 Viewcrest Road
Studio City, CA 91604
"Actress"

David Naughton
3500 West Olive #1400
Burbank, CA 91505
"Actor, Singer"

James Naughton
8942 Wilshire Blvd.
Beverly Hills, CA 90211
"Actor"

Naughty by Nature
155 Morgan Street
Jersey City, NJ 07302
"Music Group"

Martina Navratilova
133 - 1st Street NE
St. Petersburg, FL 33701
"Tennis Player"

Patricia Neal
45 East End Avenue #4C
New York, NY 10028
"Actress"

Kevin Nealon
5039 1/2 Rosewood Avenue
Los Angeles, CA 90004
"Comedian"

Christopher Neame
Guild House
Upper St. Martin's Lane
London WC2H 9EG ENGLAND
"Actor"

Ronald Neame
2317 Kimridge Drive
Beverly Hills, CA 90210
"Film Director"

Holly Near
1222 Preservation Parkway
Oakland, CA 94612
"Singer"

Lynn Neary
c/o National Public Radio
2025 "M" Street NW
Washington, DC 20036
"News Correspondent"

Connie Needham
19721 Castlebar Drive
Rowland Heights, CA 91748
"Actress"

Hal Needham
2220 Avenue of the Stars #302
Los Angeles, CA 90067
"Writer, Producer"

Tracey Needham
9229 Sunset Blvd. #311
Los Angeles, CA 90069
"Actress"

Liam Neeson
9830 Wilshire Blvd.
Beverly Hills, CA 90212
"Actress"

Taylor Negron
9000 Sunset Blvd. #1200
Los Angeles, CA 90069
"Actor"

Noel Neill
331 Sage Lane
Santa Monica, CA 90402
"Actress"

Sam Neill
P.O. Box 153, Noble Park
Victoria 3174 AUSTRALIA
"Actor"

LeRoy Neiman
1 West 67th Street
New York, NY 10023
"Artist"

Stacey Nelkin
2770 Hutton Drive
Beverly Hills, CA 90210
"Actress"

Kate Nelligan
Prince of Wales Theatre
Coventry Street
London W1 ENGLAND
"Actress"

Barry Nelson
134 West 58th Street
New York, NY 10019
"Actor"

Byron Nelson
Fairway Ranch, Rt. 2
Roanoke, TX 76262
"Golfer"

Craig Richard Nelson
8271 Melrose Avenue, #110
Los Angeles, CA 90046
"Actor"

Craig T. Nelson
9171 Wilshire Blvd. #436
Beverly Hills, CA 90210
"Actor, Writer"

David Nelson
4179 Valley Meadow Road
Encino, CA 91316
"Actor, Director"

Ed Nelson
124 Old Pecan Grove
Waveland, MS 39576
"Actor"

Frank Nelson
8906 Evanview Drive
Los Angeles, CA 90069
"Actor"

Gene Nelson
835 Catamaran Street #1
Forster City, CA 94404
"Actor, Director"

John Allen Nelson
10100 Santa Monica Blvd.
25th Floor
Los Angeles, CA 90067
"Actor"

Judd Nelson
P.O. Box 5617
Beverly Hills, CA 90210
"Actor"

Lori Nelson
10643 Riverside Drive
Toluca Lake, CA 91602
"Actress"

Tracy Nelson
405 Sycamore Road
Santa Monica, CA 90402
"Actress"

Willie Nelson
P.O. Box 3280
Austin, TX 78764
"Singer, Songwriter"

Corin "Corkey" Nemec
8942 Wilshire Blvd.
Beverly Hills, CA 90211
"Actor"

Franco Nero
Via di Monte del Gallo 26
I-00165 Rome, ITALY
"Actor"

Peter Nero
4114 Royal Crest Place
Encino, CA 91436
"Pianist"

Michael Nesmith
11858 LeGrange Avenue
Los Angeles, CA 90025
"Singer, Producer"

Benjamin Netanyahue
Hakirya Romema
Jerusalem 91950 ISRAEL
"Prime Minister"

Graig Nettles
13 North Lane
Del Mar, CA 92014
"Ex-Baseball Player"

Lois Nettleton
11762-G Moorpark Street
Studio City, CA 91604
"Actress"

Dorothy Neumann
10860 Kingsland Street
Los Angeles, CA 90034
"Actress"

Bebe Neuwirth
25 Richard Court
Princeton, NJ 08540
"Actress"

Aaron Neville
P.O. Box 750187
New Orleans, LA 70130
"Singer"

Nancy Nevinson
23 Mill Close, Fishbourne
Chichester ENGLAND
"Actress"

George Newbern
9150 Wilshire Blvd. #205
Beverly Hills, CA 90212
"Actor"

New Christy Minstrels
1484 S. Beverly Drive #309
Los Angeles, CA 90035
"Vocal Group"

New Editon
P.O. Box 77505
San Francisco, CA 94107
"R&B Group"

New Grass Revival
P.O. Box 128037
Nashville, TN 37212
"C&W Group"

Bob Newhart
420 Amapola Lane
Los Angeles, CA 90077
"Actor, Comedian"

Samuel I. Newhouse, Jr.
950 Fingerboard Road
Staten Island, NY 10305
"Publishing Executive"

Anthony Newley
60 Old Brompton Road
London SW7 3LQ ENGLAND
"Singer, Actor, Writer"

Barry Newman
425 North Oakhurst Drive
Beverly Hills, CA 90210
"Actor"

Laraine Newman
10480 Ashton Avenue
Los Angeles, CA 90024
"Actress"

Nanette Newman
Seven Pines, Wentworth
Surrey GU25 4QP ENGLAND
"Actress"

Paul Newman
9830 Wilshire Blvd.
Beverly Hills, CA 90212
"Actor"

Phyllis Newman
529 West 42nd Street #7
New York, NY 10036
"Actress"

Randy Newman
1880 Century Park West, #900
Los Angeles, CA 90067
"Singer, Songwriter"

Robert Newman
9200 Sunset Blvd. #710
Los Angeles, CA 90069
"Actor"

Julie Newmar
204 South Carmelina Avenue
Los Angeles, CA 90049
"Actress, Model"

New Order
86 Palatin Road
Dudsbury, Manchester 20
ENGLAND
"Rock & Roll Group"

New Riders of the Purple Sage
145 Third Street
San Rafael, CA 94901
"Rock & Roll Group"

David Newsom
924 Westwood Blvd. #900
Los Angeles, CA 90024
"Actor"

Tommy Newson
19315 Wells Drive
Tarzana, CA 91356
"Conductor"

Juice Newton
P.O. Box 2993323
Lewisville, TX 75029
"Singer"

Wayne Newton
6629 South Pecos
Las Vegas, NV 89120
"Singer, Actor"

Olivia Newton-John
P.O. Box 2710
Malibu, CA 90265
"Singer, Actress"

Richard Ney
800 South San Rafael Avenue
Pasadena, CA 91105
"Actor"

Dustin Nguyen
218 1/4 S. Poinsettia Place
Los Angeles, CA 90036
"Actor"

Michelle Nicastro
1800 Avenue of the Stars, #400
Los Angeles, CA 90067
"Actress"

Denise Nicholas
9300 Wilshire Blvd. #555
Beverly Hills, CA 90212
"Actress, Singer"

Fayard Nicholas
23388 Mulholland Drive #5
Woodland Hills, CA 91364
"Dancer"

Harold Nicholas
789 West End Avenue
New York, NY 10025
"Dancer"

Thomas Ian Nicholas
1801 Avenue of the Stars, #1250
Los Angeles, CA 90067
"Actor"

Bobby Nichols
8681 Glenlyon Coourt
Fort Meyers, FL 33912
"Golfer"

Mike Nichols
15 East 69th Street
New York, NY 10021
"Film Writer, Director"

Nichelle Nichols
23281 Leonora Drive
Woodland Hills, CA 91367
"Actress"

Stephen Nichols
6287 Vine Way
Los Angeles, CA 90068
"Actor"

Terry Nichols
#08157-031
9595 West Quincy Avenue
Littleton, CO 80123
"Convict"

Jack Nicholson
15760 Ventura Blvd. #1730
Encino, CA 91436
"Actor"

Jack Nicklaus
11760 U.S. Highway 1 #6
North Palm Beach, FL 33408
"Golfer"

Sen. Don Nickles (OK)
Senate Hart Bldg. #133
Washington, DC 20510
"Politician"

Stevie Nicks
P.O. Box 7855
Alhambra, CA 91802
"Singer, Songwriter"

Julia Nickson
2232 Moreno Drive
Los Angeles, CA 90039
"Actress"

Alex Nicol
1496 San Leandro Park
Santa Barbara, CA 93108
"Actor"

Joe Niekro
39 Shadow Lane
Lakeland, FL 33813
"Ex-Baseball Player"

Brigitte Nielsen
P.O. Box 57593
Sherman Oaks, CA 91403
"Actress"

Leslie Nielsen
3476 Consuelo Drive
Calabasas, CA 91302
"Actor"

Night Ranger
P.O. Box 1000
Glen Ellen, CA 95442
"Rock & Roll Group"

Birgit Nilsson
P.O. Box 527
Stockholm, SWEDEN
"Soprano"

Leonard Nimoy
2300 W. Victory Blvd., #C-384
Burbank, CA 91506
"Actor, Writer, Director"

Yvette Nipar
9300 Wilshire Blvd. #410
Beverly Hills, CA 90212
"Actress"

Paul Nitze
1619 Massachusetts Ave. N.W.
Suite #811
Washington, DC 20036
"Statesman"

Mrs. Hjordis Niven
Chateau D'Oex
Vaud SWITZERLAND
"David Niven's Widower"

David Niven, Jr.
1457 Blue Jay Way
Los Angeles, CA 90069
"Son of David Niven"

Kip Niven
9200 Sunset Blvd. #710
Los Angeles, CA 90069
"Actor"

Agnes Nixon
774 Conestoga Road
Rosemont, PA 19010
"TV Writer, Producer"

Marni Nixon
1747 Van Buren Street, #790
Hollywood, FL 33020
"Singer, Actress"

Norm Nixon
607 Marguerita Avenue
Santa Monica, CA 90402
"Ex-Basketball Player"

Yannick Noah
20 rue Billancourt
F-92100 Boulogne FRANCE
"Tennis Player"

Chelsea Noble
P.O. Box 8665
Calabasas, CA 91372
"Actress"

James Noble
80 Baavater Lane
Black Rock, CT 06605
"Actor"

Lyn Nofziger
2000 Pennsylvania Ave. NW #365
Washington, DC 20037
"Political Advisor"

Dr. Thomas Noguchi
1110 Avoca Avenue
Pasadena, CA 91105
"Coroner"

Philippe Noiret
104 rue des Sablons
F-78750 Mareil-Marly FRANCE
"Actor"

Christopher Nolan
158 Vernon Avenue
Dublin, IRELAND
"Poet, Author"

Jeanette Nolan
940 Locust Avenue
Charlottesville, VA 22901
"Actress"

Kathleen Nolan
360 East 55th Street
New York, NY 10022
"Actress"

Tom Nolan
1335 North Ontario Street
Burbank, CA 91505
"Writer"

Chuck Noll
300 Stadium Circle
Pittsburg, PA 15212
"Ex-Football Coach"

Nick Nolte
6174 Bonsall Drive
Malibu, CA 90265
"Actor"

Hideo Nome
1000 Elysian Park Avenue
Los Angeles, CA 90012
"Baseball Player"

Kathleen Noone
12747 Riverside Drive #208
Valley Village, CA 91607
"Actress"

Peter Noone
9265 Robin Lane
Los Angeles, CA 90069
"Singer"

Clayton Norcross
951 Galloway Street
Pacific Palisades, CA 90272
"Actor"

Gen. Manuel Noriega
#38699-079
P.O. Box 979132
Miami, FL 33197
"Prisoner of War"

Greg Norman
P.O. Box 1189
Hobe Sound, FL 33475
"Golfer"

Jessye Norman
1900 Broadway
New York, NY 10023
"Soprano"

Maide Norman
455 E. Charleston Road #132-B
Palo Alto, CA 94306
"Actress"

Christopher Norris
822 South Robertson Blvd., #200
Los Angeles, CA 90035
"Actress"

Chuck Norris
P.O. Box 872
Navosota, TX 77868
"Actor"

Jay North
RR #2
Lake Butler, FL 32054
"Actor"

Oliver North
RR #1, Box 560
Bluemont, VA 22012
"Former Military Lt. Col."

Sheree North
1467 Palisades Drive
Pacific Palisades, CA 90272
"Actress"

Wayne Northrup
21919 West Canon Drive
Topanga, CA 90290
"Actor"

Ken Norton
16 South Peck Drive
Laguna Niguel, CA 92677
"Boxer, Actor"

Judy Norton-Taylor
6767 Forest Lawn Drive #115
Los Angeles, CA 90068
"Actress, Model"

Deborah Norville
P.O. Box 426
Mill Neck, NY 11765
"TV Show Host"

Chris Noth
10683 Santa Monica Blvd.
Los Angeles, CA 90025
"Actor"

Michael Nouri
108 Mira Mesa
Rancho Santa Margarita, CA 92688
"Actor"

Lou Nova
2900 South Valley View #1
Las Vegas, NV 89102
"Boxing Promoter"

William Novack
3 Ashton
Newton, MA 02159
"Author"

Robert Novak
1750 Pennsylvania Avenue N.W.
Suite #1312
Washington, DC 20006
"News Journalist, Columnist"

Don Novello
P.O. Box 245
Fairfax, CA 94930
"Actor, Writer, Comedian"

Eddie Nugent
P.O. Box 1266
New York, NY 10150
"Actor"

Ted Nugent
8000 Eckert
Concord, MI 49237
"Singer, Guitarist"

Sam Nunn
915 Main Street
Perry, GA 31060
"Politician"

France Nuyen
9255 Sunset Blvd., #515
Los Angeles, CA 90069
"Actress"

Carrie Nye
200 West 57th Street #900
New York, NY 10019
"Actress"

Louis Nye
1241 Corsica Drive
Pacific Palisadaes, CA 90272
"Actor, Comedian"

Russell Nype
178 East 78th Street
New York, NY 10021
"Actor"

Laura Nyro
59 Parsons Street
West Newton, MA 02165
"Singer, Songwriter"

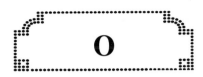

Oak Ridge Boys
2102 West Linden Avenue
Nashville, TN 37212
"C&W Group"

Randi Oakes
11750H Moorpark
Studio City, CA 91604
"Actress"

Oasis
8A Wyndham Place
London W1X 1PP ENGLAND
"Gospel Group"

John Oates
130 West 57th Street #12B
New York, NY 10019
"Singer, Songwriter"

Hugh O'Brian
10880 Wilshire Blvd. #1500
Los Angeles, CA 90024
"Actor"

Austin O'Brien
40 West 57th Street
New York, NY 10019
"Actor"

Conan O'Brien
30 Rockefeller Plaza
New York, NY 10019
"Talk Show Host"

Dan O'Brien
517 N. Robertson Blvd., #200
Los Angeles, CA 90048
"Decathlete"

Margaret O'Brien
1250 La Peresa Drive
Thousand Oaks, CA 91362
"Actress"

Billy Ocean
Ascot
Berkshire ENGLAND
"Singer"

Jerry O'Connell
160 Perth Avenue
Toronto, Ontario
M6P 3X5 CANADA
"Actor"

Mark O'Conner
P.O. Box 150245
Nashville, TN 37215
"Violinist"

Carroll O'Connor
30826 Broad Beach Road
Malibu, CA 90265
"Actor, Writer, Director"

Des O'Connor
23 Eyot Gardens
London W6 9TR ENGLAND
"Singer"

Donald O'Connor
P.O. Box 20204
Sedona, AZ 86341
"Actor, Director"

Glynnis O'Connor
8955 Norma Place
W. Hollywood, CA 90069
"Actress"

Sandra Day O'Connor
1-1st Street, Northeast
Washington, DC 20543
"Supreme Court Justice"

Sinead O'Connor
3 E. 54th Street #1400
New York, NY 10022
"Singer"

Tim O'Connor
10000 Santa Monica Blvd. #305
Los Angeles, CA 90067
"Actor"

Anita O'Day
R.D. 1, Box 91
Tannersville, PA 18372
"Entertainer, Singer"

Molly O'Day
P.O. Box 2123
Avila Beach, CA 93424
"Actress"

Tony O'Dell
417 Griffith Park Drive
Burbank, CA 91506
"Actor"

Chris O'Donnell
1724 N. Vista Street
Los Angeles, CA 90046
"Actor"

Rosie O'Donnell
4116 Bellington Avenue
Studio City, CA 91602
"Actress"

Martha O'Driscoll
22 Indian Creek Village
Miami Beach, FL 33154
"Actress"

Al Oerter
5485 Avenieda Pescadera
Ft. Meyers, FL 33931
"Executive, Discus Thrower"

Ian Ogilvy
68 St. James's Street
London SW1A 1LE ENGLAND
"Actor"

Soon-Teck Oh
4150 Riverside Drive, #212
Burbank, CA 91505
"Actress"

Jenny O'Hara
50 West 13th Street
New York, NY 10011
"Actress"

Maureen O'Hara
P.O. Box 1400
Christiansted 00820
St. Croix, VIRGIN ISLANDS
"Actress"

Dan O'Herlihy
24 W. 40th Street #1700
New York, NY 10018
"Actor"

John O'Hurley
6310 San Vincente Blvd. #407
Los Angeles, CA 90048
"Actor"

Michael O'Keeffe
1344 North Spaulding
Los Angeles, CA 90046
"Actor"

Miles O'Keeffe
P.O. Box 216
Malibu, CA 90265
"Actor"

Ken Olandt
3500 West Olive #1400
Burbank, CA 91505
"Actor"

Mike Oldfield
Singes House
32 Galena Road
London W6 OLT ENGLAND
"Musician, Composer"

Sally Oldfield
100 Chalk Farm Road
London NW1 ENGLAND
"Singer"

Gary Oldman
76 Oxford Street
London W1R 1RB ENGLAND
"Actor"

Michael O'Leary
8075 West 3rd Street #303
Los Angeles, CA 90048
"Actress"

Ken Olefson
6720 Hillpark Drive #301
Los Angeles, CA 90068
"Actor"

Ken Olin
11840 Chapparal Street
Los Angeles, CA 90049
"Actor"

Lena Olin
40 West 57th Street
New York, NY 10019
"Actress"

Gordon Oliver
200 North Swall Drive #453
Beverly Hills, CA 90210
"Actor, Director"

Edward James Olmos
18034 Ventura Blvd. #228
Encino, CA 91316
"Actor"

Gerald O'Loughlin
P.O. Box 340832
Arleta, CA 91334
"Actor, Director"

Ashley Olsen
8916 Ashcroft Avenue
Los Angeles, CA 90048
"Actress"

Mary Kate Olsen
8916 Ashcroft Avenue
Los Angeles, CA 90048
"Actress"

Nancy Olsen
945 North Alpine Drive
Beverly Hills, CA 90210
"Actress"

Susan Olsen
3580 Wilshire Blvd.
Los Angeles, CA 90010
"Actress"

James Olson
250 West 57th Street #803
New York, NY 10019
"Actor"

Peter O'Malley
1000 Elysian Park Avenue
Los Angeles, CA 90012
"Baseball Executive"

Saltan of Oman
The Palacc
Muslat OMAN
"Royalty"

Kate O'Mara
11 Southwick Mews
London W2 1JG ENGLAND
"Actress"

Sydney Omarr
201 Ocean Avenue #1706-B
Santa Monica, CA 90402
"Astrologer, Writer"

Griffin O'Neal
21368 Pacific Coast Highway
Malibu, CA 90265
"Screenwriter"

Ryan O'Neal
21368 Pacific Coast Highway
Malibu, CA 90265
"Actor"

Shaquille O'Neal
One Magic Place
Orlando, FL 32801
"Basketball Player"

Tatum O'Neal
200 East End Avenue #16H
New York, NY 10128
"Actress"

Dick O'Neil
230 South Lasky Drive
Beverly Hills, CA 90212
"Actor"

Jennifer O'Neil
32356 Mulholland Highway
Malibu, CA 90265
"Actress, Model"

Ron O'Neil
10100 Santa Monica Blvd., #2500
Los Angeles, CA 90067
"Actor"

Ed O'Neill
2607 Grand Canal
Venice, CA 90291
"Actor"

Kitty O'Neill
P.O. Box 604
Medina, OH 44256
"Stuntwoman, Auto Racer"

Yoko Ono Lennon
1 West 72nd Street
New York, NY 10023
"Singer, Songwriter"

Michael Ontkean
P.O. Box 1212
Malibu, CA 90265
"Actor"

David Opatashu
4161 Dixie Canyon Avenue
Sherman Oaks, CA 91423
"Actor, Writer"

Marcel Ophuls
10 rue Ernst-Deloison
92200 Neuilly, FRANCE
"Director, Producer"

Peter Oppegard
2331 Century Hill
Los Angeles, CA 90067
"Skater"

Jerry Orbach
10100 Santa Monica Blvd., #2490
Los Angeles, CA 90067
"Actor"

Cyril O'Reilly
8091 Selma Avenue
Los Angeles, CA 90046
"Actor"

Tony Orlando
3220 Falls Parkway
Branson, MO 65616
"Singer"

Yuri Orlov
Cornell University
Newman Laboratory
Ithica, NJ 14853
"Scientist"

Julia Ormond
308 Regent St.
London W1R 5AL ENGLAND
"Actress"

Bobby Orr
647 Summer Street
Boston, MA 02210
"Ex-Hockey Player"

Brian Orser
1600 James Naismith Dr.
Gloucester Ontario
K1B 5N4 CANADA
"Skater"

Joan Osbourne
11150 Santa Monica Blvd., 10th Flr.
Los Angeles, CA 90025
"Singer"

Jeffrey Osbourne
5800 Valley Oak Drive
Los Angeles, CA 90068
"Singer, Songwriter"

Ozzy Osbourne
184 Sutherland Avenue, #2
London W9 ENGLAND
"Singer, Songwriter"

Tom Osburne
University of Nebraska Football
Lincoln, NE 68588
"Football Coach"

Milo O' Shea
40 West 72nd Street #17-A
New York, NY 10023
"Actor"

Nagisa Osima
4-11-5, Kugenuma-Matsugaoka
Fujisawa-Shi 251 JAPAN
"Director"

K.T. Oslin
1103-16th Avenue
Nashville, TN 37212
"Singer"

Cliff Osmond
630 Bienvenida
Pacific Palisades, CA 90272
"Screenwriter"

Donny Osmond
36 Avignon
Newport Beach, CA 92657
"Singer"

Ken Osmond
9863 Wornom Avenue
Sunland, CA 91040
"Actor"

Marie Osmond
P.O. Box 1990
Branson, MO 65616
"Singer, Actress"

The Osmonds
P.O. Box 7122
Branson, MO 65616
"Vocal Group"

Jeff Osterhage
210-D North Cordova
Burbank, CA 91505
"Actor"

Bibi Osterwald
341 Carrol Park West
Long Beach, CA 90815
"Actress"

Maureen O'Sullivan
1839 Union Street
Schnectady, NY 12309
"Actress"

Annette O'Toole
360 Morton Street
Ashland, OR 97520
"Actress"

Peter O'Toole
31/32 Soho Square
London W1V 5DG ENGLAND
"Actor"

Merlene Ottey
P.O. Box 2902
CH-5001 Aarau SWITZERLAND
"Track & Field"

Otto of Austria
Hindenburger- Strasse 15
8134 Pocking GERMANY
"Ex-King"

Park Overall
4843 Arcola Avenue
North Hollywood, CA 91601
"Actress"

Paul Overstreet
P.O. Box 2977
Hendersonville, TN 37077
"Singer"

Michael Ovitz
457 Rockingham
Los Angeles, CA 90049
"Talent Agent"

Randy Owen
Rt. #4
Ft. Payne, AL 35967
"Guitarist, Singer"

Buck Owens
3223 Sillect Avenue
Bakersfield, CA 93308
"Singer, Songwriter"

Gary Owens
17856 Via Vallarta
Encino, CA 91316
"Radio/TV Performer"

Geoffrey Owens
19 West 44th Street #1500
New York, NY 10036
"Newspaper Editor"

Earl Owensby
P.O. Box 184
Shelby, NC 28150
"Director, Producer"

Catherine Oxenberg
1800 Century Park East #600
Los Angeles, CA 90067
"Actress, Model"

Frank Oz
P.O. Box 20750
New York, NY 10023
"Puppeteer"

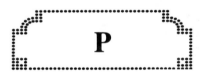

Jack Paar
9 Chateau Ridge Drive
Greenwich, CT 06830
"Ex-TV Show Host

Pablo Cruise
P.O. Box 779
Mill Valley, CA 94941
"Rock & Roll Group"

Judy Pace
4139 Cloverdale
Los Angeles, CA 90008
"Actress"

Al Pacino
350 Park Avenue #900
New York, NY 10022
"Actor"

Vance Packard
Mill Road
New Canaan, CT 06840
"Author"

Joanna Pacula
P.O. Box 5617
Beverly Hills, CA 90210
"Actress"

Anita Page
929 Rutland Avenue
Los Angeles, CA 90042
"Actress"

Bettie Page
P.O. Box 56176
Chicago, IL 60656
"50's Pin-up Girl"

Genevieve Page
52 rue de Vaugirard
75006 Paris FRANCE
"Actress"

Jimmy Page
29/33 Berner's Street
London W1P 4AA ENGLAND
"Guitarist"

LaWanda Page
1056 West 84th Street
Los Angeles, CA 90044
"Actress"

Patti Page
1412 San Lucas Court
Solana Beach, CA 92075
"Singer"

Debra Paget
737 Kuhlman Road
Houston, TX 77024
"Actress"

Ashraf Pahlavi
12 Avenue Montaigne
75016 Paris FRANCE
"Royalty"

Elaine Paige
Arlon, Pinewood Road
Iver. Buckinghamshire
SL0 0NH ENGLAND
"Actress"

Janis Paige
1700 Rising Glen Road
Los Angeles, CA 90069
"Actress"

Rev. Ian Paisley
The Parsonage
17 Cyprus Avenue
Belfast BT5 5NT IRELAND
"Clergyman"

Alan Pakula
330 West 58th Street #5-H
New York, NY 10019
"Writer, Producer"

Holly Palance
2753 Roscomare
Los Angeles, CA 90077
"Actress"

Jack Palance
P.O. Box 6201
Tehachapi, CA 93561
"Actor, Director"

Ron Palillo
448 W. 44th Street
New York, NY 10036
"Actor"

Michael Palin
68A Delancey Street
London W1 ENGLAND
"Actor, Writer"

Arnold Palmer
P.O. Box 52
Youngstown, PA 15696
"Golfer"

Betsy Palmer
40 Jordan Drive
River Edge, NJ 07661
"Actress"

Gregg Palmer
5726 Graves Avenue
Encino, CA 91316
"Actor"

Gretchen Palmer
10637 Burbank Blvd.
North Hollywood, CA 91601
"Actress"

Jim Palmer
P.O. Box 145
Brooklandville, MD 21022
"Ex-Baseball Player, Model"

Peter Palmer
478 Severn
Tampa, FL 33606
"Actor"

Robert Palmer
P.O. Box 1463
Culver City, CA 90232
"Singer, Songwriter"

Scott Palmer
4455 Saltillo Street
Woodland Hills, CA 91364
"Actor"

Tony Palmer
4 Kensington Park Gardens
London W11 3HB ENGLAND
"Writer, Producer"

Chazz Palminteri
375 Greenwich St.
New York, NY, 10013
"Actor"

Gwyneth Paltrow
9830 Wilshire Blvd.
Beverly Hills, CA 90212
"Actress"

Sec. Leon. Panetta
Office of Management & Budget
Washington, DC 20503
"Government Official"

May Pang
1619 Third Avenue #9D
New York, NY 10128
"John Lennon's Mistress"

Stuart Pankin
9150 Wilshire Blvd. #350
Beverly Hills, CA 90212
"Actor"

Joe Pantaliano
2313-30th Street
Santa Monica, CA 90405
"Actor"

Irene Papas
Xenokratous 39
Athens-Kolanaki, GREECE
"Actress"

Anna Paquin
P.O. Box 9585
Wellington, New Zealand
"Actress"

Ara Paraseghian
1212 St. Joseph Bank Building
South Bend, IN 46601
"Former College Coach"

Jack Pardee
6910 Fannin Street
Houston, TX 77030
"Football Coach"

Michael Pare
2804 Pacific Avenue
Venice, CA 90291
"Actor"

Gail Parent
2001 Mandeville Canyon
Los Angeles, CA 90024
"Screenwriter"

Johnny Paris
1764 Parkway Drive South
Maumee, OH 43537
"Singer"

Corey Parker
10431 Scenario Lane
Los Angeles, CA 90077
"Actor"

Dave Parker
7864 Ridge Road
Cincinnati, OH 45237
"Ex-Baseball Player"

Eleanor Parker
2195 La Paz Way
Palm Springs, CA 92262
"Actress"

Fess Parker
P.O. Box 908
Los Olivos, CA 93441
"Actor"

Jameson Parker
1604 North Vista Avenue
Los Angeles, CA 90046
"Actor"

Lara Parker
1441 Bonnell
Topanga, CA 90290
"Actress"

Mary Louise Parker
151 El Camino Drive
Beverly Hills, CA 90212
"Actress"

Sarah Jessica Parker
9830 Wilshire Blvd.
Beverly Hills, CA 90212
"Actress"

Suzy Parker
770 Hot Springs Road
Santa Barbara, CA 93103
"Actress"

Willard Parker
74580 Fairway Drive
Indian Wells, CA 92260
"Actor"

Camilla Parker Bowles
Middlewick House
nr. Corsham, Wiltshire ENGLAND
"Prince Charles' Friend"

Heather Parkhurst
11684 Ventura Blvd.
Studio City, CA 91604
"Actress"

Barbara Parkins
10100 Santa Monica Blvd., #2490
Los Angeles, CA 90067
"Actress"

Dian Parkinson
4655 Natick Avenue #1
Sherman Oaks, CA 91403
"Actress, Model"

Michael Parkinson
58 Queen Anne Street
London W1M 0DX ENGLAND
"Writer"

Andrew Parks
1830 Grace Avenue
Los Angeles, CA 90028
"Actor"

Michael Parks
11684 Ventura Blvd. #476
Studio City, CA 91604
"Actor"

Rosa Parks
9336 Wildemere Street
Detroit, MI 48206
"Mother of Civil Rights"

Lee Roy Parnell
P.O. Box 120073
Nashville, TN 37212
"Singer"

Van Dyke Parks
837 Melrose Hill Court
Los Angeles, CA 90036
"Actress"

Julie Parrish
P.O. Box 247
Santa Monica, CA 90406
"Actress"

Peter Parros
15 Carter Road
West Orange, NJ 07052
"Actor"

Estelle Parsons
505 West End Avenue
New York, NY 10024
"Actress"

Karyn Parsons
3208 Cahuenga Blvd. West, #16
Los Angeles, CA 90068
"Actress"

Nancy Parsons
121 North San Vicente Blvd.
Beverly Hills, CA 90211
"Actress"

Dolly Parton
P.O. Box 150307
Nashville, TN 37215
"Singer, Actress"

Stella Parton
P.O. Box 120295
Nashville, TN 37212
"Singer"

Derek Partridge
96 Broadway
Bexley Heath
Kent DA6 7DE ENGLAND
"Actor"

Francoise Pascal
89 Riverview Gardens
London SW12 ENGLAND
"Actress"

Mary Ann Pascal
9744 Wilshire Blvd. #308
Beverly Hills, CA 90212
"Actress"

Adrian Pasdar
4250 Wilshire Blvd.
Los Angeles, CA 90010
"Actor"

Robert Pastorelli
2751 Holly Ridge Drive
Los Angeles, CA 90068
"Actor"

Michael Pate
21 Bukdarra Road
Bellevue Hill 2023
AUSTRALIA
"Actor"

Mandy Patinkin
200 West 90th Street
New York, NY 10024
"Actress"

Jason Patric
10683 Santa Monica Blvd.
Los Angeles, CA 90025
"Actor"

Butch Patrick
P.O. Box 587
Farmingville, NY 11738
"Actor"

Robert Patrick
9560 Wilshire #500
Beverly Hills, CA 90211
"Playwright"

Floyd Patterson
Springtown Road
P.O. Box 336
New Paltz, NY 12561
"Boxer"

Lorna Patterson
10100 Santa Monica Blvd.
Suite 2500
Los Angeles, CA 90067
"Actress"

Neva Patterson
2498 Maneville Canyon Road
Los Angeles, CA 90049
"Actress"

Sandi Patti
P.O. Box 2940
Anderson, IN 46018
"Singer"

Adrian Paul
16027 Ventura Blvd., #206
Encino, CA 91436
"Actor"

Alexandra Paul
9229 Sunset Blvd., #710
Los Angeles, CA 90069
"Actress"

Don Michael Paul
3104 Walnut Avenue
Manhattan Beach, CA 90266
"Actor"

Les Paul
78 Deerhaven Road
Mahwah, NJ 07430
"Guitarist"

Richard Paul
3614 Willowcrest Avenue
Studio City, CA 91604
"Actor"

Jane Pauley
271 Central Park West #10-E
New York, NY 10024
"TV Show Host"

Pat Paulsen
P.O. Box 10
Tujunga, CA 91043
"Comedian, Actor

Marisa Pavan
4 Allee des Borouillards
F-75018 Paris, FRANCE
"Actress"

Luciano Pavarotti
941 Via Giardini
I-41040 Saliceta
Panaro ITALY
"Tenor"

Ria Pavia
3500 West Olive Avenue, #1400
Burbank, CA 91505
"Actress"

Bill Paxton
151 El Camino Drive
Beverly Hills, CA 90212
"Actor"

Johnny Paycheck
1321 Murfreesboro Road, #600
Nashville, TN 37217
"Singer"

David Paymer
121 N. San Vicente Blvd.
Beverly Hills, CA 90211
"Actor"

Freda Payne
245 S. Spalding Drive #302
Beverly Hills, CA 90212
"Singer"

Amanda Pays
3541 North Knoll Drive
Los Angeles, CA 90068
"Actress, Model"

Walter Payton
1251 East Golf Road
Schaumburg, IL 60195
"Ex-Football Player"

Octavio Paz
Avenue Reforma 369-104
Col Cuauhtemoc, Mexico
06500 DF MEXICO
"Poet, Diplomat"

Vinnie Pazienda
64 Waterman Avenue
Cranston, RI 02910
"Boxer"

E. J. Peaker
4935 Densmore Avenue
Encino, CA 91436
"Actress"

Pearl Jam
417 Denny Way, #200
Seattle, WA 98109
"Rock & Roll Group"

Durk Pearson
P.O. Box 1067
Hollywood, FL 33022
"Scientist, Author"

Patsy Pease
13538 Valley Heart Drive
Sherman Oaks, CA 91403
"Actress"

Gregory Peck
P.O. Box 837
Beverly Hills, CA 90213
"Actor"

Nia Peeples
P.O. Box 218033
Waco, TX 76702
"Actress"

I. M. Pei
600 Madison Avenue
New York, NY 10022
"Architect"

Ashley Peldon
924 Westwood Blvd., #900
Los Angeles, CA 90024
"Actress"

Pele
Praca dos Tres Poderes
Palacio de Planalto BR
70150900 Brasilia DF BRAZIL
"Soccer Player"

Lisa Pelikan
P.O. Box 57444
Sherman Oaks, CA 91403
"Actress"

Sen. Claiborne Pell (RI)
335 Russell Bldg.
Washington, DC 20510
"Politician"

Meeno Peluce
2713 North Keystone
Burbank, CA 91504
"Actor"

Elizabeth Pena
10100 Santa Monica Blvd.
Suite #2500
Los Angeles, CA 90067
"Actress"

Teddy Pendergrass
1505 Flat Rock Road
Narberth, PA 19072
"Singer, Songwriter"

Austin Pendleton
155 East 76th Street
New York, NY 10021
"Comedian"

Thao Penghlis
7187 Macapa Drive
Los Angeles, CA 90068
"Actor"

The Penguins
708 West 137th Street
Gardena, CA 90247
"Vocal Group"

Susan Penhaligon
109 Jermyn Street
London SW1 ENGLAND
"Actress"

Bruce Penhall
319A - 36th Street
Manhattan Beach, CA 90266
"Actor"

Ce Ce Peniston
1700 Broadway #500
New York, NY 10019
"Singer"

Leo Penn
6728 Zumirez Drive
Malibu, CA 90265
"Filmwriter, Director"

Sean Penn
2049 Century Park East #2500
Los Angeles, CA 90067
"Actor"

Penn & Teller
1325 Avenue of the Americas
New York, NY 10019
"Magicians"

Jonathan Penner
1800 Avenue of the Stars, #400
Los Angeles, CA 90067
"Actor"

Ann Pennington
701 North Oakhurst Drive
Beverly Hills, CA 90210
"Actress, Model"

Janice Pennington
433 N. Camden Drive #600
Beverly Hills, CA 90210
"Model, Actress"

Michael Pennington
41 Marlborough Hill
London NW8 ENGLAND
"Actor"

Chris Pennock
25150 1/2 Malibu Road
Malibu, CA 90265
"Actor"

Joe Penny
10453 Sarah
North Hollywood, CA 91602
"Actor"

Sidney Penny
6894 Parson Trail
Tujunga, CA 91042
"Actress"

Roger Penske
13400 Outer Drive West
Detroit, MI 48239
"Auto Racing Executive"

Willie Pep
166 Bunce Road
Wethersfield, CT 06109
"Boxer"

Joe Pepitone
32 Lois Lane
Farmingdale, NY 11735
"Ex-Baseball Player"

Lance Percival
25 Whitehall
London SW1A 2BS ENGLAND
"TV Personality"

Charles Percy
900 19th Street N. #700
Washington, DC 20006
"Ex-Senator"

Shimon Peres
10 Hayarkon Street
Box 3263
Tel Aviv 3263 ISRAEL
"Politician"

Rosie Perez
10683 Santa Monica Blvd.
Los Angeles, CA 90025
"Actress"

Vincent Perez
10 avenue George V
F-75008 Paris, France
"Actor"

Carl Perkins
27 Sunnymeade Drive
Jackson, TN 38305
"Singer, Songwriter"

Elizabeth Perkins
9830 Wilshire Blvd.
Beverly Hills, CA 90212
"Actress"

Millie Perkins
2511 Canyon Drive
Los Angeles, CA 90068
"Actress"

Rhea Perlman
P.O. Box 491246
Los Angeles, CA 90049
"Actress"

Ron Perlman
P.O. Box 5617
Beverly Hills, CA 90210
"Actress"

Ytzhak Perlman
40 West 57th Street
New York, NY 10019
"Violinist"

Mme. Isabel Peron
Moreto 3
Los Jeronimos
Madrid SPAIN
"Politician"

H. Ross Perot
1700 Lakeside Square
Dallas, TX 75251
"Data Executive"

Gigi Perreau
268 North Bowling Green Way
Los Angeles, CA 90049
"Actress"

Valerie Perrine
Via Toscana 1
I-00187 Rome ITALY
"Actress, Model"

Barbara Perry
6926 La Presa Drive
Los Angeles, CA 90068
"Actress"

Felton Perry
540 South St. Andrews Place
Suite #5
Los Angeles, CA 90020
"Actor"

Gaylord Perry
320 East Jefferies Street
Gaffney, SC 29342
"EX-Baseball Player"

Jeff Perry
8458 Ridpath Avenue
Los Angeles, CA 90046
"Actor"

John Bennett Perry
606 N. Larchmont Blvd. #309
Los Angeles, CA 90004
"Actor"

Luke Perry
19528 Ventura Blvd. #533
Tarzana, CA 91356
"Actor"

Matthew Perry
9911 W. Pico Blvd. PH I
Los Angeles, CA 90035
"Actor"

Steve Perry
1401 Pathfinder Avenue
Westlake Village, CA 91362
"Singer, Composer"

William Perry
The Pentagon
Washington, DC 20301
"Secretary of Defense"

Bill Pertwee
25 Whitehall
London SW1A 2BS ENGLAND
"Actor"

Jon Pertwee
24 Calthope Gardens, Sutton
Surrey SM1 3DF ENGLAND
"Actor, Comedian"

Nehemia Persoff
5847 Tampa Avenue
Tarzana, CA 91356
"Actor"

Joe Pesci
P.O. Box 6
Lavallette, NJ 08735
"Actor"

Donna Pescow
2179 West 21st Street
Los Angeles, CA 90018
"Actress"

Pet Shop Boys
20 Manchester Square
London W1 ENGLAND
"Rock & Roll Group"

Peter, Paul & Mary
27 West 67th Street
New York, NY 10023
"Vocal Trio"

Bernadette Peters
323 West 80th Street
New York, NY 10024
"Actress"

Brock Peters
1420 Rising Glen Road
Los Angeles, CA 90069
"Actor, Writer, Director"

Jean Peters
507 North Palm Drive
Beverly Hills, CA 90210
"Actress"

Jon Peters
9 Beverly Park
Beverly Hills, CA 90210
"Film Producer"

Roberta Peters
64 Garden Road
Scarsdale, NY 10583
"Singer"

Pat Petersen
1634 Veteran Avenue
Los Angeles, CA 90025
"Actor"

Paul Petersen
14530 Denker Avenue
Gardena, CA 90247
"Actor"

William L. Petersen
8942 Wilshire Blvd.
Beverly Hills, CA 90211
"Actor"

Wolfgang Petersen
10202 W. Washington Blvd. #224
Culver City, CA 90232
"Film Director"

Amanda Peterson
11350 Ventura Blvd. #206
Studio City, CA 91604
"Actress"

Dan Petry
1808 Carlen Drive
Placentia, CA 92670
"Ex-Baseball Player"

Joanna Pettit
10100 Santa Monica Blvd. #700
Los Angeles, CA 90067
"Actress"

Kyle Petty
4341 Finch Farm Road
Trinity, NC 27370
"Race Car Driver"

Lori Petty
12301 Wilshire Blvd. #200
Los Angeles, CA 90025
"Actress"

Richard Petty
Rt. #4, Box 86
Randleman, NC 27317
"Race Car Driver"

Tom Petty
8209 Melrose Avenue, #200
Los Angeles, CA 90046
"Rock & Roll Singer"

Penny Peyser
22039 Alizondo Drive
Woodland Hills, CA 91367
"Actress"

Michelle Pfeiffer
231 N. Orchard Drive
Burbank, CA 91506
"Actress"

Jo Ann Pflug
118 Bospirit Drive
North Palm Beach, FL 33408
"Actress"

Regis Philbin
955 Park Avenue
New York, NY 10028
"TV Show Host"

HRH Prince Philip
Duke of Edinburgh
Buckingham Palace
London SW1 ENGLAND
"Royalty"

Chynna Phillips
938-2nd Street #302
Santa Monica, CA 90403
"Actress, Singer"

Joseph C. Phillips
8730 Sunset Blvd. #480
Los Angeles, CA 90069
"Actor"

Julia Phillips
2534 Benedict Canyon
Beverly Hills, CA 90210
"Film Producer"

Julianne Phillips
10390 Santa Monica Blvd.
Suite #300
Los Angeles, CA 90025
"Actress, Model"

Lou Diamond Phillips
11766 Wilshire Blvd. #1470
Los Angeles, CA 90025
"Actor"

Mackenzie Phillips
805 3rd Avenue #2900
New York, NY 10022
"Actress, Singer"

Michelle Phillips
9150 Wilshire Blvd. #175
Beverly Hills, CA 90212
"Actress, Singer"

Sam Phillips
729 7th Avenue #1600
New York, NY 10019
"Singer"

Sian Phillips
14 Petherton Road
London N5 ENGLAND
"Actress"

Robert Picardo
P.O. Box 5617
Beverly Hills, CA 90210
"Actor"

Paloma Picasso
37 West 57th Street
New York, NY 10019
"Designer"

Michel Piccoli
11 rue de Lions St. Paul
4e Paris, FRANCE
"Actor"

Paul Picerni
19119 Wells Drive
Tarzana, CA 91356
"Actor"

Donald Pickering
Back Court
Manor House
Eastleach, Glos. ENGLAND
"Actor"

Cindy Pickett
151 El Camino Drive
Beverly Hills, CA 90212
"Actress"

Wilson Pickett
1560 Broadway #1308
New York, NY 10036
"Singer"

Christina Pickles
137 South Westgate Avenue
Los Angeles, CA 90049
"Actress"

Vivian Pickles
91 Regent Street
London W1R 8RU ENGLAND
"Actress"

Ronald Pickup
54 Crouch Hall Road
London N8 ENGLAND
"Actor"

Charles Pierce
4445 Cartwright Avenue #309
North Hollywood, CA 91602
"Impersonator"

David Hyde Pierce
9255 Sunset Blvd. #710
Los Angeles, CA 90069
"Actor"

Mary Pierce
1 Erieview Plaza, #1300
Cleveland, OH 44114
"Tennis Player"

Eric Pierpoint
10929 Morrison Street #14
North Hollywood, CA 91601
"Actor"

Jimmy Piersall
1105 Oakview Drive
Wheaton, IL 60187
"Ex-Baseball Player"

Tim Pigott-Smith
125 Gloucester Road
London SW7 4TE ENGLAND
"Actor"

Ray Pillow
Rt. 4, New Hwy. 96 West
Franklin, TN 37064
"Singer"

Bronson Pinchot
9150 Wilshire Blvd. #350
Beverly Hills, CA 90212
"Actor"

Philip Pine
7034 Costello Avenue
Van Nuys, CA 91405
"Actor"

Robert Pine
3975 Van Noord Avenue
Studio City, CA 91604
"Actor, Director"

Lou Piniella
P.O. Box 4100
Seattle, WA 98104
"Baseball Manager"

Jada Pinkett
10683 Santa Monica Blvd.
Los Angeles, CA 90025
"Actor"

Pink Floyd
729 7th Avenue, #1600
New York, NY 10019
"Rock & Roll Group"

Gordon Pinsent
180 Bloor Street West
Toronto, Ontario
M5S 2V6 CANADA
"Actor, Writer"

Vada Pinson
710 31st Street
Oakland, CA 94609
"Baseball Player"

Sir Harold Pinter
16 Cadogan Lane
London SW1 ENGLAND
"Screenwriter"

Scottie Pippen
980 N. Michigan Avenue #1600
Chicago, IL 60611
"Basketball Player"

Joe Piscopo
8665 Burton Way, PH #5
Los Angeles, CA 90048
"Actor"

Marie-France Pisier
3, Quai Malaquais
75006 Paris, FRANCE
"Actress"

Dean Pitchford
1701 Queens Road
Los Angeles, CA 90069
"Lyricist, Producer"

Gene Pitney
8901 - 6 Mile Road
Caledonia, WI 53108
"Singer"

Brad Pitt
9150 Wilshire Blvd. #350
Beverly Hills, CA 90212
"Actor"

Ingrid Pitt
2-4 Noel Street
London W1V 3RB ENGLAND
"Actress"

Mary Kay Place
2739 Motor Avenue
Los Angeles, CA 90064
"Actress, Writer"

Robert Plant
8942 Wilshire Blvd.
Beverly Hills, CA 90211
"Singer, Songwriter"

Scott Plant
151 El Camino Drive
Beverly Hills, CA 90212
"Actor"

Platinum Blonde
P.O. Box 1223, Station F.
Toronto, Ontario
M4Y 2T8 CANADA
"Rock & Roll Group"

Dana Plato
6442 Coldwater Canyon, #211
North Hollywood, CA 91606
"Actress"

The Platters
P.O. Box 39
Las Vegas, NV 89101
"Vocal Group"

Gary Player
P.O. Box 785629
Sandton 2146 SOUTH AFRICA
"Golfer"

John Pleshette
2643 Creston Drive
Los Angeles, CA 90068
"Actor, Writer"

Suzanne Pleshette
P.O. Box 1492
Beverly Hills, CA 90213
"Actress"

George Plimpton
541 East 72nd Street
New York, NY 10021
"Author"

Martha Plimpton
40 West 57th Street
New York, NY 10019
"Model, Actress"

Joan Plowright
76 Oxford Street
London W1R 1RB ENGLAND
"Actress"

Eve Plumb
280 South Beverly Drive #400
Beverly Hills, CA 90212
"Actress"

Amanda Plummer
49 Wampum Hill Road
Weston, CT 06883
"Actress"

Christopher Plummer
49 Wampum Hill Road
Weston, CT 06883
"Actor"

Glenn Plummer
924 Westwood Blvd. #900
Los Angeles, CA 90024
"Actor"

Scotty Plummer
909 Parkview Avenue
Lodi, CA 95240
"Singer"

Jim Plunkett
51 Kilroy Way
Atherton, CA 94025
"Ex-Football Player"

Steve Plytas
70 Lansbury Avenue, Feltham
Middlesex TW14 OJR ENGLAND
"Actor"

Rosanna Podesta
Via Bartolemeo Ammanatti 8
00187 Rome, ITALY
"Actress"

Sylvia Poggioli
c/o National Public Radio
2025 "M" Street NW
Washington, DC 20036
"News Correspondent"

Buster Poindexter
200 West 58th Street
New York, NY 10019
"Singer"

Anita Pointer
12060 Crest Court
Beverly Hills, CA 90210
"Singer"

Priscilla Pointer
151 El Camino Drive
Beverly Hills, CA 90211
"Actress"

Pointer Sisters
1900 Avenue of the Stars, #1640
Los Angeles, CA 90067
"Vocal Trio"

Poison
P.O. Box 6668
San Francisco, CA 94101
"Rock & Roll Group"

Sydney Poitier
1221 Stone Canyon Road
Los Angeles, CA 90077
"Actor, Writer, Producer"

Roman Polanski
43 Avenue Montaigne
75008 Paris, FRANCE
"Actor, Writer, Director"

The Police
194 Kensington Park Road
London W11 2ES ENGLAND
"Rock & Roll Group"

Sydney Pollack
13525 Lucca Drive
Pacific Palisades, CA 90272
"Writer, Producer"

Cherl Pollak
P.O. Box 5617
Beverly Hills, CA 90210
"Model"

Tracy Pollan
10468 Llona
Los Angeles, CA 90064
"Actress"

Jonathan Pollard
Federal Reformatory
Marion, IL 62959
"Israeli Spy, Traitor"

Michael J. Pollard
520 S. Burnside Avenue #12-A
Los Angeles, CA 90036
"Actor"

Danny Ponce
14539 Teton Drive
Hacienda Heights, CA 91745
"Actor"

LuAnne Ponce
3500 West Olive Avenue, #1400
Burbank, CA 91505
"Actress"

Carlo Ponti
rue Charles Bonnet 6
Geneve, SWITZERLAND
"Film Producer"

Iggy Pop
449 South Beverly Drive #102
Beverly Hills, CA 90212
"Singer"

Albert Popwell
1427 - 3rd Street #205
Santa Monica, CA 90401
"Actor"

Paulina Porizkova
9830 Wilshire Blvd.
Beverly Hills, CA 90212
"Model"

Don Porter
2049 Century Park East #2500
Los Angeles, CA 90067
"Actor, Director"

Jean Porter
3945 Westfall Drive
Encino, CA 91436
"Actress"

Nyree Dawn Porter
28 Berkeley Square
London W1X 6HD ENGLAND
"Actress"

Vladimir Posner
1125-16th Street N.W.
Washington, DC 20036
"Russian Spokesman"

Markie Post
10153 1/2 Riverside Drive
Suite #333
Toluca Lake, CA 91602
"Actress"

Tom Poston
2930 Deep Canyon Drive
Beverly Hills, CA 90210
"Actor"

Carol Potter
151 El Camino Drive
Beverly Hills, CA 90210
"Actress"

Annie Potts
7920 Sunset Blvd. #350
Los Angeles, CA 90046
"Actress"

Cliff Potts
8383 Wilshire Blvd. #954
Beverly Hills, CA 90211
"Actor"

Ely Pouget
2190 Beach Knoll Road
Los Angeles, CA 90049
"Actor"

CCH Pounder
121 North San Vicente Blvd.
Beverly Hills, CA 90211
"Actor"

Paula Poundstone
1027 Chelsea Avenue
Santa Monica, CA 90403
"Comedienne, TV Show Host"

Maury Povich
250 West 57th Street #26-W
New York, NY 10019
"TV Show Host"

Gen Colin L. Powell
310 South Henry Street
Alexandria, VA 22314
"Ex-Military Leader"

Jane Powell
150 West End Avenue #26C
New York, NY 10023
"Actress"

Randolph Powell
2644 Highland Avenue
London W1 ENGLAND
"Actor"

Robert Powell
10 Pond Place
London SW3 ENGLAND
"Actor"

Mrs. William Powell
c/o Diane Lewis
383 Verde Norte
Palm Springs, CA 92262
"Wife of William Powell"

Romina Power
Cellino San Marco
Provinz Brindise ITALY
"Actress"

Taryn Power
621 N. Orlando Ave. #8
W. Hollywood, CA 90069
"Actress"

Tyrone Power, Jr.
2298 Gloaming Way
Beverly Hills, 90210
"Son of Tyrone Power"

Udana Power
1962 Beachwood Drive #202
Los Angeles, CA 90068
"Actress"

Mala Powers
10543 Valley Spring Lane
North Hollywood, CA 91602
"Actress"

Stefanie Powers
P.O. Box 5087
Sherman Oaks, CA 91403
"Actress"

Susan Powter
2220 Colorado Avenue #1
Santa Monica, CA 90404
"Talk Show Host"

Laurie Prange
1519 Sargent Place
Los Angeles, CA 90026
"Actress"

Joan Prather
31647 Sea Level Drive
Malibu, CA 90265
"Actress"

Judson Pratt
8745 Oak Park Avenue
Northridge, CA 91325
"Actor"

Josephine Premice
755 West End Avenue
New York, NY 10023
"Actress, Singer, Dancer"

Paula Prentiss
719 North Foothill Road
Beverly Hills, CA 90120
"Actress"

Micheline Presle
6 rue Antoine Dubois
F 75006 Paris, FRANCE
"Actress"

Lisa-Marie Presley-Jackson
1167 Summit Drive
Beverly Hills, CA 90210
"Elvis' Daughter"

Priscilla Presley
1167 Summit Drive
Beverly Hills, CA 90210
"Actress, Model"

Vester Presley
3764 Elvis Presley Blvd.
Memphis, TN 38116
"Elvis's Dad"

Sen. Larry Pressler (SD)
Senate Russell Bldg. #243
Washington, DC 20510
"Politician"

Lawrence Pressman
15033 Encanto Drive
Sherman Oaks, CA 91403
"Actor"

Billy Preston
4271 Garthwaite Avenue
Los Angeles, CA 90008
"Singer"

Kelly Preston
12522 Moorpark Street #109
Studio City, CA 91604
"Actress"

The Pretenders
3 East 54th Street #1400
New York, NY 10022
"Vocal Group"

Andre Previn
8 Sherwood Lane
Bedford Hills, NY 10507
"Composer, Conductor"

Francoise Previne
5 rue Brenzin
75015 Paris, FRANCE
"Actor"

Hermann Prey
Fichtenstr. 12
D-82152 Krailling/Obb.
GERMANY
"Baritone"

Leontyne Price
9 Van Dam Street
New York, NY 10003
"Soprano"

Marc Price
8444 Magnolia Drive
Los Angeles, CA 90046
"Actor"

Mark Price
2923 Streetsboro Road
Richfield, OH 44286
"Basketball Player"

Ray Price
P.O. Box 1986
Mt. Pleasant, TX 75230
"Singer"

Nancy Priddy
329 N. Wetherly Drive #101
Beverly Hills, CA 90211
"Actress"

Charlie Pride
3198 Royal Lane #204
Dallas, TX 75229
"Singer"

Pat Priest
P.O. Box 1298
Hatley, ID 83333
"Actor"

Jason Priestley
333 South Beverly Drive, #201
Beverly Hills, CA 90212
"Actor"

Barry Primus
2735 Creston Drive
Los Angeles, CA 90068
"Actor, Director"

Prince (formely known as)
9401 Kiowa Trail
Chanhassen, MN 55317
"Singer, Songwriter, Actor"

Clayton Prince
3500 West Olive Avenue, #1400
Burbank, CA 91505
"Actor"

Jonathan Prince
10340 Calvin Avenue
Los Angeles, CA 90025
"Actor"

William Prince
750 North Kings Road
Los Angeles, CA 90069
"Actor"

Victoria Principal
8942 Wilshire Blvd.
Beverly Hills, CA 90211
"Actress"

Andrew Prine
3364 Longridge Avenue
Sherman Oaks, CA 91403
"Actor"

Joan Pringle
3500 West Olive #1400
Burbank, CA 91505
"Actress"

Sir Victor S. Pritchett
12 Regent's Park Terrace
London NW1 ENGLAND
"Author"

Jurgen Prochnow
8942 Wilshire Blvd.
Beverly Hills, CA 90211
"Actor"

The Proclaimers
P.O. Box 309
Edinburgh EH9 1JE SCOTLAND
"Rock & Roll Group"

Ronnie Prophet
1227 Saxon Drive
Nashville, TN 37215
"Singer, Songwriter"

Robert Prosky
306 - 9th Street
Washington, DC 20003
"Actor"

Paul Provenza
2838 Lambert Drive
Los Angeles, CA 90068
"Actor"

Dorothy Provine
8832 Ferncliff N.E.
Bainbridge Island, WA 98110
"Actress"

Dave Prowse
12 Marshalsea Road
London SE1 1HL ENGLAND
"Actor"

Juliet Prowse
343 South Beverly Glen
Los Angeles, LA 90024
"Actress, Dancer"

Jeanne Pruett
1300 Division Street #103
Nashville, TN 37203
"Singer"

Jonathan Pryce
233 Park Avenue South
10th Floor
New York, NY 10003
"Actor"

Sen. David Pryor (AR)
Senate Russell Bldg. #267
Washington, DC 20510
"Politician"

Nicholas Pryor
8787 Shoreham Drive #302
Los Angeles, CA 90069
"Actor"

Rain Pryor
846 N. Clybourn Avenue
Burbank, CA 91505
"Actress, Musician"

Richard Pryor
16030 Ventura Blvd. #380
Encino, CA 91436
"Actor, Comedian"

Public Enemy
298 Elizabeth Street
New York, NY 10012
"Rap Group"

Wolfgang Puck
805 North Sierra Drive
Beverly Hills, CA 91765
"Chef, Restaurateur"

Kirby Puckett
501 Chicago Avenue South
Minneapolis, MN 55415
"Baseball Player"

Tito Pueett
15 Gregg Court
Tappan, NY 10983
"Jazz Musician"

Tommy Puett
23441 Golden Springs #199
Diamond Bar, CA 91765
"Actor"

Keshia Knight Pulliam
P.O. Box 866
Teaneck, NJ 07666
"Actress"

Bill Pullman
9560 Wilshire Blvd., #500
Beverly Hills, CA 90212
"Actor"

Liselotte Pulver
Villa Bip, Perroy
Kanton Vandois SWITZERLAND
"Actress"

Dr. Bernard Punsley
1415 Granvia Altemeia
Rancho Palos Verdes, CA 90274
"Actor"

Lee Purcell
1317 N. San Fernando Rd. #167
Burbank, CA 91504
"Actress"

Edmund Purdom
via Giosue Carducci
I0-00187 Rome ITALY
"Actor"

Linda Purl
10417 Ravenwood Court
Los Angeles, CA 90077
"Actress"

John Putch
5750 Wilshire Blvd. #512
Los Angeles, CA 90036
"Actor"

Mario Puzo
866 Manor Lane
Bay Shore, NY 11706
"Author, Screenwriter"

Denver Pyle
10614 Whipple Street
North Hollywood, CA 91602
"Actor, Writer, Director"

Natasha Pyne
43A Princess Road
Regent's Park
London NW1 8JS ENGLAND
"Actress"

Monty Python
68a Delancy Street
London NW1 70W ENGLAND
"Comedy Group"

Dennis Quaid
9034 Sunset Blvd. #200
Los Angeles, CA 90069
"Actor"

Randy Quaid
P.O. Box 17372
Beverly Hills, CA 90209
"Actor"

Robert Quarry
11032 Moorpark St. #A-3
No. Hollywood, CA 91602
"Actor"

Suzi Quatro
Hellkamp 17
D-20255 Hamburg GERMANY
"Singer"

Anna Quayle
4 Guilford Road, Brighton
Essex ENGLAND
"Actress"

Dan Quayle
11711 N. Pennsylvania Street, #100
Carmel, IN 46032
"Ex-Vice President U.S.A."

Marilyn Tucker-Quayle
11711 N. Pennsylvania Street, #100
Carmel, IN 46032
"Wife of Dan Quayle"

Queen
16A High St. Barnes
London SW13 9LW ENGLAND
"Rock & Roll Group"

Mae Questel
27 East 65th Street
New York, NY 10021
"Actress"

Diana Quick
162 Wardour Street
London W1V 3AT ENGLAND
"Actress"

Quiet Riot
3208 Cahuenga Blvd. West #107
Los Angeles, CA 90068
"Rock & Roll GrouP"

Joan Quigley
1055 California Street #14
San Francisco, CA 94108
"Astrologer"

Linnea Quigley
12710 Blythe Street
North Hollywood, CA 91605
"Actress, Model"

Denis Quilley
22 Willow Road
London NW3 ENGLAND
"Actor, Singer"

Kathleen Quinlan
8942 Wilshire Blvd.
Beverly Hills, CA 90211
"Actress"

Adrian Quinn
9830 Wilshire Blvd.
Beverly Hills, CA 90212
"Actor"

Aileen Quinn
170 West End Avenue #3K
New York, NY 10023
"Actress"

Anthony Quinn
60 East End Avenue
New York, NY 10028
"Actor, Director"

Bill Quinn
16302 Village #16
Camarillo, CA 93010
"Actor"

Danny Quinn
1630 Marmont Avenue, #A
Los Angeles, CA 90069
"Actor"

Francesco Quinn
1230 North Horn Avenue #730
Los Angeles, CA 90069
"Actor"

Glenn Quinn
1999 Avenue of the Stars #2850
Los Angeles, CA 90067
"Actor"

Martha Quinn
7920 Sunset Blvd., #400
Los Angeles, CA 90046
"TV Personality"

Sally Quinn
3014 "N" Street NW
Washington, DC 20007
"Journalist"

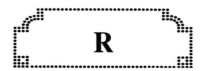

Eddie Rabbitt
P.O. Box 35286
Cleveland, OH 44135
"Singer"

Alan Rachins
1274 Capri
Pacific Palisades, CA 90272
"Actor, Writer, Director"

Lee Radziwell
9255 Sunset Blvd. #901
Los Angeles, CA 90069
"Society Leader"

Cassidy Rae
1801 Ave. of the Stars #902
Los Angeles, CA 90067
"Actress"

Charlotte Rae
P.O. Box 49991
Los Angeles, CA 90049
"Actress"

Frances Rafferty Baker
221411 Burbank Blvd. #4
Woodland Hills, CA 91367
"Actress"

Deborah Raffin
2630 Eden Place
Beverly Hills, CA 90210
"Actress"

Kaye Lani Rae Rafko
4932 Frary Lane
Monroe, MI 48161
"Former Miss America"

Hashemi Rafsanjani
The Majlis
Tehran, IRAN
"President of Iran"

Gerald Rafshoon
3028 "Q" Street N.W.
Washington, DC 20006
"Former Presidential Aide"

John S. Ragin
5706 Briarcliff Road
Los Angeles, CA 90068
"Actor"

Bobby Rahal
P.O. Box 39
Hilliard, OH 43026
"Race Car Driver"

Steve Railsback
P.O. Box 1308
Los Angeles, CA 90078
"Actor"

Gillian Raine
13 Billing Road
London SW10 ENGLAND
"Actress"

Luise Rainer
CH-6921 Vocp
Morcote SWITZERLAND
"Actress"

Cristina Raines-Crowe
15250 Ventura Blvd. #720
Studio City, CA 91604
"Actress"

Ford Rainey
3821 Carbon Canyon
Malibu, CA 90265
"Actor"

Bonnie Raitt
1344 Spaulding
Los Angeles, CA 90046
"Singer"

John Raitt
1164 Napoli Drive
Pacific Palisades, CA 90272
"Actor"

Sheryl Lee Ralph
938 South Longwood
Los Angeles, CA 90019
"Actress"

Vera Hruba Ralston
4121 Crecienta Drive
Santa Barbara, CA 93110
"Actress"

Raul Ramirez
Avenida Ruiz
65 Sur Ensenda
Baja California, MEXICO
"Tennis Player"

Harold Ramis
12921 Evanston Street
Los Angeles, CA 90049
"Actor, Writer, Director"

Pres. Fidel Ramos
Malacanang Palace
Manila PHILIPPINES
"Politician"

Charlotte Rampling
1 Ave. Emile Augier
F-78290 Croissy-Sur Seine
FRANCE
"Actress"

Logan Ramsey
12932 Killion Street
Van Nuys, CA 91401
"Actor"

Tony Randall
1 West 81st Street #6-D
New York, NY 10024
"Actor, Director"

Teddy Randazzo
5254 Oak Island Road
Orlando, FL 32809
"Singer"

Boots Randolph
P.O. Box 110379
Nashville, TN 37222
"Saxophonist"

John Randolph
1850 North Whitley Place
Los Angeles, CA 90028
"Actor"

Joyce Randolph
295 Central Park West #18-A
New York, NY 10024
"Actress"

Willie Randolph
648 Juniper Place
Franklin Lakes, NJ 07417
"Ex-Baseball Player"

Rep. Charles B. Rengel (NY)
House Rayburn Bldg. #2252
Washington, DC 20515
"Politician"

Crown Price Ranier III
Grimaldi Palace
Monte Carlo, MONACO
"Royalty"

Kenny Rankin
4347 Mammoth Avenue, #4
Sherman Oaks, CA 91423
"Singer, Songwriter"

Prunella Ransome
59 Frith Street
London W1 ENGLAND
"Actress"

Sally Jessy Raphael
510 West 57th Street #200
New York, NY 10019
"TV Show Host"

David Rasche
P.O. Box 5617
Beverly Hills, CA 90210
"Actor"

Ahmad Rashad
30 Rockefeller Plaza #1411
New York, NY 10020
"Ex-Football Player, Sportcaster"

Phylicia Rashad
130 West 42nd Street #1804
New York, NY 10036
"Actress"

Thalmus Rasulala
4837 Clybourn Avenue #5
Hollywood, CA 91601
"Actor"

Dan Rather
524 West 57th Street
New York, NY 10019
"Newscaster"

RATT
1818 Illion Street
San Diego, CA 92110
Rock & Roll Group"

John Ratzenberger
7080 Hollywood Blvd., #1118
Los Angeles, CA 90028
"Actor"

Eddy Raven
P.O. Box 1402
Hendersonville, TN 37075
"Singer, Songwriter"

Lou Rawls
109 Fremont Place
Los Angeles, CA 90005
"Singer"

James Earl Ray
Station A West
Tennessee State Prison
Nashville, TN 37203
"Martin Luthur King, Jr.'s Assassin"

Gene Rayburn
245 Fifth Avenue
New York, NY 10016
"TV Show Host"

Collin Raye
612 Humboldt Street
Reno, NV 89509
"Singer"

Marguerite Raye
1329 North Vista #106
Los Angeles, CA 90046
"Actress"

Gene Raymond
250 Trino Way
Pacific Palisades, CA 90272
"Actor"

Guy Raymond
550 Erskine Drive
Pacific Palisades, CA 90272
"Actor"

Paula Raymond
P.O. Box 86
Beverly Hills, CA 90213
"Actress"

Peggy Rea
1801 Avenue of the Stars, #902
Los Angeles, CA 90067
"Actress"

Stephen Rea
108 Leonard Street
London EC2A 4RH ENGLAND
"Actor"

James Read
12635 Hortense Street
Studio City, CA 91604
"Actor"

Ralph Read
P.O. Box 1990
Chesapeake, VA 23327
"Christian Spokesman"

Maureen Reagan
10317 Dunleer
Los Angeles, CA 90064
"Ex-President's Daughter"

Michael Reagan
4740 Allott Avenue
Sherman Oaks, CA 91403
"Ex-President's Son"

Nancy Reagan
668 St. Cloud Road
Los Angeles, CA 90077
"Ex-First Lady, Actress"

Ronald Reagan
668 St. Cloud Road
Los Angeles, CA 90077
"Actor, Ex-President"

Ron Reagan, Jr.
1283 Devon Avenue
Los Angeles, CA 90024
"TV Show Host, Dancer"

Jeff Reardon
4 Martwood Lane
Palm Beach Gardens, FL 33410
"Baseball Player"

Rex Reason
20105 Rhapsody Road
Walnut, CA 91789
"Actor"

Rhodes Reason
409 Winchester Avenue
Glendale, CA 914201
"Actor"

Charles "Bebe" Rebozo
524 Fernwood Drive
Key Biscayne, FL 33149
"Financier"

Peter Reckell
8033 Sunset Blvd. #4016
Los Angeles, CA 90046
"Actor"

Leon Redbone
179 Aquestong Road
New Hope, PA 18938
"Singer, Guitarist"

Juli Reddy
115 North Carolwood Drive
Los Angeles, CA 90077
"Actress"

Helen Reddy
820 Stanford
Santa Monica, CA 90403
"Singer"

Quinn Redeker
17931 Welby Way
Reseda, CA 91335
"Actor, Writer"

Robert Redford
1101-E Montana Avenue
Santa Monica, CA 90403
"Actor, Director"

Lynn Redgrave
21342 Colina Drive
Topanga, CA 90290
"Actress"

Vanessa Redgrave
15 Golden Square #300
London W1R 3AG ENGLAND
"Actress"

Red Hot Chili Peppers
11116 Aqua Vista #39
North Hollywood, CA 91602
"Music Group"

Marge Redmond
420 Madison Avenue #1400
New York, NY 10017
"Actress"

Sumner Redstone
200 Elm Street
Dedham, MA 02026
"Media Executive"

Alaina Reed-Hall
10636 Rathburn
Northridge, CA 91326
"Actress"

Andre Reed
One Bill Drive
Orchard Park, NY 14127
"Football Player"

Jerry Reed
153 Rue De Grande
Brentwood, TN 37027
"Singer, Actor"

Margaret Reed
524 West 57th Street #5330
New York, NY 10019
"Actress"

Oliver Reed
Houmit Lane
Houmit Vale, Guernsey
CHANNEL ISLANDS (UK)
"Actor"

Pamela Reed
1875 Century Park East #1300
Los Angeles, CA 90067
"Actress"

Philip Reed
969 Bel Air Road
Los Angeles, CA 90077
"Actor"

Rex Reed
1 West 72nd Street #86
New York, NY 10023
"Film Critic"

Della Reese
P.O. Box 2812
Beverly Hills, CA 90210
"Singer, Actress"

Christopher Reeve
Kessler Institute
Pleasant Valley Way
West Orange, NJ 07052
"Actor"

Dan Reeves
c/o Giants Stadium
East Rutherford, NJ 07073
"Football Coach"

Del Reeves
2804 Opryland Drive
Nashville, TN 37214
"Singer"

Keanu Reeves
9460 Wilshire Blvd., #700
Beverly Hills, CA 90212
"Actor"

Martha Reeves
P.O. Box 1987
Paramount, CA 90723
"Singer"

Steve Reeves
P.O. Box 807
Valley Center, CA 92082
"Actor, Bodybuilder"

Joe Regalbuto
724-24th Street
Santa Monica, CA 90402
"Actor"

Donald T. Regan
11 Canal Center Plaza #301
Alexandria, VA 22314
"Former Secretary of Treasury"

Duncan Regehr
2501 Main Street
Santa Monica, CA 90405
"Actor"

Paul Regina
4243 Colfax Avenue #C
Studio City, CA 91604
"Actor"

Regine
502 Park Avenue
New York, NY 10022
"Singer"

William Rehnquist
1-1st Street N.E.
Washington, DC 20543
"Supreme Court Chief Justice"

Beryl Reid
36 Michaelham Gardens
Strawberry Hill
Twick TW1 ENGLAND
"Actor, Comedian"

Daphne Maxwell Reid
11342 Dona Lisa Drive
Studio City, CA 91604
"Actress"

Elliott Reid
1850 N. Whitley Avenue
Los Angeles, CA 90028
"Actor, Writer"

Frances Reid
9165 Sunset Blvd. #202
Los Angeles, CA 90069
"Actress"

J.R. Reid
Two First Union Center #2600
Charlotte, NC 28282
"Basketball Player"

Tim Reid
11342 Dona Lisa Drive
Studio City, CA 91604
"Actor"

Charles Nelson Reilly
2341 Gloaming Way
Beverly Hills, CA 90210
"Actor"

John Reilly
602 North Las Palmas Avenue
Los Angeles, CA 90004
"Actor"

Tom Reilly
8200 Wilshire Blvd. #218
Beverly Hills, CA 90211
"Actor"

Carl Reiner
714 North Rodeo Drive
Beverly Hills, CA 90210
"Actor, Director"

Rob Reiner
255 Chadbourne Avenue
Los Angeles, CA 90049
"Actor, Director"

Judge Reinhold
1341 Ocean Avenue #113
Santa Monica, CA 90401
"Actor"

Ann Reinking
366 Madison Avenue, #1603
New York, NY 10017
"Actor"

Paul Reiser
11845 West Olympic Blvd. #1125
Los Angeles, CA 90064
"Actor"

R.E.M.
250 West Clayton Street
Atlanta, GA 30601
"Rock & Roll Group"

Bert Remsen
5722 Mammoth Avenue
Van Nuys, CA 91401
"Actor"

Line Renaud
5 rue de Bois de Boulogne
F-75016 Paris FRANCE
"Actress"

Liz Renay
3708 San Angelo Avenue
Las Vegas, NV 89102
"Burlesque"

Brad Renfro
P.O. Box 53454
Knoxville, TN 37950
"Actor"

Janet Reno
Department of Justice
10th & Constitution
Washington, DC 20530
"U.S. Attorney General"

Faye Resnick
301 N. Canon Drive #203
Beverly Hills, CA 90210
"Nicole Brown-Simpson's Friend"

Alain Resnis
70 rue des Plantes
75014 Paris, FRANCE
"Film Director"

James Reston
1804 Kallorama Square N.W.
Washington, DC 20008
"Columnist"

Mary Lou Retton
322 Via El Prado #209
Redondo Beach, CA 90277
"Gymnast, Actress"

Paul Reubens
P.O. Box 29373
Los Angeles, CA 90029
"Actor"

Gloria Reubin
9229 Sunset Blvd. #710
Los Angeles, CA 90069
"Actress"

Paul Revere & The Raiders
P.O. Box 544
Graingeville, ID 83530
"Rock & Roll Group"

Clive Revill
15029 Encanto Drive
Sherman Oaks, CA 91403
"Actor"

Ernie Reyes, Jr.
1800 Avenue of the Stars, #400
Los Angeles, CA 90067
"Actor"

Burt Reynolds
16133 Jupiter Farms Road
Jupiter, FL 33478
"Actor, Director"

Debbie Reynolds
305 Convention Center Drive
Las Vegas, NV 89109
"Actress"

Gene Reynolds
2034 Castillian Drive
Los Angeles, CA 90068
"Actor, Director"

James Reynolds
1925 Hamscom Drive
South Pasadena, CA 91109
"Actor"

Alicia Rhett
50 Tradd Street
Charleston, SC 29401
"Actress"

Barbara Rhoades
12366 Ridge Circle
Los Angeles, CA 90049
"Actress"

Betty (Jane) Rhodes
10693 Chalon Road
Los Angeles, CA 90024
"Actress"

Cynthia Rhodes
15250 Ventura Blvd. #900
Sherman Oaks, CA 91403
"Actress, Dancer"

Donnelly Rhodes
9744 Wilshire Blvd. #308
Beverly Hills, CA 90212
"Actor"

Dusty Rhodes
8577A Boca Glades Blvd. W.
Boca Raton, FL 33434
"Wrestler"

Madlyn Rhue
148 South Maple Drive, Apt. #D
Beverly Hills, CA 90212
"Actress"

John Rhys-Davies
1933 Cold Canyon Road
Calabasas, CA 91302
"Actor"

Abraham Ribicoff
425 Park Avenue
New York, NY 10022
"Ex-Senator"

Christina Ricci
8942 Wilshire Blvd.
Beverly Hills, CA 90211
"Actress"

Anne Rice
1239 First Street
New Orleans, LA 70130
"Writer"

Bobby G. Rice
505 Canton Pass
Madison, TN 37115
"Singer"

Donna Rice
P.O. Box 773
Great Falls, VA 22066
"Actress, Model"

Jerry Rice
4949 Centennial Blvd.
Santa Clara, CA 95054
"Football Player"

Jim Rice
RR #8
Anderson, SC 29621
"Ex-Baseball Player"

Tim Rice
196 Shaftesbury Avenue
London WC2 ENGLAND
"Lyricist"

Adam Rich
21848 Vantage Avenue
Chatsworth, CA 91311
"Actor"

Christopher Rich
15760 Ventura Blvd. #1730
Encino, CA 91436
"Actor"

Elaine Rich
500 South Sepulveda Blvd.
Los Angeles, CA 90049
"Producer"

John Rich
2501 Colorado Ave. #350
Santa Monica, CA 90404
"Writer, Producer"

Matty Rich
9560 Wilshire Blvd. #500
Beverly Hills, CA 90210
"Director"

Cliff Richard
Portsmouth Road
Box 46A, Esher
Surrey KT10 9AA ENGLAND
"Singer, Actor"

Maurice Richard
10950 Peloquin
Montreal PQ H2C 2KB CANADA
"Hockey Player"

Ann Richard
P.O. Box 684746
Austin, TX 78768
"Ex-Governor"

Ariana Richards
9255 Sunset Blvd., #710
Los Angeles, CA 90069
"Actress"

Beah Richards
1842 South Sycamore Avenue
Los Angeles, CA 90019
"Actress"

Evan Richards
1800 Avenue of the Starts, #400
Los Angeles, CA 90067
"Actor"

Kieth Richards
"Redlands" West Whittering
Near Chichester Sussex
ENGLAND
"Actor"

Michael Richards
8942 Wilshire Blvd.
Beverly Hills, CA 90211
"Actor"

Elliot Richardson
1100 Crest Lane
McLean, VA 22101
"Diplomat"

Ian Richardson
131 Lavender Sweep
London SW11 ENGLAND
"Actor"

Miranda Richardson
Forest Hill
195 Devonshire Road
London SE 23 ENGLAND
"Actress"

Natasha Richardson
30 Brackenburg Avenue
London W6 ENGLAND
"Actress, V. Redgrave's Daughter"

Patricia Richardson
253 - 26th Street #A-312
Santa Monica, CA 90402
"Actress"

Salli Richardson
1518 Crowe Avenue
Deerfield, IL 60015
"Actress"

Lionel Richie
8000 Beverly Blvd.
Los Angeles, CA 90048
"Singer, Songwriter"

Peter Mark Richman
5114 Del Moreno Drive
Woodland Hills, CA 91364
"Actor"

Branscombe Richmond
5706 Calvin Avenue
Tarzana, CA 91356
"Actor/Stuntman"

Jason James Richter
10683 Santa Monica Blvd.
Los Angeles, CA 90025
"Actor"

Don Rickles
925 North Alpine Drive
Beverly Hills, CA 90210
"Comeidan, Actor"

Alan Rickman
76 Oxford Street
London W1N 0AX ENGLAND
"Actor"

Dr. Sally Ride
9500 Gillman Drive
MS 0221
La Jolla, CA 92093
"Astronaut"

Andrew Ridgeley
8800 Sunset Blvd. #401
Los Angeles, CA 90069
"Singer, Composer"

Leni Riefenstahl
Tengstrasse 20
D-8000 Munich
GERMANY
"Film Director"

Lisa Rieffel
9200 Sunset Blvd. #710
Los Angeles, CA 90069
"Actress"

Peter Riegert
8730 Sunset Blvd., #490
Los Angeles, CA 90069
"Actor"

Joshua Rifkind
1939 Pinehurst Road
Los Angeles, CA 90068
"Conductor"

Cathy Rigby
110 East Wilshire #200
Fullerton, CA 92632
"Gymnast"

Diana Rigg
2-4 Noel Street
London W1V 3RB ENGLAND
"Actress"

Bobby Riggs
1834 Parliament Road
Encintas, CA 92024
"Tennis Player"

Righteous Brothers
9841 Hot Springs Drive
Huntington Beach, CA 92646
"Vocal Group"

Robin Riker-Halsey
1089 North Oxford Avenue
Los Angeles, CA 90029
"Actress"

Meshulam Riklis
23720 Malibu Colony Road
Malibu, CA 90265
"Film Producer"

Jeaniie C. Riley
P.O. Box 23256
Nashville, TN 37202
"Singer"

Pat Riley
34 Simmons Lane
Greenwich, CT 06840
"Basketball Coach"

Molly Ringwald
9454 Wilshire Blvd. #405
Beverly Hills, CA 90212
"Actress"

Lisa Rinna
3500 W. Olive #1400
Burbank, CA 91505
"Actress"

Mayor Richard Riordan
200 North Spring Street
Los Angeles, CA 90012
"Mayor of Los Angeles"

Cal Ripken, Jr.
335 West Camden Street
Baltimore, MD 21201
"Baseball Player"

Rodney Allen Rippey
4900 Clair Del Avenue #113
Long Beach, CA 90807
"Actor"

Robby Rist
P.O. Box 867
Woodland Hills, CA 91365
"Actor"

Clint Ritchie
10000 Riverside Drive #6
Toluca Lake, CA 91602
"Actor"

Michael Ritchie
22 Miller Avenue
Mill Valley, CA 94947
"Director, Producer"

The Ritchie Family
4100 West Flagler #B-2
Miami, FL 33134
"Vocal Group"

Lee Ritenour
P.O. Box 6774
Malibu, CA 90265
"Guitarist"

John Ritter
4024 Radford Avenue
Studio City, CA 91604
"Actor"

Mrs. Tex Ritter
14151 Valley Vista
Sherman Oaks, CA 91423
"Tex Ritter's Widower"

Chita Rivera
1325 Avenue of the Americas
New York, NY 10019
"Actress, Singer, Dancer"

Geraldo Rivera
555 West 57th Street #1100
New York, NY 10019
"TV Show Host, Author"

Jorge Rivero
Salvador Novo 71
Cuyoacan 21 D.F. MEXICO
"Actor"

Joan Rivers
1 East 62nd Street
New York, NY 10021
"Comedienne, TV Show Host"

Johnny Rivers
3141 Coldwater Canyon Lane
Beverly Hills, CA 90210
"Singer, Songwriter"

Mickey Rivers
350 N.W. 48th Street
Miami, FL 33127
"Ex-Baseball Player"

Jacques Rivette
20 Blvd. de la Bastille
75012 Paris, FRANCE
"Film Director"

Phil Rizzuto
912 Westminister Avenue
Hillside, NJ 07205
"Ex-Baseball Player"

Adam Roarkd
4520 Aida Place
Woodland Hills, CA 91364
"Actor"

Jason Robards
200 West 57th Street, #900
New York, NY 10019
"Actor"

Sam Robards
2530 Riverbend Drive
Crested Butte, CO 81224
"Actor"

Sen. Charles Robb (VA)
Senate Dirksen Bldg. #493
Washington, DC 20510
"Politician"

Lynda Bird Johnson-Robb
3050 Chain Bridge Raod
Mc Lean, VA 22101
"Ex-President's Daughter"

Seymour Robbie
9980 Liebe Drive
Beverly Hills, CA 90210
"TV Director"

Brian Robbins
752 North Orange Drive
Los Angeles, CA 90038
"Actor"

Harold Robbins
601 West Camino Sur
Palm Springs, CA 92262
"Novelist"

Jerome Robbins
117 East 81st Street
New York, NY 10028
"Choreographer"

Mrs. Marty Robbins
713-18th Avenue South
Nashville, TN 37203
"Marty Robbins's Widower"

Tim Robbins
40 West 57th Street
New York, NY 10019
"Actor"

Beverly Roberts
30912 Ariana Lane
Laguna Niguel, CA 92677
"Actress"

Cokie Roberts
1717 DeSales Street NW
Washington, DC 20036
"News Correspondent"

Doris Roberts
6225 Quebec Drive
Los Angeles, CA 90068
"Actress, Director"

Eric Roberts
2605 Ivanhoe Drive
Los Angeles, CA 90039
"Actor"

Jake "The Snake" Roberts
P.O. Box 3859
Stamford, CT 06905
"Wrestler"

Julia Roberts
6220 Del Valle Drive
Los Angeles, CA 90048
"Actress"

Louie Roberts
2401-12th Avenue South
Nashville, TN 37203
"Singer, Guitarist"

Oral Roberts
7777 Lewis Street
Tulsa, OK 74130
"Evangelist"

Pernell Roberts
20395 Seaboard Road
Malibu, CA 90265
"Actor"

Robin Roberts
504 Terrace Hill Road
Temple Terrace, FL 33617
"Ex-Baseball Player"

Tanya Roberts
7436 Del Zuro Drive
Los Angeles, CA 90046
"Actress"

Tony Roberts
970 Park Avenue #8-N
New York, NY 10028
"Actor"

Cliff Robertson
325 Dunmere Drive
La Jolla , CA 92037
"Actor, Writer, Director"

Oscar Robertson
P.O. Box 179
Springfield, MA 01101
"Ex-Basketball Player"

Pat Robertson
1000 Centerville Turnpike
Virginia Beach, VA 23463
"Evangelist"

Andrew Robinson
2671 Byron Place
Los Angeles, CA 90046
"Actor"

Brooks Robinson
36 S. Charles Street #2000
Baltimore, MD 21201
"Ex-Baseball Player"

Chris Robinson
9300 Wilshire Blvd. #410
Beverly Hills, CA 90212
"Actor, Director"

David Robinson
P.O. Box 530
San Antonio, TX 78292
"Basketball Player"

Eddie Robinson
Grambling Football
Grambling, LA 71245
"Football Coach"

Frank Robinson
15557 Aqua Verde Drive
Los Angeles, CA 90024
"Ex-Baseball Player & Manager"

Glen Robinson
1001 North Fourth Street
Milwaukee, WI 53203
"Basketball Player"

Holly Robinson
10683 Santa Monica Blvd.
Los Angeles, CA 90025
"Actress"

Jay Robinson
13757 Milbank Avenue
Sherman Oaks, CA 91403
"Actor"

Pres. Mary Robinson
Phoenix Park
Dublin IRELAND
"Politician"

Randall Robinson
1744 "R" Street NW
Washington, DC 20009
"Social Activist"

Smokey Robinson
17085 Rancho Street
Encino, CA 91316
"Singer, Songwriter"

Andy Robustelli
74 Wedgemere Road
Stamford, CT 06901
"Ex-Football Player"

Alex Rocco
1755 Ocean Oaks Road
Carpinteria, CA 93013
"Actor"

Eugene Roche
9911 West Pico Blvd., #PH-A
Los Angeles, CA 90035
"Actor"

Lela Rochon
6310 San Vicente Blvd., #407
Los Angeles, CA 90048
"Actress"

David Rockefeller, Jr.
30 Rockefeller Plaza #5600
New York, NY 10112
"Businessman"

Sen. John D. Rockefeller IV (WV)
Senate Hart Bldg. #109
Washington, DC 20510
"Politician"

Mrs. Nelson Rockefeller
812 Fifth Avenue
New York, NY 10024
"Wife of Nelson Rockefeller"

Sharon Rochefeller
2121 Park Road N.W.
Washington, DC 20010
"Wife of John D. Rockefeller"

Robert Rockwell
650 Toyopa Drive
Pacific Palisades, CA 90272
"Actor"

Marcia Rodd
11738 Moorpark Street #C
Studio City, CA 91604
"Actress"

Anton Rodgers
The White House
Lower Basildon
Berkshire ENGLAND
"Actor"

Jimmie Rodgers
P.O. Box 685
Forsyth, MO 65653
"Singer, Songwriter"

Dennis Rodman
980 N. Michigan Avenue, #1600
Chicago, IL 60611
"Basketball Player"

Chi Chi Rodriguez
1720 Merriman Road
P.O. Box 5118
Akron, OH 44334
"Golfer"

Johnny Rodriguez
P.O. Box 120725
Nashville, TN 37212
"Singer, Songwriter"

Paul Rodriguez
435 N. Camden Drive, #400
Beverly Hills, CA 90210
"Comedian"

Tommy Roe
P.O. Box 26037
Minneapolis, MN 55426
"Singer, Songwriter"

Daniel Roebuck
15221 Kingsbury Street
Mission Hills, CA 91345
"Actor"

Nicholas Roeg
14 Courtnell Street
London W2 5BX ENGLAND
"Film Director"

Maurice Roeves
1800 Avenue of the Stars, #400
Los Angeles, CA 90067
"Actor"

Joe Rogan
9200 Sunset Blvd., #625
Los Angeles, CA 90069
"Actor"

Bill Rogers
353 The Marketplace
Fanuil Hall
Boston, MA 02109
"Runner"

Charles "Buddy" Rogers
1147 Pickfair Way
Beverly Hills, CA 90210
"Actor"

Mr. Rogers (Fred)
4802 - 5th Avenue
Pittsburgh, PA 15213
"TV Show Host"

Joy Rogers
4141 West Kling Street #3
Burbank, CA 91505
"Actress"

Kenny Rogers
Rt 1, Box 100
Colbert, GA 30628
"Singer, Songwriter"

Melody Rogers
2051 Nicols Canyon
Los Angeles, CA 90046
"Actress, TV Show Host"

Mimi Rogers
11693 San Vicente Blvd. #241
Los Angeles, CA 90049
"Actress"

Paul Rogers
9 Hillside Gardens
London N6 5SU ENGLAND
"Actor"

Roy Rogers
15650 Seneca Road
Victorville, CA 92392
"Actor, Singer, Guitarist"

Suzanne Rogers
11266 Canton Drive
Studio City, CA 91604
"Actress"

Tristan Rogers
8550 Hollyway Drive #301
Los Angeles, CA 90069
"Actor"

Wayne Rogers
11828 La Grange Avenue
Los Angeles, CA 90025
"Actor, Writer, Director"

Fred Roggin
3000 West Alameda Avenue
Burbank, CA 91523
"TV Show Host"

Eric Rohmer
26 Ave. Pierre-Ler-De-Serbie
F-75016 Paris, FRANCE
"Film Director"

Roxie Roker
9255 Sunset Blvd. #515
Los Angeles, CA 90069
"Actress"

Rolanda (Watts)
1456 2nd Avenue, #202
New York, NY 10021
"Talk Show Host"

Ether Rolle
P.O. Box 8986
Los Angeles, CA 90008
"Actress"

Rolling Stones
P.O. Box 6152
New York, NY 10028
"Rock & Roll Group"

Ed Rollins
510 King Street, #302
Alexandria, VA 22314
"Political Consultant"

Howard E. Rollins, Jr.
123 West 85th Street #4-F
New York, NY 10024
"Actor"

Sonny Rollins
Rt. 9-G
Germantown, NY 12526
"Saxophonist"

Freddie Roman
101 West 57th Street
New York, NY 10019
"Comedian"

Roman Holiday
P.O. Box 475
London W1 ENGLAND
"Rock & Roll Group"

Lulu Roman
P.O. Box 140400
Nashville, TN 37214
"Actress"

Ruth Roman
1225 Cliff Drive
Laguna Beach, CA 92651
"Actress"

Richard Romanus
1840 Camino Palmero
Los Angeles, CA 90046
"Actor"

Sydne Rome
Via di Porta Piniciana 14
I-00100 Rome, ITALY
"Actress"

Gov. Roy Romer (CO)
136 State Capitol Bldg.
Denver, CO 80203
"Governor"

George Romero
3364 Lake Road North
Sanibel, FL 33957
"Filmmaker, Screenwriter"

Ned Romero
9255 Sunset Blvd. #515
Los Angeles, CA 90069
"Actor"

Linda Ronstadt
644 North Doheny
Los Angeles, CA 90069
"Singer"

Andy Rooney
254 Rowayton Avenue
Rowayton, CT 06853
"Writer, Actor, Director"

Mickey Rooney
1400 Red Sail Circle
Westlake Village, CA 91361
"Actor"

Axl Rose
15250 Ventura Blvd. #900
Sherman Oaks, CA 91403
"Singer"

Charlie Rose
499 Park Ave., 15th Floor
New York, NY 10022
"Talk Show Host"

Jamie Rose
8380 Melrose Avenue, #207
Los Angeles, CA 90069
"Actress"

Rose Marie
6916 Chisholm Avenue
Van Nuys, CA 91406
"Singer"

Murray Rose
3305 Carse Drive
Los Angeles, CA 90028
"Swimmer"

Pete Rose
6248 N.W. 32nd Terrace
Boca Raton, FL 33496
"Ex-Baseball Player"

Sherrie Rose
1758 Laurel Canyon Blvd.
Los Angeles, CA 90046
"Actress"

Roseanne
12424 Wilshire Blvd. #740
Los Angeles, CA 90025
"Actress"

Alan Rosenberg
10468 Ilona Ave.
Los Angeles, CA 90064
"Actor"

Barney Rosenzweig
308 North Sycamore #502
Los Angeles, CA 90036
"TV Writer, Producer"

Ken Rosewall
111 Pentacost Avenue
Turramurra NSW 2074
AUSTRALIA
"Tennis Player"

Francesco Rosi
Via Gregoriana 36
I-00187 Rome, ITALY
"Film Director"

Charlotte Ross
8715 Burton Way #1
Los Angeles, CA 90048
"Actress"

Diana Ross
P.O. Box 11059
Glenville Station
Greenwich, CT 06831
"Singer, Actress"

Herbert Ross
9830 Wilshire Blvd.
Beverly Hills, CA 90210
"Producer"

Jonathan Ross
34/42 Cleveland Street
London W1P 5SB ENGLAND
"Actor"

Katherine Ross
33050 Pacific Coast Hwy.
Malibu, CA 90265
"Actress"

Marion Ross
14159 Riverside Drive #101
Sherman Oaks, CA 91423
"Actress"

Stan Ross
1410 North Gardner
Los Angeles, CA 90046
"Actor"

Tracey Ross
12304 Santa Monica Blvd., #104
Los Angeles, CA 90025
"Actress"

Isabella Rossellini
745 Fifth Avenue #814
New York, NY 10151
"Actress"

Carol Rossen
1119-23rd Street #8
Santa Monica, CA 90403
"Actress"

Norman Rossington
27 Parliament Hill
London NW3 ENGLAND
"Actor"

Dan Rostenkowski
1372 West Evergreen Street
Chicago, IL 60027
"Ex-Congressman"

Walt Rostow
1 Wildwind Point
Austin, TX 78746
"Economist"

Miklos Rosza
2936 Montcalm Drive
Los Angeles, CA 90046
"Composer"

Kyle Rote
24700 Deepwater Pt. Drive #14
St. Michaels, MD 21663
"Ex-Football Player"

David Lee Roth
455 Bradford Street
Pasadena, CA 91105
"Singer, Songwriter"

Matt Roth
10390 Santa Monica Blvd. #300
Los Angeles, CA 90025
"Actor"

Tim Roth
4 Windmill Street
London, W1P 1HF England
"Actor"

Sen. William Roth, Jr. (DE)
Senate Hart Bldg. #104
Washington, DC 20510
"Politician"

Cynthia Rothrock
4654B East Avenue South, #190
Palmdale, CA 93552
"Martial Arts Superstar"

Richard Roundtree
28843 Wagon Road
Agoura Hills, CA 91301
"Actor"

Mickey Rourke
9150 Wilshire Blvd., #350
Beverly Hills, CA 90212
"Actor"

The Roustabouts
P.O. Box 25371
Charlotte, NC 28212
"Bluegrass Group"

Carl T. Rowan
3251-C Sutton Place NW
Washington, DC 20016
"Columnist"

Alan Rowe
8 Sherwood Close
London SW13 ENGLAND
"Actor"

Misty Rowe
161 West 61st Street #16B
New York, NY 10023
"Actress"

Nicholas Rowe
200 Fulham Road
London SW 10 ENGLAND
"Poet, Dramatist"

Betty Rowland
125 N. Barrington Avenue #103
Los Angeles, CA 90049
"Burlesque"

Dave Rowland
P.O. Box 121089
Nashville, TN 37212
"Singer"

Gena Rowlands
7917 Woodrow Wilson Drive
Los Angeles, CA 90046
"Actress"

Patsy Rowlands
265 Liverpool Rd.
London N1 1LX ENGLAND
"Actress"

Steve Roxton
6 Thornton Road, Leytonstone
London E11 ENGLAND
"Actor"

Billy Joe Royal
48 Music Square East
Nashville, TN 37203
"Singer, Songwriter"

Darrell Royal
10507 La Costa Drive
Austin, TX 78747
"Ex-Football Coach"

Kenneth Royce
3 Abbott's Close, Andover
Hants. SP11 7NP ENGLAND
"Author"

Mike Royko
435 North Michigan Avenue
Chicago, IL 60611
"Columnist"

Pamela Roylance
10635 Santa Monica Blvd., #130
Los Angeles, CA 90025
"Actress"

Pete Rozelle
P.O. Box 9686
Rancho Santa Fe, CA 92067
"Former Football Commissioner"

Mike Rozier
I-85 & Suwanee Road
Suwanee, GA 30174
"Football Player"

Jennifer Rubin
9560 Wilshire Blvd. #500
Beverly Hills, CA 90212
"Actress"

Zelda Rubinstein
9250 Wilshire Blvd. #208
Beverly Hills, CA 90212
"Actress"

Paul Rudd
15760 Ventura Blvd., #1730
Encino, CA 91436
"Actor"

Al Ruddy
1601 Clearview Drive
Beverly Hills, CA 90210
"Film Writer, Producer"

Herbert Rudley
13056 Maxella Ave. #1
Marina del Rey, CA 90292
"Actor"

Rita Rudner
2934 Beverly Glen Circle #389
Los Angeles, CA 90077
"Comedienne"

Mercedes Ruehl
P.O. Box 178
Old Chelsea Station
New York, NY 10011
"Actress"

Rufus
7250 Beverly Blvd #200
Los Angeles, CA 90036
"R&B Group"

Tracy Ruiz-Conforto
14314-174th Avenue N.E.
Redmond, WA 98052
"Swimmer"

Janice Rule
105 West 72nd Street #12B
New York, NY 10023
"Actress"

Donald Rumsfeld
135 South La Salle Street #3910
Chicago, IL 60603
"Ex-Government Official"

Dr. Robert Runcie
Archbishop of Canterbury
Lambeth Palace
London SW1 7JU ENGLAND
"Archbishop"

Run D.M.C.
160 Varick Street
New York, NY 10013
"Rap Group"

Jennifer Runyon
3113 Thatcher Avenue
Marina del Rey CA 90292
"Actress"

RuPaul
2001 Wayne Avenue, #103
San Leandro, CA 94577
"Singer"

Barbara Rush
1709 Tropical Avenue
Beverly Hills, CA 90120
"Actress"

Jennifer Rush
145 Central Park West
New York, NY 10023
"Singer"

Salman Rushdie
c/o Gillon Aitken
29 Fernshaw Road
London SW10 OTG ENGLAND
"Author"

Patrice Rushen
1090 South La Brea Avenue
Los Angeles, CA 90010
"Singer"

Jared Rushton
326 County Club Drive #B
Simi Valley, CA 93065
"Actor"

Robert Rusler
10683 Santa Monica Blvd.
Los Angeles, CA 90025
"Actor"

Betsy Russell
13926 Magnolia Blvd.
Sherman Oaks, CA 91423
"Actress"

Bill Russell
11430 S. Fulton Avenue
Tulsa, OK 74137
"Basketball Player"

Bing Russell
229 E. Gainsborough Road
Thousand Oaks, CA 91360
"Actor"

Brenda Russell
9000 Sunset Blvd. #1200
Los Angeles, CA 90069
"Singer"

Harold Russell
34 Old Town Road
Hyannis, MA 02601
"Government Official"

Jane Russell
2934 Torito Road
Santa Barbara, CA 93108
"Actress"

Johnny Russell
P.O. Box Drawer 37
Hendersonville, TN 37075
"Singer, Songwriter"

Ken Russell
7 Bellmount Wood Land
Watford, Hert. ENGLAND
"Film Director"

Kimberly Russell
11617 Laurelwood
Studio City, CA 91604
"Actress"

Kurt Russell
1900 Avenue of the Stars #1240
Los Angeles, CA 90067
"Actor"

Mark Russell
2800 Wisconsin Avenue #810
Washington, DC 20007
"Satirist, Comedian"

Nipsey Russell
353 West 57th Street
New York, NY 10019
"Comedian, Writer, Director"

Theresa Russell
9454 Lloyd Crest Drive
Beverly Hills, CA 90210
"Actress"

Rene Russo
8046 Fareholm Drive
Los Angeles, CA 90046
"Actress"

Ann Rutherford
826 Greenway Drive
Beverly Hills, CA 90210
"Actress"

Johnny Rutherford
4919 Black Oak Lane
Fort Worth, TX 76114
"Race Car Driver"

Kelly Rutherford
PO Box 492266
Los Angeles, CA 90049
"Actress"

Susan Ruttan
2677 La Cuesta Drive
Los Angeles, CA 90046
"Actress"

Frank Ryan
4204 Woodland
Burbank, CA 91505
"Actress"

Lisa Dean Ryan
11684 Ventura Blvd. #475
Studio City, CA 91604
"Actress"

John P. Ryan
1422 N. Sierra Bonita Avenue
Los Angeles, CA 90046
"Actor"

Meg Ryan
11718 Barrington Court #508
Los Angeles, CA 90049
"Actress"

Mitchell Ryan
30355 Mulholland Drive
Cornell, CA 91301
"Actor"

Nolan Ryan
719 Dezzo Drive
Alvin, TX 77511
"Ex-Baseball Player"

Peggy Ryan
1821 East Oakley Blvd.
Las Vegas, NV 89104
"Actress"

Bobby Rydell
917 Bryn Mawr Avenue
Narberth, PA 19072
"Singer"

Christopher Rydell
911 North Sweetzer #C
Los Angeles, CA 90069
"Actor"

Mark Rydell
1 Topsail
Marina del Rey, CA 90292
"Actor, Director"

Winona Ryder
10345 West Olympic Blvd.
Los Angeles, CA 90064
"Actress"

Ann Ryerson
935 Gayley Avenue
Los Angeles, CA 90024
"Actress"

Leony Rysanek
8201 Altenbeuren/Obb
GERMANY
"Soprano"

Jim Ryun
Rt. 3, Box 62-B
Lawrence, KS 66044
"Track Athlete"

Gabriela Sabatini
217 East Redwood Street #1800
Baltimore, MD 21202
"Tennis Player"

Michael Sabatino
9300 Wilshire Blvd. #555
Beverly Hills, CA 90212
"Actor"

Brett Saberhagen
19229 Arminta Street
Reseda, CA 91335
"Baseball Player"

Robert Sacchi
232 South Windsor Blvd.
Los Angeles, CA 90004
"Actor"

Andrew Sachs
25 Whitehall
London SW1A 2BS ENGLAND
"Actor"

Madame Jehan El-Sadat
2310 Decatur Place N.W.
Washington, DC 20008
"Widower of Anwar"

Sade
37 Limerston Street
London SW10 ENGLAND
"Singer, Songwriter"

William Sadler
918 - 6th Street #5
Santa Monica, CA 90405
"Actor"

Morley Safer
51 West 52nd Street
New York, NY 10019
"News Journalist"

William Safire
6200 Elmwood Road
Chevy Chase, MD 20815
"Columnist"

Jean Sagal
8383 Wilshire Blvd. #954
Beverly Hills, CA 90211
"Actress"

Katey Sagal
7095 Hollywood Blvd. #792
Los Angeles, CA 90028
"Actress"

Liz Sagal
4526 Wilshire Blvd.
Los Angeles, CA 90046
"Actress"

Dr. Carl E. Sagan
Cornell University
Space-Science Bldg.
Ithaca, NY 14853
"Astronomer, Writer"

Francoise Sagan
Equemauville 14600
Honfleur FRANCE
"Author"

Jeff Sagansky
145 Ocean Avenue
Santa Monica, CA 90402
"TV Executive"

Carole Bayer Sager
658 Nimes Road
Los Angeles, CA 90077
"Singer, Songwriter"

Bob Saget
9150 Wilshire Blvd., #350
Beverly Hills, CA 90212
"Comedian"

Mort Sahl
2325 San Ysidro Drive
Beverly Hills, CA 90210
"Comedian, Writer"

Eva Marie Saint
10590 Wilshire Blvd. #408
Los Angeles, CA 90024
"Actress"

Lili St. Cyr
624 North Plymouth Blvd. #7
Los Angeles, CA 90004
"Entertainer"

Susan Saint James
9830 Wilshire Blvd.
Beverly Hills, CA 90212
"Actress"

Jill St. John
1500 Old Oak Road
Los Angeles, CA 90077
"Actress"

Yves St. Laurent
15 Columbus Circle
New York, NY 10023
"Fashion Designer"

Buffy Sainte-Marie
2729 Westshire Drive
Los Angeles, CA 90068
"Singer, Songwriter"

Pat Sajak
3400 Riverside Drive
Burbank, CA 91505
"TV Show Host"

Theresa Saldana
104-60 Queens Blvd. #10C
Forest Hills, NY 11375
"Actress"

Meredith Salenger
12700 Ventura Blvd. #100
Studio City, CA 91604
"Actress"

Soupy Sales
245 East 35th Street
New York, NY 10016
"Actor, Comedian"

J. D. Salinger
RR #3, Box 176
Cornish Flat, NH 03746
"Author"

Matt Salinger
21604 Paseo Serra
Malibu, CA 90265
"Actor"

Pierre Salinger
1850 "M" Street NW #900
Washington, DC 20036
"News Correspondent"

Alexander Salkind
Iver Heath
Bucks. SLO ONH ENGLAND
"Film Producer"

Jennifer Salt
9045 Elevado Street
West Hollywood, CA 90069
"Actress"

Salt-N-Pepa
215 E. Orangethorpe Ave. #363
Fullerton, CA 92632
"Rap Group"

Emma Samms
2934 1/2 N. Beverly Glen Circle
Suite #417
Los Angeles, CA 90077
"Actress"

Pete Sampras
6352 Maclaurin Drive
Tampa, FL 33647
"Tennis Player"

Jeffrey D. Sams
9200 Sunset Blvd., #625
Los Angeles, CA 90069
"Actor"

Ron Samuels
120 S. El Camino Drive #116
Beverly Hills, CA 90212
"Talent Agent"

Paul Sand
924 Westwood Blvd., #900
Los Angeles, CA 90024
"Actor"

Casey Sander
8271 Melrose Avenue #202
Los Angeles, CA 90046
"Actor"

Barry Sanders
1200 Featherstone Road
Pontiac, MI 48057
"Football Player"

Deion Sanders
P.O. Box 4064
Atlanta, GA 30302
"Football & Baseball Player"

Doug Sanders
8828 Sandringham
Houston, TX 77024
"Golfer"

Jay O. Sanders
9229 Sunset Blvd. #710
Los Angeles, CA 90069
"Actor"

Marlene Sanders
175 Riverside Drive
New York, NY 10024
"Actress"

Richard Sanders
P.O. Box 1644
Woodinville, WA 98072
"Actor, Writer"

Summer Sanders
730 Sunrise Avenue
Roseville, CA 95661
"Swimmer"

William Sanderson
8271 Melrose Avenue #110
Los Angeles, CA 90046
"Actor"

Adam Sandler
9000 Sunset Blvd., #1200
Los Angeles, CA 90069
"Actor"

Jay Sandrich
610 North Maple Drive
Beverly Hills, CA 90210
"Actor, Director"

Tommy Sands
4312 Troost Avenue
North Hollywood, CA 91604
"Actor, Singer"

Baby Sandy
(Sandra Lee Henville Magee)
6846 Haywood
Tujunga, CA 91042
"Actress"

Isabel Sanford
9000 Sunset Blvd. #1200
Los Angeles, CA 90069
"Actress"

Laura San Giacomo
335 North Maple Drive #254
Beverly Hills, CA 90210
"Actress"

Olga San Juan
4845 Willowcrest Avenue
Studio City, CA 91604
"Dancer, Comedienne"

Santana
P.O. Box 881630
San Francisco, CA 94188
"Rock & Roll Group"

Carlos Santana
121 Jordan Street
San Rafael, CA 94901
"Singer"

Benito Santiago
2267 NW 199th Street
Miami, FL 33056
"Baseball Player"

Ron Santo
1303 Somerset
Glenview, IL 60025
"Ex-Baseball Player"

Penny Santon
1918 North Edgemont Street
Los Angeles, CA 90027
"Actress"

Reni Santoni
247 South Beverly Drive #102
Beverly Hills, CA 90212
"Actor"

Joe Santos
10100 Santa Monica Blvd. #700
Los Angeles, CA 90067
"Actor"

Carolyn Sapp
1211 Farr Lane
Honolulu, HI 96819
"Former Miss America"

Mia Sara
222 North Norton
Los Angeles, CA 90004
"Actress"

HRH Sarah, Dutchess of York
Romenda Lodge
Wentworth, Surrey, ENGLAND
"Royalty"

Chris Sarandon
107 Glasco Turnpike
Woodstock, NY 12498
"Actor"

Susan Sarandon
40 West 57th Street
New York, NY 10019
"Actress"

Gene Sarazen
Emerald Beach
P.O. Box 677
Marco, FL 33937
"Golfer"

Sen. Paul Sarbanes (MD)
Senate Hart Bldg. #309
Washington, DC 20510
"Politician"

Vincent Sardi, Jr.
234 West 44th Street
New York, NY 10036
"Restaurateur"

Michael Sarrazin
9920 Beverly Grove
Beverly Hills, CA 90210
"Actor"

Vidal Sassoon
1163 Calle Vista
Beverly Hills, CA 90210
"Hair Stylist"

Paul Satterfield
P.O. Box 6945
Beverly Hills, CA 90212
"Actor"

Van Gordon Sauter
9240 Swallow Drive
Los Angeles, CA 90069
"TV Executive"

Ann Savage
8218-B DeLongpre Avenue
Los Angeles, CA 90069
"Actress"

Fred Savage
9830 Wilshire Blvd.
Beverly Hills, CA 90212
"Actor"

John Savage
9465 Wilshire Blvd., #405
Beverly Hills, CA 90212
"Actor"

Randy Savage
P.O. Box 3859
Stamford, CT 06905
"Wrestler"

Tracie Savage
6212 Banner Avenue
Los Angeles, CA 90038
"Actress"

Doug Savant
1015 East Angelo Avenue
Burbank, CA 91501
"Actor"

Jennifer Savidge
2705 Glendower Avenue
Los Angeles, CA 90027
"Actress"

David Saville
28 Colomb Street
London SW10 9EW ENGLAND
"Actor"

Sawyer Brown
4295 Hillsboro Road #208
Nashville, TN 37215
"Rock & Roll Group"

Diane Sawyer
77 West 66th Street
New York, NY 10023
"Broadcast Journalist"

John Saxon
2432 Banyan Drive
Los Angeles, CA 90049
"Actor, Writer"

Peggy Say
438 Lake Shore Drive
Cadiz, KY 42211
"Sister Of American Hostage"

Gale Sayers
624 Buch Road
Northbrook, IL 60062
"Ex-Football Player"

Raphael Sbarge
4526 Wilshire Blvd.
Los Angeles, CA 90010
"Actor"

Greta Scacchi
121 North San Vicente Blvd.
Beverly Hills, CA 90211
"Actress"

Boz Scaggs
8900 Wilshire Blvd. #300
Beverly Hills, CA 90211
"Singer, Songwriter"

Prunella Scales
18-21 Jermyn Street
London SW1 ENGLAND
"Actress"

Antonin Scalia
1-1st Street N.E.
Washington, DC 20543
"Supreme Court Justice"

Jack Scalia
2150 Cold Canyon
Calabasas, CA 91302
"Actor"

Michele Scarabelli
4720 Vineland Avenue #216
North Hollywood, CA 91602
"Actress"

Glenn Scarpelli
3480 Barham Blvd. #320
Los Angeles, CA 90068
"Actor"

Diana Scarwid
P.O. Box 3614
Savannah, GA 31404
"Actress"

Francesco Scavullo
216 East 63rd Street
New York, NY 10021
"Photographer"

Wendy Schaal
9255 Sunset Blvd. #515
Los Angeles, CA 90069
"Actress"

William Schallert
14920 Ramos Place
Pacific Palisades, CA 90272
"Actor"

Anne Schedeen
4526 Wilshire Blvd.
Beverly Hills, CA 90210
"Actress"

Roy Scheider
P.O. Box 364
Sagaponack, NY 11962
"Actor"

John Schelessinger
76 Oxford Street
London WIN OAX ENGLAND
"Film Director"

Catherine Schell
Postfache 8000504 D-51005
Kain, GERMANY
"Actress"

Maria Schell
9400 Wolfsberg/Karnsten
AUSTRIA
"Actress"

Maximilian Schell
P.O. Box 7426
Beverly Hills, CA 90212
"Actor"

Ronnie Schell
4024 Sapphire Drive
Encino, CA 91316
"Comedian, Actor"

John Schelessinger
76 Oxford Street
London WIN OAX ENGLAND
"Film Director"

Bo Schembechler
1000 South State Street
Ann Arbor, MI 48109
"Ex-Football Coach, Baseball"

Paul Scherrer
9000 Sunset Blvd. #1200
Los Angeles, CA 90069
"Actor"

Vincent Schiavelli
450 N. Rossmore Avenue #206
Los Angeles, CA 90004
"Actor"

Bob Schieffer
2020 "M" Street NW
Washington, DC 20036
"Broadcast Journalist"

Claudia Schiffer
5 Union Square West #500
New York, NY 10003
"Model"

Lalo Schifrin
710 North Hillcrest Road
Beverly Hills, CA 90210
"Composer, Conductor"

William Schilling
626 North Valley Street
Burbank, CA 91505
"Actor"

G. David Schine
626 South Hudson
Los Angeles, CA 90005
"Businessman"

Walter M. Schirra, Jr.
16834 Via de Santa Fe
Rancho Santa Fe, CA 92067
"Astronaut"

Phyllis Schlafly
68 Fairmont
Alton, IL 62002
"Author, Politician"

Charlie Schlatter
13501 Contour Drive
Sherman Oaks, CA 91423
"Actor"

George Schlatter
400 Robert Lane
Beverly Hills, CA 90210
"Writer, Producer"

Arthur Schlesinger, Jr.
33 West 42nd Street
New York, NY 10036
"Historian, Author"

Edwin Schlossberg
641 Avenue of the Americas
New York, NY 10011
"Artist"

Max Schmeling
Sonnenweg 1
D-21279 Hollenstedt
Nordheide GERMANY
"Boxer"

Harold Schmid
Schlag 2, D-6467
Hasselroth 3 Germany
"T.V. Show Host"

Helmut Schmidt
Adenaunerallee 139-141
53 Bonn 1 GERMANY
"Chancellor"

Mike Schmidt
P.O. Box 32
Rydal, PA 19046
"Ex-Baseball Player"

John Schneider
2644 E. Chevy Chase Drive
Glendale, CA 91401
"Actor, Writer, Singer"

Stephen Schnetzer
448 West 44th Street
New York, NY 10036
"Actor"

Gina Schock
P.O. Box 4398
North Hollywood, CA 91617
"Drummer, Singer"

Carolyn Hunt Schoellkopf
100 Crescent #1700
Dallas, TX 75201
"Businesswoman"

Daniel Schorr
3113 Woodley Road
Washington, DC 20008
"Broadcast Journalist"

Marge Schott
100 Riverfront Stadium
Cincinnati, OH 45202
"Baseball Team Owner"

David Schramm
3521 Berry Drive
Studio City, CA 91604
"Actor"

Tex Schramm
9355 Sunnybrook
Dallas, TX 75220
"Football Team Executive"

Avery Schreiber
6612 Ranchito
Van Nuys, CA 91405
"Actor, Comedian"

Barbet Schroeder
1478 North Kings Road
Los Angeles, CA 90069
"Film Director"

Patricia Schroeder
1600 Emerson
Denver, CO 80218
"Politician"

Rick Schroeder
9560 Wilshire Blvd. #500
Beverly Hills, CA 90212
"Actor"

Mark Schubb
9744 Wilshire Blvd. #308
Beverly Hills, CA 90212
"Actor"

John Schuck
702 California Court
Venice, CA 90291
"Actor"

Budd Schulberg
P.O. Box 707, Brookside
Westhampton Beach, NY 11978
"TV Writer"

Dr. Robert Schuller
464 South Esplanade
Orange, CA 92669
"Evangelist"

Dwight Schultz
2179 West 21st Street
Los Angeles, CA 90010
"Actor"

Charles Schulz
1 Snoopy Place
Santa Rosa, CA 95401
"Cartoonist

Joel Schumacher
4000 Warner Blvd.
Bldg. 81 #117
Burbank, CA 91522
"Writer, Producer"

Diane Schuur
9000 Sunset Blvd. #1200
Los Angeles, CA 90069
"Singer"

Neil Schwartz
23427 Schoolcraft Avenue
Canoga Park, CA 91304
"Actor"

Sherwood Schwartz
1865 Carla Ridge Dr.
Beverly Hills, CA 90210
"TV Writer, Producer"

Arnold Schwarzenegger
3110 Main Street #300
Santa Monica, CA 90405
"Actor"

Elisabeth Schwarzkopf
Rebhusstr. 29
8126 Zunnikon
Zurich, SWITZERLAND
"Opera Singer"

Gen. Norman Schwarzkopf
400 North Ashley Drive #3050
Tampa, FL 33609
"Military Leader"

Eric Schweig
P.O. Box 5163
Vancouver BC V7B 1M4 CANADA
"Actor"

David Schwimmer
10390 Santa Monica Blvd. #300
Los Angeles, CA 90025
"Actor"

Hanna Schygulla
17 rue Dumont-d'Urville
F-75016 Paris FRANCE
"Actress"

Patti Scialfa
11 Gimbel Place
Ocean, NJ 07712
"Singer"

Leonard Sciascia
Viale Scaduto 10/B
I-00144 Palermo, ITALY
"Author"

Annabella Sciorra
132 S. Rodeo Drive, #300
Beverly Hills, CA 90212
"Actress"

Dean Scofield
12304 Santa Monica Blvd. #104
Los Angeles, CA 90025
"Actor"

Paul Scofield
The Gables
Balcombe, Sussex ENGLAND
"Actor"

Tracy Scoggins
1131 Alta Loma Road #515
Los Angeles, CA 90069
"Actress, Model"

Peter Scolari
1104 Foothill Blvd.
Ojai, CA 93023
"Actor"

The Scooters
15190 Encanto Drive
Sherman Oaks, CA 91403
"Rock & Roll Group"

Scorpions
P.O. Box 5220
3000 Hanover, GERMANY
"Rock & Roll Group"

Martine Scorsese
445 Park Avenue #700
New York, NY 10022
"Film Writer, Producer"

Campbell Scott
3211 Retreat Court
Malibu, CA 90265
"Actor"

Dr. Gene Scott
1615 Glendale Avenue
Glendale, CA 91205
"TV Show Host, Teacher"

Geoffrey Scott
1801 Ave. of the Stars #1250
Los Angeles, CA 90067
"Actor"

George C. Scott
3211 Retreat Court
Malibu, CA 90265
"Actor, Director"

Jacqueline Scott
12456 Ventura Blvd. #1
Studio City, CA 91604
"Actress"

Judson Scott
10000 Santa Monica Blvd. #305
Los Angeles, CA 90067
"Actor"

Kathryn Leigh Scott
P.O. Box 17217
Beverly Hills, CA 90209
"Actress"

Lizabeth Scott
P.O. Box 5522
Beverly Hills, CA 90213
"Actress"

Martha Scott
14054 Chandler Blvd.
Van Nuys, CA 91401
"Actress"

Pippa Scott
414 Avondale Avenue
Los Angeles, CA 90049
"Actress"

Ridley Scott
5555 Melrose Avenue #117
Los Angeles, CA 90038
"Film Director"

Ronnie Scott
47 Frith Street
London W1V 5TE ENGLAND
"Saxophonist"

Williard Scott
30 Rockerfeller Plaza #304
New York, NY 10012
"TV Weatherman"

Vito Scotti
5456 Vanalden Avenue
Tarzana, CA 91356
"Actor"

Renato Scotto
61 West 62nd Street #6F
New York, NY 10023
"Soprano"

Gen. Brent Scowcroft
350 Park Avenue #2600
New York, NY 10022
"Ex-Military, Politician"

Earl Scruggs
P.O. Box 66
Madison, TN 37115
"Banjoist, Songwriter"

Vin Scully
1555 Capri Drive
Pacific Palisades, CA 90272
"Sportscaster"

Glenn T. Seaborg
1 Cyclotron Road
Berkeley, CA 94720
"Chemist"

The Seachers
P.O. Box 262
Carteret, NJ 07008
"Vocal Group"

Steven Seagal
344 E. 59th Street
New York, NY 10022
"Actor"

Jenny Seagrove
2-4 Noel Street
London W1V 3RB ENGLAND
"Actress"

Bobby Seale
302 West Chelton Avenue
Philadelphia, PA 19144
"Activist, Author"

Dan Seals
153 Saunders Ferry Rd.
Hendersonville, TN 37075
"Singer, Songwriter"

Junior Seau
9449 Friars Road
San Diego, CA 92108
"Football Player"

Tom Seaver
Larkspur Lane
Greenwich, CT 06830
"Ex-Baseball Player"

John Sebastian
11846 Balboa Boulevard, #204
Granada Hills, CA 91344
"Singer, Songwriter"

Jon Secada
P.O. Box 4417
Miami, FL 33269
"Singer"

Sir Harry Secombe
46 St. James's Place
London SW1 ENGLAND
"Actor, Singer"

Kyle Secor
538 North Mansfield Avenue
Los Angeles, CA 90036
"Actor"

Gen. Richard Secord
1 Pennsylvania Plaza #2400
New York, NY 10119
"Miltary Leader"

Neil Sedaka
888 - 7th Avenue #1600
New York, NY 10106
"Singer, Songwriter"

Frank Sedgman
28 Bolton Avenue
Hampton, Victoria 3188
AUSTRALIA
"Tennis Player"

Kyra Sedgwick
1724 North Vista
Los Angeles, CA 90046
"Actress"

Pete Seeger
P.O. Box 431
Duchess Junction
Beacon, NY 12508
"Singer, Songwriter"

Erich Segal
53 The Pryors
East Heath Road
London NW3 1BP ENGLAND
"Author"

George Segal
810 Holmby Avenue
Los Angeles, CA 90224
"Actor"

Jonathan Segal
P.O. Box 3059
Tel Aviv 61030 ISRAEL
"Actor"

Michael Segal
27 Cyprus Avenue, Finchley
London N3 1SS ENGLAND
"Actor"

Pamela Segall
9560 Wilshire Blvd. #500
Beverly Hills, CA 90212
"Actress"

Bob Seger
567 Purdy
Birmingham, MI 48009
"Singer"

Pancho Segura
La Costa Hotel & Spas
Costa Del Mar Road
Carlsbad, CA 92008
"Tennis Player"

Emmanuella Seigner
210 rue du Faubourg St. Honore
F-75008 Paris FRANCE
"Actress"

Jerry Seinfeld
147 El Camino Drive #205
Beverly Hills, CA 90212
"Comedian, Actor"

David Selby
15152 Encanto Drive
Sherman Oaks, CA 91403
"Actor"

Monica Seles
7751 Beeridge Road
Sarasota, FL 34241
"Tennis Player"

Bud Selig
c/o County Coliseum
Milwaukee, WI 53214
"Baseball Team Owner"

Connie Selleca
14755 Ventura Blvd. #1-916
Sherman Oaks, CA 91403
"Actress"

Tom Selleck
331 Sage Lane
Santa Monica, CA 90402
"Actor"

Milton Selzer
575 San Juan Street
Santa Paul, CA 93060
"Actor"

The Serendipity Singers
P.O. Box 399
Lisle, IL 60532
"Vocal Group"

Yahoo Serious
12/33 East Crescent Street
McMahons Point NSW 2060
AUSTRLIA
"Actor, Director"

Pepe Serna
2321 Hill Drive
Los Angeles, CA 90041
"Actor"

Sesame Street
One Lincoln Plaza
New York, NY 10022
"Children TV Show"

Brian Setzer
113 Wardour Street
London W1 ENGLAND
"Musician"

Johnny Seven
11213 McLennan Avenue
Granada Hills, CA 91344
"Actor, Director"

Joan Severance
9000 Sunset Boulevard, #1200
Los Angeles, CA 90069
"Actress, Model"

Doc Severinsen
4275 White Pine Lane
Santa Ynez, CA 93460
"Trumpeter"

Jane Seymour
P.O. Box 548
Agoura, CA 91376
"Actress, Model"

Stephanie Seymour
12626 High Bluff Drive, #200
San Diego, CA 92130
"Model"

Ted Shackelford
12305 Valleyheart Drive
Studio City, CA 91604
"Actor"

Paul Shaffer
1697 Broadway
New York, NY 10019
"Keyboardist"

Peter Shaffer
200 Fulham Road
London SW10 ENGLAND
"Screenwriter"

Steve Shagan
10390 Wilshire Blvd. #705
Los Angeles, CA 90024
"Writer, Producer"

Sec. Donna Shalala
200 Independence Avenue S.W.
Washington, DC 20201
"Sec. Health & Human Service"

Shalamar
9229 Sunset Boulevard, #319
Los Angeles, CA 90069
"R&B Group"

Gen. John Shalikashvilli
The Pentagon, Room 2E872
Washington, DC 20301
"Joint Chief of Staff"

Gene Shalit
225 East 79th Street
New York, NY 10021
"Film Critic"

Yitzhak Shamir
Kiriyat Ben Gurian
Jerusalem 91919 ISRAEL
"Politician"

Sha Na Na
1720 N. Ross Street
Santa Ana, CA 92706
"Rock & Roll Group"

Garry Shandling
9150 Wilshire Boulevard, #350
Beverly Hills, CA 90212
"Comedian, Actor, Director"

Shanice
8455 Fountain Avenue #530
Los Angeles, CA 90069
"Singer"

Ravi Shankar
17 Warden Court
Gowalia Tank Road
Bombay 36 INDIA
"Satarist"

Esther Shapiro
617 North Alta Drive
Beverly Hills, CA 90210
"TV Writer, Producer"

Richard Shapiro
617 North Alta Drive
Beverly Hills, CA 90210
"TV Writer, Producer"

Robert Shapiro
2121 Avenue of the Stars
Los Angeles, CA 90067
"Attorney"

Omar Sharif
18 rue Troyan
F-75017 Paris FRANCE
"Actor"

Barbara Sharma
P.O. Box 29125
Los Angeles, CA 90029
"Actress"

Don Sharp
80 Castelnau
London SW13 9EX ENGLAND
"TV Writer, Executive"

Rev. Al Sharpton
1133 Bedford Avenue
Brooklyn, NY 11216
"Social Activist"

William Shatner
P.O. Box 7401725
Studio City, CA 91604
"Actor"

Grant Shaud
8738 Applan Way
Los Angeles, CA 90046
"Actor"

Charles Shaughnessy
2215 Malcolm Avenue
Los Angeles, CA 90064
"Actor"

Mel Shavelson
11947 Sunshine Terrace
North Hollywood, CA 91604
"Writer, Producer"

Helen Shaver
P.O. Box 5617
Beverly Hills, CA 90210
"Actress"

Artie Shaw
2127 West Palos Court
Newbury Park, CA 91320
"Orchestra Leader"

Bernard Shaw
111 Massachusetts N.W.
Washington, DC 20001
"News Correspondent"

Martin Shaw
204 Belswins Lane
Hemel, Hempstead
Hertfordshire, ENGLAND
"Actor"

Stan Shaw
4526 Wilshire Blvd.
Los Angeles, CA 90010
"Actor"

Tommy Shaw
1790 Broadway PH
New York, NY 10019
"Singer, Songwriter"

David Shawyer
16 Rylett Road
London W12 ENGLAND
"Actor"

George Beverly Shea
1300 Harmon Place
Minneapolis, MN 55403
"Singer"

John Shea
955 South Carrillo Drive #300
Los Angeles, CA 90048
"Actor"

Rhonda Shear
317 North Palm Drive
Beverly Hills, CA 90210
"Actress, Model"

Harry Shearer
119 Ocean Park Blvd.
Santa Monica, CA 90405
"TV Writer, Director"

Moira Shearer
2 Powls Mews
London, W11 1JN England
"Actress"

George Shearing
605 Market Street #1350
San Francisco, CA 94105
"Actor"

Ally Sheedy
P.O. Box 523
Topanga, CA 90290
"Actress"

Doug Sheehan
4019-137 Goldfinch Street
San Diego, CA 92103
"Actor"

Gail Sheehy
300 East 57th Street #18-D
New York, NY 10022
"Author, Journalist"

Charlie Sheen
1845 Olivera Drive
Agoura Hills, CA 91301
"Actor"

Martin Sheen
6916 Dune Drive
Malibu, CA 90265
"Actor, TV Director"

Craig Sheffer
5699 Kanan Road #275
Agoura, CA 91301
"Actor"

Johnny Sheffield
834 First Avenue
Chula Vista, CA 92011
"Actor"

David Sheiner
601 N. Orange Drive
Los Angeles, CA 90036
"Actor"

Sen. Richard C. Shelby (AL)
Senate Hart Bldg. #110
Washington, DC 20515
"Politician"

Deborah Sheldon
1690 Coldwater Canyon
Beverly Hills, CA 90210
"Actress"

Reid Sheldon
1524 Labaig Avenue
Los Angeles, CA 90028
"Actor"

Sidney Sheldon
10250 Sunset Blvd.
Los Angeles, CA 90077
"Writer"

Art Shell
30816 rue de la Pierre
Rancho Palos Verdes, CA 90274
"Football Player & Coach"

Carole Shelley
333 West 56th Street
New York, NY 10019
"Actress"

Adm. Alan B. Shepard, Jr.
6225 Vectorspace Boulevard
Titusville, FL 32780
"Astronaut"

Cybill Shepherd
16037 Royal Oak Road
Encino, CA 91436
"Actress, Model"

T.G. Sheppard
916 South Byrne #2
Toledo, OH 43609
"Singer"

Jamey Sheridan
8942 Wilshire Blvd.
Beverly Hills, CA 90211
"Actor"

Nicollette Sheridan
2131 Roscomare Road
Los Angeles, CA 90077
"Actress"

Bobby Sherman
1870 Sunset Plaza Drive
Los Angeles, CA 90069
"Singer, Actor"

Jenny Sherman
P.O. Box 73
Los Angeles, CA 90078
"Actress, Model"

Richard Sherman
9030 Harratt Street
Los Angeles, CA 90069
"Composer, Lyricist"

Robert Sherman
9030 Harratt Street
Los Angeles, CA 90069
"Composer, Lyricist"

Madeline Sherwood
32 Leroy Street
New York, NY 10014
"Actress"

Roberta Sherwood
14155 Magnolia Blvd. #126
Sherman Oaks, CA 91423
"Singer, Actress"

Pres. Edward Shevardnadze
c/o State Council
Tbilisi GEORGIA
"Politician"

Brooke Shields
P.O. Box 18
Las Vegas, NV 89125
"Actress, Model"

James Shigeta
8917 Cynthia #1
Los Angeles, CA 90069
"Actor"

Yoko Shimada
7245 Hillside Avenue #415
Los Angeles, CA 90046
"Actress"

Armin Shimerman
8730 Sunset Boulevard, #480
Los Angeles, CA 90069
"Actor"

Joanna Shimkus
1221 Stone Canyon Road
Los Angeles, CA 90077
"Actress"

John Wesley Shipp
P.O. Box 5617
Beverly Hills, CA 90210
"Actor"

Talia Shire
16633 Ventura Blvd. #1450
Encino, CA 91436
"Actress"

The Shirelles
P.O. Box 100
Clifton, NJ 07011
"Singing Group"

William Shockley
2062 Glencoe Way
Los Angeles, CA 90068
"Actor"

Bill Shoemaker
2553 Fairfield Place
San Marino, CA 91108
"Horse Racer"

Pauly Shore
1375 North Doheny Drive
Los Angeles, CA 90069
"Actor"

Lonnie Shorr
141 S. El Camino Drive #205
Beverly Hills, CA 90212
"Comedian"

Bobby Short
444 East 57th Street #9E
New York, NY 10022
"Actor, Singer"

Martin Short
15907 Alcima Avenue
Pacific Palisades, CA 90272
"Actor"

Frank Shorter
890 Willowbrook Road
Boulder, CO 80302
"Track Athlete"

Steve Shortridge
1707 Clearview Drive
Beverly Hills, CA 90210
"Actor"

Grant Show
937 South Tremaine
Los Angeles, CA 90019
"Actor"

Max Showalter
5 Gilbert Hill Road
Chester, CT 06412
"Actor"

Kathy Shower
8383 Wilshire Blvd. #954
Beverly Hills, CA 90210
"Actress"

Jean Shrimpton Cox
Abbey Hotel
Penzance
Cornwall ENGLAND
"Actress"

Kin Shriner
3915 Benedict Canyon
Sherman Oaks, CA 91423
"Actor"

Wil Shriner
5313 Quakertown Avenue
Woodland Hills, CA 91364
"Actor, Writer, Comedian"

Eunice Kennedy Shriver
1350 New York Avenue NW
Washington, DC 20005
"Ex-President's Sister"

Maria Shriver
3110 Main Street #300
Santa Monica, CA 90405
"Broadcast Journalist"

Pam Shriever
133 1st Street N.E.
St. Petersburg, FL 33701
"Tennis Player"

R. Sargent Shriver
1350 New York Avenue N.W.
Washington, DC 20005
"Politician"

Sonny Shroyer
12725-F Ventura Blvd.
Studio City, CA 91604
"Actor"

Andrew Shue
151 El Camino Drive
Beverly Hills, CA 90212
"Actor"

Elisabeth Shue
P.O. Box 464
South Orange, NJ 07079
"Actress"

Don Shula
16 Indian Creek Island
Miami Lakes, FL 33154
"Football Coach"

Richard B. Shull
16 Gramercy Park
New York, NY 10003
"Actor"

George P. Shultz
776 Dolores Street
Stanford, CA 94305
"Ex-Government Official"

Michael Shuster
c/o National Public Radio
2025 "M" Street NW
Washington, DC 20036
"New Correspondent"

Jane Sibbett
2144 Nichols Canyon Road
Los Angeles, CA 90046
"Actress"

Jane Siberry
41 Britain St. #200
Toronto, Ont. M5A 1R7
CANADA
"Singer, Guitarist"

Hugh Sidey
1050 Connecticut Avenue
Washington, DC 20036
"Columnist"

Sylvia Sidney
9744 Wilshire Blvd. #308
Beverly Hills, CA 90212
"Actress"

Charles Sieberg
15301 Ventura Blvd. #345
Sherman Oaks, CA 91403
"Actor, Director"

Robert Siegel
c/o National Public Radio
2025 "M" Street NW
Washington, DC 20036
"News Correspondent"

Siegfried & Roy
1639 North Valley Drive
Las Vegas, NV 89109
"Circus Act"

Casey Siemaszko
9830 Wilshire Blvd.
Beverly Hills, CA 90212
"Actor"

Gregory Sierra
10000 Santa Monica Blvd. #305
Los Angeles, CA 90067
"Actor"

Sanford Sigoloff
320 Cliffwood Avenue
Los Angeles, CA 90049
"Business Executive"

Cynthia Sikes
250 Delfern Drive
Los Angeles, CA 90077
"Actress"

James B. Sikking
4526 Wilshire Blvd.
Beverly Hills, CA 90210
"Actor"

Karen Sillas
P.O. Box 5617
Beverly Hills, CA 90210
"Actress"

Beverly Sills
211 Central Park West #4F
New York, NY 10024
"Soprano"

Henry Silva
5226 Beckford
Tarzana, CA 91356
"Actor"

Fred Silverman
12400 Wilshire Blvd. #920
Los Angeles, CA 90025
TV Executive, Producer"

Jonathan Silverman
7920 Sunset Blvd. #400
Los Angeles, CA 90046
"Actor"

Alicia Silverstone
P.O. Box 16539
Beverly Hills, CA 90209
"Actress"

Dick Simmons
3215 Silver Cliff Drive
Prescott, AZ 86303
"Actor"

Gene Simmons
12424 Wilshire Blvd. #1000
Los Angeles, CA 90025
"Singer, Actor, Composer"

Jaason Simmons
5433 Beethoven Street
Los Angeles, CA 90066
"Actor"

Jean Simmons
636 Adelaide Way
Santa Monica, CA 90402
"Actress"

Richard Simmons
P.O. Box 5403
Beverly Hills, CA 90209
"Exercise Instructor"

Larry Simms
P.O. Box 85
Gray River, WA 98621
"Actor"

Carly Simon
135 Central Park West
New York, NY 10023
"Singer, Songwriter"

Neil Simon
10745 Chalon Road
Los Angeles, CA 90077
"Dramatist"

Sen. Paul Simon (IL)
Senate Dirksen Bldg.#462
Washington, DC 2051
"Politician"

Paul Simon
1619 Broadway #500
New York, NY 10019
"Singer, Songwriter

Scott Simon
c/o National Public Radio
2025 "M" Street NW
Washington, DC 20036
"News Correspondent"

Simone Simon
5 rue de Tilsitt
75008 Paris, FRANCE
"Actress"

William Simon
330 South Street
Morristown, NJ 07960
"Former Secretary of Treasury"

Nina Simone
7250 Franklin Avenue #115
Los Angeles, CA 90046
"Singer, Pianist"

Simple Minds
63 Frederic Street
Edinburgh EH2 1LH SCOTLAND
"Rock & Roll Group"

Simply Red
48 Princess Street
Manchester M1 6HR
ENGLAND
"Rock & Roll Group"

Sen. Alan K. Simpon (WY)
Senate Dirksen Bldg. #261
Washington, DC 20510
"Politician"

Arnelle Simpson
11661 San Vicente Blvd. #632
Los Angeles, CA 90049
"O.J.'s Daughter"

Jason Simpson
11661 San Vicente Blvd. #632
Los Angeles, CA 90049
"O.J.'s Son"

O.J. Simpson
360 Rockingham Avenue
Los Angeles, CA 90049
"Ex-Football Player"

Joan Sims
17 Esmond Court
Thackery Street
London W8 ENGLAND
"Actress"

Frank Sinatra
915 N. Foothill Road
Beverly HIls, CA 90210
"Singer, Actor"

Frank Sinatra, Jr.
2211 Florian Place
Beverly Hills, CA 90210
"Singer"

Nancy Sinatra, Jr.
P.O. Box 69453
Los Angeles, CA 90069
"Singer, Actress"

Tina Sinatra
9461 Lloydcrest Drive
Beverly Hills, CA 90210
"Singer"

Sinbad
21704 Devonshire #13
Chatsworth, CA 91311
"Comedian, Actor"

Sinceros
25 Buliver Street
Shephards Bush
London W12 ENGLAND
"Rock & Roll Group"

Madge Sinclair
P.O. Box 5617
Beverly Hills, CA 90210
"Actress"

Donald Sinden
60 Temple Fortune Lane
London NW11 ENGLAND
"Actor"

Lori Singer
9830 Wilshire Blvd.
Beverly Hills, CA 90212
"Actress"

Marc Singer
11218 Canton Drive
Studio City, CA 91604
"Actor"

John Singleton
4223 Don Carlos Drive
Los Angeles, CA 90008
"Director"

Margie Singleton
P.O. Box 567
Hendersonville, TN 37077
"Singer, Guitarist"

Penny Singleton
13419 Riverside Drive #C
Sherman Oaks, CA 91423
"Actress"

Gary Sinise
P.O. Box 6704
Malibu, CA 90264
"Actor"

Curt Siomak
Old Southfork Ranch
43422 South Fork Drive
Three Rivers, CA 93271
"Writer, Producer"

Sirhan Sirhan #B21014
Corcoran State Prison
P.O. Box 8800
Corcoran, CA 93212
"Robert Kennendy's Killer"

Marina Sirtis
2436 Creston Way
Los Angeles, CA 90068
"Actress"

Siskel & Ebert
108 W. Grand Avenue
Chicago, IL 60610
"Movie Critics"

Gene Siskel
1301 North Astor
Chicago, IL 60610
"Film Critic"

Jeremy Sisto
1724 North Vista Street
Los Angeles, CA 90046
"Actor"

Emil Sitka
18124 Village #18
Camarillo, CA 93012
"Actor"

Sister Sledge
151 El Camino Drive
Beverly Hills, CA 90212
"Vocal Group"

Ricky Skaggs
380 Forest Retreat
Hendersonville, TN 37075
"Singer, Guitarist"

Red Skelton
37801 Thompson Road
Rancho Mirage, CA 92270
"Comedian, Actor"

Tom Skerritt
335 N. Maple Drive #360
Beverly Hills, CA 90210
"Actor"

Skid Row
240 Central Park South #2-C
New York, NY 10019
"Rock & Roll Group"

Moose Skowron
1118 Beachcomber Drive
Schaumburg, IL 60193
"Ex-Baseball Player"

Ione Skye
8794 Lookout Mountain Avenue
Los Angeles, CA 90046
"Actress"

Mark Slade
38 Joppa Road
Worcester, MA 01602
"Actor"

Christian Slater
150 So. Lasky Drive, #220
Beverly Hills, CA 90212
"Actor"

Helen Slater
1999 Avenue of the Stars, #2850
Los Angeles, CA 90067
"Actress"

Richard X. Slattery
P.O. Box 2410
Avalon, CA 90704
"Actor"

Robert F. Slatzer
3033 Hollycrest Drive #2
Los Angeles, CA 90068
"Writer, Producer"

Enos Slaughter
Rt. #2, Box 159
Roxboro, NC 27573
"Ex-Baseball Player"

Dr. Frank Slaughter
P.O. Box 14, Ortega Station
Jacksonville, FL 32210
"Author, Surgeon"

Percy Sledge
2513 Denny Avenue
Pascagoula, MS 39567
"Singer"

Erika Slezak
40 W. 57th St.
New York, NY 10019
"Actress"

Grace Slick
2548 Laurel Pass
Los Angeles, CA 90046
"Singer, Songwriter"

Curtis Sliwa
628 West 28th Street
New York, NY 10001
"Guardian Angles Founder"

Lisa Sliwa
628 West 28th Street
New York, NY 10001
"Guardian Angeles Co-Founder"

Mary Small
165 W. 66th Street
New York, NY 10023
"Actress"

Jean Smart
151 El Camino Drive
Beverly Hills, CA 90212
"Actress"

Yakov Smirnoff
1990 South Bundy Drive #200
Los Angeles, CA 90025
"Comedian"

Allison Smith
9000 Sunset Blvd. #1200
Los Angeles, CA 90069
"Actress"

Anna Nicole Smith
200 Ashdale Avenue
Los Angeles, CA 90049
"Actress, Playmate"

Bruce Smith
4385 Twilight Lane
Hamburg, NY 14075
"Football Player"

Bubba Smith
5178 Sunlight Place
Los Angeles, CA 90016
"Actor, Football Player"

Buffalo Bob Smith
500 Overlook Drive
Flat Rock, NC 28731
"Actor"

Charlie Martin Smith
31515 Germaine Lane
Westlake Village, CA 91361
"Actor"

Connie Smith
1300 Division Street #103
Nashville, TN 37203
"Singer"

Cotter Smith
15332 Antioch Street #800
Pacific Palisades, CA 90272
"Actor"

Emmitt Smith
1 Cowboy Parkway
Irving, TX 78063
"Football Player"

Harry Smith
524 West 57th Street
New York, NY 10019
"TV Show Host"

Ian Smith
Gwenoro Farm
Shurugwi ZIMBABWE
"Ex-Government Official"

Ilan Mitchell Smith
104-60 Queens Blvd. #10-C
Fox Hills, NY 11375
"Actor"

Jaclyn Smith
10398 Sunset Blvd.
Los Angeles, CA 90077
"Actress, Model"

Karin Smith
2300 Palisades Street
Los Osos, CA 93402
"Actress"

Kathy Smith
117 South Laxton Drive
Los Angeles, CA 90049
"Actress"

Keely Smith
3434 Oneida Way
Las Vegas, NV 89109
"Actress"

Kurtwood Smith
635 Frontenac Avenue
Los Angeles, CA 90065
"Actor"

Lane Smith
10000 Santa Monica Blvd. #305
Los Angeles, CA 90067
"Actor"

Lewis Smith
8271 Melrose Avenue #110
Los Angeles, CA 90046
"Actor"

Liz Smith
160 East 38th Street
New York, NY 10016
"Film Critic, Columnist"

Madeline Smith
76 Oxford Street
London W1N 0AX ENGLAND
"Actress"

Dame Maggie Smith
76 Oxford Street
London W1N 0AX ENGLAND
"Actress"

Margo Smith
1802 Williamson Court, #200
Brentwood, TN 37027
"Singer"

Martha Smith
P.O. Box 2241
Beverly Hills, CA 90213
"Actress, Model"

Rex Smith
9000 Sunset Blvd. #1200
Los Angeles, CA 90069
"Actor, Singer"

Roger Smith
2707 Benedict Canyon
Beverly Hills, CA 90210
"Actor, Writer"

Shawnee Smith
43 Navy Street #300
Venice, CA 90291
"Actress"

Shelley Smith
182 South Mansfield Avenue
Los Angeles, CA 90036
"Actress"

Susan Smith
#94g-4901-1104
Women's Correctional Facility
4450 Broad River Road
Columbia, SC 29210
"Convicted Child Killer"

Vince Smith
P.O. Box 1221
Pottsville, PA 17901
"Singer, Songwriter"

Wendy Smith
2925 Tuna Canyon Road
Topanga, CA 90290
"Actress"

Will Smith
330 Bob Hope Drive
Burbank, CA 91523
"Actor"

William Smith
3250 West Olympic Blvd. #67
Santa Monica, CA 90404
"Actor"

Dr. William Kennedy Smith
345 East Superior Street
Chicago, IL 60611
"Sen. Ted Kennedy's Nephew"

William Smithers
11664 Laurelcrest Drive
Studio City, CA 91604
"Actor"

Bill Smitrovich
5052 Rubio Avenue
Encino, CA 91436
"Actor"

Jimmy Smits
P.O. Box 49922
Barrington Station
Los Angeles, CA 90049
"Actor"

Dick Smothers
8489 W. 3rd Street, #1063
Los Angeles, CA 90048
"Comedian, Actor"

Tom Smothers
8489 W. 3rd Street, #1063
Los Angeles, CA 90048
"Comedian, Actor"

Marcus Smythe
12212 Califa Street
North Hollywood, CA 91607
"Actor"

Reggie Smythe
Whiteglass Caladonian Road
Hartlepool Cleveland, ENGLAND
"Cartoonist"

J.C. Snead
P.O. Box 2047
Ponte Verde Beach, FL 32082
"Golfer"

Sam Snead
P.O. Box 777
Hot Springs, VA 24445
"Golfer"

Tom Sneva
3301 East Valley Vista Lane
Paradise Valley, AZ 85253
"Race Car Driver"

Mike Snider
P.O. Box 140710
Nashville, TN 37214
"Bluegrass Musician"

Wesley Snipes
9830 Wilshire Blvd.
Beverly Hills, CA 90212
"Actor"

Carrie Snodgress
3025 Surry Street
Los Angeles, CA 90027
"Actress"

Snoop Doggy Dog
10900 Wilshire Blvd. #1230
Los Angeles, CA 90024
"Rap Singer"

Hank Snow
P.O. Box 1084
Nashville, TN 37202
"Singer, Songwriter"

Lord Snowdon
22 Lauceston Place
London, W1 England
"Photographer"

Tom Snyder
1225 Beverly Estates Drive
Beverly Hills, CA 90210
"Talk Show Host"

Barry Sobel
9000 Sunset Blvd. #1200
Los Angeles, CA 90069
"Comedian"

Steve Sohmer
2625 Larmar Road
Los Angeles, CA 90068
"TV Director"

Stephen Solarz
241 Dover Street
Brooklyn, NY 11235
"Ex-Congressman"

P.J. Soles
20940 Almazon
Woodland Hills, CA 91364
"Actress"

Sir George Solti
Chalet Haut Pre
1884 Villars-sur-Ollon
SWITZERLAND
"Conductor"

Suzanne Somers
8899 Beverly Blvd., #713
Los Angeles, CA 90048
"Actress, Singer"

Julie Sommars
9744 Wilshire Blvd. #308
Los Angeles, CA 90212
"Actress"

Elke Sommer
540 North Beverly Glen
Los Angeles, CA 90024
"Actress"

Stephen Sondheim
246 East 49th Street
New York, NY 10017
"Composer, Lyricist"

Kevin Sorbo
8033 Sunset Blvd., #920
Los Angeles, CA 90046
"Actor"

Louise Sorel
10808 Lindbrook Drive
Los Angeles, CA 90024
"Actress"

Ted Sorenson
1285 Avenue of the Americas
New York, NY 10019
"Former Government Official"

Arleen Sorkin
100 South Doheny Drive #605
Los Angeles, CA 90048
"Writer, Producer"

Paul Sorvino
110 East 87th Street
New York, NY 10128
"Actor"

Ann Sothern
P.O. Box 2285
Ketchum, ID 83340
"Actress"

Talisa Soto
9000 Sunset Blvd., #1200
Los Angeles, CA 90069
"Actress, Model"

David Soul
2232 Moreno Drive
Los Angeles, CA 90039
"Actor, Singer, Director"

Soundgarden
207 1/2 First Avenue So., #00
Seattle, WA 98104
"Rock & Roll Group"

David Souter
1-1st Street N.E.
Washington, DC 20543
"Supreme Court Justice"

Joe South
3051 Claremont Road NE
Atlanta, GA 30329
"Singer, Songwriter"

J.D. Souther
P.O. Box 5617
Beverly Hills, CA 90210
"Singer, Songwriter"

Southern Belles
11150 West Olympic Blvd.
Suite #1100
Los Angeles, CA 90064
"Wrestling Tag Team"

Terry Southern
RFD
East Canaan, CT 06020
"TV Writer"

Shawn Southwick
15250 Ventura Blvd. #720
Sherman Oaks, CA 91403
"Actress"

Catherine Spaak
Viale Parioli 59
00197 Rome, ITALY
"Actress"

Sissy Spacek
Rt. 22, #640
Cobham, VA 22929
"Actress"

Kevin Spacey
200 East 58th Street #7H
New York, NY 10022
"Actor"

James Spader
8942 Wilshire Blvd.
Beverly Hills, CA 90211
"Actor"

Warren Spahn
RD #2
Hartshorne, OK 74547
"Ex-Baseball Player"

Joe Spano
9056 Santa Monica Blvd. #307
Los Angeles, CA 90069
"Actor"

Vincent Spano
7920 Sunset Blvd., #400
Los Angeles, CA 90046
"Actor"

Camilla Spary
957 North Cole Avenue
Los Angeles, CA 90038
"Actress"

Boris Spassky
Skatertny Pereulok 5
Moscow RUSSIA
"Chess Player"

Jeff Speakman
18935 Granada Circle
Northridge, CA 91326
"Actor"

Billy Joe Spears
2802 Columbine Place
Nashville, TN 37204
"Singer"

Sen. Arlen Specter (PA)
Senate Hart Bldg. #303
Washington, DC 20510
"Politician"

Phil Spector
1210 South Arroyo Blvd.
Pasadena, CA 91101
"Record Producer"

Ronnie Spector
7 Maplecrest Drive
Danbury, CT 06810
"Singer"

Aaron Spelling
594 North Mapleton Drive
Los Angeles, CA 90077
"TV Producer"

Tori Spelling
5700 Wilshire Blvd. #575
Los Angeles, CA 90036
"Actress"

Gerry Spence
15 South Jackson
Jackson, WY 83001
"Attorney"

Bud Spencer
Via Cortina d'Ampezzo 156
00191 Rome, ITALY
"Actor"

Victor Spencer-Churchill
6 Cumberland Mansions
George Street
London W1 ENGLAND
"Viscount"

Wendy Jo Sperber
12424 Wilshire Blvd., #840
Los Angeles, CA 90025
"Actress"

Penelope Spheeris
P.O. Box 5617
Beverly Hills, CA 90210
"Director, Producer"

David Spielberg
3531 Bentley Avenue
Los Angeles, CA 90034
"Actor"

Steven Spielberg
P.O. Box 8520
Universal City, CA 91608
"Director, Producer"

Mickey Spillane
c/o General Delivery
Marrells Inlet, SC 22117
"Writer"

Sandy Spillman
1353 Alvarado Terrace
Los Angeles, CA 90017
"Actor"

Spinal Tap
15250 Ventura Blvd., #1215
Sherman Oaks, CA 91403
"Rock & Roll Group"

Brent Spiner
P.O. Box 5617
Beverly HIlls, CA 90210
"Actor"

Michael Spinks
250 West 57th Street
New York, NY 10107
"Boxer"

Spinners
65 West 55th Street #6C
New York, NY 10019
"Vocal Group"

Mark Spitz
383 Dalehurst
Los Angeles, CA 90077
"Swimmer"

Split Ends
136 New Kings Road
London SW6 ENGLAND
"Rock & Roll Group"

Dr. Benjamin Spock
P.O. Box 1890
St. Thomas 00803 V.I.
"Physician"

Michael Spound
1800 Avenue of the Stars #400
Los Angeles, CA 90067
"Actor"

Jerry Springer
P.O. Box 4118
Chicago, IL 60654
"Talk Show Host"

Dusty Springfield
7 Oak Thorpe Road
Palmer's Green
London N13 5HV ENGLAND
"Singer"

Rick Springfield
9200 Sunset Blvd. PH.-15
Los Angeles, CA 90069
"Singer, Guitarist"

Bruce Springsteen
1224 Benedict Canyon
Beverly Hills, CA 90210
"Singer, Guitarist"

Steve Spurrier
P.O. Box 14485
Gainesville, FL 32661
"Football Coach"

Spyro Gyro
P.O. Box 7308
Carmel, CA 93921
"Jazz Group"

Billy Squier
P.O. Box 1251
New York, NY 10023
"Singer, Guitarist"

Ken Stabler
Rt. Box, Gen. Del.
Orange Beach, AL 36561
"Ex-Football Player"

Robert Stack
321 St. Pierre Road
Los Angeles, CA 90077
"Actor"

Jim Stafford
P.O. Box 6366
Branson, MO 65616
"Singer"

Jo Stafford
2339 Century Hill
Los Angeles, CA 90067
"Singer"

Nancy Stafford
13080 Mindanao Way #69
Marina del Rey, CA 90292
"Actress"

Susan Stafford
101 California Avenue, PH
Santa Monica, CA 90405
"Actress"

Thomas Strafford
3212 East Interstate #240
Oklahoma City, OK 73135
"Astronaut, Businessman"

Lesley Stahl
524 West 57th Street
New York, NY 10019
"Journalist"

Lisa Stahl
9229 Sunset Blvd., #710
Los Angeles, CA 90069
"Actress"

Joan Staley
24516-B Windsor Drive
Valencia, CA 91355
"Actress"

Lynn Stallmaster
9911 West Pico Blvd. #1580
Los Angeles, CA 90035
"Casting Director"

Frank Stallone
10668 Eastborne #206
Los Angeles, CA 90025
"Actor"

Sasha Stallone
9 Bevery Park
Beverly Hills, CA 90210
"Ex-Wife of Sylvester Stallone"

Sylvester Stallone
8800 Sunset Blvd. #214
Los Angeles, CA 90069
"Actor"

Susan Stamberg
c/o National Public Radio
2025 "M" Street NW
Washington, DC 20036
"News Correspondent"

John Stamos
2319 St. George Street
Los Angeles, CA 90027
"Actor"

Terrence Stamp
The Albany, Piccadilly
London W1 ENGLAND
"Actor"

John Standing
28 Broomhouse Road
London SW6 ENGLAND
"Actor"

Dennis Stanfill
908 Oak Grove Avenue
San Marino, CA 91108
"Business Executive"

Arnold Stang
P.O. Box 786
New Canaan, CT 06840
"Actor"

Eddie Stanky
2100 Spring Hill Road
Mobile, AL 36607
"Ex-Baseball Manager"

Kim Stanley
3640 Monon Street, #111
Los Angeles, CA 90027
"Actress"

Maurice Stans
211 South Orange Grove
Pasadena, CA 91105
"Government Official"

Lisa Stansfield
Box 59, Ashwall
Herfordshire SG 5NG ENGLAND
"Singer"

Harry Dean Stanton
14527 Mulholland Drive
Los Angeles, CA 90077
"Actor"

Jean Stapleton
635 Perugia Way
Los Angeles, CA 90024
"Actress"

Maureen Stapleton
1-14 Morgan Manor
Lenox, MA 01240
"Actress"

Koo Stark
52 Shaftesbury Avenue
London W1 ENGLAND
"Actress"

Ray Stark
232 South Mapleton Drive
Los Angeles, CA 90077
"TV Producer"

Bart Starr
1400 Urban Center Drive, #400
Birmingham, AL 35242
"Ex-Football Player"

Kay Starr
223 Ashdale Avenue
Los Angeles, CA 90077
"Singer"

Kenneth Starr
6455 Madison Court
McLean, VA 22101
"Attorney"

Ringo Starr
1541 Ocean Avenue, #200
Santa Monica, CA 90401
"Drummer, Actor"

Starship (Jefferson Airplane)
2051 Third Street
San Francisco, CA 94107
"Rock & Roll Group"

Harold E. Stassen
310 Salem Church Road
Sunfish Lake, MN 55118
Ex-Governor"

Statler Brothers
P.O. Box 492
Hernando, MS 38632
"Vocal Group"

Roger Staubach
6750 LBJ Freeway
Dallas, TX 75109
"Football Player"

Eleanor Steber
P.O. Box 342
Port Jefferson, NY 11777
"Soprano"

Amy Steel
331 North Martel Avenue
Los Angeles, CA 90036
"Actress"

Dawn Steel
1033 Gayley Avenue #208
Los Angeles, CA 90024
"Producer"

Barbara Steele
442 South Bedford Drive
Beverly Hills, CA 90212
"Actress"

Danielle Steele
330 Bob Hope Drive
Burbank, CA 90212
"Novelist"

Tommy Steele
76 Oxford Street
London W1N 0AX ENGLAND
"Actor, Singer"

Mary Steenburgen
1325 Avenue of the Americas
New York, NY 10019
"Actress"

Rod Steiger
6324 Zumirez Drive
Malibu, CA 90265
"Actor"

Ben Stein
4549 Via Vienta
Malibu, CA 90265
"Writer"

David Steinberg
4406 Haskell Avenue
Encino, CA 91436
"Comedian, Actor, Writer"

George Steinbrenner
River Avenue & East 16th Street
New York, NY 100451
"Baseball Executive"

Gloria Steinem
118 East 73rd Street
New York, NY 10021
"Author, Feminist"

Jake Steinfeld
622 Toyopa Drive
Pacific Palisades, CA 90272
"Actor, Bodybuilder"

Ingemar Stenmark
Tarnaby, SWEDEN
"Skier"

Princess Stephanie
Grimaldi Palace
Monte Carlo PM MONACO
"Royalty"

George Stephanopoulos
1600 Pennsylvania Avenue
Washington, DC 20500
"White House Official"

James Stephens
822 South Robertson Blvd. #200
Los Angeles, CA 90035
"Actor, Director"

Laraine Stephens
1900 Avenue of the Stars
Suite #2270
Los Angeles, CA 90067
"Actress"

Jan Stephenson
7601 Della Drive #276
Orlando, FL 32819
"Golfer"

Steppenwolf
315 South Beverly Drive, #206
Beverly Hills, CA 90212
"Rock & Roll Group"

Jan Sterling
245 Woodlawn Avenue #H-6
Chula Vista, CA 91910
"Actress"

Philip Sterling
4114 Benedict Canyon
Beverly Hills, CA 90210
"Actor"

Robert Sterling
121 South Bentley Avenue
Los Angeles, CA 90049
"Actor"

Daniel Stern
9830 Wilshire Blvd.
Beverly Hills, CA 90212
"Actor"

Howard Stern
10 East 44th Street #500
New York, NY 10017
"Shock Radio Host"

Isaac Stern
211 Central Park West
New York, NY 10024
"Violinist"

Frances Sternahgen
152 Sutton Manor Road
New Rochelle, NY 10805
"Actress"

Andrew Stevens
9300 Wilshire Blvd. #400
Beverly Hills, CA 90212
"Actor"

Brinke Stevens
8033 Sunset Blvd. #556
Los Angeles, CA 90046
"Actress, Model"

Cat Stevens
(aka Yusef Islam)
Steinhauser Str. 3
81677 Munich GERMANY
"Singer, Songwriter"

Connie Stevens
8721 Sunset Blvd., PH 1
Los Angeles, CA 90069
"Actress, Singer"

Craig Stevens
25 Central Park West
New York, NY 10023
"Actor"

Fisher Stevens
151 El Camino Drive
Beverly Hills, CA 90212
"Actor"

George Stevens, Jr.
John F. Kennedy Center
Washington, DC 20566
"Director, Producer"

Kay Stevens
3518 Cahuenga Blvd. W. #216
Los Angeles, CA 90068
"Actress"

Morgan Stevens
14348 Roblar Place
Sherman Oaks, CA 91423
"Actor"

Ray Stevens
1708 Grand Avenue
Nashville, TN 37212
"Singer, Songwriter"

Rise Stevens
930 Fifth Avenue
New York, NY 10021
"Mezzo-Soprano"

Shadow Stevens
2570 Benedict Canyon
Beverly Hills, CA 90210
"Radio-TV personality"

Shawn Stevens
11355 Camarillo Street
North Hollywood, CA 91602
"Actor"

Stella Stevens
2180 Coldwater Canyon
Beverly Hills, CA 90210
"Actress"

Sen. Ted Stevens (AK)
Senate Hart Bldg. #522
Washington, DC 20510
"Politician"

Warren Stevens
14155 Magnolia Blvd. #44
Sherman Oaks, CA 91403
"Actor"

Adlai Stevenson III
231 South La Salle Street
Chicago, IL 60604
"Ex-Governor"

Parker Stevenson
4526 Wilshire Blvd.
Los Angeles, CA 90010
"Actor"

Teofilo Stevenson
Hotel Havana Libre
Havana, CUBA
"Boxer"

Alana Stewart
12824 Evanston Street
Los Angeles, CA 90049
"Actress"

Catherine Mary Stewart
350 DePont Street
Toronto Ontario
M5R 1Z9 CANADA
"Actress"

Emanuel Stewart
19600 W. McNichol Street
Detroit, MI 48219
"Boxing Trainer"

Jackie Stewart
24 Rte. de Divonne
1260 Nyon, SWITZERLAND
"Ex-Race Car Driver"

James Stewart
P.O. Box 90
Beverly Hills, CA 90213
"Actor, Director"

Jermaine Stewart
4A Lauceston Place
Kensington
London W8 5RL ENGLAND
"Singer"

Martha Stewart
10877 Wilshire Blvd. #900
Los Angeles, CA 90024
"Society Caterer, Author"

Patrick Stewart
8942 Wilshire Blvd.
Beverly Hills, CA 90211
"Actor"

Payne Stewart
390 North Orange Avenue
Suite #2600
Orlando, FL 32801
"Golfer"

Peggy Stewart
11139 Hortense Street
North Hollywood, CA 91602
"Actress"

Rod Stewart
23 Beverly Park
Beverly Hills, CA 90210
"Singer, Songwriter"

Michael Stich
Ernst-Barlach Street 44
DW-2200 Elmshorn GERMANY
"Tennis Player"

Dorothy Stickney
13 East 94th Street
New York, NY 10023
"Actress"

David Ogden Stiers
121 North San Vicente Blvd.
Beverly Hills, CA 90211
"Actor, Director"

Robert Stigwood
1775 Broadway
New York, NY 10023
"Film Producer"

Ben Stiller
10390 Santa Monica Blvd. #300
Los Angeles, CA 90025
"Actor"

Jerry Stiller
118 Riverside Drive, #5A
New York, NY 10024
"Comedian, Actor, Writer"

Stephen Still
191 North Phelps Avenue
Winter Park, FL 32789
"Singer"

Sting
2 The Grove
Highgate Village
London N16 ENGLAND
"Singer, Actor, Composer"

Barbara Stock
12424 Wilshire Blvd., #840
Los Angeles, CA 90025
"Actress"

Adm. James B. Stockdale
Hoover Institution
Stanford, CA 94305
"Ross Perot's V.P. Select"

Karl-Heinz Stockhausen
Stockhausen-Verlag
5067 Kuerten, GERMANY
"Composer"

Dean Stockwell
145 S. Fairfax Avenue #310
Los Angeles, CA 90036
"Actor"

Guy Stockwell
4924 Cahuenga Blvd.
North Hollywood, CA 91601
"Actor"

Brandon Stoddard
241 North Glenroy Avenue
Los Angeles, CA 90049
"Film-TV Executive

Rep. Louis Stokes (OH)
House Rayburn Bldg. #2365
Washington, DC 20515
"Politician"

Eric Stoltz
5200 Lankershim Blvd. #260
North Hollywood, CA 91601
"Actor"

Christopher Stone
23035 Cumorah Crest Drive
Woodland Hills, CA 91364
"Actor, Writer"

Cliffie Stone
P.O. Box 2033
Canyon Country, CA 91386
"Musician"

Doug Stone
P.O. Box 943
Springfield, TN 37172
"Singer"

Marianne Stone
46 Abbey Road
London NW8 ENGLAND
"Actress"

Oliver Stone
201 Santa Monica Blvd. #601
Santa Monica, CA 90401
"Film Writer, Director"

Rob Stone
8033 Sunset Blvd. #450
Los Angeles, CA 90046
"Actor"

Sharon Stone
P.O. Box 7304
North Hollywood, CA 91603
"Actress, Model"

Sly Stone
145 West 57th Street, #1400
New York, NY 10019
"Singer/Musician"

Tom Stoppard
Iver Grove, Iver
Bucks. ENGLAND
"Dramatist"

Larry Storch
330 West End Avenue #17-F
New York, NY 10023
"Actor"

Gale Storm
308 North Sycamore Avenue #104
Los Angeles, CA 90036
"Actress, Singer"

John Stossel
211 Central Park West #15K
New York, NY 10024
"Broadcast Journalist"

Damon Stoudamire
150 York Street, #1100
Toronto, Ontario
MSH 355 CANADA
"Basketball Player"

Madeleine Stowe
10345 W. Olympic Blvd. #200
Los Angeles, CA 90064
"Actress"

Michael Stoyanov
8271 Melrose Avenue #110
Los Angeles, CA 90046
"Actor"

Beatrice Straight
30 Norford Road
Soughfield, MA 01259
"Actress"

Julie Strain
602 De La Vista Avenue
Santa Barbara, CA 93103
"Actress"

George Strait
1000-18th Avenue South
Nashville, TN 37212
"Singer, Songwriter"

David Straithairn
9200 Sunset Blvd. #625
Los Angeles, CA 90069
"Actor"

Hank Stram
194 Belle Terre Blvd.
Covington, LA 70483
"Ex-Football Coach"

Robin Strand
4118 Elmer
North Hollywood, CA 91607
"Actor"

Susan Strasberg
P.O. Box 847
Pacific Palisades, CA 90272
"Actress"

Robin Strasser
10100 Santa Monica Blvd.
Suite #2500
Los Angeles, CA 90067
"Actress"

Marcia Strassman
520 - 18th Street
Santa Monica, CA 90402
"Actress"

Gil Stratton
4227-B Colfax Avenue #B
Studio City, CA 91604
"Sportscaster"

Peter Straub
53 West 85th Street
New York, NY 10026
"Novelist"

Peter Strauss
609 North Palm Drive
Beverly Hills, CA 90210
"Actor"

Robert Strauss
1333 New Hampshire Ave. NW
Suite #400
Washington, DC 20005
"Politician"

Darryl Strawberry
P.O. Box 17868
Encino, CA 91868
"Baseball Player"

Stray Cats
113 Wardour Street
London W1 ENGLAND
"Rock & Roll Group"

Meryl Streep
130 Paradise Cove Road
Malibu, CA 90265
"Actress"

Rebecca Street
247 S. Beverly Drive #102
Beverly Hills, CA 90212
"Actress"

Barbara Streisand
301 N. Carolwood
Los Angeles, CA 90077
"Singer, Actress, Director"

Amzie Strickland
1329 North Ogden Drive
Los Angeles, CA 90046
"Actress"

Gail Strickland
14732 Oracle Place
Pacific Palisades, CA 90272
"Actress"

Ray Stricklyn
852 North Genesee Avenue
Los Angeles, CA 90046
"Actor"

Sherry Stringfield
4000 Warner Blvd.
Bldg. 1, #204
Burbank, CA 91505
"Actress"

Elaine Stritch
1 Bennett Street
Cambridge, MA 02138
"Actress"

Don Stroud
17020 Sunset Blvd. #20
Pacific Palisades, CA 90272
"Actor"

Sally Struthers
9100 Wilshire Blvd., #1000
Beverly Hills, CA 90212
"Actress"

Gloria Stuart
884 South Bundy Drive
Los Angeles, CA 90049
"Actress"

Marty Stuart
119 17th Avenue South
Nashville, TN 37203
"Singer, Songwriter"

Maxine Stuart
9744 Wilshire Blvd. #308
Beverly Hills, CA 90212
"Actress"

Roy Stuart
4948 Radford Avenue
North Hollywood, CA 91602
"Actor"

Rep. Garry Studds (MA)
House Cannon Bldg. #237
Washington, DC 20515
"Politician"

Wes Studi
8380 Melrose Avenue #207
Los Angeles, CA 90069
"Actor"

Shannon Sturges
1518 Hill Street
Santa Monica, CA 90405
"Actress"

William Styron
RFD
Roxbury, CT 06783
"Author"

David Suchet
169 Queensgate #8A
London SW7 5EH ENGLAND
"Actor"

Alan Sues
9014 Dorrington Avenue
Los Angeles, CA 90048
"Actor"

Burt Sugarman
150 South El Camino Drive #303
Beverly Hills, CA 90212
"Rock & Roll Producer"

Helena Sukova
1 Avenue Grande Bretagne
Monte Carlo, Monaco
"Tennis Player"

Danny Sullivan
2811 Arizona Avenue
Santa Monica, CA 90404
"Race Car Driver"

Kathleen Sullivan
5670 Wilshire Blvd. #213
Los Angeles, CA 90036
"Broadcast Journalist"

Gov. Mike Sullivan (WY)
State Capitol
Cheyenne, WY 82002
"Governor"

Susan Sullivan
8642 Allenwood Road
Los Angeles, CA 90046
"Actress"

Tom Sullivan
30 Glenmoor Drive
Englewood, CO 80110
"Singer, Songwriter"

Sultan of Brunei
Hassanal Bolkiah Nuda
Bandar Seri Begawan
BRUNEI
"Royalty"

Arthur Ochs Sulzberger
229 West 43rd Street
New York, NY 10036
"Newspaper Publisher"

Yma Sumac
1524 La Baig Avenue
Los Angeles, CA 90028
"Singer"

Cree Summer
131 South Orange Drive
Los Angeles, CA 90036
"Actress"

Donna Summer
18165 Eccles
Northridge, CA 91324
"Singer"

Pat Summerall
10036 Sawgrass Drive
Ponte Verde, FL 32082
"Sportscaster"

Eleanor Summerfield
10 Kildare Terrace
London W2 ENGLAND
"Actress"

Andy Summers
21A Noel Street
London W1V 3PD ENGLAND
"Singer, Songwriter"

Yale Summers
9490 Cherokee Lane
Beverly Hills, CA 90210
"Actor"

John Sununu
24 Samoset Drive
Salem, NH 03079
"Former Governor"

Nicolas Surovy
8942 Wilshire Blvd.
Beverly Hills, CA 90211
"Actor"

Survivor
2114 West Pico Blvd.
Santa Monica, CA 90405
"Rock & Roll Group"

Todd Susman
10340 Keokuk Avenue
Chatsworth, CA 91311
"Actor"

Rick Sutcliff
313 N.W. North Shore Drive
Parkville, MO 64151
"Baseball Player"

Donald Sutherland
760 North La Cienega Blvd. #300
Los Angeles, CA 90069
"Actor"

Joan Sutherland
111 West 57th Street
New York, NY 10019
"Soprano"

Kiefer Sutherland
132 So. Rodeo Drive, #300
Beverly Hills, CA 90212
"Actor"

James Sutorius
10100 Santa Monica Blvd., #2500
Los Angeles, CA 90067
"Actor"

Janet Suzman
11 Keats Grove
Faircroft, Hampsted
London NW3 ENGLAND
"Actress"

Bo Svenson
1434 Princeton Street, #D
Santa Monica, CA 90404
"Actor"

Jimmy Swaggart
P.O. Box 2550
Baton Rouge, LA 70821
"Evangelist"

Caskey Swaim
1605 North Cahuenga Blvd. #202
Los Angeles, CA 90028
"Actor"

Michael Swan
1535 Magnolia Blvd. #429
Sherman Oaks, CA 91403
"Actor"

Lynn Swann
1720 Kelton Avenue
Los Angeles, CA 90024
"Ex-Football Player"

Jackie Swanson
847 Iliff Street
Pacific Palisades, CA 90272
"Actress"

Kristy Swanson
145 S. Fairfax Avenue #310
Los Angeles, CA 90036
"Actress"

Don Swayze
247 S. Beverly Drive #102
Beverly Hills, CA 90212
"Actor"

Patrick Swayze
132 S. Rodeo Drive, #300
Beverly HIlls, CA 90212
"Actor"

Inga Swenson
3475 Cabrillo
Los Angeles, CA 90066
"Actress"

Jo Swerling, Jr.
25745 Vista Verde Drive
Calabasas, CA 91302
"Writer, Producer"

Nora Swinburne
52 Crammer Court
Whitehead's Grove
London SW3 3HW ENGLAND
"Actress"

Loretta Swit
6363 Wilshire Blvd. #600
Los Angeles, CA 90048
"Actress"

Barry Switzer
1 Cowboy Parkway
Irving, TX 78063
"Football Coach"

Ken Swofford
144 South Beverly Drive #405
Beverly Hills, CA 90212
"Actor"

Eric Sykes
9 Orme Court
London W2 ENGLAND
"Actor, Writer, Director"

Tom Sykes
P.O. Box 29543
Atlanta, GA 30359
"Singer"

The Sylvers
1900 Ave. of the Stars #1600
Los Angeles, CA 90067
"Vocal Group"

Sylvia Syms
47 West Square
London SE11 4SP ENGLAND
"Actress"

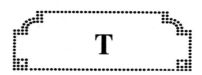

Mr. T
395 Green Bay Road
Lake Forest, IL 60045
"Actor"

Kristoffer Tabori
172 East 95th Street
New York, NY 10028
"Actor"

Cary-Hiroyuki Tagawa
6464 Sunset Blvd., #1130
Los Angeles, CA 90028
"Actor"

Taj Mahal
1671 Appian Way
Santa Monica, CA 90401
"Musician"

Paul Tagliabueruss
410 Park Avenue
New York, NY 10022
"Football [NFL] Commissioner"

Miiko Taka
14560 Round Valley Drive
Sherman Oaks, CA 91403
"Actress"

Take Six
4404 Sumatra Drive
Nashville, TN 37218
"Vocal Group"

George Takei
3518 Cahuenga Blvd. #301
Los Angeles, CA 90068
"Actor"

Nita Talbot
3420 Merrimac Road
Los Angeles, CA 90049
"Actress"

Gloria Talbott
2066 Montecito Drive
Glendale, CA 91208
"Actress"

Gay Talese
154 East Atlantic Blvd.
Ocean City, NJ 08226
"Writer"

Maria Tallchief
2739 Elston Avenue
Chicago, IL 60747
"Ballerina"

Russ Tamblyn
1221 N. Kings Road PH 405
West Hollywood, CA 90064
"Actor"

Jeffrey Tambor
5526 Calhoun Avenue
Van Nuys, CA 91401
"Actor"

Amy Tan
3315 Sacramento St. #127
San Francisco, CA 94118
"Novelist"

Tangerine Dream
Via Giosue Carducci
10-00187 ITALY
"Rock & Roll Group"

Yoko Tani
29 rue des Vignes
75018 Paris, FRANCE
"Actress"

Alain Tanner
Chemin Pt. du-jour 12
1202 Geneva, SWITZERLAND
"Film Director"

Roscoe Tanner
1109 Gnome Trail
Lookout Mountain, TN 37350
"Tennis Player"

Quentin Tarantino
151 El Camino Drive
Beverly Hills, CA 90212
"Actor, Director"

Jimmy Tarbuck
118 Beaufort Street
London SW3 6BU ENGLAND
"Comedian"

Fran Tarkington
3345 Peachtree Road N.E.
Atlanta, GA 30326
"Ex-Football Player"

Brandon Tartikoff
1479 Lindacrest Drive
Beverly Hills, CA 90210
"TV Executive"

Bernie Taupin
1422 Devlin Drive
Los Angeles, CA 90069
"Lyricist"

Benedict Taylor
4 Great Queen Street
London WC28 5DG ENGLAND
"Actor"

Buck Taylor
2899 Agoura Road #275
Westlake Village, CA 91361
"Actor"

Clarice Taylor
35 Hamilton Terrace
New York, NY 10031
"Actress"

Don Taylor
1111 San Vicente Blvd.
Santa Monica, CA 90402
"Film Director"

Elizabeth Taylor
700 Nimes Road
Los Angeles, CA 90077
"Actress"

Holland Taylor
1355 North Laurel Avenue #7
Los Angeles, CA 90046
"Actress"

James Taylor
644 North Doheny Drive
Los Angeles, CA 90069
"Singer"

Josh Taylor
422 S. California Avenue
Burbank, CA 91505
"Actor"

Lawrence Taylor
1055 Summer Street
Stamford, CT 06905
"Football Player"

Leigh Taylor-Young
9229 Sunset Blvd. #710
Los Angeles, CA 90069
"Actress"

Lili Taylor
151 El Camino Drive
Beverly Hills, CA 90212
"Actress"

Meldrick Taylor
2917 North 4th Street
Philadelphia, PA 19132
"Boxer"

Meshach Taylor
10100 Santa Monica Blvd
25th Floor
Los Angeles, CA 90067
"Actor"

Niki Taylor
8362 Pines Blvd., #334
Hollywood, FL 33024
"Model"

Regina Taylor
151 El Camino Drive
Beverly Hills, CA 90212
"Actress"

Renee Taylor
16830 Ventura Blvd. #326
Encino, CA 91436
"Actress, Writer"

Rip Taylor
1133 North Clark Street
Los Angeles, CA 90069
"Actor"

Rod Taylor
2375 Bowmont Drive
Beverly Hills, CA 90210
"Actor"

Roger Taylor
Salterwwell Farm
Moreton-In -The-Marsh
Gloucestershire ENGLAND
"Drummer"

Ludmilla Tcherina
42 cours Albert ler
75008 Paris, FRANCE
"Ballerina"

Lewis Teague
2190 N. Beverly Glen Blvd.
Los Angeles, CA 90077
"Film Director"

Tears For Fears
50 New Bond Street
London 1W ENGLAND
"Rock & Roll Group"

Renata Tebaldi
1 Piazza Guastalla 20100
Milan ITALY
"Opera Singer"

Teenage Mutant Ninja Turtles
1700 Broadway #500
New York, NY 10019
"Fighting Team"

Dr. Edward U. Teller
Radiation Laboratory
P.O. Box 808
Livermore, CA 94550
"Physicist, Author"

Shirley Temple-Black
115 Lakeview Drive
Woodside, CA 94062
"Actress, Ex-Ambassador"

Christopher Templeton
11333 Moorpark Street
North Hollywood, CA 91602
"Actress"

The Temptations
1325 Avenue of the Americas
New York, NY 10019
"R&B Group"

Victoria Tennant
4526 Wilshire Blvd.
Los Angeles, CA 90010
"Actress"

Toni Tennille
3612 Lake View Road
Carson City, NV 89703
"Singer"

Judy Tenuta
950 - 2nd Street #101
Santa Monica, CA 90403
"Comedienne"

Mother Teresa
54A Acharya J. Chandara
Bose Road
Calcutta 70010 INDIA
"Missionary"

Studs Terkel
850 West Castlewood
Chicago, IL 60640
"Novelist"

Malcolm Terris
14 England's Lane
London NW3 ENGLAND
"Actor"

Clark Terry
218-14 36th Avenue
Bayside, NY 11361
"Musician"

John Terry
10100 Santa Monica Blvd. #2500
Los Angeles, CA 90067
"Actor"

John Tesh
14755 Ventura Blvd. #1-916
Sherman Oaks, CA 91403
"TV Show Host"

Vinny Testaverde
P.O. Box 10628
Green Bay, WI 54307
"Football Player"

Lauren Tewes
1110 W. Howe Street, #101
Seattle, WA 98119
"Actress"

Baroness Margaret Thatcher
Chester Square Belgravia
London ENGLAND
"Former Prime Minister"

John Thaw
5 Denmark Street
London, WC2H 8LP England
"Actor"

Phyllis Thaxter
10000 Santa Monica Blvd. #305
Los Angeles, CA 90067
"Actress"

Brynn Thayer
956 Kagawa Street
Pacific Palisades, CA 90272
"Actress"

Joe Theismann
5912 Leesburg Pike
Falls Church, VA 22041
"Football Player"

Brooke Theiss
9744 Wilshire Blvd. #308
Beverly Hills, CA 90212
"Actress"

Alan Thicke
10505 Sarah
Toluca Lake, CA 91602
"Actor, TV Show Host, Singer"

Ursula Thiess
1940 Bel Air Road
Los Angeles, CA 90077
"Actress"

Tiffani-Amber Thiessen
4227 Greenbush Avenue
Sherman Oaks, CA 91423
"Actress"

Roy Thinnes
9200 Sunset Blvd., #625
Los Angeles, CA 90069
"Actor"

Third World
151 El Camino Drive
Beverly Hills, CA 90212
"Raggae Band"

Betty Thomas
P.O. Box 1130
Studio City, CA 91604
"Actress"

B.J. Thomas
P.O. Box 120003
Arlington, TX 76012
"Singer, Songwriter"

Cal Thomas
2200 Fletcher Drive
Fort Lee, NJ 07024
"Christian Leader"

Clarence Thomas
1-1st Street N.E.
Washington, DC 20543
"Supreme Court Justice"

Damien Thomas
31 Kings Road
London SW3 ENGLAND
"Actor"

Debi Thomas
22 East 71st Street
New York, NY 10021
"Ice Skater"

Frank Thomas
333 West 35th Street
Chicago, IL 60616
"Baseball Player"

Frankie Thomas
13939 Riverside Drive
Sherman Oaks, CA 91423
"Actor"

Heather Thomas
1433 San Vicente Blvd.
Santa Monica, CA 90402
"Actress, Model"

Helen Thomas
2501 Calvert Street N.W.
Washington, DC 20008
"News Correspondent"

Henry Thomas
9255 Sunset Blvd. #710
Los Angeles, CA 90069
"Actor"

Isaiah Thomas
150 York Street #1100
Toronto, Ontario
M5H 3S5 CANADA
"Basketball Executive & Player"

Jay Thomas
1800 Avenue of the Stars, #400
Los Angeles, CA 90067
"Singer, Songwriter"

Jonathan Taylor Thomas
1717 N. Highland Avenue #414
Los Angeles, CA 90028
"Actor"

Marlo Thomas
420 East 54th Street #22-F
New York, NY 10022
"Actress, Writer"

Melody Thomas-Scott
20620 Kingsboro Way
Woodland Hills, CA 91364
"Actress"

Philip Michael Thomas
12615 West Dixie Hwy.
North Miami, FL 33161
"Actor"

R. David Thomas
4288 Dublin Erunville Road
Dublin, OH 43017
"Owner of Wendy's Restaurants"

Richard Thomas
5676 Hollyoak Drive
Los Angeles, CA 90068
"Actor, Director"

Thurman Thomas
One Bill Drive
Orchard Park, NY 14127
"Football Player"

Harry Thomason
9220 Sunset Blvd. #11
Los Angeles, CA 90069
"Film Producer"

Tim Thomerson
2440 Long Jack Road
Encinitas, CA 92024
"Actor, Comedian"

Tony Thomopoulos
1280 Stone Canyon
Los Angeles, CA 90077
"Film Executive"

Bobby Thompson
122 Sunlit Drive
Watchung, NJ 07060
"Banjoist"

Daley Thompson
1 Church Row
Wandsworth Plain
London SW18 ENGLAND
"Track Athlete"

Emma Thompson
56 King's Road
Kingston-upon-Thames
KT2 5HF ENGLAND
"Actress"

Ernest Thompson
Rt. 1, Box 3248
Ashland, NH 03217
"Screenwriter"

Hank Thompson
5 Rushing Creek Court
Roanoke, TX 76262
"Singer, Songwriter"

Jack Thompson
12754 Sarah Street
Studio City, CA 91604
"Actor"

John Thompson
Georgetown University Basketball
Washington, DC 20057
"Basketball Coach"

Kay Thompson
300 East 57th Street
New York, NY 10022
"Actress"

Lea Thompson
P.O. Box 5617
Beverly Hills, CA 90210
"Actress"

Linda Thompson
3365 Cahuenga Blvd. W., #450
Los Angeles, CA 90068
"Actress"

Sada Thompson
P.O. Box 490
Southbury, CT 06488
"Actress"

Shawn Thompson
9057A Nemo Street
West Hollywood, CA 90069
"Actor"

The Thompson Twins
9 Eccleston Street
London SW1 ENGLAND
"Rock & Roll Trio"

Gov. Tommy Thompson (WI)
115 East State Capitol
P.O. Box 7863
Madison, WI 53707
"Governor"

Gordon Thomson
629 Eastern Avenue
Toronto, Ontario
M4M 1E4 CANADA
"Actor"

Courtney Thorne-Smith
10100 Santa Monica Blvd.
Suite #2500
Los Angeles, CA 90067
"Actress"

Jeremy Thorpe
2 Orme Square Bayswater
London W2 ENGLAND
"Political Leader"

Linda Thorson
145 West 45th Street #1204
New York, NY 10036
"Actress"

Three Degrees
19 The Willows
Maidenhead Road
Winsor, Berk. ENGLAND
"Rock & Roll Group"

Malachi Throne
11805 Mayfield Avenue #306
Los Angeles, CA 90049
"Actor"

Ingrid Thulin
Kevingerstrand 7b
Danderyd, SWEDEN
"Actress"

Uma Thurman
9830 Wilshire Blvd.
Beverly Hills, CA 90212
"Actress"

Sen. Strom Thurmond (SC)
211 York Street NE
Alken, SC 29801
"Politician"

Greta Thyssen
444 East 82nd Street
New York, NY 10228
"Actress"

Paul W. Tibbets
5574 Knollwood Drive
Columbus, OH 43227
"Singer"

Cheryl Tiegs
1060 Channel Drive
Santa Barbara, CA 93108
"Model"

Lawrence Tierney
33 Brooks Avenue, #3
Venice, CA 90291
"Actor"

Maura Tierney
P.O. Box 5617
Beverly Hills, CA 90210
"Actress"

Tiffany
2165 East Lemon Height Drive
Santa Ana, CA 92705
"Singer"

Pamela Tiffin
15 West 67th Street
New York, NY 10023
"Actress, Model"

Kevin Tighe
P.O. Box 453
Sedro Woolley, WA 98284
"Actor"

Nadja Tiller
Via Tamporiva 26
CH6976 Castagnola
SWITZERLAND
"Actress"

Mel Tillis
P.O. Box 1626
Branson, MO 65616
"Singer"

Pam Tillis
P.O. Box 120073
Nashville, TN 37212
"Singer"

Floyd Tillman
4 Music Square East
Nashville, TN 37203
"Singer"

Johnny Tillotson
17530 Ventura Blvd. #108
Encino, CA 91316
"Singer"

Jennifer Tilly
4526 Wilshire Blvd.
Beverly Hills, CA 90210
"Actress"

Meg Tilly
321 South Beverly Drive #M
Beverly Hills, CA 90212
"Actress"

Charlene Tilton
22050 Galvez Street
Woodland Hills, CA 91364
"Actress"

Martha Tilton
760 Lausanne Road
Los Angeles, CA 90077
"Singer, Actress"

Grant Tinker
531 Barnaby Road
Los Angeles, CA 90077
"TV Executive"

Tiny Tim
Hotel Savoy
4th & Locust
Des Moines, IA 50309
"Singer, Songwriter"

Wayne Tipitt
8730 Sunset Blvd. #220W
Los Angeles, CA 90069
"Actor"

Sir Michael Tippett
48 Great Marlborough Street
London W1V 2BN ENGLAND
"Composer, Conductor"

Aaron Tippin
2100 West End Avenue, #1000
Nashville, TN 37203
"Singer"

Laurence Tisch
Island Drive North
Rye, NY 10580
"TV Executive"

TLC
3350 Peachtree St. #1500
Atlanta, GA 30362
"Music Group"

Kenneth Tobey
14155 Magnolia Blvd.
Sherman Oaks, CA 91403
"Actor"

Oliver Tobias
Geranienstrasse 3
8022 Grunwald GERMANY
"Actor"

Beverly Todd
4888 Valley Ridge
Los Angeles, CA 90043
"Actress"

Hallie Todd
10100 Santa Monica Blvd.
Suite #700
Los Angeles, CA 90067
"Actress"

Richard Todd
Chinham Farm
Faringdon, Oxfordshire
ENGLAND
"Actor"

Alvin Toffel
2323 Bowmont Drive
Beverly Hills, CA 90210
"Author"

Tokyo Rose (Iva Toguri)
851 West Belmont Avenue
Chicago, IL 60611
"Traitor"

Michael Tolan
9229 Sunset Blvd. #311
Los Angeles, CA 90069
"Actor"

John Toland
1 Long Ridge Road
Danbury, CT 06810
"Author"

Berlinda Tolbert
1800 Ave. of the Stars #400
Los Angeles, CA 90067
"Actress"

Susan Tolsky
10815 Acama Street
North Hollywood, CA 91602
"Actress"

David Toma
P.O. Box 854
Clark, NJ 07066
"Writer"

Alberto Tomba
Castell de Britti
Bologna ITALY
"Skier"

Concetia Tomei
121 North San Vicente Blvd.
Beverly Hills, CA 90211
"Actress"

Marisa Tomei
7920 Sunset Blvd., #350
Los Angeles, CA 90046
"Actress"

Lily Tomlin
P.O. Box 27700
Los Angeles, CA 90027
"Comedian, Actress, Writer"

David Tomlinson
Brook Cottage
Mursley, Bucks. ENGLAND
"Actor"

Angel Tompkins
9812 Video Drive, #101
Los Angeles, CA 90035
"Actress"

Bruce Toms
9200 Sunset Blvd. #710
Los Angeles, CA 90069
"Actor"

James Toney
6305 Wellesley
West Bloomfield, MI 48322
"Boxer"

Tony! Toni! Tone!
484 Lake Park Avenue #21
Oakland, CA 94610
"Music Group"

Bill Toomey
1750 East Boulder Street
Colorado Springs, CO 80909
"Track Athlete"

Chaim Topol
22 Vale Court, Maidville
London W9 ENGLAND
"Actor, Director"

Peter Tork
1551 South Robertson Blvd.
Los Angeles, CA 90035
"Musician"

Mel Torme
1734 Coldwater Canyon
Beverly Hills, CA 90210
"Singer, Actor, Writer"

Rip Torn
130 West 42nd Street #2400
New York, NY 10036
"Actor, Director"

Dean Torrence
18932 Gregory Lane
Huntington Beach, CA 92646
"Singer, Songwriter"

Gwen Torrence
1712 Rock Springs Road NE
Atlanta, GA 30324
"Track & Field"

Liz Torres
1711 North Avenue #53
Los Angeles, CA 90042
"Singer, Actress"

Robert Torti
13609 Chandler Blvd.
Van Nuys, CA 91401
"Actor"

Torvill & Dean
Box 16, Beeston
Nottingham NG9 ENGLAND
"Skating Duo"

Nina Totenberg
c/o National Public Radio
2025 "M" Street NW
Washington, DC 20036
"News Correspondent"

Toto
50 West Main Street
Ventura, CA 93001
"Rock & Roll Group"

Audrey Totter
1945 Glendon Avenue #301
Los Angeles, CA 90025
"Actress"

Tamara Toumanova
305 North Elm Drive
Beverly Hills, CA 90210
"Dancer, Actress"

Constance Towers
10651 Chalon Road
Los Angeles, CA 90077
"Actress"

Robert Towne
1417 San Remo Drive
Pacific Palisades, CA 90272
"Film Writer, Director"

Harry Townes
251 Burton Way
Palm Springs, CA 92262
"Actor"

Barbara Townsend
1930 Century Park West #303
Los Angeles, CA 90067
"Actress"

Claire Townsend
2424 Laurel Pass
Los Angeles, CA 90046
"Actress"

Colleen Townsend
508 Seward Square S.E.
Washington, DC 20003
"Actress"

Robert Townsend
2034 1/2 N. Beverly Glen Circle,
#407
Los Angeles, CA 90077
"Director, Actor, Comedian"

Arthur Tracy
350 West 57th Street
New York, NY 10019
"Actor"

The Tramps
P.O. Box 82
Great Neck, NY 10021
"R&B Group"

Fred Travalana
4515 White Oak Place
Encino, CA 91316
"Comedian, Actor, Writer"

Daniel J. Travanti
1077 Melody Road
Lake Forest, IL 60045
"Actor"

Kylie Travis
3500 W. Olive Ave. #1400
Burbanks, CA 91505
"Actress"

Nancy Travis
9869 Portola Drive
Beverly Hills, CA 90210
"Actress"

Randy Travis
P.O. Box 121712
Nashville, TN 37212
"Singer, Songwriter"

Ellen Travolta
5832 Nagle Avenue
Van Nuys, CA 91401
"Actress"

Joey Travolta
4975 Chimineas Avenue
Tarzana, CA 91356
"Actor"

John Travolta
1504 Live Oak Lane
Santa Barbara, CA 93105
"Actor, Singer"

Terri Treas
9000 Sunset Blvd. #1200
Los Angeles, CA 90069
"Actress"

Alex Trebek
3405 Fryman Road
Studio City, CA 91604
"Game Show Host"

Les Tremayne
901 South Barrington Avenue
Los Angeles, CA 90049
"Actor"

Anne Tremko
924 Westwood Blvd. #900
Los Angeles, CA 90024
"Actress"

Charles Trenet
2 rue Anatole FRANCE
F-11100 Narbonne, FRANCE
"Singer, Songwriter"

Lee Trevino
5757 Alpha Road #620
Dallas, TX 75240
"Golfer"

Claire Trevor
Hotel Pierre
2 East 61st Street
New York, NY 10022
"Actress"

Jean-Louis Trintignant
10 Ave. George V
75008 Paris FRANCE
"Actor"

Jean Tripplehorn
9830 Wilshire Blvd.
Beverly Hills, CA 90212
"Actress"

Travis Tritt
1112 North Sherbourne Drive
Los Angeles, CA 90069
"Singer"

Bobby Troup
16074 Royal Oaks
Encino, CA 91436
"Actor, Comedian, Singer"

Tom Troup
8829 Ashcroft Avenue
Los Angeles, CA 90048
"Actor"

Garry Trudeau
459 Columbus Avenue #113
New York, NY 10024
"Cartoonist"

Mrs. Ernest Truex
3263 Via Altamura
Fallbrook, CA 92028
"Wife of Ernest Truex"

Margaret Truman (Daniel)
830 Park Avenue
New York, NY 10028
"Authoress"

Douglas Trumbull
Box 847
Riverview Road
Lenox, MA 01240
"Writer, Producer"

Donald Trump
721 Fifth Avenue
New York, NY 10022
"Real Estate Executive"

Ivana Trump
725 Fifth Avenue
New York, NY 10022
"Ex-Wife of Donald Trump"

Natalie Trundy
6140 Lindenhurst Avenue
Los Angeles, CA 90048
"Actress"

Paul Tsongas
1 Post Office Square
Boston, MA 02109
"Former Senator"

Irene Tsu
2760 Hutton Drive
Beverly Hills, CA 90210
"Actress"

Barry Tubb
121 North San Vicente Blvd.
Beverly Hills, CA 90211
"Actor"

Marshall Tucker Band
315 S. Beverly Drive, #206
Beverly Hills, CA 90212
"Rock & Roll Group"

Michael Tucker
2183 Mandeville Canyon
Los Angeles, CA 90049
"Actor"

Tanya Tucker
5200 Maryland Way
Brentwood, TN 37027
"Singer"

Tommy Tune
50 East 89th Street
New York, NY 10128
"Dancer, Director"

John Tunney
1819 Ocean Avenue
Santa Monica, CA 90401
"Ex-Senator"

HRM King Tupou IV
Palace Officiale
Nuku'alofa TONGA
"Royalty"

Paige Turco
121 N. San Vincente Blvd.
Beverly Hills, CA 90211
"Actress"

Ann Turkel
9877 Beverly Grove
Beverly Hills, CA 90210
"Actress"

Christy Turlington
344 East 59th Street
New York, NY 10022
"Model"

Glynn Turman
9000 Sunset Blvd. #1200
Los Angeles, CA 90069
"Actor"

Dr. Debbye Turner
P.O. Box 12450
St. Louis, MO 63132
"Beauty Contest Winner"

Dame Eva Turner
26 Palace Court
London W2 ENGLAND
"Opera Singer"

Grant Turner
P.O. Box 414
Brentwood, TN 37027
"Singer"

Janine Turner
8455 Beverly Blvd. #505
Los Angeles, CA 90048
"Actress"

Kathleen Turner
163 Amsterdam Avenue #210
New York, NY 10023
"Actress"

Ted Turner
1050 Techwood Drive
Atlanta, GA 30318
"Broadcast & Sports Executive"

Tina Turner
14755 Ventura Blvd., #772
Sherman Oaks, CA 91403
"Singer"

Stanley Turrentine
P.O. Box 396
Kensington, MD 20895
"Musician"

John Turturro
16 North Street #2A
Ventura, CA 93001
"Actor"

Rita Tushingham
2-4 Noel Street
London W1V 3RB ENGLAND
"Actress"

Dorothy Tutin Browne
13 St. Martins Road
London SW9 ENGLAND
"Actress"

Desmond Tutu
Bishopscourt
Claremont 7700
Johannesburg, SOUTH AFRICA
"Arch-Bishop"

Shannon Tweed
9300 Wilshire Blvd. #410
Beverly Hills, CA 90212
"Actress, Model"

2 Live Crew
8400 N.E. 2nd Avenue
Miami, FL 33138
"Rap Group"

Twiggy
4 St. George's House
15 Hanover Square
London W1R 9AJ ENGLAND
"Actress, Singer"

Beverly Tyler
14585 Geronimo Trail
Reno, NV 89551
"Actress"

Bonnie Tyler
17-19 Soho Square
London W1 ENGLAND
"Singer, Songwriter"

Willie Tyler
9955 Balboa Blvd.
Northridge, CA 91325
"Ventriloquist"

Hunter Tylo
7660 Beverly Blvd., #107
Los Angeles, CA 90036
"Model"

Michael Tylo
7660 Beverly Blvd. #107
Los Angeles, CA 90026
"Actor"

Susan Tyrell
1489 Scott Avenue
Los Angeles, CA 90026
"Actress"

Cicely Tyson
315 West 70th Street
New York, NY 10023
"Actress"

Mike Tyson
6740 Tomiyasu Lane
Las Vegas, NV 89120
"Boxer"

Richard Tyson
9200 Sunset Blvd. #625
Los Angeles, CA 90069
"Actor"

U2
119 Rockland Center #350
Nanvet, NY 10954
"Rock & Roll Group"

Peter Ueberroth
184 Emerald Bay
Laguna Beach, CA 92651
"Former Baseball Executive"

Bob Uecker
c/o Milwaukee County Stadium
Milwaukee, WI 53214
"Actor, Baseball Announcer"

UFO
10 Sutherland
London W9 24Q ENGLAND
"Rock & Roll Group"

Leslie Uggams
3 Lincoln Center
New York, NY 10023
"Singer, Actress"

Anneliese Uhlig
1519 Escalona Drive
Santa Cruz, CA 95060
"Actress"

Dr. Art Ulene
10810 Via Verona
Los Angeles, CA 90024
"TV Medical Reporter"

Liv Ullman
15 West 81st Street
New York, NY 10024
"Actress"

Tracey Ullman
P.O. Box 9720
Glendale, CA 91226
"Actress, Singer"

Blair Underwood
5200 Lankershim Blvd. #260
North Hollywood, CA 91601
"Actor"

Jay Underwood
145 S. Fairfax Avenue #310
Los Angeles, CA 90036
"Actor"

Johnny Unitas
5607 Patterson Road
Baldwin, MD 21013
"Football Player"

Al Unser
7625 Central N.W.
Albuquerque, NM 87105
"Race Car Driver"

Al Unser, Jr.
73243 Calle de Deborah N.W.
Albuquerque, NM 87104
"Race Car Driver"

Bobby Unser
7700 Central S.W.
Albuquerque, NM 87105
"Race Car Driver"

John Updike
675 Hale Street
Beverly Farm, MA 01915
"Author"

Gene Upshaw
1102 Pepper Tree Drive
Great Falls, VA 22066
"Football Executive"

Robert Urich
P.O. Box 5973-1006
Sherman Oaks, CA 91403
"Actor, Writer"

Loen Uris
P.O. Box 1559
Aspen, CO 81611
"Author"

Peter Ustinov
11 rue de Silly
92100 Boulogne, FRANCE
"Actor, Writer, Director"

Garrick Utely
8 Carburton Street
London W1P 7DT ENGLAND
"News Correspondent"

Brenda Vaccaro
17641 Tarzana Street
Encino, CA 91316
"Actress"

Roger Vadim
316 Alta Avenue
Santa Monica, CA 90402
"Film Director"

Vanessa Vadim
316 Alta Avenue
Santa Monica, CA 90402
"Daughter of Jane Fonda"

Jerry Vale
1100 N. Alta Loma Rd., #1404
Los Angeles, CA 90069
"Singer"

Nancy Valen
10000 Santa Monica Blvd.
Suite #305
Los Angeles, CA 90067
"Actress"

Jack Valenti
1600 Eye Street N.W.
Washington, D C 20006
"Film Director"

Karen Valentine
P.O. Box 1410
Washington Depot, CT 06793
"Actress"

Scott Valentine
662 N. Van Ness Avenue, #305
Los Angeles, CA 90004
"Actor"

Valentino
2 East 70th Street
New York, NY 100021
"Singer"

Fernando Valenzuela
3004 North Beachwod Drive
Los Angeles, CA 90027
"Baseball Player"

Alida Valli
Viale Liegi 42
00100 Rome, ITALY
"Actress"

Frankie Valli
25934 W. Manley Court
Calabasas, CA 91302
"Singer"

Raf Vallone
Viale R. Bacone #14
Rome, ITALY
"Actor"

Richard Van Allen
18 Octavia Street
London SW11 3DN ENGLAND
"Singer"

Joan Van Ark
10950 Alta View Drive
Studio City, CA 91604
"Actress"

Abigail Van Buren
P.O. Box 69440
Los Angeles, CA 90069
"Columnist"

Cyrus Vance
425 Lexington Avenue
New York, NY 10017
"Government Official"

Jean-Claude Van Damme
P.O. Box 4149
Chatsworth, CA 91313
"Actor"

Gloria Vanderbilt
1349 Eagle Cove Road
Jacksonville, FL 32218
"Fashion Designer"

Trish Van Devere
3211 Retreat Court
Malibu, CA 90265
"Actress"

Kiki Vandeweghe
4 Pennsylvania Plaza
New York, NY 10019
"Ex-Basketball Player"

Titos Vandis
1930 Century Park East #303
Los Angeles, CA 90067
"Actor"

Mamie Van Doren
428-31st Street
Newport Beach, CA 92663
"Actress, Singer"

Luther Vandross
P.O. Box 5542
Beverly Hills, CA 90209
"Singer"

Barry Van Dyke
27800 Blythdale Road
Agoura, CA 91301
"Actor"

Dick Van Dyke
23215 Mariposa De Oro
Malibu, CA 90265
"Actor"

Jerry Van Dyke
145 S. Fairfax Avenue #310
Los Angeles, CA 90036
"Actor"

Charles Van Eman
12304 Santa Monica Blvd., #104
Los Angeles, CA 90025
"Actor"

Jo Van Fleet
54 Riverside Drive
New York, NY 10024
"Actress"

Vangelis
195 Queens Gate
London W1 ENGLAND
"Composer"

Van Halen
10100 Santa Monica Blvd.
Suite #2460
Los Angeles, CA 90067
"Rock & Roll Group"

Alex Van Halen
12024 Summit Circle
Beverly Hills, CA 90210
"Musician"

Eddie Van Halen
31736 Broad Beach Rd.
Malibu, CA 90265
"Guitarist, Songwriter"

Vanilla Ice
1290 Ave. of the Americas #4200
New York, NY 10104
"Rap Singer"

Vanity (Denise Mathews)
1871 Messino Drive
San Jose, CA 95132
"Singer, Actress"

Merete Van Kemp
10000 Santa Monica Blvd. #305
Los Angeles, CA 90067
"Actress"

Dick Van Patten
13920 Magnolia Blvd.
Sherman Oaks, CA 91423
"Actor"

James Van Patten
14411 Riverside Drive #15
Sherman Oaks, CA 91423
"Actor"

Joyce Van Patten
1321 North Hayworth #C
Los Angeles, CA 90046
"Actress"

Nels Van Patten
14411 Riverside Drive #18
Sherman Oaks, CA 91423
"Actor"

Tim Van Patten
13920 Magnolia Blvd.
Sherman Oaks, CA 91423
"Actor"

Vincent Van Patten
13926 Magnolia Blvd.
Sherman Oaks, CA 91423
"Actor"

Mario Van Peebles
11 Tuxedo
Glenridge, NJ 07028
"Actor, Writer, Director"

Melvin Van Peebles
353 West 56th Street #10-F
New York, NY 10019
"Actor, Writer, Director"

Ricky Van Shelton
818 - 19th Avenue South
Nashville, TN 37203
"Singer"

Deborah Van Valkenburgh
2025 Stanley Hills Drive
Los Angeles, CA 90046
"Actress"

Monique Van Vooren
165 East 66th Street
New York, NY 10021
"Actress, Singer"

Randy Vanwarmer
65 Music Square West
Nashville, TN 37203
"Singer, Songwriter"

Steve Van Zandt
322 West 57th Street
New York, NY 10019
"Singer, Guitarist"

The Vapors
44 Valmoral Drive
Woking, Surrey, ENGLAND
"Rock & Roll Group"

Jim Varney
1200 McGovock Street
Nashville, TN 37203
"Actor"

Victor Vasarely
83 re aux Reliaues
Annet-sur-Marne, FRANCE
"Artist"

Robert Vaughn
162 Old West Mountain Road
Ridgefield, CT 06877
"Actor, Director"

Bobby Vee (Velline)
P.O. Box 41
Saulk Rapids, MN 56379
"Singer, Songwriter"

Suzanne Vega
30 West 21st Street, #700
New York, NY 10010
"Singer"

Jorge Velasquez
770 Allerton Avenue
Bronx, NY 10467
"Horse Racer"

Eddie Velez
5439 Ellenvale Avenue
Woodland Hills, CA 91367
"Actor"

Reginald Vel Johnson
8637 Allenwood Drive
Los Angeles, CA 90046
"Actor"

Vendela
344 East 59th Street
New York, NY 10022
"Model"

Ken Venturi
P.O. Box 5118
Akron, OH 44334
"Golf Instructor"

Gwen Verdon
26 Latimer Lane
Bronxville, NY 10708
"Actress, Dancer"

Elena Verdugo
P.O. Box 2048
Chula Vista, CA 92012
"Actress"

Ben Vereen
924 Westwood Blvd., #900
Los Angeles, CA, 90024
"Dancer, Actor"

Dick Vermeil
77 West 66th Street
New York, NY 10023
"Sportcaster"

Henri Verneuil
21 rue du Bois-de-Boulogne
92200 Neuilly-sur-Seine
FRANCE
"Film Director"

John Vernon
15125 Mulholland Drive
Los Angeles, CA 90077
"Actor"

Kate Vernon
1999 Avenue of the Stars #2850
Los Angeles, CA 90067
"Actress"

Gianni Versace
Via della Spige 25
Milan, I-20121 ITALY
"Fashion Designer"

Yvette Vickers
P.O. Box 664
Pinon Hills, CA 92372
"Actress"

James Victor
1944 N. Whitley Avenue #306
Los Angeles, CA 90036
"Actor"

Gore Vidal
1201 Alta Loma Road
Los Angeles, CA 90069
"Writer"

Peter Vidmar
6 Flores
Foothill Ranch, CA 92610
"Gymnast"

Abe Vigoda
8500 Melrose Avenue #208
West Hollywood, CA 90069
"Actor"

Richard Viguerie
7777 Leesburg Pike
Falls Church, VA 22043
"Professional Fund Raiser"

Bob Vila
10877 Wilshire Blvd. #900
Los Angeles, CA 90024
"Home Repair TV Host"

Guillermo Vilas
Avenue Foch 86
Paris, FRANCE
"Tennis Player"

The Village People
1560 Broadway, #1308
New York, NY 10036
"Music Group"

Jan-Michael Vincent
11693 San Vicente Blvd., #296
Los Angeles, CA 90049
"Actor"

Virginia Vincent
1001 Hammond Street
Los Angeles, CA 90069
"Actress"

Melanie Vincz
2212 Earle Court
Redondo Beach, CA 90278
"Actress, Model"

Helen Vinson
2213 Carol Woods
Chapel Hill, NC 27514
"Actress"

Jesse Vint
10637 Burbank Blvd.
No. Hollywood, CA 91601
"Actress"

Bobby Vinton
P.O. Box 6010
Branson, MO 65616
"Singer"

Frank Viola
844 Sweetwater Island Circle
Longwood, FL 32779
"Baseball Player"

Lasse Viren
Piltihuset
Helsingfors (Helsinki)
FINLAND
"Track Athlete"

Sal Visculo
6491 Ivarene Avenue
Los Angeles, CA 90068
"Actor"

Nana Visitor
P.O. Box 5617
Beverly Hills, CA 90210
"Actress"

Monica Vitti
Via F. 38, Siacci
00197 Rome, ITALY
"Actress"

Marina Vlady
10 Avenue de Marivauz
78800 Mission Lafitte
FRANCE
"Actress"

Virgil Vogel
5550 Colbath Avenue
Van Nuys, CA 91401
"Fim Director"

Karl Micheal Vogler
Auweg 8, Seehof
D-82418 Seehausen
GERMANY
"Actor"

Jon Voight
13340 Galewood Drive
Sherman Oaks, CA 91423
"Actor"

Paul Volcker
International Economic Dept.
Princeton University
Princeton, NJ
"Former Monetary Treasurer"

Nedra Volz
615 Tulare Way
Upland, CA 91786
"Actress"

Helene von Damm-Gurtler
Hotel Sacher bei der Oper
1010 Vienna, AUSTRIA
"Diplomat"

Erich Von Daniken
Baselstrasse 1
4532 Feldbrunen, SWITZERLAND
"Author"

Lenny Von Dohlen
2271 Betty Lane
Beverly Hills, CA 90210
"Actor"

Betsy Von Fursterberg
230 Central Park West
New York, NY 10028
"Actress"

Diane von Furstenberg
745 Fifth Avenue
New York, NY 10151
"Fashion Designer"

Veola Vonn
8906 Evanview Drive
Los Angeles, CA 90069
"Actress"

Kurt Vonnegut, Jr.
P.O. Box 27
Sagaponack, NY 11962
"Author"

Max Von Sydow
avd C-G Rissberg
Box 5209
Stockholm 10245 SWEDEN
"Actor"

Richard von Weizsacker
Meisenstr. 6
D-14195 Berlin GERMANY
"Ex-President of Germany"

Lark Voorhies
10635 Santa Monica Blvd., #130
Los Angeles, CA 90025
"Actress"

Adam Wade
118 East 25th Street #600
New York, NY 10010
"Actor, Singer"

Russell Wade
47-287 West Eldorado Drive
Indian Wells, CA 92260
"Actor"

Virginia Wade
Sharstead Court
Sittingbourne
Kent, ENGLAND
"Tennis Player"

Lanny Wadkins
P.O. Box 673
Richmond, VA 23206
"Golfer"

Lyle Waggoner
4450 Balboa Avenue
Encino, CA 91316
"Actor"

Chuck Wagner
1419 N. Hollywood Way
Burbank, CA 91505
"Actor"

Jack Wagner
1134 Alta Loma Road #115
West Hollywood, CA 90069
"Actor, Singer"

Jane Wagner
P.O. Box 27700
Los Angeles, CA 90027
"Writer, Producer"

Lindsay Wagner
P.O. Box 188
Pacific Palisades, CA 90272
"Actress"

Robert Wagner
2121 Avenue of the Stars, #1240
Los Angeles, CA 90067
"Actor"

Porter Wagoner
P.O. Box 290785
Nashville, TN 37229
"Singer, Songwriter"

Ken Wahl
480 Westlake Blvd.
Malibu, CA 90265
"Actor"

Mark Wahlberg
63 Pilgrim Road
Braintree, MA 02184
"Actor, Talk Show Host"

Bea Wain
9955 Durant Drive, #305
Beverly Hills, CA 90212
"Singer"

Ralph Waite
73317 Ironwood Street
Palm Desert, CA 92260
"Actor, Director"

Terry Waite
Lambeth Palace
London SE1 7JU ENGLAND
"Clergy"

Tom Waits
P.O. Box 498
Valley Ford, CA 94972
"Singer, Songwriter"

Grete Waitz
Postboks 51, Jjan
1113 Oslo NORWAY
"Track Athlete"

Andrzej Wajda
ul-Jezefa Hauke Bosaka 14
01-540 Warsaw POLAND
"Director"

Jeff Wald
227 Toyopa Drive
Pacific Palisades, CA 90272
"Talent Agent"

Robert Walden
1450 Arroyo View Drive
Pasadena, CA 91103
"Actor"

Kurt Waldheim
Hofburg, Bullhausplatz
1010 Vienna, AUSTRIA
"President of Austria"

Janet Waldo
15725 Royal Oak Road
Encino, CA 91316
"Actress"

Lech Walesa
Polskistr. 53
Gdansk - (Danzig) POLAND
"Politician"

Christopher Walken
8969 Sunset Blvd.
Los Angeles, CA 90069
"Actor"

Ally Walker
7920 Sunset Blvd. #400
Los Angeles, CA 90046
"Actress"

Arnetia Walker
20738 Deforest Street
Woodland Hills, CA 91364
"Actress"

Bree Walker
3347 Tareco Drive
Los Angeles, CA 90068
"Newscaster"

Clint Walker
Rodeo Flat Road
Auburn, CA 95603
"Actor"

Doak Walker
P.O. Box TT
Steamboat Springs, CO 80477
"Ex-Football Player"

Fiona Walker
13 Despard Road
London N19 ENGLAND
"Actress"

Hershell Walker
1 Cowboy Parkway
Irving, TX 75063
"Football Player"

Jimmy Walker
8265 Sunset Blvd. #100
Los Angeles, CA 90046
"Actor, Comedian"

Junior Walker
141 Dunbar Avenue
Fords, NJ 08863
"Saxophonist"

Kim Walker
15760 Ventura Blvd. #1730
Encino, CA 91436
"Actress"

Marcy Walker
4403 Clybourn Avenue
North Hollywood, CA 91602
"Actress"

Mort Walker
61 Studio Court
Stamford, CT 06903
"Cartoonist"

Nicholas Walker
6925 Tuna Canyon Road
Topanga, CA 90290
"Actor"

Polly Walker
8730 Sunset Blvd., #490
Los Angeles, CA 90069
"Actress"

Robert Walker, Jr.
20828 Pacific Coast Hwy.
Malibu, CA 90265
"Actor"

Chris Wallace
1717 DeSales Street
Washington, DC 20036
"Broadcast Journalist"

Dee-Wallace Stone
9000 Sunset Blvd. #1200
Los Angeles, CA 90069
"Actress"

George Wallace
P.O. Box 4419
Montgomery, AL 36104
"Former Governor"

George Wallace
8455 Fountain Avenue #401
W. Hollywood, CA 90069
"Comedian"

Marcia Wallace
1312 South Genesee Avenue
Los Angeles, CA 90019
"Actress"

Mike Wallace
555 West 57th Street
New York, NY 10019
"Broadcast Journalist"

Eli Wallach
90 Riverside Drive
New York, NY 10024
"Actor"

The Great Wallendas
138 Frog Hollow Road
Churchville, PA 18966
"High Wire Act"

Deborah Walley
P.O. Box 1226
Sedona, AZ 86339
"Actress"

Jon Walmsley
13810 Magnolia Blvd.
Sherman Oaks, CA 91403
"Actor"

Martin Walser
Zum Hecht 36
7700 Uberlingen, GERMANY
"Author, Dramatist"

Bill Walsh
Stanford University Football
Stanford, CA 94305
"Football Coach"

John Walsh
5151 Wisconsin Avenue
Washington , DC 20016
"Actor"

M. Emmet Walsh
4173 Motor Avenue
Culver City, CA 90232
"Actor"

Ray Walston
423 South Rexford Drive #205
Beverly Hills, CA 90212
"Actor"

Jessica Walter
10530 Strathmore Drive
Los Angeles, CA 90024
"Actress"

Tracey Walter
257 North Rexford Drive
Beverly Hills, CA 90210
"Actor"

Barbara Walters
33 West 60th Street
New York, NY 10021
"News Journalist"

Hugh Walters
15 Christ Church Avenue
London NW6 7QP ENGLAND
"Actor"

Jaime Walters
9560 Wilshire Blvd. #500
Beverly Hills, CA 90212
"Actor"

Julie Walters
265 Liverpool Road
London N1 1LX ENGLAND
"Actress"

Laurie Walters
13428 Maxella #224
Marina del Rey, CA 90292
"Actress"

Susan Walters
151 El Camino Drive
Beverly Hills, CA 90212
"Actress"

Jess Walton
4702 Ethel Avenue
Sherman Oaks, CA 91423
"Actress"

Darrell Waltrip
P.O. Box 855
Franklin, TN 37065
"Race Car Driver"

Joseph Wambaugh
3520 Kellogg Way
San Diego, Ca 92106
"Novelist"

Joseph A. Wapner
16616 Park Lane Place
Los Angeles, CA 90049
"TV Show Judge"

Fred Ward
1214 Cabrillo Avenue
Venice, CA 90291
"Actor"

Megan Ward
1999 Avenue of the Stars #2850
Los Angeles, CA 90067
"Actress"

Rachel Ward
110 Queen Street
Woollahra
NSW 2025 AUSTRALIA
"Actress"

Sela Ward
2102 Century Park East #202
Los Angeles, CA 90067
"Actress"

Skip Ward
P.O. Box 755
Beverly Hills, CA 90210
"Actor"

Jack Warden
23604 Malibu Colony Drive
Malibu, CA 90265
"Actor"

Clyde Ware
1252 North Laurel Avenue
Los Angeles, CA 90046
"Writer, Producer"

Herta Ware
P.O. Box 151
Topanga, CA 90290
"Actress"

Marsha Warfield
P.O. Box 691713
Los Angeles, CA 90069
"Actress, Comedienne"

Dr. William Warfield
P.O. Box 1573
Champaign, IL 61824
"Actor, Singer"

Steve Wariner
P.O. Box 1209
Nashville, TN 37135
"Singer"

Richard Waring
1 Chester Close
Queens Ride
London SW13 OJE ENGLAND
"TV Writer"

Todd Waring
10 East 44th Street #500
New York, NY 10017
"Actor"

Billy Warlock
9229 Sunset Blvd. #315
Los Angeles, CA 90069
"Actor"

Cornelius Warmerdam
3976 North 1st Street
Fresno, CA 93726
"Track Athlete"

David Warner
68 St. James's Street
London SW1A 1LE ENGLAND
"Actor"

Sen. John Warner (VA)
Senate Russell Bldg. #225
Washington, DC 20510
"Politician"

Julie Warner
639 North Larchmont Blvd. #207
Los Angeles, CA 90004
"Actress"

Malcolm-Jamal Warner
P.O. Box 69646
Los Angeles, CA 90069
"Actor"

Jennifer Warren
1675 Old Oak Road
Los Angeles, CA 90049
"Actress"

Lesley Ann Warren
8942 Wilshire Blvd.
Beverly Hills, CA 90212
"Actress"

Michael Warren
189 Greenfield Avenue
Los Angeles, CA 90049
"Actor"

Ruth Warrick
903 Park Avenue
New York, NY 10021
"Actress"

Dionne Warwick
1583 Lindacrest Drive
Beverly Hills, CA 90210
"Singer"

Don Was
12831 Mulholland Drive
Beverly Hills, CA 90210
"Producer"

Denzel Washington
4701 Sancola
Toluca Lake, CA 91602
"Actor"

Ted Wass
7667 Seattle Place
Los Angeles, CA 90046
"Actor"

Dale Wasserman
1680 Valecroft Avenue
Westlake Village, CA 91361
"Playwright"

Lew Wasserman
911 North Foothill Road
Beverly Hills, CA 90210
"Film Executive"

Craig Wasson
P.O. Box 735
McCall, ID 83638
"Actor"

Gedde Watanabe
3855 Lankershim Blvd.
Studio City, CA 91604
"Actor"

Waterboys
3 Monmouth Road
London W2 ENGLAND
"Rock & Roll Group"

John Waters
8942 Wilshire Blvd.
Beverly Hills, CA 90211
"Director, Writer"

Sam Waterson
RR Box 232
West Cornwell, CT 06796
"Actor"

Carlene Watkins
104 Fremont Place
Los Angeles, CA 90005
"Actress"

Jody Watley
16130 Ventura Blvd. #550
Encino, CA 91436
"Singer"

Mills Watson
1930 Century Park West #403
Los Angeles, CA 90007
"Actor"

Tom Watson
1901 West 47th Place #200
Westwood, KS 66205
"Golfer"

James G. Watt
P.O. Box 3705
Jackson Hole, WY 83001
"Former Secretary of Interior"

Al Waxman
87 Forrest Hill Road
Toronto, Ontario
M4V 2L6 CANADA
"Actor"

Rep. Henry A. Waxman (CA)
House Rayburn Bldg. #2408
Washington, DC 20515
"Politician"

Damon Wayans
12140 Summit Court
Beverly Hills, CA 90210
"Actor"

Dwayne Wayans
16405 Mulholland
Los Angeles, CA 90049
"Actor"

Keenan Ivory Wayans
16405 Mulholland Drive
Los Angeles, CA 90049
"Actor"

Kim Wayans
1742 Granville Avenue #2
Los Angeles, CA 90025
"Actress"

Marlon Wayans
9200 Sunset Blvd. #106
Los Angeles, CA 90069
"Actor"

Fredd Wayne
117 Strand Street
Santa Monica, CA 90405
"Actor, Writer"

Michael Wayne
10425 Kling Street
North Hollywood, CA 91602
"Film Executive"

Patrick Wayne
10502 Whipple Street
North Hollywood, CA 91602
"Actor"

Pilar Wayne
30801 S. Coast Hwy. #9
Laguna Beach, CA 92651
"Widow of John Wayne"

Shawn Weatherly
12203 Octagon Street
Los Angeles, CA 90049
"Actress, Model"

Carl Weathers
10960 Wilshire Blvd. #826
Los Angeles, CA 90024
"Actor"

Bob Weatherwax
16133 Soledad Canyon Road
Canyon Country, CA 91351
"Animal Trainer"

Dennis Weaver
P.O. Box 257
Ridgeway, CO 81432
"Actor"

Earl Weaver
501 Cypress Point Drive West
Pembroke Pines, FL 33027
"Ex-Baseball Manager"

Fritz Weaver
161 West 75th Street
New York, NY 10023
"Actor"

Sigourney Weaver
200 West 57th Street #1306
New York, NY 10019
"Actress"

Jimmy Webb
1560 North Laurel Avenue #109
Los Angeles, CA 90046
"Singer, Composer"

Lucy Webb
1360 N. Crescent Heights #3-B
Los Angeles, CA 90046
"Actress, Comedienne"

Andrew Lloyd Webber
Trump Tower
725 Fifth Avenue
New York, NY 10022
"Composer"

Chris Webber
1 Harry S. Truman Drive
Landover, MD 20785
"Basketball Player"

Steven Weber
2881 Hollyridge Drive
Los Angeles, CA 90068
"Actor"

Ann Wedgeworth
10100 Santa Monica Blvd. #2500
Los Angeles, CA 90067
"Actress"

Gene Weed
10405 Oklahoma Avenue
Chatsworth, CA 91311
"Writer, Producer"

Caspar Weinberger
60 Fifth Avenue
New York, NY 10011
"Former Government Official"

Scott Weinger
417 S. Beverly Drive #201
Beverly Hills, CA 90212
"Actor"

Carl Weintraub
10390 Santa Monica Blvd. #300
Los Angeles, CA 90025
"Actor"

Jerry Weintraub
27740 Pacific Coast Hwy.
Malibu, CA 90265
"Film Producer"

Peter Weir
Post Office
Palm Beach 2108 AUSTRALIA
"Film Director"

Tom Weiskepf
7580 East Gray Road
Scottsdale, AZ 85260
"Golfer"

Sam Weisman
4448 Tujunga Avenue
No. Hollywood, CA 91602
"Actor"

Michael T. Weiss
151 South El Camino Drive
Beverly Hills, CA 90212
"Actor"

Morgan Weisser
1443 N. Hayworth Avenue
Los Angeles, CA 90046
"Actor"

Bruce Weitz
5030 Arundel Drive
Woodland Hills, CA 91364
"Actor"

Ezer Weizman
26 Hagiffen Street
Ramat, Haseram, ISRAEL
"Politician"

Raquel Welch
540 Evelyn Place
Beverly Hills, CA 90210
"Actress, Singer, Writer"

Tahnee Welch
134 Duane Street #400
New York, NY 10013
"Actress"

Tuesday Weld
P.O. Box 367
Valley Streem, NY 11582
"Actress"

Ann Weldon
11555 Dona Teresa Drive
Studio City, CA 91604
"Actress"

Mary Louise Weller
1416 North Havenhurst Drive #11
Los Angeles, CA 90046
"Actress"

Peter Weller
37 Riverside Drive
New York, NY 10021
"Actor"

Robb Weller
4249 Beck Avenue
Studio City, CA 91604
"TV Show Host"

William Wellman, Jr.
410 North Barrington Avenue
Los Angeles, CA 90049
"Actor"

Dawn Wells
4616 Ledge Avenue
North Hollywood, CA 91602
"Actress"

Kitty Wells
240 Old Hickory Blvd.
Madison, TN 35115
"Singer"

Sen. Paul Wellstone
702 Hart Office Bldg.
Washington, DC 20510
"Politician"

Eudora Welty
1119 Pinehurst Street
Jackson, MS 39202
"Author"

Ming-Na Wen
9200 Sunset Blvd., #625
Los Angeles, CA 90069
"Actress"

Señor Wences
204 West 55th Street #701A
New York, NY 10019
"Ventriliquist"

Rudolph Wendelin
4516-7th Avenue North
Arlington, VA 22203
"Illustrator"

George Wendt
3856 Vantage Avenue
Studio City, CA 91604
"Actor"

Lina Wertmuller
via Principessa Clotilde 5
00196 Rome, ITALY
"Film Director"

Dick Wesson
4444 Lankershim Blvd., #207
North Hollywood, CA 91602
"Actor, Writer"

Adam West
P.O. Box 3446
Ketchum, ID 83340
"Actor"

Jerry West
P.O. Box 10
Inglewood, CA 90306
"Ex-Basketball Player"

Red West
10637 Burbank Blvd.
Hollywood, CA 91601
"Actor, Author"

Shelly West
P.O. Box 2977
Hendersonville, TN 37077
"Singer"

Timothy West
46 North Side
Wandsworth Common
London SW18 ENGLAND
"Actor"

✓ **Dr. Ruth Westheimer**
900 West 190th Street
New York, NY 10040
"Sex Theapist"

James Westmoreland
8019 1/2 West Norton Avenue
Los Angeles, CA 90046
"Actor"

Gen. William Westmoreland
107 1/2 Tradd Street
P.O. Box 1059
Charleston, SC 29401
"Military Leader"

David Weston
123A Grosvenor Road
London SW1 ENGLAND
"Actor"

Jack Weston
420 Madison Avenue #1400
New York, NY 10017
"Actor"

Paul Weston
2339 Century Hill
Los Angeles, CA 90067
"Musician, Composer"

Patricia Wetting
11840 Chaparal Street
Los Angeles, CA 90049
"Actress"

Joanne Whaley-Kilmer
P.O. Box 362
Tesuque, NM 87574
"Actress"

Frank Whaley
151 El Camino
Beverly Hills, CA 90212
"Actor

Justin Whalin
9000 Sunset Blvd., #1200
Los Angeles, CA 90069
"Actor"

Wil Wheaton
P.O. Box 12567
La Crescenta, CA 91214
"Actor"

Jill Whelan
6767 Forest Lawn Drive #101
Los Angeles, CA 90069
"Actress"

Lisa Whelchel
17647 Orna Drive
Granada Hills, CA 91344
"Actress"

Shannon Whirry
8091 Selma Drive
Los Angeles, CA 90046
"Actress"

Forest Whitaker
1990 South Bundy Drive #200
Los Angeles, CA 90025
"Actor"

Johnny Whitaker
525 North Kings Road #2
Los Angeles, CA 90048
"Actor"

Ian Whitcomb
P.O. Box 451
Altadena, CA 91001
"Singer, Actor, Producer"

Barry White
3395 S. Jones Blvd. #176
Las Vegas, NV 89102
"Singer, Songwriter"

Betty White
P.O. Box 3713
Granada Hills, CA 91344
"Actress"

Jaleel White
1450 Belfast Drive
Los Angeles, CA 90069
"Actor"

Jesse White
1944 Glendon Avenue #304
Los Angeles, CA 90025
"Actor"

Karyn White
3300 Warner Blvd.
Burbank, CA 91505
"Singer"

Reggie White
P.O. Box 10628
Green Bay, WI 54307
"Football Player"

Sharon White
380 Forest Retreat
Hendersonville, TN 37075
"Singer, Guitarist"

Slappy White
1055 Flamingo Road #819
Las Vegas, NV 89109
"Comedian"

Vanna White
3400 Riverside Drive
Burbank, CA 91505
"TV Personality, Model"

Geoffrey Whitehead
81 Shaftesbury Avenue
London W1 ENGLAND
"Actor"

Billie Whitelaw
535 King's Road
19 The Plaza #2
London SW10 0SZ ENGLAND
"Actress"

The White's
P.O. Box 2158
Hendersonville, TN 37075
"C&W Group"

Heather Whitestone
1325 Boardwalk
Atlantic City, NJ 08401
"Former Miss America"

Lynn Whitfield
8942 Wilshire Blvd.
Beverly Hills, CA 90211
"Actress"

Barbara Whiting
1085 Waddington Street
Birmingham, MI 48009
"Actress"

Margaret Whiting
41 West 58th Street #5A
New York, NY 10019
"Singer"

Slim Whitman
1300 Divison Street #103
Nashville, TN 37203
"Singer"

Stuart Whitman
749 San Ysidro Road
Santa Barbara, CA 93108
"Actor"

James Whitmore
4990 Puesta Del Sol
Malibu, CA 90265
"Actor"

James Whitmore, Jr.
1284 La Brea Drive
Thousand Oaks, CA 91362
"Actor"

Jane Whitney
5 TV Place
Needham, MA 02192
"TV Talk Show Host"

Phyllis Whitney
310 Madison Avenue #607
New York, NY 10017
"Actress"

Roger Whittaker
P.O. Box 1655-GB
London W8 5HZ ENGLAND
"Singer, Songwriter"

Dick Whittinghill
11310 Valley Spring Lane
Toluca Lake, CA 91602
"Radio Personality"

Margaret Whitton
250 N. Robertson Blvd., #518
Beverly Hills, CA 90211
"Actress"

The Who
48 Harley House
London NW1 ENGLAND
"Rock & Roll Group"

Tom Wicker
229 West 43rd Street
New York, NY 10036
"Columnist"

Mary Wickes
10000 Santa Monica Blvd. #305
Los Angeles, CA 90067
"Actress"

Kathleen Widdoes
200 West 57th Street #900
New York, NY 10019
"Actress"

Elie Wiesel
745 Common Wealth Avenue
Boston, MA 02115
"Author, Journalist"

Simon Wiesenthal
Salvtorgasse 6
1010 Vienna 1 AUSTRIA
"Jewish Leader"

Dianne Wiest
59 East 54th Street #22
New York, NY 10022
"Actress"

Mats Wilander
Vickersvagen 2
Vaxjo, SWEDEN
"Tennis Player"

The Wilburn Brothers
P.O. Box 50
Goodlettsville, TN 37072
"C&W Group"

Larry Wilcox
10 Appaloosa Lane
Bell Canyon
Canoga Park, CA 91304
"Actor, Director"

Shannon Wilcox
105 South Medio
Los Angeles, CA 90049
"Actress"

Jack Wild
68 Old Brompton Road
London SW7 3LQ ENGLAND
"Actor"

Kim Wilde
1 Stevenage Road
Nebworth, Herts. ENGLAND
"Singer, Songwriter"

Billy Wilder
10375 Wilshire Blvd.
Los Angeles, CA 90024
"Writer, Producer"

Gene Wilder
1511 SAwtelle Blvd. #155
Los Angeles, CA 90025
"Actor, Writer, Director"

James Wilder
8601 Wilshire Blvd. #801
Beverly, Hills, CA 90211
"Actor"

Michael Wilding, Jr.
8428-C Melrose Place
Los Angeles, CA 90069
"Actor"

Hoyt Wilhelm
3102 North Himes Avenue
Tampa, FL 33607
"Ex-Baseball Player"

Donna Wilkes
3802 North Earl Avenue
Rosemead, CA 91770
"Actress"

Jamaal Wilkes
7846 West 81st Street
Playa del Rey, CA 90291
"Ex-Basketball Player"

June Wilkinson
1025 N. Howard Street
Glendale, CA 91207
"Actress"

George Will
1150-15th Street N.W.
Washington, DC 20071
"Columnist, Writer"

Jo Ann Willette
9300 Wilshire Blvd. #400
Beverly Hills, CA 90212
"Actress"

Williams & Ree
P.O. Box 163
Hendersonville, TN 37077
"Vocal Duo"

Andy Williams
2500 West Highway 76
Branson, MO 65616
"Singer, Actor"

Anson Williams
24615 Skyline View Drive
Malibu, CA 90265
"Actor"

Barry Williams
3646 Reina Court
Calabasas, CA 91302
"Actor"

Billy Williams
586 Prince Edward Road
Glen Ellyn, IL 60137
"Ex-Baseball Player"

Billy Dee Williams
2114 Beech Knoll Road
Los Agneles, CA 90046
"Actor"

Bruce Williams
P.O. Box 547
Elfers, FL 34680
"Radio Personality"

Cara Willaims Dann
146 South Peck Drive
Beverly Hills, CA 90212
"Actress"

Cindy Williams
6712 Portshead Road
Malibu, CA 90265
"Actress"

Clarence Williams III
9057A Nemo Street
Los Angeles, CA 90069
"Actor"

Darnell Williams
1930 Century Park West #403
Los Angeles, CA 90067
"Actor"

Deniece Williams
1414 Seabright
Beverly Hills, CA 90210
"Singer"

Don Williams
1103-16th Avenue South
Nashville, CA 37203
"Singer, Songwriter"

Edy Williams
1638 Blue Jay Way
Los Angeles, CA 90069
"Actress, Model"

Esther Williams
9377 Readcrest Drive
Beverly Hills, CA 90210
"Actress"

Hal Williams
8485E Melrose Place
Los Angeles, CA 90069
"Actor"

Hank Williams, Jr.
Hwy. 79 East
Box 1350
Paris, TN 38242
"Singer, Guitarist"

Jobeth Williams
3529 Beverly Glen Blvd.
Sherman Oaks, CA 91423
"Actress"

Joe Williams
3337 Knollwood Court
Las Vegas, NV 89121
"Singer"

John Williams
333 Loring Avenue
Los Angeles, CA 90024
"Composer, Conductor"

Kimberly Williams
415 North Camden Drive, #200
Beverly Hills, CA 90210
"Actress"

Mary Alice Williams
30 Rockefeller Plaza #508
New York, NY 10020
"Broadcast Journalist"

Mason Williams
P.O. Box 5105
Eugene, OR 97405
"Singer, Songwriter"

Montel William
1500 Broadway #1107
New York, NY 10036
"TV Show Host"

Paul Williams
8545 Franklin Avenue
Los Angeles, CA 90069
"Singer, Songwriter"

Robin Williams
1100 Wall Road
Napa, CA 94558
"Actor, Comedian, Writer"

Roger Williams
16150 Clear Valley Place
Encino, CA 91436
"Pianist"

Stephanie Williams
1269 South Orange #1
Los Angeles, CA 90019
"Actress"

Ted Williams
2455 N. Citrus Hills Blvd.
Hernando, FL 33442
"Ex-Baseball Player"

Treat Williams
215 West 78th Street #10-A
New York, NY 10024
"Actor"

Van Williams
1630 Ocean Park Blvd.
Santa Monica, CA 90405
"Actor"

Vanessa Williams
50 Old Farm Road
Chappaqua, NY 10514
"Singer"

Willie Williams
150 N. Los Angeles St. #615
Los Angeles, CA 90012
"Police Chief"

Fred Williamson
733 Seward Street PH
Los Angeles, CA 90038
"Actor, Director"

Marianne Williamson
565 Valley Club Rd.
Montecito, CA 93108
"Singer"

Mykelti Williamson
151 El Camino Drive
Beverly Hills, CA 90212
"Actor"

Nicol Williamson
76 Oxford Street
London W1N OAX ENGLAND
"Actor"

Bruce Willis
1453 Third Street #420
Santa Monica, CA 90401
"Actor, Singer"

Brian Wilson
14042 Aubrey Road
Beverly Hills, CA 90210
"Musician"

Carl Wilson
8860 Evan View Drive
Los Angeles, CA 90069
"Singer, Songwriter"

Carnie Wilson
13601 Ventura Blvd. #286
Sherman Oaks, CA 91423
"Actress"

Demond Wilson
Church of God in Christ
Ft. Washington, MD 20022
"Actor, Evangelist"

Don Wilson
6605 Hollywood Blvd. #220
Los Angeles, CA 90028
"Actor, Kick Boxer"

Elizabeth Wilson
200 West 57th Street #900
New York, NY 10019
"Actress"

Flip Wilson
21970 Pacific Coast Hwy.
Malibu, CA 90265
"Comedian, Actor, Writer"

Jeannie Wilson
10358-A Riverside Drive
North Hollywood, CA 91602
"Actress"

Jennifer Wilson
1947 Lakeshore Drive
Branson, MO 65616
"Actress"

Lambert Wilson
91 rue Saint-Honore
75001 Paris FRANCE
"Actor"

Mara Wilson
3500 West Olive, #1400
Burbank, CA 91505
"Actress"

Mary Wilson
11684 Ventura Blvd., #809
Studio City, CA 91604
"Singer"

Melanie Wilson
10100 Santa Monica Blvd., #2500
Los Angeles, CA 90067
"Actress"

Nancy Wilson
202 San Vicente Blvd. #4
Santa Monica, CA 90402
"Heart Lead Singer"

Gov. Pete Wilson (CA)
State Capitol
Sacramento, CA 95814
"Governor"

Wilson Phillips
1290 Ave. of the Americas #4200
New York, NY 10104
"Rock & Roll Group"

Rita Wilson
23414 Malibu Colony Road
Malibu, CA 90265
"Actress"

Sheree J. Wilson
7218 South Jan Mar Drive
Dallas, TX 75230
"Actress"

Brian Wimmer
641 Swarthmore Avenue
Pacific Palisades, CA 90272
"Actor"

The Winans
P.O. Box 150245
Nashville, TN 37215
"Gospel Group"

Paul Winchell
32262 Oakshore Drive
Westlake Village, CA 91361
"Actor"

Jeff Wincott
3880-B Fredonia Drive
Los Angeles, CA 90068
"Actor"

William Windom
6535 Langden
Van Nuys, CA 91406
"Actor"

Marie Windsor
9501 Cherokee Lane
Beverly Hills, CA 90210
"Actress"

Dave Winfield
11809 Gwynne Lane
Los Angeles, CA 90077
"Baseball Player"

Paul Winfield
14970 Hickory Greens Court
Ft. Meyers, FL 33912
"Actor"

Oprah Winfrey
P.O. Box 909715
Chicago, IL 60690
"TV Show Host, Actress"

Debra Winger
P.O. Box 9078
Van Nuys, CA 91409
"Actress"

Jason Wingreen
4224 Teesdale Avenue
North Hollywood, CA 91604
"Actor"

Henry Winkler
P.O. Box 49914
Los Angeles, CA 90049
"Actor, Producer"

Michael Winner
31 Melbury Road
London W14 8AB ENGLAND
"Writer, Producer"

Mare Winningham
9560 Topanga Canyon Blvd., #103
Chatsworth, CA 91311
"Actress"

Kate Winslet
31/32 Soho Square
London, W1V 5DF England
"Actress"

Alex Winter
107 West 25th Street #6B
New York, NY 10001
"Actor"

Edward Winter
181 North Saltair Avenue
Los Angeles, CA 90049
"Actor"

Johnny Winter
208 East 51th Street #151
New York, NY 10022
"Singer"

Judy Winter
Lamonstrasse 9
8000 Munich 80 GERMANY
"Singer"

Jonathan Winters
4310 Arcola Avenue
Toluca Lake, CA 91602
"Comedian, Actor"

Shelley Winters
457 N. Oakhurst Drive
Beverly Hills, CA 90210
"Actress"

Steve Winwood
9200 Sunset Blvd. PH 15
Los Angeles, CA 90069
"Singer, Songwriter"

Billy Wirth
9255 Sunset Blvd., #1010
Los Angeles, CA 90069
"Actor"

Norman Wisdom
19 Denmark Street
London W2 ENGLAND
"Actor"

Ernie Wise
306-16 Euston Road
London NW13 ENGLAND
"Comedian"

Robert Wise
315 S. Beverly Drive, #214
Beverly Hills, CA 90212
Director, Producer"

Googie Withers
1740 Pittwater Road
Bay View NSW 2104 AUSTRALIA
"Actress"

Jane Withers
4249 Stern Avenue
Sherman Oaks, CA 91423
"Actress"

Jimmy Witherspoon
223 1/2 E. 48th Street
New York, NY 10017
"Singer, Musician"

Reese Witherspoon
8942 Wilshire Blvd.
Beverly Hills, CA 90211
"Actress"

Katarina Witt
Lindenstr. 8
16244 Altenhof GERMANY
"Ice Skater"

Paul Junger Witt
1438 North Gower Street
Los Angeles, CA 90028
"TV Producer"

Kevin Wixted
10100 Santa Monica Blvd.
Suite #700
Los Angeles, CA 90067
"Actor"

Mr. Wizard (Don Herbert)
P.O. Box 83
Canoga Park, CA 91305
"TV Personality"

Charles Wolcott
P.O. Box 155
Haifa, ISRAEL
"Composer

Scott Wolf
9300 Wilshire Blvd. #555
Beverly Hills, CA 90210
"Actor"

Michael Wolfe
41 Landowne Road
London W11 26Q ENGLAND
"Actor"

Tom Wolfe
21 East 79th Street
New York, NY 10021
"Writer"

David L. Wolper
1833 Rising Glen
Los Angeles, CA 90069
"Film Director"

Bobby Womack
504 W. 168th Street
New York NY 10032
"Singer"

Stevie Wonder
4616 Magnolia Blvd.
Burbank, CA 91505
"Singer, Songwriter"

Elijah Wood
9150 Wilshire Blvd., #350
Beverly Hills, CA 90212
"Actor"

Judith Wood
1300 1/2 N. Sycamore Avenue
Los Angeles, CA 90028
"Actress"

Lane Wood
4129 Woodman Avenue
Sherman Oaks, CA 91423
"Actress"

Tiger Wood
Stanford University Golf Dept.
Stanford, CA 94305
"Golfer"

Alfre Woodard
8942 Wilshire Blvd.
Beverly Hills, CA 90211
"Actress"

John Wooden
17711 Margate Street #102
Encino, CA 91316
"Basketball Coach"

Cynthia Woodhead
P.O. Box 1193
Riverside, CA 92501
"Swimmer"

Frank Woodruff
170 North Crescent Drive
Beverly Hills, CA 90210
"Director, Producer"

Judy Woodruff
P.O. Box 2626
Washington, DC 20013
"Broadcast Journalist"

Donald Woods
690 North Camino Real
Palm Springs, CA 92262
"Actor"

James Woods
760 N. La Cienega Blvd.
Los Angeles, CA 90069
"Actor, Director"

Michael Woods
P.O. Box 5617
Beverly Hills, CA 90210
"Actor"

Robert S. Woods
227 Central Park W. #5-A
New York, NY 10024
"Actor"

Rosemary Woods
1194 West Cambridge Street
Alliance, OH 44601
"Secretary to President Nixon"

Bob Woodward
1150-15th Street N.W.
Washington, DC 20005
"News Corespondent"

Edward Woodward
Ravens Court, Calstock
Cornwall PL18 9ST ENGLAND
"Actor"

Joanne Woodward
40 West 57th Street
New York, NY 10019
"Actress, Director"

Marjorie Woodworth
807 North La Brea Avenue
Inglewood, CA 90301
"Actress"

Chuck Woolery
620 North Linden Drive
Beverly Hills, CA 90210
"TV Show Host"

Sheb Wooley
Route 3, Box 231
Sunset Island Trail
Gallatin, TN 37066
"Singer"

Tom Wopat
2614 Woodlawn Drive
Nashville, TN 37212
"Actor, Director"

Joanne Worley
4714 Arcola
Toluca Lake, CA 91602
"Actress"

Cal Worthington
3815 Florin Road
Sacramento, CA 95823
"Car Dealer"

Irene Worty
333 West 56th Street
New York, NY 10018
"Actress"

Herman Wouk
3255 "N" Street N.W.
Washington, DC 20007
"Author"

Steve Wozniak
475 Alberto Way
Los Gatos, CA 95030
"Computer Builder"

Fay Wray
2160 Century Park East #1901
Los Angeles, CA 90067
"Actress"

Clare Wren
5750 Wilshire Blvd. #512
Los Angeles, CA 90036
"Actress"

Cobina Wright, Jr.
1326 Dove Meadow Road
Solvang, CA 93463
"Actress"

Jenny Wright
245 West 104th Street
New York, NY 10025
"Actress"

Jim Wright
9A10 Lanham Federal Bldg.
819 Taylor Street
Fort Worth, TX 76102
"Former House Speaker"

Robin Wright
2049 Century Park E., #2500
Los Angeles, CA 90067
"Actress"

Steven Wright
9000 Sunset Blvd. #1200
Los Angeles, CA 90069
"Comedian"

Teresa Wright
948 Rowayton Wood Drive
Norwalk, CT 06854
"Actress"

William Wrigley
410 North Michigan Avenue
Chicago, IL 60611
"Chewing Gum & Baseball Executive"

Robert Wuhl
10590 Holman Avenue
Los Angeles, CA 90024
"Comedian, Actor, Writer"

Kari Wuhrer
2447 Benedict Canyon
Beverly Hills, CA 90210
"Actress"

Jane Wyatt
651 Siena Way
Los Angeles, CA 90024
"Actress"

Shannon Wyatt
8949 Falling Creek Court
Annandale, VA 22003
"Actress"

Sharon Wyatt
24549 Park Grande
Calabasas, CA 91302
"Actress"

Andrew Wyeth
c/o General Delivery
Chadds Ford, PA 19317
"Artist"

Noah Wyle
8730 Sunset Blvd., #490
Los Angeles, CA 90069
"Actor"

Gretchen Wyler
15215 Weddington Street
Van Nuys, CA 91411
"Actress"

Jane Wyman
P.O. Box 1317
Elfers, FL 34690
"Actress"

H.M. Wynant
1021 North Beverly Glen
Los Angeles, CA 90077
"Actor"

George Wyner
3450 Laurie Place
Studio City, CA 91604
"Actor"

Tammy Wynette
P.O. Box 6532
Richboro, PA 18059
"Singer, Actress"

Early Wynn
P.O. Box 218
Nakomis, FL 33555
"Ex-Baseball Player"

Amanda Wyss
9229 Sunset Blvd., #311
Los Angeles, CA 90069
"Actress"

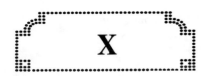

Chairman Deng Xiaoping
Office of the Chairman
Beijing (Peking)
PEOPLES REPUBLIC OF CHINA
"Politician"

Xuxa
7800 Beverly Blvd. #202
Los Angeles, CA 90036
"Actress"

Frank Yablans
100 Bull Path
East Hampton, NY 11937
"Film Writer, Producer"

Andrea Yaeger
P.O. Box 10970
Aspen, CO 81612
"Tennis Player"

Jeff Yagher
10100 Santa Monica Blvd. #2500
Los Angeles, CA 90067
"Actor"

Kristi Yamaguchi
3650 Montecito Drive
Fremont, CA 94536
"Ice Skater"

Emily Yancey
247 South Beverly Drive #102
Beverly Hills, CA 90212
"Actress"

Wierd Al Yankovic
8842 Hollywood Blvd.
Los Angeles, CA 90069
"Singer, Songwriter"

Yanni
5443 Beethoven Street
Los Angeles, CA 90066
"Rock & Roll Group"

Cale Yarborough
9617 Dixie River Road
Charlotte, NC 28270
"Race Car Driver"

Mollie Yard
1000-16th Street N.W.
Washington, DC 20036
"Feminist Leader"

Claire Yarlett
9300 Wilshire Blvd. #410
Beverly Hills, CA 90212
"Actress"

Amy Yasbeck
606 N. Larchmont Blvd. #309
Los Angeles, CA 90004
"Actress"

Carl Yastrzemski
4621 S. Ocean Blvd.
Highland Beach, FL 33431
"Ex-Baseball Player"

Cassie Yates
520 Washington Blvd., #175
Marina del Rey, CA 90292
"Actress"

Peter Yates
334 Caroline Avenue
Culver City, CA 90230
"Film Director"

General Chuck Yeager
P.O. Box 128
Cedar Ridge, CA 95924
"Military Test Pilot, Actor"

Jeana Yeager
Rt. #2
P.O. Box 47
Campbell, TX 75442
"Avaitrix"

Trisha Yearwood
1112 N. Sherbourne Dr.
Los Angeles, CA 90069
"Singer"

Yellowjackets
9220 Sunset Blvd. #320
Los Angeles, CA 90069
"Jazz Group"

✓ **Boris Yeltsin**
Uliza Twerskaya
Jamskaya 2
Moscow, Russia
"President of Russia"

David Yip
15 Golden Square #315
London W1R 3AG ENGLAND
"Actor"

Dwight Yoakum
6363 Sunset Blvd. #800
Los Angeles, CA 90028
"Singer, Guitarist"

Philip Yordan
4894 Mt. Elbrus Drive
San Diego, CA 92117
"Screenwriter"

Francine York
14333 Addison Street #315
Sherman Oaks, CA 91423
"Actress"

Michael York
9100 Cordell Drive
Los Angeles, CA 90069
"Actor"

Susannah York
59 Knightsbridge
London SW1 ENGLAND
"Actress"

Bud Yorkin
250 North Delfern Drive
Los Angeles, CA 90077
"Writer, Producer"

Mayor Sam Yorty
12979 Blairwood Drivce
Studio City, CA 91604
"Ex-Mayor"

Tina Yothers
280 S. Beverly Drive #400
Beverly Hills, CA 90212
"Actress"

Alan Young
P.O. Box 67-B-69
Los Angeles, CA 90067
"Actor"

Andrew Young
1088 Veltrie Circle S.W.
Atlanta, GA 30311
"Ex-Mayor of Atlanta"

Barbara Young
59 Belsize Avenue #1
London NW3 BN ENGLAND
"Actress"

Burt Young
5820 Wilshire Blvd. #503
Beverly Hills, CA 90211
"Actor, Screenwriter""

Chris T. Young
5959 Triumph Street
Commerce, CA 90040
"Actor"

Coleman Young
2 Woodward Avenue
Detroit, MI 49226
"Ex-Mayor of Detroit"

Dean Young
235 East 45th Street
New York, NY 10017
"Cartoonist"

Faron Young
P.O. Box 526
Old Hickory, TN 37138
"Singer, Songwriter"

Jesse Colin Young
P.O. Box 130
Pt. Reyes Sta., CA 94956
"Singer, Songwriter"

Michael Young
4570 Encino Avenue
Encino, CA 91316
"Actor"

Neil Young
2644 30th St. #100
Santa Monica, CA 90405
"Singer, Songwriter"

Raymond Young
Hampton Cottage
7 Church Street
Littlehampton BN1Y ENGLAND
"Actor"

Richard Young
1275 Westwood Blvd.
Los Angeles, CA 90024
"Actor"

Robert Young
31589 Saddletree Drive
Westlake Village, CA 91261
"Actor"

Sean Young
P.O. Box 20547
Sedona, AZ 86341
"Actress"

Steve Young
4949 Centennial Blvd.
Santa Clara, CA 95054
"Football Player"

William Allen Young
1213 West 122nd Street
Los Angeles, CA 90044
"Actor"

Barrie Youngfellow
9255 Sunset Blvd. #515
Los Angeles, CA 90069
"Actress"

Henny Youngman
77 West 55th Street
New York, NY 10019
"Comedian"

Malika Yuba
230 Park Avenue #550
New York, NY 10069
"Actor"

Harris Yulin
1630 Crescent Place
Venice, CA 90291
"Actor"

William Zabka
345 North Maple Drive #183
Beverly Hills, CA 90210
"Actor, Singer"

Grace Zabriskie
1800 S. Robertson Blvd. #426
Los Angeles, CA 90035
"Actress"

John Zaccaro
22 Deepdene Road
Forest Hills, NY 11375
"Businessman"

Pia Zadora
9560 Wilshire Blvd.
Beverly Hills, CA 90212
"Actress, Singer"

Paula Zahn
524 West 57th Street
New York, NY 10019
"TV Show Host"

Steven Zaillan
1300 Marquesas Way "C" #83
Marina del Rey, CA 90292
"Screenwriter"

Roxanne Zal
1450 Belfast Drive
Los Angeles, CA 90069
"Actress"

Billy Zane
450 N. Rossmore Avenue #1001
Los Angeles, CA 90004
"Actor"

Carmen Zapata
6107 Ethel Avenue
Van Nuys, CA 91405
"Actress"

Dweezil Zappa
7885 Woodrow Wilson Drive
Los Angeles, CA 90046
"Singer"

Moon Zappa
10377 Oletha Lane
Los Angeles, CA 90077
"Singer"

Michael Zaslow
9255 Sunset Blvd. #710
Los Angeles, CA 90069
"Actor"

Franco Zefferelli
42 Barrow Street
New York, NY 10014
"Film Director"

Heidi Zeigler
150 E. Olive Avenue #304
Burbank, CA 91502
"Actress"

Jacklyn Zeman
6930 Dume Drive
Malibu, CA 90265
"Actress"

Anthony Zerbe
245 Chateaux Elise
Santa Barbara, CA 93109
"Actor"

Ian Ziering
118 South Beverly Drive #201
Beverly Hills, CA 90212
"Actress"

Efrem Zimbalist, Jr.
1448 Holsted Drive
Solvang, CA 93463
"Actor"

Stephanie Zimbalist
16255 Ventura Blvd. #1011
Encino, CA 91436
"Actress"

Don Zimmer
10124 Yacht Club Drive
St. Petersberg, FL 33706
"Ex-Baseball Player"

Kim Zimmer
25561 Almendra Drive
Santa Clarita, CA 91355
"Actress"

Adrian Zmed
22103 Avenida Morelos
Woodland Hills, CA 91364
"Actor"

Kim Zmeskal
17203 Bamwood
Houston, TX 77090
"Gymnast"

"Fuzzy" Zoeller
12 Bellewood Court
New Albany, IN 47150
"Golfer"

Louis Zorich
222 Upper Mountain Road
Montclair, NJ 07043
"Actor"

Bill Zuckert
3397 Floyd Terrace
Los Angeles, CA 90028
"Actor"

Pinchas Zuckerman
711 West End Avenue #5K-N
New York, NY 10025
"Violinist"

Adm. Elmo Zumwalt Jr.
1000 Wilson Blvd., #3105
Arlington, VA 22209
"Ex-Military Leader"

Daphne Zuniga
P.O. Box 1249
White River Junction, VT 05001
"Actress"

Other Places to write Celebrities: Movie Studios, TV Networks and Record Companies

Major Movie Studios:

Columbia Pictures
(Sony Pictures Entertainment, Inc.)
10202 West Washington Blvd.
Culver City, CA 90232

Fox, Inc.
10201 West Pico Blvd.
Los Angeles, CA 90035

Home Box Office, Inc.
2049 Century Park East, Suite 4100
Los Angeles, CA 90067

MGM-Pathe Communications Co.
10000 West Washington Blvd.
Culver City, CA 90232

Orion Pictures Corporation
1888 Century Park East
Los Angeles, CA 90067

Paramount Communication, Inc.
New York (Home Office)
15 Columbus Circle
New York, NY 10023

Paramount Communication, Inc.
West Coast Office:
5555 Melrose Avenue
Los Angeles, CA 90038

Touchstone Pictures
500 South Buena Vista Street
Burbank, CA 91521

Twentieth Century Fox
P.O. Box 900
Beverly Hills, CA 90213

Universal Pictures
100 Universal City Plaza
Universal City, CA 91608

Warner Bros., Inc.
4000 Warner Blvd.
Burbank, CA 91522

Major Television Network:

ABC
77 West 66th Street
New York, NY 10023

ABC
West Coast Studio:
2040 Avenue of the Stars
Century City, CA 90067

CBS
51 West 52nd Street
New York, NY 10019

CNN
One CNN Center
P.O. Box 105366
Atlanta, GA 30348

Fox Broadcasting Company
10201 West Pico Blvd.
Los Angeles, CA 90035

NBC
New York (Home Office)
30 Rockefeller Plaza
New York, NY 10112

NBC
West Coast Studio:
3000 Alameda Avenue
Burbank, CA 91523

ESPN
935 Middle Street
Bristol, CT 06010

Black Entertainment Network
1232 31st Street N.W.
Washington, DC 20007

C-SPAN
400 N. Capitol Street NW#650
Washington, DC 20001

PBS
1320 Braddock Place
Alexandria, VA 22314

Major Record Companies:

CBS Records, Inc.
51 West 52nd Street
New York, NY 10019

EMI
810 Seventh Avenue
8th Floor
New York, NY 10019

Emeral Records
830 Glastonbury Road
Suite 614
Nashville, TN 37217

Erika Records, Inc.
9827 Oak Street
Bellflower, CA 90706

MCA Records
70 Universal City Plaza
Universal City, CA 91608

Motown Record Company
6255 Sunset Blvd.
17th Floor
Los Angeles, CA 90028

PolyGram Records, Inc.
825 Eighth Avenue
New York, NY 10019

PolyGram Records: Nashville
901 - 18th Avenue South
Nashville, TN 37212

RCA Records, Inc.
P.O. Box 126
405 Tarrytown Road
Suite 335
Elmsford, NY 10523

SBK Records
1290 Avenue of the Americas
New York, NY 10104

Warner Music International
75 Rockefeller Plaza
New York, NY 10019

Other Places to Write Sports Celebrities: Baseball, Basketball and Football Teams

Major League Baseball
350 Park Avenue
New York, NY 10022
Commissioner:
Fay Vincent

American League Teams:

Baltimore Orioles
333 West Camden Street
Baltimore, MD 21201

Boston Red Sox
Fenway Park
Boston, MA 02215

California Angeles
P.O. Box 2000
Anaheim, CA 92803

Chicago White Sox
333 West 35th Street
Chicago, IL 60016

Cleveland Indians
Cleveland Stadium
Cleveland, OH 44114

Detroit Tigers
2121 Trumbull Avenue
Detroit, MI 48216

Kansas City Royals
P.O. Box 419969
Kansas City, MO 64141

Milwaukee Brewers
Milwaukee County Stadium
Milwaukee, WI 53214

Minnesota Twins
501 Chicago Avenue South
Minneapolis, MN 55415

New York Yankees
Yankee Stadium
Bronx, NY 10451

Oakland Athletics
Oakland Alameda County Stadium
Oakland, CA 94621

Seattle Mariners
P.O. Box 4100
Seattle, WA 98104

Texas Rangers
P.O. Box 90111
Arlington, TX 76004

Toronto Blue Jays
1 Blue Jays Way #3200
Toronto, Ont. M5V 1J1 CANADA

National League Teams:

Atlanta Braves
P.O. Box 4064
Atlanta, GA 30302

Chicago Cubs
1060 West Addison
Chicago, IL 60613

Cincinnati Reds
100 Riverfront Stadium
Cinncinnati, OH 45202

Colorado Rockies
1700 Broadway
Suite #2100
Denver, CO 80290

Florida Marlins
2267 NW 199th Street
Miami, FL 33056

Houston Astros
P.O. Box 288
Houston, TX 77001

Los Angeles Dodgers
1000 Elysian Park Avenue
Los Angeles, CA 90012

Montreal Expos
P.O. Box 500, Station M
Montreal, Que. H1V 3P2 CANADA

New York Mets
Shea Stadium
Flushing, NY 11368

Philadelphia Phillies
P.O. Box 7575
Philadelphia, PA 19101

Pittsburgh Pirates
Three Rivers Stadium
Pittsburg, PA 15212

St. Louis Cardinals
250 Stadium Plaza
St. Louis, MO 63102

San Diego Padres
P.O. Box 2000
San Diego, CA 92120

San Francisco Giants
Candlestick Park
San Francisco, CA 94124

National Basketball Association:

Olympic Tower
645 Fifth Avenue
New York, NY 10022
Commissioner:
David Stern

Atlanta Hawks
One CNN Center
South Tower, Suite 405
Atlanta, GA 30303

Boston Celtics
151 Merrimac Street, 5th Floor
Boston, MA 02114

Charlotte Hornets
100 Hive Drive
Charlotte, NC 28217

Chicago Bulls
980 North Michigan Avenue
Suite #1600
Chicago, IL 60611

Cleveland Cavaliers
Gateway Arena
1 Center Court
Cleveland, OH 44115

Dallas Mavericks
Reunion Arena
777 Sports Street
Dallas, TX 75207

Denver Nuggets
1635 Clay Street
P.O. Box 4658
Denver, CO 80204

Detroit Pistons
The Palace
3777 Lapeer Road
Auburn Hills, MI 48057

Golden State Warriors
Oakland Coliseum Arena
7000 Coliseum Way
Oakland, CA 94621

Houston Rockets
The Summit
10 Greenway Plaza East
Houston, TX 77277

Indiana Pacers
300 East Market Street
Indianapolis, IN 46204

Los Angeles Clippers
3939 South Figueroa
Los Angeles, CA 90037

Los Angeles Lakers
Great Western Forum
3900 W. Manchester Blvd.
Inglewood, CA 90306

Miami Heat
Miami Arena
701 Areana Blvd.
Miami, FL 33136

Milwaukee Bucks
The Bradley Center
1001 North Fourth Street
Milwaukee, WI 53203

New Jersey Nets
405 Murray Hill Parkway
East Rutherford, NJ 07073

New York Knickerbockers
Madison Square Garden
Two Pennsylvania Plaza
New York, NY 10121

Orlando Magic
Orlando Arena
One Magic Place
Orlando, FL 32801

Philadelphia 76ers
P.O. Box 25040
Philadelphia, PA 19147

Phoenix Suns
201 East Jefferson
Phoenix, AZ 85001

Portland Trail Blazers
700 N.E. Multnomah Street
Suite #950 - Lloyd Building
Portland, OR 97232

Sacramento Kings
One Sports Parkway
Sacramento, CA 95834

San Antonio Spurs
100 Montana Street
San Antonio, TX 78205

Seattle Supersonics
190 Queen Anne Avenue North
Suite 200
Seattle, WA 98109

Toronto Raptors
150 York Street, Suite 1100
Toronto, Ontario
M5H 3S5 CANADA

Utah Jazz
Delta Center
301 West South Temple
Salt Lake City, UT 84101

National Football League:
410 Park Avenue
New York, NY 10022
Commissioner:
Paul Tagliabue

American Football Conference:
Buffalo Bills
One Bills Drive
Orchard Park, NY 14127

Cincinnati Bengals
200 Riverfront Stadium
Cinncinnati, OH 45202

Denver Broncos
1900 West Eliot
Denver, CO 80204

Houston Oilers
Kirby & Fannin Street
Loop 610
Houston, TX 77054

Indianapolis Colts
100 South Capitol Avenue
Indianapolis, IN 46225

Jacksonville Jaguars
1 Stadium Place
Jacksonville, FL 32202

Kansas City Chiefs
One Arrowhead Drive
Kansas City, MO 64129

Miami Dolphins
Joe Robbie Stadium
2269 N.W. 199th Street
Miami, FL 33056

New England Patriots
Sullivan Stadium-Route 1
Foxboro, MA 02035

New York Jets
Giants Stadium
East Rutherford, NJ 07073

Oakland Raiders
3911 South Figueroa Street
Los Angeles, CA 90037

Pittsburgh Steelers
Three Rivers Stadium
300 Stadium Circle
Pittsburgh, PA 15212

San Diego Chargers
9449 Friars Road
San Diego, CA 92120

Seattle Seahawks
201 South King Street
Seattle, WA 98033

National Football Conference:
Atlanta Falcons
1 Georgia Drive
Atlanta, GA 30313

Baltimore Ravens
333 West Camden Street
Baltimore, MD 21201

Carolina Panters
227 West Trade Street #1600
Charlotte, NC 28202

Chicago Bears
425 McFetridge Place
Chicago, IL 60605

Dallas Cowboys
1 Cowboys Parkway
Irving, TX 75063

Detroit Lions
1200 Featherstone Road
Pontiac, MI 48057

Green Bay Packers
1265 Lombardi Avenue
Green Bay, WI 54303

St. Louis Rams
4245 North King Hwy
St. Louis, MO 63115

Minnesota Vikings
500 - 11th Avenue South
Minneapolis, MN 55415

New Orleans Saints
1500 Poydras Street
New Orleans, LA 70112

New York Giants
Giants Stadium
East Rutherford, NJ 07073

Philadelphia Eagles
Veterans Stadium
Broad Street & Pattison Avenue
Philadelphia, PA 19148

Phoenix Cardinals
Sun Devil Stadium
Fifth Street
Tempe, AZ 85287

San Francisco 49ers
Candlestick Park
San Francisco, CA 94124

Tampa Bay Buccaneers
Tampa Stadium
North Dale Mabry
Tampa, FL 33607

Washington Redskins
RFK Stadium
East Capitol Street
Washington, DC 20003